KU-436-619

DRIVE 5
pp68–79

FRANCE

DRIVE 6
pp80–89

DRIVE 7
pp90–97

DRIVE 8
pp98–107

Figueres

Girona

NAVARRA

Iruña

Bilbao

PAÍS VASCO

Vitoria Gasteiz

Logroño

A RIOJA

VE 4
5–67

Soria

Tudela

Huesca

ARAGÓN

Zaragoza

CATALONIA

Manresa

Lleida

Barcelona

Calatayud

Tarragona

DRIVE 9
pp108–117

DRIVE 10
pp118–127

Alcañiz

Tortosa

DRIVE 11
pp128–135

Teruel

Benicarló

Benicasim

Mahón

DRIVE 24
pp238–247

Palma

Cuenca

Sagunto

Requena

Valencia

PAÍS VALENCIANO

Albacete

DRIVE 25
pp248–253

Ibiza

THE BALEARIC ISLANDS

DRIVE 12
pp136–143

Xàbia

Hellín

Elda

Alicante

MEDITERRANEAN SEA

MURCIA

Murcia

Lorca

Cartagena

DRIVE 23
pp232–237

KEY

═══ Motorway

─── Dual carriageway

─── Major road

─── International border

─── Regional border

EYEWITNESS TRAVEL
BACK ROADS
SPAIN

EYEWITNESS TRAVEL

BACK ROADS
SPAIN

CONTRIBUTORS:

Mary-Ann Gallagher, Nick Inman, Phil Lee,

Chris Moss, Nick Rider, Richard Trillo,

Suzanne Wales, Greg Ward

Penguin Random House

MANAGING EDITOR Aruna Ghose
EDITORIAL MANAGER Ankita Awasthi
DESIGN MANAGER Kavita Saha
PROJECT EDITOR Trisha Bora
EDITORS Parvati M. Krishnan,
Souvik Mukherjee
PROJECT DESIGNER Shruti Singhi
DESIGNER Neha Sethi
PICTURE RESEARCH Taiyaba Khatoon
DTP DESIGNER
Rakesh Pal, Azeem Siddiqui
CARTOGRAPHY
Uma Bhattacharya,
Mohammad Hassan, Suresh Kumar,
Lovell Johns Ltd
ILLUSTRATIONS
Dev Datta, Arun Pottirayil,
Pallavi Thakur

Printed and bound in China

First published in the UK in 2010 by
Dorling Kindersley Limited,
80 Strand,
London WC2R 0RL
A Penguin Random House Company

15 16 17 18 10 9 8 7 6 5 4 3 2 1

Reprinted with revisions 2013, 2016

Copyright 2010, 2016 © Dorling
Kindersley Limited, London

A CIP catalogue record is available from
the British Library.

ISBN 978-0-2412-0809-0

*Jacket: Cala Rosella Roses, Costa Brava,
Catalonia, Spain*

CONTENTS

ABOUT THIS BOOK 6
INTRODUCING SPAIN 8
GETTING TO SPAIN 10
PRACTICAL INFORMATION 12
DRIVING IN SPAIN 16
WHERE TO STAY 22
WHERE TO EAT 24
THE FLAVOURS OF SPAIN 26
THE DRIVES 28

Drive 1

MEDIEVAL TREASURES AND
GOLDEN BAYS
**Santiago de Compostela
to Pontevedra** 30
1–2 days

Drive 2

ALONG THE SACRED SHORE
**Ourense to the Valle
del Silencio** 38
2–3 days

Drive 3

OCEAN AND MOUNTAIN
Ribadesella to Llanes 46
3–4 days

Drive 4

THE LAND OF RIOJA
**Laguardia to Quintanar
de la Sierra** 56
4–5 days

Drive 5

A CIRCUIT AROUND NAVARRA
Zangoza to Lizarra 68
4–5 days

Drive 6

TO THE ROOF OF ARAGÓN
**Castillo de Loarre to
Hecho** 80
3–4 days

Drive 7

MOUNTAINS AND VALLEYS
**La Seu d'Urgell to La
Pobla de Segur** 90
3–4 days

Drive 8

THE CATALAN HEARTLAND
Girona to Cadaqués 98
3–4 days

Drive 9

VINEYARDS AND GOTHIC
TREASURES
**Sant Sadurní d'Anoia to
Delta de l'Ebre** 108
3–4 days

Above Valldemossa monastery complex, Mallorca

Below left Pretty balcony in Beceite **Below right** Rows of olive trees in Cazorla, Andalusia

Above left Visitors relax on Cala Deia, Mallorca **Above centre** A tunnel cuts through the Catalan Pyrenees **Above right** Windmills in Consuegra, La Mancha

Drive 10

FROM THE MOUNTAINS TO THE PLAINS
Alcañiz to Albarracín 118
3–4 days

Drive 11

THE LAND OF THE TEMPLARS
Morella to Ares del Maestre 128
2–3 days

Drive 12

BEHIND THE COSTA BLANCA
Xàtiva to Xàbia 136
2–3 days

Drive 13

ALONG THE DUERO
Peñafiel to Clunia 144
2–3 days

Drive 14

THE SPINE OF CASTILE
Toros de Guisando to Ciudad Rodrigo 152
4 days

Drive 15

ROMAN RUINS AND UNSPOILT LANDSCAPES
Trujillo to Las Hurdes 162
2–3 days

Drive 16

CITIES OF THE CONQUISTADORS
Cáceres to Jerez de los Caballeros 170
3 days

Drive 17

DON QUIXOTE'S LA MANCHA
Puerto Lápice to Consuegra 178
3–4 days

Drive 18

WHITE PUEBLOS
Arcos de la Frontera to Jimena de la Frontera 188
3–4 days

Drive 19

COAST OF LIGHT
Jerez de la Frontera to Tarifa 198
3–4 days

Drive 20

THE MUDÉJAR ROUTE
Almuñécar to Salobreña 208
2 days

Drive 21

HISTORIC MOUNTAIN VILLAGES
Granada to Puente de Tablate 214
2 days

Drive 22

ANDALUSIAN RENAISSANCE AND WOODED MOUNTAINS
Baeza to Sabiote 224
2 days

Drive 23

SECRET BEACHES
Carboneras to Vela Blanca 232
1 day

Drive 24

MALLORCA'S CLIFFS AND COVES
Palma to Alcúdia 238
2 days

Drive 25

THE WHITE ISLAND
Santa Eulària des Riu to Eivissa Town 248
1–2 days

Below left Intricate arches of the Palacio de Partal in the Alhambra **Below right** Hats and dresses on sale, Xàbia

INDEX   254
ACKNOWLEDGMENTS   260
PHRASE BOOK   261
DRIVER'S PHRASE BOOK   263

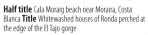

Half title Cala Moraig beach near Moraira, Costa Blanca **Title** Whitewashed houses of Ronda perched at the edge of the El Tajo gorge

About this Book

Back Roads Spain aims to get visitors off the main highways, make discoveries and to get a real feel of the life and riches of Spain. The drives take visitors across Spain around all kinds of enthralling corners that lie off the well-trodden routes – fascinating old towns, placid villages in exquisite settings, and a prodigious variety of scenery, from dramatic mountain peaks and vast brown plains to idyllic green valleys and hidden beaches. On the byways of Spain you can find many of its most ancient monuments and most rumbustious local festivals, as well as the vineyards that produce its finest wines, rich traditional foods, innovative restaurants in remote places and delightful small hotels.

Getting Started
The guide begins with all the practical information you need to plan a driving holiday in Spain. This includes an overview of the best times to visit, ways to get there, the documentation that you will need, important motoring advice, and places to eat and stay. A language section at the back lists essential words and phrases, including key driving-related vocabulary.

The Drives
The 25 drives featured in this guide are spread across the whole of mainland Spain, Mallorca and Ibiza. They take visitors on leisurely tours through Spain's many and varied regions on country roads, avoiding main highways unless it is absolutely unavoidable. The drives have been selected to be accessible from different parts of the country, and to give a taste of the huge diversity of Spain – so some take you through the steep green valleys of Galicia or the Alpine mountains of Asturias or the Pyrenees, while others visit the sun-toasted villages of Don Quixote's La Mancha or the beaches and coastal villages of Andalusia. Some drives include celebrated towns and attractions like Santiago de Compostela or Granada, but then they show you how to get to the next stop along quiet, minor roads. Throughout the emphasis is given to exploring places that have a real feel of being away from it all.

All of the featured drives in this guide can be explored with a standard-model car, and by any normally experienced driver. Country roads can be narrow, and in mountain areas they will twist and turn, but there are no great risks in getting around them, at least in good weather. In Spain, even remote valley roads are generally in fine condition.

Each of the drives presents a range of possible activities to try – market shopping, wine tasting, exploring the mountains or keeping the kids entertained on the beach – and each one also includes a route for a walk, in a special town or beautiful countryside. Drives of more than one day can also be divided into single day trips which allow visitors to return to their starting point at the end of each day. Places to stay and eat listed with each drive have been carefully selected for

Using the Sheet Map
A pull-out road map of the entire country is attached at the back. This map contains all the information you need to drive around the country and to navigate between the tours. All motorways, major roads, airports, both domestic and international, plus all the ferry ports are easily identified. This makes the pull-out map an excellent addition to the drive itinerary maps within the book. There is a map index to help you find the places. The map is further supplemented by a clear distance chart, so you can gauge the distances between the major cities.

individuality, quality and charm. And after each stop there are clear road directions to continue the drive to the next stop.

Top left Blooming bougainvillea in Salobreña
Top right Fascinating rock formation of the Mallos de Riglos in Aragón **Middle left** Maro cliffs in Cerro Gordo **Middle right** Terrace bar in medieval Potes **Below left** Museo Cueva in Guadix **Below right** Bullring in Las Virtudes **Right** Rocky coastline of Mallorca

Introducing Spain

The essence of Spain lies in the variety it has to offer. It is the most mountainous country in Europe, and has western Europe's only real desert, in Almería. Behind the Atlantic coasts of Galicia and Asturias there are still bears and wild boars in the deep-green forests of oak and beech, while to the south the summer sun roasts the bare, rugged hills golden brown between the olive groves. In different parts of Spain three languages – Catalan, Basque and Galician – enjoy official status with Castilian Spanish. This linguistic variety is further reflected in the vigour of local festivals and traditions, and the delicious range of regional cuisines.

When to Go

Late March to early July is an ideal time for visiting most parts of Spain, as temperatures remain pleasantly warm. In "dry Spain", from the Cantabrian mountains to Andalusia, spring sees a burst of new life before the torrid heat of summer, with flashes of wild flowers by the roadsides. Temperatures rise sharply in July and August, above all in the centre and south, and while there is plenty going on – especially local festivals – whether visitors wish to travel then may depend on how much they like the heat, and the crowds. September into October is another delightful time to visit, with clear, warm skies, and the grape harvest beginning in vine-growing areas. In late autumn, from mid-October on, the weather gets chillier and wetter in the north, but many areas have seasonal attractions at this time too, often to do with special foods. From December to March, snow and ice can make travel more difficult in mountain areas, but this is also the winter sports season.

Times to Avoid

The majority of Spain's population takes its holidays in late July or August, and this is also the most popular time for foreign visitors – so roads are congested, prices go up and hotel rooms are harder to come by. Added to that, in many areas the temperature lingers above 30° C (86° F) . Country areas not far from major cities can get very busy on fine weekends at any time of year. Some monuments, museums and other attractions in country areas are closed from November to February or March, so check before travelling. In mountain areas such as Asturias or the Pyrenees, the transitional times between the summer and winter are often rainy with poor visibility, and hence not ideal for touring.

Festivals

Easter is the most widely marked religious festival, above all in Valencia, Andalusia, central Spain and Alicante. The eve of the **Feast of St John the Baptist**, 23 June, is known for loud revelry with bonfires and fireworks. Early July sees the **bull-running** of San Fermín in Pamplona, one of Spain's most famous festivals. The summer months are the most popular time for each town or village to have its *fiesta mayor*. From September cultural programmes get going in cities and towns, and many country areas have celebrations of their special products such as wine, mushrooms or ham. **Christmas** has a special touch, with traditional fairs in many places. Winter comes to an end in several towns with the raucous partying of **Carnaval**, in late February or March.

Public Holidays

New Year's Day (1 Jan)
Día de Reyes (6 Jan)
Good Friday (Mar/Apr)
May Day (1 May)
Feast of the Assumption (15 Aug)
Día de la Hispanidad (12 Oct)
All Saints' Day (1 Nov)
Día de la Constitución (6 Dec)
Immaculate Conception (8 Dec)
Christmas Day (25 Dec)

Climate

"Green Spain", extending from Galicia through Asturias and the Basque Country, and along the Pyrenees, has plenty of rain, chilly winters and warm but moderate summers. The Mediterranean coast has cold winters but the spring is generally superb, and summers are pleasant. In the south, across Andalusia to Murcia, winters are warmer, but the full summer heat is often intense. In the central Castilian plain, winter temperatures can drop to freezing, but summers can easily be as hot as further south.

Getting to Spain

As one of Europe's most popular destinations, Spain is easy to reach from any part of the world. There are several major hub airports in different parts of the country, and even many small regional airports have direct international flights. Spain's excellent railways are well connected to the European high-speed train network, and fast motorways cross over from France at either end of the Pyrenees. Direct ferry services run to the north coast from Britain. In the Mediterranean there are frequent ferries from mainland ports to the Balearic Islands and to North Africa.

Above Funicular train up to Catalonia

Arriving by Air

Spain's main hub airports are Madrid, Barcelona, Málaga and Palma de Mallorca, and each has a huge range of direct flights with major and low-cost airlines, above all from the UK, Ireland and every part of Europe. In addition, the growth of low-cost airlines using smaller airports has made it very easy to fly straight to the part of Spain you wish to visit, especially from the UK, Ireland, France, Italy and Germany. Airline routes can change, but currently **Ryanair** has flights to 23 airports in Spain, including Santiago de Compostela, Santander, Valladolid, Zaragoza, Girona, Reus (near Tarragona) and Jerez de la Frontera; **easyJet** to 18, including Valencia, Seville, Ibiza, Asturias, Bilbao and Murcia; **Flybe** to Alicante, Madrid, Malaga and Mallorca; while **Vueling** serves 25 airports.

Direct flights from North America run by **Air Canada**, **American Airlines** and **Delta**, and flights from other countries outside Europe, generally arrive in Barcelona or Madrid. From these cities visitors can take a connecting flight on to any of Spain's islands or regional destinations, or take a train to see more of the country. Many of the international low-cost airlines now operate internal flights within Spain.

Flight times to Madrid or Barcelona from different cities are: London, 2 hours; Paris, 2 hours; Amsterdam, 2.5 hours; Berlin, 2.5 hours; New York, 8 hours; Buenos Aires, 12 hours; Los Angeles, 15 hours.

Arriving by Sea

There are two direct car ferry services between Britain and northern Spain. **Brittany Ferries** sails twice each week from Plymouth and Portsmouth to Santander (with a journey time of approximately 20–24 hours) and twice each week from Portsmouth to Bilbao (one- and two-night crossings, taking approximately 24 and 32 hours respectively). Since these are long sailings, the ships are "cruise ferries": small cruise liners with comfortable berths, swimming pools and a big choice of entertainment on board. Several Mediterranean car ferry routes connect Spain with Italy and North Africa. From Barcelona **Grimaldi Ferries** sails several times each week to Civitavecchia and Livorno (taking approximately 20 hours), and **Grande Navi Veloci** sails to Genoa (with a travel time of approximately 18 hours). The same company also has a weekly ferry to Tangiers in Morocco (taking around 26 hours), and there are several ferries serving the ports in Algeria and Morocco from Alicante, Almería, Málaga, Algeciras and Tarifa.

Balearic Islands Ferries

The ports for car and passenger ferries to the Balearic Islands are Barcelona (which has the most services), Valencia, Alicante and Denia on the Costa Blanca, which offers the shortest crossing to Ibiza. Services on most routes are frequent and are operated by several different companies, so prices are competitive. **Acciona Trasmediterranea** is the largest company and has daily sailings to Mallorca from Barcelona (about 8 hours), Menorca and Ibiza

Left Police officers in Cangas de Onís, Asturias **Right** Spanish police car

your nearest consulate for a list of recommended doctors, or call for an **ambulance**.

Pharmacies, identified by large green or red illuminated crosses, are plentiful, and there is at least one in nearly every town. Pharmacists are highly trained and can often advise on treatments for minor ailments, sunburn, bites and so on. Many pharmacists also now speak some English. In the windows of each pharmacy there will be a list of pharmacies in the area that are open at night.

Disabled Travellers

Major efforts have been made to improve access and facilities for disabled people in Spain in the last few years, and many hotels have adapted rooms. There are good access facilities at most city museums and access ramps on many beaches, but in small towns and at monuments with uneven paths things may still be more difficult. **Tourism for All** in the UK is a good source of information for disabled travellers.

Personal Security

Violent crime and even petty theft is rare in rural Spain, but as anywhere you should avoid leaving bags or valuables in view when you park your car. In crowded areas and at the bigger fiestas be aware that there may be pickpockets and bag-snatchers around. When sitting at a pavement café, always keep your bag in view, either on the table or in your lap.

If you are robbed or become a victim of any other crime, report it immediately to the nearest police station or call the **emergency** number. In cases of theft, you must get a police statement to make an insurance claim. Spain has several police forces with varying responsibilities. In most cities the main force responsible for dealing with crime is the **Policía Nacional** (national police), but nearly every town also has its own local force (usually called **Policía Local**, Policía Municipal or Guardia Urbana), which is mainly concerned with traffic, parking and various local regulations. In most rural districts and on main highways, all areas of policing are the responsibility of the green-uniformed **Guardia Civil** (civil guard). However, in two of Spain's autonomous regions most rural and city policing has now been taken over by separate local forces, the red-uniformed Ertzaintza in the Basque Country and the blue-clad Mossos d'Esquadra in Catalonia.

DIRECTORY

PASSPORTS AND VISAS
Australia
913 536 600; www.spain.embassy. gov.au

Canada
913 828 400; www.spain.gc.ca

United Kingdom
917 146 300; www.ukinspain.com

United States
915 872 200; http://spanish.madrid. usembassy.gov

DISABLED TRAVELLERS
Tourism for All
www.tourismforall.org.uk

EMERGENCY
Emergencies: all services
112

Ambulance
061

Policía Nacional
091

Policía Local (most towns)
092

Guardia Civil
062

Below far left Pharmacy sign **Below left** Sign indicating beach with wheelchair access, Costa Blanca **Below middle** Tourist office sign **Below right** Street signs in Gaucín

Communications

Standard Spanish phone numbers have nine digits, and incorporate the local area code. Numbers that begin with 900 are free phone lines; those beginning 902, 906 or other combinations are premium-rate lines. Spanish mobile phone numbers all start with a 6.

Spain's former monopoly phone company Telefónica now has to compete with other phone service providers, especially for mobile phones, but it still dominates the market for landlines and provides nearly all payphones. Payphones are increasingly rare, but can still be found at train stations, airports and other transport hubs. Most now operate with credit cards or phone-cards (tarjetas telefónicas), which can be purchased from tobacco shops (estancos). Many bars have coin-operated phones, but these tend to be expensive, as do the surcharges levied by most hotels for making a call from your room.

Mobile/cell phones (móviles) are enormously popular in Spain and the coverage is pretty good in every part of the country, except perhaps the most remote mountain valleys. Most mobile phones from other European countries will work in Spain via a roaming facility, but charges can be higher. It may be more economical just to buy a cheap, pay-as-you-go local mobile or a Spanish SIM card while in Spain. Spanish mobiles all operate on the standard European wave band, so North American phones will only work here if they have a tri- or quad-band facility.

Wi-Fi is widely available, either through your mobile phone service provider, or in cafés, restaurants and hotels, even in the smallest towns. Some of the bigger cities, such as Barcelona, offer free Wi-Fi hot spots, and free Wi-Fi is also available on most of RENFE's high-speed trains.

The Spanish postal service (Correos) has post offices all over the country, and large offices in every main town. Postboxes (buzones) are yellow, with a crown-and-horn insignia. Stamps can be bought at post offices, but it is generally easier to get them from tobacco shops. Larger offices provide a wide range of services and are generally open all day, Monday to Saturday; smaller offices are more limited and are often closed in the afternoons. As well as by regular post, letters and packages can be sent by express (urgente) or registered (certificado) mail.

Money and Banks

Spain is one of the many European Union countries that has adopted the euro (€) as its currency. Each euro is divided into 100 cents (céntimos in Spain). Euro notes are identical throughout the euro area, and are issued for €5, €10, €20, €50, €100, €200 and €500. Euro coins have a distinctive design for the issuing country on one side, and come in values of 1, 2, 5, 10, 20 and 50 cents, and €1 and €2.

Banks (virtually always with an ATM cash machine) are plentiful in all major towns and tourist areas. In the mountains and countryside, there is at least one bank branch and ATM in the largest town of each district, but they are scarce in villages, so plan accordingly. Banks

Above Painted sign for various facilities, Andalusia

generally open Monday to Friday from 8:30am to 2pm, and often on Saturdays from 8:30am to 1pm. Banking hours vary; however, some branches in larger towns may open on a few afternoons each week.

Outside of banking hours, in airports, main rail stations and most tourist areas there will be a range of late-opening small bureaux de change for changing money. However, these may give poorer rates than banks.

Cash Passports, prepaid currency cards that are loaded before travelling and can be used in shops and ATMs abroad, are also gaining popularity. They are available from **Thomas Cook**, **Travelex** and various banks. Credit and debit cards are widely accepted, but note that when you use a card in shops you may be asked to show your passport or other photo ID. Given the restrictive opening times of banks, the most convenient way to obtain cash can also be by withdrawing it from an ATM with a card. Most Spanish ATMs accept all the major international cards (**American Express**, **Visa**, **MasterCard** and others), and display instructions in English and other languages.

Above left A credit card reader in Spain **Above middle** Old town hall in a town in La Rioja **Above right** An information kiosk

Tourist Information

The Spanish national tourist office has offices around the world, but tourist information within Spain is generally provided by individual cities and the various autonomous regions, which produce a huge range of information and maps about attractions and activities in their area. All major towns and many small ones have a tourist office *(oficina de turismo)*. In national parks and nature reserves there are special visitor centres which provide a range of walking maps.

Opening Hours

Most monuments and museums close on one day each week, usually Monday, although some close on Tuesdays. On other days smaller sights are generally open from 10am to 2pm and from 5 to 8pm, but the biggest, most famous buildings and museums are often open all day. Admission is normally charged, but many museums are free on Sundays. Local and smaller shops usually open from 9am to 1–2pm, and again from 4–5 to 8–9pm, Monday to Saturday, with hours tending to be later in summer. Markets open earlier, from around 7am, and often close down by 2pm. Larger city stores and shopping malls, however, are open through the day without a break. This pattern has been copied by many shops in cities. Traditionally, only news-stands, bakeries *(panaderías)* and cake shops *(pastelerías)* stayed open on Sundays, but nowadays the big stores also stay open on some Sundays.

Tipping

It is common to leave around 5–10 per cent in restaurants. In bars, customers often leave small change. Tips are usually given to hotel porters and toilet attendants. Taxi drivers do not expect tips, but appreciate them when they are given, and a common practice is to round up the fare to the nearest euro or more, leaving a bit more for longer journeys or if the driver has helped with luggage.

Time

Spain (except for the Canary Islands) is 1 hour ahead of GMT during winter. It changes to and from daylight saving time on the last Sunday in March and on the last Sunday in October respectively.

Below far left Telephone booth in Andalusia **Below left** Telephone shop in Xàbia **Below middle** An automatic teller machine in Andalusia **Below right** Yellow postbox of the Spanish postal service **Below far right** A terrace bar in La Pobla de Segur

DIRECTORY

COMMUNICATIONS
Directory Enquiries
11888

To call Spain from abroad
International access code (usually 00) +34 followed by the full 9-digit number

To call home from Spain
Dial 00, then the country code, and then the area code where necessary. Omit the first 0 in numbers in the UK, France and some other countries

Country Codes
Australia: 61; Ireland: 353; New Zealand: 64; UK: 44; USA and Canada: 1

MONEY AND BANKS
American Express
900 814 500;
www.americanexpress.com

MasterCard
900 971 231;
www.mastercard.com

Thomas Cook
www.thomascook.com

Travelex
900 948 971

Visa
900 991 124;
www.visa.com

TOURIST INFORMATION
Ireland
0163 502 00;
www.spain.info

UK
64 North Row, London W1K 7DE;
020 7317 2011;
www.spain.info

USA
60 East 42nd Street, Suite 5300, New York 10165-0039;
(212) 265 8822;
www.spain.info

Driving in Spain

At peak times on multilane highways around Madrid or Barcelona you can get caught up in horrendous congestion, but by getting off the main roads you can escape onto placid lanes between craggy hillsides and stupendous views. Carry on further, and the same road may get narrower still and wind tightly up to a tiny village. Exploring these byways is a delight, but to get the most out of your trip it is advisable to make some preparations first.

Above Sign for *autopista*, a toll motorway

Insurance and Breakdown Cover

All car insurance policies in the EU automatically include minimum third-party insurance cover valid in any EU country. However, it is advisable to have wider cover too. For holders of fully comprehensive car insurance, most companies provide full European cover for a small extra premium; some do not charge for this, but still require you to notify them before travelling. An international Green Card confirming your car is insured is no longer a legal requirement, but is still useful to have, and most companies issue them when you obtain European cover.

It is also advisable to have breakdown cover with one of the Europe-wide networks with English-speaking phone lines. This can be arranged with your European insurance cover, or through a motoring organization such as the **AA** *(see p19)* or **RAC** *(see p19)*.

What to Take

You must carry your driving licence, passport, the vehicle registration document and a certificate of insurance (with a Green Card if you have one). If you are taking your own car, get it serviced before you leave your home country. If you are not the registered owner, you must have a letter of authorization from the owner. You must also carry a set of spare light bulbs and a red warning triangle. It is not yet obligatory for foreign vehicles to carry a second warning triangle or a luminous vest, but it is strongly recommended. Drivers who wear glasses should carry a spare pair. The car's country of registration should be displayed on a sticker or as part of the registration plate, and right-hand-drive cars need headlamp deflectors for driving on the right, available at ferry ports and on ferries. Additional requirements apply when towing caravans or trailers *(see p20)*.

Road Systems

Main highways in Spain are either *autopistas* or *autovías*. *Autopistas* (AP2, AP7 etc) are multilane toll *(peaje)* motorways. Wherever there is a toll motorway it is flanked by a toll-free *carretera nacional* on the same route. *Autovías* (A2, A7 etc) are also multilane and generally of the same standard as *autopistas*, but they are toll-free. Several highways change between stretches of *autopista* and *autovía*, and around cities many highways are toll-free. European route numbers are also shown in green on signs alongside the Spanish numbers.

The next grade of road is the *carreteras nacionales* or national highways (N25, N230 etc). Some are just two-lane roads, but many have passing lanes. Numbering of other roads varies according to the authority responsible for them (regional, provincial or local), so it changes as you cross from one area to another. Distances along all roads (and exit numbers on motorways) are marked in kilometres from the theoretical start point of the road.

Paying Tolls

On short stretches of *autopista* the toll is a flat fee, but elsewhere you take a ticket as you enter the motorway, and pay by the distance driven when you exit or leave a toll section of road. Tolls are also charged at some tunnels. At toll stations, there are three sets of lanes: *telepago/telepeaje*, for holders of prepaid *autopista* cards; *automático*, for paying by credit card or with the exact amount in cash; and, simplest to use, *manual* lanes with staffed booths. *Autopista* tolls are quite high (€7.55 for Girona–Barcelona) which is why they are often pretty empty, while nearby non-toll roads are congested.

Left Sign for a toll motorway **Right** Cars and lorries on a highway in Granada, Andalusia

Rules of the Road

Seat belts must be worn by everyone in the car, front and back. It is illegal to use a mobile phone when driving, and to sound a horn in urban areas except in an emergency. Only dipped headlights can be used in urban areas, and dipped headlights must be switched on when in tunnels.

Common in small towns is a type of traffic light with electronic sensors: it normally flashes yellow, but if you approach it at excessive speed it will turn to red and stop you; if you slow down, it turns back to flashing yellow. Entrances and exits on *autopistas* and *autovías* can be abrupt, so extra care is necessary, above all in a right-hand-drive car. Take special care on *autovías*, because some still have junctions with quite minor roads.

If oncoming drivers flash their lights at you, this usually means they are claiming right of way. However, this can be a friendly warning that there is a police spotcheck ahead. For advice on driving or travelling abroad, visit the Foreign and Commonwealth Office website *(see p19)*.

Speed Limits and Fines

Standard speed limits are 50 km/h (30 mph) in built-up areas, 80 km/h (50 mph) on urban dual carriageways, 90 km/h (55 mph) on most country roads, 100 km/h (60 mph) on dual carriageways and 120–130 km/h (75–80 mph) on *autopistas* and *autovías*. These can be modified by signs, and in many residential areas there is a limit of 30 km/h (19 mph).

Electronic speed traps and video speed checks are common in Spain. Fines are levied on the spot according to a fixed scale of charges. The legal limit for alcohol in the blood is 0.05 per cent.

Buying Fuel

Fuel stations have two or three grades of unleaded petrol (95, 97 and 98 octane) and diesel *(gas-oil* or *gasóleo-A)*. Many have two grades of diesel, and some offer LPG fuel *(autogas)* and biodiesel. Normal diesel is a little more expensive than unleaded petrol in Spain.

Petrol stations are plentiful in cities and on main highways, but in rural areas there may only be one in the district's main town. Country stations may be closed on Sundays. Many stations have automatic pumps open 24 hours operated by credit card, but some reject non-Spanish cards. On self-service pumps you often have to tap in the amount you wish to pay before it will release fuel.

INSTRUCTIONS FOR DRIVERS

Given here in Spanish only. In the Basque Country, Galicia and Catalan-speaking regions, these signs may be written in the local languages.

Calle sin salida
Dead end, no through road

Camino/Carril cerrado
Road/lane closed

Ceda el paso
Give way, yield

Modere su velocidad
Slow down

Desviación
Detour

Precaución – Obras
Caution – road works

Salida
Exit

Sentido único
One way

Uso de cadenas obligatorio
Snow chains compulsory

Below far left Road winding past a cliff in Mallorca **Below left** Fuel station **Below middle** Sign warning drivers to use the horn **Below right** High-altitude road near the Pyrenees **Below far right** A deer-crossing road sign to caution motorists

Road Conditions

A great deal has been spent on upgrading Spain's roads, and even country roads are generally in very good condition. Dust can make roads slippery at speed in the full summer heat, and rain, when it comes, can be very heavy and make roads treacherous, so extra care is necessary.

Spain's main cities are all relatively small in area. Hence they and their access highways are often congested, especially on weekday mornings and evenings, and on Sunday nights. If you visit Spain's cities (above all, Madrid and Barcelona), it will be more relaxing and save time to leave your car at a hotel or car park and use public transport, which is excellent. If you hire a car in a city, ask the rental company for clear directions onto highways out of town. Away from major cities, congestion is far less common, and long-distance roads often seem very empty. Exceptions are coastal roads and those leading to popular countryside areas, which get very busy in the holiday season.

Signs on country roads can be inconsistent, but are generally quite straightforward. It is not always so in towns, where local signs are often small and hard to find. Try to look for a *centro urbano* sign when entering a town, and for *todas direcciones* when you want to leave, which should lead you to a main highway.

Information on road conditions is available in Spanish only from the **Dirección General de Tráfico** (DGT) website and phone line. For Catalonia, there is more information on the regional government website. For weather information check the **Weather Channel** or **BBC Weather**.

Above Road winding under an old stone viaduct in Mallorca

Mountain Roads

Discovering many of Spain's most spectacular places involves venturing up its remarkable mountain roads, with long series of switchback hairpins. Even very remote roads now have good surfaces, with crash barriers on the sharpest bends, and have space to allow two vehicles to pass with care, but they are unavoidably steep and narrow. The main thing to take into account on mountain roads is to take time, as average speeds will often be around 40 km/h (25 mph). Drive cautiously around blind bends, and if in doubt use your horn when approaching, as many local drivers do. If you want to stop to take in the often breathtaking views, wait for a stopping place or viewpoint.

Warning sign for danger of snow

Driving in Winter

From December to March, roads in mountain areas can be coated with snow and ice. Motorways are kept clear, but minor roads may be closed completely, and access to other roads may only be permitted for vehicles fitted with snow chains (*cadenas*). This includes many highways over mountain passes. When a road is closed or chains are required, it is signposted well in advance. The state of mountain roads in winter is assessed daily, so check websites before travelling.

Taking a Break

There are service areas (*areas de servicio*) with ample facilities at intervals along *autopistas* and *autovías*. Along the main highways it is easy to find roadside café-restaurants. On other roads there are frequent lay-bys (with a "P" sign), with more on picturesque and mountain roads, indicated as a *mirador* (viewpoint).

Breakdowns and Accidents

If you have a breakdown or accident, put hazard lights on and try to get the car off the main carriageway. Place your warning triangle about 30 m (100 ft) behind the car; you should also wear a luminous jacket, but this is not obligatory for drivers of foreign-registered cars. There are free orange emergency telephones every 5 km (3 miles) along *autopistas* and *autovías*, and operators often take calls in English. Otherwise, use your mobile to call your breakdown service. In case of accidents,

Left Road signs in Andalusia **Middle** Sign for Puerto de Artesiaga in the Pyrenees **Right** Shops carved out of rocks in Mallorca

your insurance company should have supplied copies of the **European Accident Statement**. You and the other driver should each fill in the form, and each should keep a copy to accompany an insurance claim.

It is only required to notify the police if someone has been injured or there is a dispute over what has happened. If there is a serious disagreement over an accident, each driver must make a statement at the local police station.

Parking

In most Spanish towns parking space is at a premium. Parking is prohibited where the kerb is painted yellow; on-street pay-and-display spaces are marked in blue, with a ticket machine nearby. Parking on the street or in municipal car parks is usually free during lunch hours. In many narrow streets there is free parking on different sides of the street at different times: a no-parking sign with "1–15" beneath it means parking is prohibited during the first half of each month, while on the other side a similar sign will say "16–30", for the second half. Parking space is especially scarce in the old centres of cities and towns, and in cities it is best to use one of the big paid car parks. Smaller

towns have at least a few paid and free car parks.

Do not park in front of any *vado permanente* sign (*gual permanent* in Catalan), which means an entry with 24-hour right of access. If the local police tow your car away, they will leave a sticker on the kerb with a phone number and the address where you must pay a fine before retrieving the car.

Maps

The official **Instituto Geográfico Nacional (IGN)** publishes a comprehensive road atlas, the *Mapa Oficial de Carreteras*. Also of high quality are the maps and road atlases of Michelin, Repsol and Planeta. The IGN produces regional and hiking maps, and the **Institut Cartogràfic de Catalunya** has a detailed series on Catalonia. The best maps for walking and exploring the countryside are by Editorial Adrados (for Asturias, Cantabria, the Sierra de Gredos) and **Editorial Alpina** (Catalonia, Andalusia, the Pyrenees). Tourist offices also provide good maps.

Below far left Road signs near Najera **Below left** Cars parked in Murillo de Reino **Below middle** Parking ticket machine **Below right** Road sign warning of falling rocks **Below far right** Visitors enjoying views of Gorg-Blau, Mallorca

DIRECTORY

INSURANCE AND BREAKDOWN COVER
AA
0800 085 7253;
www.theaa.com
RAC
www.rac.co.uk

RULES OF THE ROAD
Foreign and Commonwealth Office
www.gov.uk/driving-abroad

ROAD CONDITIONS
BBC Weather
www.bbc.co.uk/weather

Dirección General de Tráfico (DGT)
011 (road information);
www.dgt.es

The Weather Channel
www.weather.com

BREAKDOWN OR ACCIDENTS
European Accident Statement
http://cartraveldocs.com

MAPS
Editorial Alpina
www.editorialalpina.com

Institut Cartogràfic de Catalunya (ICC)
www.icc.es

Instituto Geográfico Nacional (IGN)
www.ign.es

Caravans and Motorhomes

Basic driving rules and speed limits are the same for caravans and motorhomes as for standard cars, with the addition that cars towing a caravan must have a yellow triangle on a blue backing near the front number plate. Also, if car and caravan or trailer have a combined length of 12 m (40 ft) or more, there must be yellow reflector triangles either side of the rear number plate. On roads with three or more lanes, towing vehicles can only use the two right lanes, and vehicles or combinations with a total length over 10 m (33 ft) must keep a distance of at least 50 m (165 ft) from the vehicle in front of them. Drivers towing caravans should be wary of taking on minor mountain roads, and ask at local tourist offices on their level of accessibility.

Parking a caravan or mobile home is usually only permitted in authorized sites, but there are well-equipped camp sites throughout Spain. In the peak holiday season they are very busy, so book early. Electrical voltage at sites is generally 220v, but can be less. Due to different national systems, reverse polarity can occasionally be a problem when the site's live cable connects to a caravan's neutral one, so it may be advisable to take a polarity tester, and an adaptor to use if this occurs. Calor gas is not available in Spain, but it is easy to find Campingaz, and Repsol and Cepsa petrol stations sell butane gas cylinders. You will need an adaptor to connect them to UK Calor gas equipment.

The best source of information of all kinds on travelling in Spain with a caravan or motorhome is the *Caravan*

Above Caravan parked at a camp site in Cádiz

Europe guide from **Caravan Club**, which includes a site guide. Volume 1 covers Spain, Portugal and France.

Motorcycles

The main traffic laws, speed limits and so on for motorcyclists are the same as for car drivers. In addition, helmets are compulsory for riders and passengers on all bikes, and dipped headlights must be switched on at all times. *Autopista* and tunnel tolls are less for bikes, and in many towns bikes and scooters can be parked for free, so long as they do not take up a car parking space. In many towns it is legal (and free) to park bikes on the pavement if it is over 3 m (10 ft) wide, but check to see what local bike users do, as in some towns this can attract a fine.

Cycling

Cycling in Spain's cities can be terrifying, but out in the countryside conditions are ideal, and mountain biking especially is extremely popular. Officially, all riders must wear helmets, but this is loosely enforced. Tourist offices often have free guides to local mountain-biking routes, and more extensive guides are published by companies such as **Editorial Alpina** *(see p19)*.

Many companies now offer mountain-biking tours in Spain. If you do not come with a tour or have your own bike, shops offering cycle hire *(alquiler de bicicletas)* are easy to find, especially near popular bike routes.

Driving with Children

Children under age 12 and/or less than 1.35 m (4 ft 5 in) in height may not travel in the front seat of a car. In the back, children of any age less than 1.35 m (4 ft 5 in) tall must use a child seat, not just booster cushions. Seat belts must be worn at all times.

Autopista service areas, and the less formal restaurant-petrol station drive-ins beside national highways, often have good play areas for children.

Disabled Drivers

The European-standard blue badge for disabled drivers is also valid in Spain. However, this does not mean you can disregard parking restrictions: instead, you must use a designated disabled parking space, indicated by the usual wheelchair symbol. There are disabled spaces in all public and most private car parks, and usually some among on-street pay-and-display (parking ticket machines from which the customer must buy a ticket to display on his dashboard) spaces.

Left Instructions to visitors in Parque Natural del Cap de Creus **Right** Pedestrianized street in Alcúdia, Mallorca

They are usually free, but sometimes you must pay for them at a reduced rate. The **AA** *(see p19)* provides a guide to using the blue badge around Europe (downloadable free from the AA website), and more information can be obtained from **Tourism for All**.

Car, Bike and Motorhome Hire

All the major car rental chains operate in Spain; there are at least a few car hire offices in every provincial capital, and many more in cities. However, if you wish to collect or drop off a car on a Sunday, you may find you can only do so at an airport or in a major city. Prices are competitive, so check around. In general, **Europcar** and **Enterprise** have the most extensive network throughout Spain. To get the very best deals, it is best to book a car in advance through one of the online rental brokers, such as **Auto Europe** or **Argus**.

Precise conditions vary, but in general to hire a car in Spain you must be over 21 and have had a driving licence for at least a year, and must present your licence, passport and a credit card against a deposit. The price quoted to you should include all taxes and unlimited mileage *(kilometraje ilimitado)*, which nowadays is usual practice. By law

rental contracts include basic third-party insurance, but some companies now include comprehensive insurance for no extra charge. If not, it can be worth paying a bit more for comprehensive insurance and collision damage waiver (CDW) cover.

When you collect the car you will be given an emergency contact number and/or the number of a breakdown service. As well as checking the general condition of the car, check that it has the equipment required by law in Spanish-registered vehicles: a set of spare bulbs, two warning triangles and a luminous jacket. If the police discover that the car does not have them, the driver is liable for a fine, not the rental company. If you require extras such as child seats or snow chains, indicate when booking.

Motorcycle rental agencies are less common, so you have less choice of starting point. **BMW Bikerental**, based in Malaga, has offices in Barcelona and Madrid and can arrange bike collection at airports across Spain. **Spain Motorent** has offices in Barcelona, Madrid and Alicante. Helmet rental is usually extra.

Motorhomes can also be rented in Spain: reliable agencies include **CaravanEuropa** and **Euromotorhome**. Minimum age for drivers is usually 25.

DIRECTORY

CARAVANS AND MOTORHOMES
Caravan Club
www.caravanclub.co.uk

DISABLED DRIVERS
Tourism for All
www.tourismforall.org.uk

CAR, BIKE AND MOTORHOME HIRE
Argus
933 801 204; www.arguscarhire.com

Auto Europe
900 801 789; www.autoeurope.com

BMW Bikerental
952 748 141; www.bmwbikerentals.com

CaravanEuropa
www.caravaneuropa.com

Enterprise
902 100 101; www.enterprise.com

Euromotorhome
www.euromotorhome.es

Europcar
www.europcar.com

Spain Motorent
965 656 754; www.spainmotorent.com

Below far left Municipal camp site in Agüero **Below left** Entrance to camp site, Agüero **Below right** Cyclists along a trail near La Mancha **Below far right** Motorcyclist on a road in Sierra de Gredos

Where to Stay

The range of accommodation for travellers in the Spanish countryside has broadened enormously in the last few years. The long-established mix of luxurious paradors in historic buildings, beach resorts, business hotels and simple but cheap *pensiones* has been livened up with the addition of small, family-run *casas rurales* bed-and-breakfasts, allowing you to get much closer to the landscape. Even in placid old towns and remote valleys, you can find distinctive small hotels, often in stunning locations.

Above Sign for the *casas rurales* in Valencia

Hotels

Hotels in Spain are regulated by regional governments, so details of categorization vary. In general accommodation is divided between *hoteles* (identified by a blue plaque with an "H" on it), *hostales* ("HS") and *pensiones* ("P"). Hotels have *en suite* bathrooms in every room; *hostales* and *pensiones* do not always, but in fact many do now offer *en suite* facilities in most or even all rooms. Usually, *hostales* and *pensiones* are cheaper and have fewer facilities than hotels. A *hostal* is not the same as a hostel in English, it is actually a small hotel or guesthouse; a hostel is an *albergue*. Two other traditional names still widely used are *posada* and *fonda*. They generally indicate a traditional-inn atmosphere, but can also be used for quite grand hotels.

Hoteles are star-rated one to five. The differences between *hostales* and *pensiones* are pretty vague and they are star-rated one to two. Star ratings in all regions are based on a checklist of facilities, so are not an automatic guide to a hotel's attractiveness. A four- or five-star hotel must have extensive facilities such as swimming pools, meeting rooms and so on, but the rating will not take into account quality of service, location or charm. Hence a good two-star can be more enjoyable than a functional three-star, and a distinctive *pensión* more attractive than a basic hotel. Many midrange hotels are owned by chains, such as **NH Hoteles** or **Sol Meliá**. They can be relied on for modern comforts, but not usually with much character.

Paradors and Other Distinctive Hotels

There are also hotels that stand out for their special appeal, many of which are conveniently grouped together in chains or associations. Oldest and best-known are the government-owned **paradors**, the first of which opened in 1928. Spread around the country, the most enticing paradors are in finely renovated castles and other historic buildings. Others, especially in the mountains, are in modern buildings in spectacular locations. All paradors have very comfortable, often luxurious rooms, and provide a high level of traditional service and comfort, with restaurants that showcase regional cuisine.

In addition there are now many smaller yet unique hotels around Spain, usually for lower prices. Many are represented by the **Rusticae** group, a quality benchmark that is a handy shortcut to finding attractive small hotels in any part of Spain. Some Rusticae hotels are boutique-style, while others have a more traditional charm, making the most of old houses and lovely settings.

Several regions have local *clubes de calidad* or small hotel associations, such as **Casonas Asturianas** in Asturias and **Cantabria Infinita** and the **Posadas Reales** in Castilla y León, while others have local quality-labelling schemes for hotels (indicated by Q de Calidad Turística).

Casas Rurales

The hotel range is supplemented by family-run *casas rurales*, country homes in villages or farms. Every Spanish region now has rural tourism schemes: classifications and local names are again confusingly varied, but usually homes are listed under *turismo rural*, *agroturismo* or something similar on regional tourism websites. This includes both bed-and-breakfast-type homes with rooms for overnight stays, and separate, fully equipped self-catering cottages that can usually only be rented for a few

Left Outside the charming Posada el Bosque in Potes, *see p52* **Middle** Room in the Posada el Bosque, Potes, *see p52* **Right** Logo of Paradores de Turismo

nights. Some bed-and-breakfasts are grand manor houses, while others are more rustic. Many offer home-cooked evening meals with local produce. *Casas rurales* are listed on Spain-wide sites such as **Guíarural** and **Toprural** as well as on regional websites.

Facilities and Prices

Spanish hotels mostly have double rooms with a double bed (*cama de matrimonio*) or twin beds (*con dos camas*); single rooms are scarce except in business hotels. Only a few cheap *hostales* and *pensiones* still have shared bathrooms. Many hotels now have accessible rooms for disabled travellers, but these are more common in larger hotels. Breakfast is charged separately in most hotels, but included in the room price in *casas rurales* and many small hotels. Rates are generally quoted per room, not per person, but quoted prices do not normally include IVA tax (VAT), at 10 per cent. Prices vary between high season (Easter and July–August, and December–February in winter sports areas) and other times of year, and some hotels have three price seasons (high, medium, low: *alta, media, baja*). In country areas seasonal price differences are relatively modest, but they are far more acute on the coast.

Booking

In low season you can often get a room in country hotels without any prior notice, but booking is always advisable. It is essential to book well in advance on weekends, Easter and in July and August. Reservations are also necessary at nearly all *casas rurales* and the most attractive small hotels. For non-Spanish speakers the best way is to book online. If you arrive without a booking, local tourist offices may be able to assist.

Camping

Well-equipped campsites are plentiful, especially around the coasts and popular mountain ranges. In summer, sites must be booked well ahead. Nearly all large sites admit caravans and motorhomes (*see p20*). Two annual guides to camping sites across Spain are the government-produced *Guía Oficial de Campings* and the *Guía Camping* of the Spanish camping federation **FECC**.

Below far left El Habana around Llanes, *see p55* **Below left** Interior of Casa Leonardo in Vall Fosca, *see p97* **Below middle** Stunning exterior of Marqués de Riscal in Elciego, *see p62* **Below right** Parador de Santo Estevo de Ribas de Sil in Galicia, *see p42* **Below far right** Sign for Bodegas Arzuaga in La Ribera del Duero, *see p149*

DIRECTORY

HOTELS

NH Hoteles
902 115 116 (Spain), 020 3499 8271 (UK); www.nh-hotels.com

Sol Meliá
912 764 757 (Spain), 0808 345 1953 (UK); www.solmelia.com

PARADORS AND OTHER DISTINCTIVE HOTELS

Cantabria Infinita
www.clubcalidadcantabriainfinita.es

Casonas Asturianas
www.casonasasturianas.com

Paradors
902 547 979 (Spain), 020 7953 3020 (UK); www.parador.es; www.keytel.co.uk

Posadas Reales
902 203 030; www.turismocastillayleon.com; www.posadasdecastilla.com

Rusticae
902 103 892; www.rusticae.es

CASAS RURALES

Guíarural
www.guiarural.com

Toprural
www.toprural.com

CAMPING

Federación Española de Clubes Campistas (FECC)
961 399 009; www.guiacampingfecc.com

PRICE CATEGORIES

The following price ranges are for a standard double room in high season:

inexpensive: under €70;
moderate: €70–€120;
expensive: over €120

Where to Eat

Eating out in Spain is a very social activity, and one to be enjoyed at your own pace. You can choose between lingering over a full menu for a relaxing lunch, picking and mixing tapas on a café terrace or just knocking back a beer and a *bocadillo* sandwich while sitting at a bar. The food of Spain is also enormously varied, with specialities in each region. In the last few years, refined restaurants have cropped up even in apparently out-of-the-way places, joining the satisfying traditional country restaurants.

Above Sign for Comercios a Mano

Practical Information

The first thing to adapt to in Spain is local mealtimes. Spaniards traditionally have only a light breakfast, a snack mid-morning and lunch around 2pm, followed by dinner around 9pm or later. Except in touristy areas, where restaurants often follow an "international" timetable, most restaurants only serve a full menu from about 1:30 to 4pm in the afternoons, and 8:30 to11pm at night. For those who find this restrictive, the natural alternatives to go for are tapas *(see pp26–7)*, available all day.

It is not usually necessary to book in mid- or lower-range restaurants, except on Friday and Saturday nights and Sunday lunchtimes, when reservations are a must. It is always a good idea to book ahead in more expensive restaurants. There is rarely any pressure to vacate a table once you have finished eating. A time-honoured part of a Spanish meal is the *sobremesa*, the time when you sit back to chat after a meal over coffee and liqueurs.

Restaurants are often closed on Sunday evenings and for one day each week, usually Monday. Many also close for a few weeks in low season or in August. Credit and debit cards are accepted in virtually all restaurants and even many bars and cafés, but cash is preferred for paying small bills. All restaurant bills are liable to IVA (VAT) tax. This is usually included in menu prices, but some restaurants only add it to the final bill. A growing number of restaurants include a service charge *(servicio incluído)* in bills, but elsewhere tipping is expected. Usually 7 per cent is enough in most restaurants.

Casual clothing is acceptable virtually everywhere except the smartest city restaurants. Children are also generally welcome. Not many restaurants have special menus for children, but most provide smaller portions on request. A growing number of restaurants have facilities for disabled diners, but this is still a problem in older buildings, so it is worth phoning to check.

Smoking has been banned in bars and restaurants since January 2011 but is still permitted on outdoor terraces. If you are a smoker, consider booking a terrace table, as these areas are usually very busy.

Restaurants

Restaurante in Spain covers a wide range of places to eat. Most local and village restaurants also have a bar attached, as a *bar-restaurante*, and are open through the day; their full table menu will usually only be available around Spanish mealtimes *(see above)*. A restaurant without a bar will normally only be open at these times.

Restaurants presenting Spain's acclaimed contemporary cuisine do not have a specific label, but are often indicated in listings as *restaurante gastronómico* or *cocina creativa* or *moderna*. A *marisquería* features fish and seafood *(mariscos)*. Old names for local inns – *venta*, *posada*, *fonda* and especially *mesón* – are widely used and generally go with traditional oak-beam decor and tasty regional dishes. Some restaurants are typical of certain regions. An *arrocería* showcases *paella* and other rice *(arroz)* dishes of Valencia and southern Catalonia; an *asador* specializes in roast *(asado)* meats, typical of Castile.

Monday to Friday, most restaurants offer a set *menú del día* for lunch, with a starter *(primer plato* or *entrada)*, main course *(segundo plato)*, dessert *(postre)*, bread and a drink for €8–€20. Gourmet restaurants may have a *menú de degustación* or tasting menu, at the top end of the price scale.

Left The Cal Sastre restaurant in Santa Pau, *see p104* **Middle** Sign of a bar in Teruel **Right** Vegetables on sale in the Costa Blanca

Tapas, Bars and Cafés

Nearly all bars in Spain offer some kind of food – the only ones that regularly do not are nightclub-style pubs. Bar-restaurants offer a selection of tapas available at all times, as well as their table menus. In many bars small complimentary tapas – olives, chunks of cheese – are served whenever you order a drink, but more elaborate tapas must be ordered and paid for. A *ración* is a larger serving, almost as big as a restaurant course. Tapas, like everything, vary around the country: in many areas they are fairly simple, but Basque bars are renowned for their arrays of intricate snacks.

Other kinds of food can be ordered in bars. A *bocadillo* or *bocata* is a hefty sandwich, made with a large chunk of Spanish bread filled with cold meats, cheese, Spanish omelette and so on. Many cafés also offer *platos combinados*, single dishes with meat or fish, salad and other vegetables all on the same plate.

Wine and Other Drinks

Upper- and mid-range restaurants take increasing care over their wine lists, but in others the choice is more limited, and it is often best to stay with the *vino de la casa* or house wine. Similarly, outside the main wine and sherry areas the wine range in bars that do not specialize in wine is often fairly plain.

Sidra (cider) is popular across northern Spain, and beer *(cerveza)* is available everywhere. Mineral water *(agua con gas*, sparkling, or *sin gas*, still*)* is always an option too. Excellent coffee can be ordered as an espresso *(café solo)*, an espresso with a dash of milk *(cortado)*, or a white coffee *(café con leche)*. An *americano* is an espresso with twice the amount of water, and a *carajillo* is a *solo* with a dash of brandy or other spirits.

Shopping for a Picnic

Before heading into the countryside, buy picnic ingredients in the district's main town, especially, of course, on market days. At other times, the best one-stop shop is a *colmado* or grocery store (or *alimentación general*, or *queviures* in Catalan-speaking areas), which will have fresh fruit and vegetables, cold meats *(charcutería)*, cheeses *(quesos)*, wine, beers and water. For bread, *panaderías* have *pan de barra*, the normal Spanish white baguette-style bread, country breads and sometimes brown bread *(pan integral)*. There are also small supermarkets in many towns.

DIRECTORY

PRICE BANDS

The following price ranges are for a three-course meal for one person, including tax and service:

inexpensive: under €20;
moderate: €20–€40;
expensive: over €40

Below far left Tapas bar in Valderrobres **Below left** Inventive signs at a restaurant in Andalusia **Below middle** Restaurants, bars and other attractions advertised on a wall in Andalusia **Below right** Parador de Cambados, *see p36* **Below far right** Van selling snacks in Xàbia, Costa Blanca

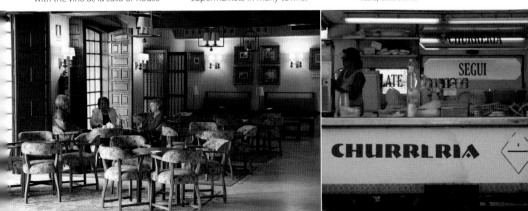

The Flavours of Spain

Every part of Spain has its own distinctive dishes. Regions such as the Basque Country and Catalonia have complete cuisines of their own. Spain's adventurous modern chefs may experiment with ideas from around the world, but their creativity is nearly always rooted in traditions from their home region. Some favourites such as *tortilla* (potato omelette) and *chorizo* sausages are found in every part of Spain, but the more intriguing dishes have a strong local flavour. This creates a rich culinary landscape that is immensely enjoyable to explore.

Above Menu displaying the day's specials outside a restaurant

DIRECTORY

ON THE MENU

Ajoblanco (Andalusia)
Cold soup of garlic, almonds and often a range of other ingredients

Arròs negre (Catalan)
Black rice with squid, cooked in squid ink

Bacalao al pil-pil (Basque)
Salt cod fried in very hot oil with garlic

Botifarra amb mongetes (Catalan)
Sausage with haricot beans

Cochinillo asado (Castile)
Roast suckling pig

Empanada gallega (Galicia)
Pastry pie filled with tuna, meat or shellfish, and peppers and onions

Fabada (Asturias)
A rich stew of haricot beans, chorizo and pork

Fideuà (Catalonia and Valencia)
Similar to a paella, but made with noodles instead of rice

Gazpacho (Andalusia, with variations all across the south)
Cold tomato soup, usually served sprinkled with chopped cucumbers, peppers, onions and bread

Lacón con grelos (Galicia)
Pork joint with Swiss chard and potatoes

Merluza a la vasca (Basque)
Hake cooked in white wine with prawns, clams, peppers and other ingredients

The North

With its rocky Atlantic coast, Galicia is famed above all for superb fish and seafood, especially hake, mussels, scallops and octopus, accompanied by the region's crisp white wines. Other Galician favourites such as *caldo gallego* (a stew made of greens, potatoes, bacon and other meats), reflect the bracing ocean climate and the often chilly, wet winter.

Neighbouring Asturias and Cantabria also draw excellent fish from the sea, and just inland is Spain's best dairy country, producing distinctive cheeses such as Asturias' pungent *cabrales*, helped down with *sidra* (cider). Hearty mountain stews are another hallmark. Asturian restaurants are also renowned for generous portions, and tapas can be as big as a restaurant course.

Refined, distinctive and subtle, Basque cuisine has traditionally been the most prestigious of all Spain's culinary traditions. It has served as an inspiration to a whole line of famous chefs. Fish and seafood such as salt cod, hake and crab, often with red peppers, are again mainstays. Basques also have a distinctive approach to tapas, known as *pintxos*. Instead of the relatively simple snacks, Basque bars serve impressive trays of carefully assembled and mixed tapas.

Navarra and La Rioja are known above all for superb wines, but also for many delicious dishes often featuring red peppers, nuts and river fish such as trout.

Along the Mediterranean

Catalonia is the Basque Country's main challenger in terms of culinary sophistication. Ferran Adrià (b. 1962), one of the world's most reputed chefs at the moment, is from Catalonia. Among the many Catalan specialities are unusual combinations of meat and seafood. Much more use is made of vegetables here than in many parts of Spain. Along with refined creations, there is also simpler Catalan country cooking based around meats, especially lamb, rabbit and *botifarra* sausages, grilled *a la brasa* over charcoal, and served with *all i oli* (garlic and mayonnaise).

Catalonia also produces a wide range of wines and sparkling cava. One of the most popular Catalan dishes is *pa amb tomàquet* (bread moistened by wiping it with tomatoes, olive oil, garlic and salt).

Above left Seafood on display **Above middle** Bottle of Spanish-made Ambar beer **Above right** Fish being grilled on stakes over a wood fire

The Balearic Islands also have interesting dishes, with a strongly Mediterranean flavour. Rich fish and shellfish stews are specialities.

Valencia is known above all for the international symbol of Spanish food – paella. In its Valencian homeland (and the rice lands of southern Catalonia) you can order paella in many different varieties, with a fascinating range of ingredients. Valencia is also the home of another speciality that has conquered the whole country, turrón (almond nougat). Made since Moorish times, it is an essential finale to a Spanish Christmas feast.

The Centre: Castile and Aragón

In contrast to the complicated creations of Atlantic and Mediterranean Spain, the food of the two Castiles, Castilla y León and Castilla La Mancha, puts the stress on simplicity. Meats such as the roast lamb and suckling pig of Segovia, or superb chuletón steaks in Ávila, are the centrepiece. Beans and other pulses appear in many sustaining potajes (stews). Otherwise, vegetables are scarce and usually served separately as salads or first courses, since Castilians traditionally prefer to consume good meat on its own.

Punchy hams and sausages such as chorizos, longaniza and the botillo of León are also Castilian trademarks.

In Aragón, traditional cooking is simple, but with well-flavoured country dishes featuring borage and other unusual vegetables.

The South

The best dishes of Andalusia reflect the region's Moorish past and the southern heat. Moorish influence is seen in the subtle use of almonds and honey. The characteristic cold soups such as gazpacho and the less well-known ajoblanco are deliciously refreshing in an Andalusian summer. Equally intertwined with the climate are the many salads, such as pipirrana (peppers, tomatoes, cucumber and garlic, with variations that include meat and fish). Fish and seafood such as squid and pescadilla (whiting) are generally cooked simply, either plain grilled or fried in batter. Inland, traditional cooking makes more use of strong meats and pulses such as chickpeas (garbanzos). Western Andalusia and neighbouring Extremadura are the home of the finest serrano hams. Murcia is known above all for the quality of its peppers and other Mediterranean vegetables, used in soups, salads and tapas.

DIRECTORY

ON THE TAPAS LIST

Albóndigas
Meatballs

Boquerones en vinagre
Fresh anchovies marinated in oil, lemon and vinegar

Calamares a la romana
Squid rings fried in batter

Ensaladilla rusa
Salad of potatoes, red peppers, onions, tuna and other ingredients in mayonnaise

Gambas al ajillo
Prawns cooked in garlic

Jamón serrano
Dry-cured ham

Patatas bravas
Deep-fried potatoes with a peppery sauce

Salpicón de mariscos
Seafood salad

Sobrasada (Mallorca)
Spicy, slightly soft red sausage

Below far left Sausages and cheese in a market **Below left** Varieties of olives on sale **Below middle left** Red peppers drying in the sun **Below middle right** Large pan of paella **Below right** Wine for sampling at a bodega **Below far right** Chef cooking squid over a fire

LEON

CASTILIA VETVS

CASTILIA NOVA

EXTREMADVRA

ANDALVSIA

Montes d'Occa
Villa vega
Rocedillo
Val de buentas
Burgos
Silos
S. Pedro
Cabacubia
Lara
Retuerta
S. Domingo
Padilla
Leonardos
S. Steva
S. gormes
Oradara
Villa vega
Rabe
Tramidos
Venta moral
Salduendo
Lerma
Bahabon
Cogollo
Torquema da
Peniafuel
Lavid
Froçedillo
Aranda de Duero
Torresandino
Castrill
Raa
quera
Relaux rio
Moral del reino
Palentia
Duenna
Cabecon
Villa baues
Castroyed
Rueldo
Boezillo
Castrillo
Ives
Simacos
Valpuesta
Ventosa
Auila fuente
Marçotea
Villa nueva
Ric
Rica
S. Ma de nieua
Olmedo
Don hierro
Coca
S. Pedro
Segovia
Guadarama
Pto de
Sepulueda
Escurial
Talamanca
Torre di lodones
Alarça
Madrid
Ar
Baraco
Zebreros
Aleorcoz
Redemolinos
Cadahalso
Las Ventas
S. Sylvestro
Maqueda
S. Olaja
C. d. Aquila
Cavana
Anouer
Yeyes
Bravo
Burugel
Cassalegas
Toledo
Rio Tajo
Venta de Osmo
Ocania
Bogas
Orgas
Tembleque
Villa
Puebla
Panojerbo
Yuenes
Huertas
Cosuegra
Rosatan
Malagon
Alcacer
Calatrava
Vela
Carioncilla
Almagr
Ciudad real
Villa real
Camalueches
Fardilla
Cru
El convento de calatrava
Venta la reina
Almodoar del campo
Elviso
Solan
Vila
La venta Ilerva
La venta de los Palacios
Izti
Vtches
Alhama
Ventala
Linares
Megibar
Sierra Morena
Andujar
Baeça
Jaen
Martos
Alcaudate
Aravita
Cambil
Guarda
Alcala real
Sequia
Puerto lope
Granada
Arriza
Duero rio
Xambrino
Aniago
Rodilaua
Mojadas
Guarate
Fuente sahuro
Medina del campo
Ataquines
Çorita
Fresno
Salamanca
Ventosa
Helite
Auila
Villa casti
Torre sol
Villafranca
Bonhos
Giuguelo
Martin del castagol
Cardenosa
Herra don
Paja ruz
S. Pedro
Pennaranda
Alua
La moya
Endrinas
Martin de rio
Caparra
Cuidad Rodrigo
Bodom
Aldea nueva
Laxarilla
El villar
Quacos
Xandarilla
Coria
Plazentia
Toril
Vera de Placencia
Colmenar
Porto d. pico
Paredes
Cassarubios
Cipuezelos
Esquivias
Legan
Mostoles
Mor
Bavona
Antigol
S. Martinho dos vinhos
Olgura
Capara
Cañaveral
Alcantara
Almaraz
La calsada
Talavera la reina
Velada
Oropesa
Puete del Arcobispo
Tagus flu
La barcas del coneta
Arroyo el yuercos
Caçeres
Las casas del puerto
Venta la vadera
Naval villar
Villaneto
Villar de pedrosa
Vent. d. los Nogalles
Malpartida
Licenda
Aldealcano
Venta del hospital
S. M. d. Guadalupe
Cihameros
Legrusaon
Herrera
Merida
Medelin
Trugilho
Campilho
Palazio del Rey
Rio Guadiana
S. Vincente
Venta Barachiva
Venta de los herreras
Talavera
Trugilhano
Cafra
Majadas
Campanario
La Puebla del coçer
Ruesta
Curita
Albufera
Torre de Mexia
Vil. nu. della Serena
Magazela
Calbeça del ouey
Ventas nuevas
La parra
Almendralejo
Fuente de iudofre
Alcudia
Belalcaçar
Hynojosa
Aberquerque
Enzina Sola
Ellarena
Vlaire
Alhama
Aroche
Cala
Realejo
Alanis
Ynojosa
Cumbres maiores
S. Olalla
Caffe
Cacalla
S. Niclaes
Constantino
Samosa
Fesira
S. Iuhan
Aldeo el rio
Adamuz
Torre de campo
Xabuga
Araçena
Elpodioso
Almaden
Almeria
Cordoua
Lora
Peñaflor
Guadalcaçer
Carpio
Moron
Cambil
El villar
Calamea
Elmadiono
Castilblanco
Villa nueva
C. de las guardas
Azarcolla
Gerenna
Guadaxos
La Campana
Carmona
Las posadas
Rambla
Vaena
Montemaior
Cabral
Buytron
Mança nilla
Triana
Bogodun
Santella
Eçya
Aguil
Isnasar
Priego
COND.
Niebla
Bollos
Coria
Sevilla
Puen
Lasqui
Alcamu
Zebreros
Losada
Al Furado
Cacabelos
P. de Domingo
S. Stevan Bollo
Viana
Cadahox
Lomba
Bragança
Fruadeso
Caravalbes
Chasim
Mirandela
Freres
Alfandega
Benposto
Terre de Moncorve
Pejares
Pena da francia
S. Felizes de Gallegas
Laboueda
Mezonero
Vilueste
Aldea nueva
Fuente Salim
Aldea nueva
Hermi selho
Arcediano
Aldea
Terra
Cabreya
Puebla de Sanabria
Peradela
S. Martinho
Tracossos
Alcani
Villalpando
Çamora
Mirida
Astorga
P. de Reyna
Ponferrada
Benauente
Medina de rio Seco
Castromonte
Villalat
Pedrosa
Tordezillas
Tore
Simacos
Valadolid
Villalon
Carion d. los candes
Mansilla
Calcadilla
Seldana
Villa nueva de las carctes
d'Occa
Montes d. Melger
Leon
Villa reme
Maratiiones

THE
DRIVES

Medieval Treasures and Golden Bays

Santiago de Compostela to Pontevedra

Highlights

- **The pilgrims' goal**
  Explore the architectural treasures of
  Santiago de Compostela

- **Medieval manor**
  Travel deep into the green Gallego
  countryside to visit the fairy-tale
  house and gardens of Pazo de Oca

- **Pristine beaches**
  Stroll along the lovely beaches
  around the Ría de Pontevedra

- **Charming street life**
  Visit one of the many excellent bars
  and cafés of Pontevedra's old quarter

Beaches stretch out around the
Ría de Pontevedra

Medieval Treasures and Golden Bays

The medieval city of Santiago has been a key pilgrimage destination for over a thousand years. Crammed with architectural treasures, it is less than an hour's drive from the natural beauty of Galicia's Rías Baixas. Scattered along this rugged coastline is a succession of superb beaches lining the narrow, steep-sided bays or *rías*. Pretty towns, such as Cambados and Pontevedra, offer yet more cultural gems, plus a chance to savour the area's fine cuisine and wines in their many good-value restaurants.

KEY

Drive route

0 kilometres 5

0 miles 5

Above Santiago de Compostela's grand cathedral towering over the city, *see p34*

ACTIVITIES

Forage for clams and cockles at low tide along the beach at the fishing village of Cambados

Be pampered in style at one of the luxurious spas on the tiny island of A Toxa

Soak up the sun on Galicia's longest beach, Praia de Lanzada, or rent a windsurf board and glide out into the Atlantic

Take a cruise from Sanxenxo or Portonovo out to the isolated Illa de Ons, just off the coast from Praia de Paxariñas

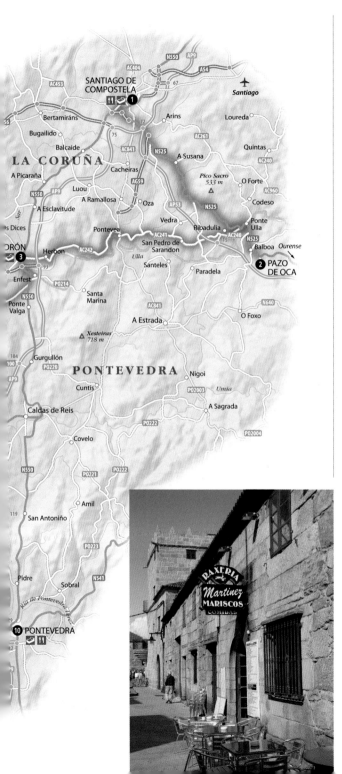

PLAN YOUR DRIVE

Start/finish: Santiago de Compostela to Pontevedra.

Number of days: 1–2, allowing half a day in Santiago.

Distance: 150 km (95 miles).

Road conditions: There are no steep climbs and roads remain passable all year round. Main roads along the coast can get crowded in summer, especially from mid-July to August.

When to go: Between May and October is the best time to visit, preferably avoiding the peak season of August.

Opening times: Most shops and museums open from 9am to 7pm daily, many closing for a couple of hours between 1 and 4pm. Churches usually stay open all day from 8am to 7pm.

Main market days: Santiago de Compostela: daily; Cambados: daily; Pontevedra: daily.

Shopping: Besides fine Albariño wines, many visitors like to take home the *tarta de Santiago* almond cakes.

Major festivals: Santiago de Compostela: Fiestas del Apóstol Santiago, 24–25 Jul; **Padrón:** Fiesta del Pimiento, first Sun Aug; **Cambados:** Festa del Vino Albariño, first Sun Aug; **A Lanzada:** Romería da Lanzada, last Sun Aug; **Pontevedra:** Fiesta dos Maios, May; Fiesta de San Benito, Jul.

DAY TRIP OPTIONS

Using Santiago de Compostela as a base, spend a **leisurely day** exploring the Rías Baixas coastline, with its golden beaches, islands and picturesque fishing villages. **Culture** and **history lovers**, however, may prefer to head straight to Pontevedra and spend a day wandering the city's medieval alleyways. For details, *see p37*.

Left One of the many restaurants in Cambados, known for local wines and seafood, *see p36*

Above Dazzling façade of Santiago's grand cathedral looms over the Praza do Obradoiro
Below Lovely gardens of the Casa-Museo Rosalía de Castro, Padrón

VISITING SANTIAGO DE COMPOSTELA

Tourist Information
Rúa do Vilar 63, 15705; 981 555 129; www.santiagoturismo.com

Parking
The most convenient car park for the cathedral is the huge Xoán XXIII car park, a short distance north.

WHERE TO STAY

SANTIAGO DE COMPOSTELA

As Artes *moderate*
This cosy hotel is located near the cathedral. It is worth paying a little extra for one of the larger of its seven beautifully furnished rooms.
Travesa Dúas Portas 2, 15707; 981 555 254; www.asartes.com

Hostal dos Reis Católicos *expensive*
One of the oldest hotels in the world, this parador is luxurious with elegant living rooms, spectacular bedrooms and a beautiful dining room.
Plaza do Obradoiro 1, 15705; 981 582 200; www.parador.es

PADRÓN

Pension Jardin *inexpensive*
At the eastern edge of old Padrón, this fine old mansion has been tastefully converted into a very comfortable little hotel.
Avda. de la Estación 3, 15900; 981 810 950

1 Santiago de Compostela
La Coruña; 15700

A ravishing ensemble of colonnaded stone lanes, vast squares and mighty medieval churches, Santiago de Compostela offers a wealth of cultural treasures, along with a whirl of great places to eat, drink and sleep.

A thousand years ago, half a million pilgrims made their way each year to Santiago, walking the route known as the Camino de Santiago. The city ranked after Jerusalem and Rome as the third holiest site in Christendom, thanks to the legend that the body of the Apostle James – Sant Yago in the local Galician language – was brought here by sea after his death. Now encircled by suburbs, the city's ancient core has changed little. In its labyrinth of alleyways, each building merges organically into the next.

Towering over the Praza do Obradoiro, a large square usually packed with pilgrims, the **Catedral de Santiago de Compostela** is an amazing spectacle. Its Baroque façade dates from the 18th century. Behind, its Romanesque predecessor, six centuries older, remains largely intact. Enter via the Pórtico de Gloria, pausing to touch the carved Tree of Jesse. Relics of St James are preserved in a crypt beneath the gilded altar.

The Romanesque **Pazo de Xelmirez** *(open daily, closed Sun afternoon)* and the Baroque church wof the **Monasterio de San Martiño Pinario** *(open daily)* in Praza da Immaculata are also worth visiting.

🚗 *From the Xoán XXIII car park, take the exit northeast on Avenue Xoán XXIII to join Santiago's ring road. Turn right at the third traffic light, following signs to Ourense onto the N525. Just past the "Km 319" marker, turn right and follow signs for Pazo de Oca.*

2 Pazo de Oca
Pontevedra; 36685

The best-preserved *pazo* (traditional country house) in Galicia, the Pazo de Oca is enchanting. The 18th-century mansion is not open to visitors. Its gardens *(open daily)* are the attraction. Part playful, part formal, they centre on a small lake that holds a couple of boat-shaped islands. Hydrangeas and magnolias blossom on all sides, and everywhere is the trickle of running water from the irrigation channels that feed vine-clad trellises. Statues and topiary abound.

🚗 *Return to the N525 and turn left towards Santiago. Go left from Ponte Ulla (direction Arzúa/Pontevea) on the AC240, which later becomes the AC241. At Pontevea, turn right and then left onto the AC242 and cross the auto-pista. Continue into Padrón. Turn right before the railway to park outside Casa-Museo Rosalía de Castro.*

3 Padrón
La Coruña; 15900

Padrón is best known for its succulent *pimientos*, little green peppers deep-fried and served whole in tapas bars across Spain. It was home to Galicia's most famous poet, Rosalía de Castro (1837–85), who wrote in both Galician and Castilian. Her charming house, opposite the town's railway station, now serves as the Casa-Museo Rosalía de Castro *(closed Mon)*, with memorabilia downstairs and her living quarters preserved upstairs.

🚗 *Continue on the AC242 and take the N550 left in Padrón. Turn right onto the PO548. Follow signs through Vilagarcía, then after 5 km (3 miles) onto the PO549, beyond Vilaxoán, turn right onto the PO307 and cross the bridge to Illa de Arousa. Follow signs for Parque Natural de Carreirón.*

❹ Parque Natural de Carreirón

Pontevedra; 36626

The Illa de Arousa, linked to the mainland by a long, low road bridge, is probably the one place in the whole of the Rías Baixas that remains closest to its original, natural state. That is why it is worth taking the time to stroll along the footpaths of the Parque Natural de Carreirón, located at the southern end of this heavily forested island. The isolated beaches, heathland and saltwater marshes of this natural park have been set aside as a sanctuary for migratory waterbirds.

Above Colourful boats used by local fishermen along the Illa de Arousa's shore

A two-hour walking tour

A placard by the car park maps out two possible loop walks around this promontory: one of 3.6 km (2 miles), and one of 2.5 km (1.5 miles) that involves taking a short cut across the middle. Visitors are, however, unlikely to regret taking the longer route, as it allows extra time in delightful surroundings. All the way around the perimeter rough-hewn granite picnic tables stand amid the pines.

Head right from the car park, through the woods lining the south shore of the Enseada da Brava. One hundred metres (110 yd) or so along, either turn left to take the shorter loop, or continue ahead to reach the mouth of the bay, to enjoy the ocean views from the **Punta da Cruz** ①. To the southwest, the town of O Grove and the linked island of A Toxa are clearly visible, while yachts and fishing boats thread their way between the lesser islets. The headland itself consists of tumbled, eroded boulders

and an abundance of tidal pools. The two loops meet again at the **Praia das Margaritas** ②, a tiny pocket of sand amid jumbled rocks. Continue south, rounding the peninsula's southern tip. Immediately inland of the **Praia Lontreira** ③ is a saltwater marsh that is a good spot to watch for wading birds, including herons and ducks. Turning up the eastern side of the peninsula, there are longer strands of beach, such as the **Praia de Salinas** ④, where swimming in summer is easy and safe. There are tremendous views along the coast from here, with the low-lying rafts that are used to cultivate mussels tethered in symmetrical rows across the *rías* and the town of Cambados sprawling along the shore over to the east. Continue on the trail to the car park.

🚗 *Drive back across the bridge to rejoin the PO549. Turn right and 5 km (3 miles) south the road enters Cambados via the Praza de Fefiñanes. Park on the far side of the square.*

VISITING PARQUE NATURAL DE CARREIRÓN

Tourist Information
There is no tourist information office – simply a noticeboard in the park – though the park management can be contacted by phone on 986 805 483

Parking
Park at the end of the road at the start of the trail.

EAT AND DRINK

SANTIAGO DE COMPOSTELA

Los Sobrinos del Padre Benito
inexpensive
This is the perfect place to try the Gallego speciality of *pulpo a feira* (octopus with potatoes and paprika).
San Miguel dos Argos 7, 15704; 981 583 566; closed Mon

O Gato Negro *inexpensive*
A traditional stalwart, unchanged in decades, this charming spot is a great place for traditional local tapas.
Travesía do Franco, 15702; 981 583 105

Don Gaiferos *expensive*
This atmospheric restaurant, beneath vaulted stone ceilings in old Santiago, has attentive service and a full menu of succulent seafood and meat dishes.
Rúa Nova 23, 15705; 981 583 984; closed Sun eve and Mon

Enseada da Brava

🛈 🅿

Punta da Cruz
①

Praia de Salinas
④

②
Praia das Margaritas

③
Praia Lontreira

0 metres 500
0 yards 500

Eat and Drink: inexpensive, under €20; moderate, €20–€40; expensive, over €40

Above Capela de San Caralampio, A Toxa
Below Capela de Nosa Señora in A Lanzada

FERRIES TO ILLA DE ONS

Ferries to the island sail from
Portonovo and Sanxenxo.

Naviera Mar de Ons
986 225 272; www.mardeons.com

Naviera Illa de Ons
986 320 048; www.isladeons.net

WHERE TO STAY

CAMBADOS

Hotel O Lagar *moderate*
A family-run hotel offering spacious
rooms in the centre of town, along
with a traditional restaurant.
C/ Pontevedra 14, 36630;
986 520 807

Parador de Cambados *expensive*
This fine old manor house is the most
comfortable hotel in Cambados, with
pleasant gardens and a good restaurant.
Plaza Calzada, 36630; 986 542 250;
www.parador.es

A LANZADA

Samar Hotel *moderate–expensive*
Perched in splendid isolation at the
north end of A Lanzada beach, this
hotel has spacious ocean-view
rooms and a large terrace restaurant.
A Lanzada 9, O Grove, 36989; 986 738
378; www.samarhotel.com

PONTEVEDRA

Hotel Ruas *inexpensive*
Smart Hotel Ruas has presentable
rooms. It is ideally positioned for nightlife in one of old Pontevedra's squares.
C/ Sarmiento 20, 36002; 986 846 416;
www.hotelruas.net

Parador Casa del Baron *expensive*
This inviting hotel is housed in a
majestic former palace in the lanes
of Pontevedra's ravishing old quarter.
Rúa del Baron 19, 36002; 986 855 800;
www.parador.es

⑤ Cambados
Pontevedra; 36630
Despite its lack of a swimming
beach, medieval Cambados is the
prettiest seaside town in the Rías
Baixas. It centres on the **Praza de
Fefiñáns**, a large flagstoned square
that is set well back from the ocean,
and is alive with bars and restaurants.
During harvest season, tractors
unload crates of the plump, white
grapes used to make Albariño wine
into the cellars of the ancient stone
mansions that line the narrow main
street. Down by the harbour, sturdy
cockle-pickers dig shellfish from the
sands exposed by each low tide.

🚗 *Head south, then right at the first
traffic light west on the PO550 from
Cambados. After 14 km (8 miles), on
reaching the peninsula that leads to A
Toxa island, turn right onto the PO316
for 4 km (2 miles) towards O Grove,
then turn right again onto the A Toxa
bridge. Head right on reaching the
island, and park alongside the hotels.*

Albariño Wine

Since Galicia's dry, elegant Albariño
was first officially standardized and
certified in 1986, it has become
firmly established internationally
as one of the most popular Spanish
wines. The Albariño grape variety
from which the wine is made was
introduced to the region by medieval German monks – the name
means "white (wine) from the
Rhine". Thousands of farmers now
grow Albariño in small-scale vineyards concentrated mainly around
Cambados. Wineries that can be
visited include Condes de Albarei,
2 km (1 mile) south of town *(www.
condesdealbarei.com)*.

---

⑥ A Toxa
Pontevedra; 36991
Reached by a short road bridge from
the fishing port of O Grove, the little
wooded island of A Toxa became
famous for its healing waters during
the 19th century. As a result, it is now
swamped by luxury spas, hotels and
holiday villas and can become a little
overcrowded, although it is still possible to enjoy a quiet walk along the
attractive seashore. The 12th-century
hermitage **Capela de San Caralampio**
(open daily), with its walls covered in
scallop shells, is well worth a visit.

🚗 *Recross the bridge from A Toxa,
turn left onto the PO316 to reach the
north end of Praia de Lanzada and
take a turn at the roundabout to a
large car park to the right of the road.*

⑦ A Lanzada
Pontevedra; 36989
The majestic golden crescent of the
Praia de Lanzada is the best known
of the Rías Baixas beaches. Stretching
for around 7 km (4 miles) along the
southern shore of a slender isthmus,
it is busy with swimmers, surfers and
sunbathers in high summer. For the
rest of the year, it is the perfect place
for a long, windswept stroll, enjoying
superb views out to the scattered
offshore islands. On the road out of
A Lanzada, between Km 27 and 26
on the PO308, turn right (following
signs for the Capela) to get to the
Capela de Nosa Señora *(open daily)*.

🚗 *Go 2 km (1 mile) south along Praia
de Lanzada and come back onto the
coastal PO308. About 10 km (6 miles)
along, at a sharp bend to the left,
follow a sign to the right, down to
the car park for Praia de Paxariñas.*

⑧ Praia de Paxariñas
Pontevedra; 36970

The tiny beach at Paxariñas is perhaps the definitive example of the kind of sheltered cove that makes the Rías Baixas so popular with holidaying families. Tucked down at the foot of small cliffs, out of sight of a coastal road that is lined with little hotels, it is a wonderful spot to while away a few hours. Take a ferry to the **Illa de Ons** from either Portonovo or Sanxenxo, east of Praia de Paxariñas. The island cradles pretty beaches on its inland side, such as the Praia das Dornas, where the boats dock. The wild hillsides facing the ocean are ideal for walking.

🚗 *Continue east on the PO308 and pass through Portonovo and above central Sanxenxo. After 15 km (9 miles) from Sanxenxo, at the west end of Poio near Casalvito, follow a signposted turning to the left to reach the car park.*

⑨ Poio
Pontevedra; 36995

Although Poio itself is only a fairly plain modern beach town, a true gem of old Galicia survives not far up the hillside – the 500-year-old Benedictine **Monasterio de Poio** *(open daily)*. As well as an imposing church, the complex includes a colonnaded cloister, decorated with a mosaic mural that depicts the history of the pilgrimage to Santiago. There is also a museum of the world's smallest books, while a newer annexe serves as a hotel.

🚗 *Return to the PO308 and turn left. Continue on this road to the end, following signs to Pontevedra. Turn right to cross Ría de Pontevedra Lérez and reach Pontevedra. Follow signs to one of the underground car parks.*

⑩ Pontevedra
Pontevedra; 36000

The old city of Pontevedra is cradled in the final bend of the Ría de Pontevedra Lérez. A stroll through its compact pedestrian core of cobbled alleys introduces visitors to a succession of charming medieval squares, ranging from the formal and spacious Praza da Ferrería to the elegant Praza de Teucro with its rows of orange trees, and the Praza da Verdura with its lively cafés and bars. Prettiest of them all is the tiny Praza da Lena, where a fascinating museum of Gallego history and culture, the **Museo de Pontevedra** *(open Tue–Sun)*, is housed in a cluster of five neighbouring historic buildings. Among the works on display are 15th-century canvases by Goya and Zurbarán. The lovely ruins of the church of San Domingo are nearby.

Above left View of the beach near Sanxenxo
Above right Praza de Teucro, Pontevedra

EAT AND DRINK

CAMBADOS

Yayo Daporta *expensive*
Try creative Galician cuisine highlighting local fresh seafood here.
Rúa Hospital 7, 36630; 986 526 062; www.yayodaporta.com; closed Sun eve, Mon and 2 weeks in Nov

POIO

Casa Solla *expensive*
Enjoy Gallego favourites and views over the bay in this elegant spot.
Avda. Sineiro 7, 36005; 986 872 884; www.restaurantesolla.com; closed Sun eve, Mon, Thu and 2 weeks in Dec

PONTEVEDRA

El Pitillo *inexpensive*
Warm, old-fashioned spot with delicious grilled scallops and other tasty tapas.
Rúa Alta 3, 36002; 986 872 322

DAY TRIP OPTIONS

To break up the drive into day trips, it is best to stay overnight in either Santiago de Compostela at the start of the trip or Pontevedra at the end, both easily accessible by the AP9.

Nature's unspoilt wonders
Spend the morning on the beach of A Lanzada ⑦. Then allow an hour to savour the wild Illa de Arousa and its Parque Natural de Carreirón ④. A stop en route in the picturesque village of Cambados ⑤, to sample fine Albariño wines at one of the bodegas, is a must.

From Santiago, head south towards Padrón on the N550. Then follow the coastal PO549 and PO550 through Cambados to A Lanzada. Return to Santiago the same way.

Medieval treasure trove
Walk around the labyrinth of ancient, winding alleyways, crammed with glorious examples of medieval architecture in Pontevedra ⑩. Beautiful squares and fine old mansions are punctuated by a stream of appealing cafés and restaurants. A short round-trip west takes in the magnificent Monasterio de Poio ⑨.

Take the N550 or AP9 motorway south from Santiago to Pontevedra. Poio is 4 km (2 miles) west of Pontevedra on the PO308.

Eat and Drink: inexpensive, under €20; moderate, €20–€40; expensive, over €40

Along the Sacred Shore

Ourense to the Valle del Silencio

Highlights

- **Medieval monastery**
  Visit the cliff top Monasterio de Santo Estevo de Ribas de Síl, which now doubles as a magnificent spa hotel

- **Majestic canyon**
  Trek through the Cañón do Síl, sculpted with ancient Roman terraced vineyards

- **Gold fever**
  Take in the extraordinary stark beauty of the Roman gold mines at Las Médulas

- **Spectacular valley**
  Walk the trails of the Valle del Silencio and explore its sanctuaries and monasteries

Magnificent golden-yellow rock formations at Las Médulas

Along the Sacred Shore

In its final stretch before meeting the Miño river, not far northeast of the provincial capital of Ourense, the Síl river has carved a stupendous canyon, cloaked with ancient forests. This tour traces the sheer green walls of the gorge, which have been sculpted since Roman times with precarious terraced vineyards. The sides of the gorge are so prized for their fine, rare soils that they are known as the Ribeira Sacra (the Sacred Shore). Continuing east towards Ponferrada, the route climbs into the eerie bad lands of Las Médulas, devastated by Roman gold-mining operations. The drive finally reaches the Valle del Silencio, where early Christian churches and monasteries, linked by ravishing foot trails, lie hidden high in the woods.

0 kilometres   10

0 miles   10

KEY

Drive route

Above Village of Peñalba de Santiago nestled in the mountains, *see p44*

ACTIVITIES

Walk through the woods by the Síl river or the mountains

Taste the exquisite wines of the Ribeira Sacra

Explore the ancient monasteries in the Valle del Silencio

Above Courtyard of the Monasterio de Santo Estevo de Ribas de Síl, *see p42*

Below Rugged rock formations at Las Médulas, *see p44*

PLAN YOUR DRIVE

Start/finish: Ourense to the Valle del Silencio.

Number of days: 2–3, allowing half a day to explore the Valle del Silencio.

Distance: 280 km (175 miles).

Road conditions: Roads in the Síl gorge and all mountain valleys are susceptible to ice in winter. The roads, especially on the Síl section and around the Valle del Silencio, are poorly paved and very narrow and winding at parts.

When to go: The ideal time to visit is spring for wild flowers or autumn for foliage. The Valle del Silencio is inaccessible in winter.

Opening hours: Most shops and monuments are open from 9am to 6pm with a break from 1 to 4pm.

Main market days: Ourense: 7th, 17th and 25th of every month.

Shopping: The major products on sale are earthy local foods such as figs, chestnuts, honey, strong cheeses and Ribeira Sacra wine.

Major festivals: Ourense: Festival de Cine Internacional, Oct; Ponferrada: San José Obrero de Cuatrovientos, 1 May.

DAY TRIP OPTIONS

Architecture enthusiasts will enjoy a trip to the monasteries on the Canón do Síl, while **adventure lovers** will enjoy a boat trip on the Síl river. **History buffs** will be fascinated by the rugged beauty of Las Médulas. For details, *see p45*.

Above Puente Romano, over the Miño river, in Ourense **Below** Monasterio de Santo Estevo de Ribas de Síl nestled in the mountains

WHERE TO STAY

OURENSE

Gran Hotel San Martín *moderate*
This very comfortable high-rise hotel overlooks the Parque San Lázaro.
Rúa Curros Enríquez 1, 32003; 988 371 811; www.granhotelsanmartin.com

MONASTERIO DE SANTO ESTEVO DE RIBAS DE SÍL

Parador de Santo Estevo de Ribas de Síl *expensive*
This magnificent monastery has rooms and a restaurant with great views over the Cañón do Síl.
Nogueira de Ramuín, 32162; 988 010 110; www.parador.es

AROUND MONASTERIO DE SANTA CRISTINA DE RIBAS DE SÍL

Reitoral de Chandrexa *inexpensive*
Near the river and 5 km (3 miles) from the monastery, this is a lovely three-room rural bed-and-breakfast.
Parada de Síl, 32747; 988 208 099; www.chandrexa.com; credit cards not accepted

CASTRO CALDELAS

Hotel Vicente Risco *inexpensive*
This charming hotel offers comfortable rooms and a good-value restaurant.
Rúa Grande 4, 32769; 988 203 360; www.pousadavicenterisco.com

A POBRA DE TRIVES

Casa Grande de Trives *inexpensive*
In a beautifully restored manor house, this bed-and-breakfast offers rooms with modern facilities.
C/ Marqués de Trives 17, 32780; 988 332 066; www.casagrandetrives.com

① Ourense
Ourense; 32000
The handsome city of Ourense was founded by the Romans on the south bank of the Miño river, around the city's well-known, mineral-rich thermal springs, **Fonte as Burgas**. Its hilltop historic core, a tangle of tiny stone lanes interspersed with arcaded squares, holds an appeal for visitors. The 12th- to 13th-century **Catedral de San Martiño** is the city's principal sight. Two contrasting bridges span the river – the much-rebuilt seven-arched **Puente Romano**, and the eye-catching **Puente Milenio**, unveiled in 2001, which offers great views.

🚗 *Take the N120 out of town, towards Monforte. After 18 km (11 miles), turn right onto the C546 to Luíntra. Just before Pereira, turn sharp left onto the OU0555, following signs to "Parador" and then left onto the OU0508. After 4 km (3 miles) turn left onto the OU0504 to reach Santo Estevo de Ribas de Síl.*

② Monasterio de Santo Estevo de Ribas de Síl
Ourense; 32164, 32747
The ancient Monasterio de Santo Estevo de Ribas de Síl *(open daily)* is perched high above an especially narrow section of the Síl river gorge. Originally built as a chapel in the 6th century, it was expanded by the Benedictine Order 400 years later, which accounts for its current majestic size. While its magnificent church and three cool, quiet cloisters remain intact, other sections have been converted into a stylish parador hotel. Walking trails lead from the end of the OU504 through a superb old chestnut forest, with tremendous

views over the canyon. Hiking 11 km (7 miles) northwest goes down to the river at Os Peares, and 17 km (11 miles) east leads to the Monasterio de Santa Cristina de Ribas de Síl.

Drive back to the OU0508 and drive eastwards left past Albeguería and Cerreda; park across the road from the **Mirador de Cabezoás**. A rare break in the woods that engulf much of the OU0508, the viewpoint provides a bird's-eye view of the river's northern shore, and of the city of Monforte de Lemos on the distant plains.

🚗 *Drive east (left) onto the OU0508. At the end of the road, turn left onto the OU0605 to Parada de Síl. Turn left towards Castro, then turn right to reach Santa Cristina de Ribas de Síl.*

③ Monasterio de Santa Cristina de Ribas de Síl
Ourense; 32747, 32765
The remote, haunting ruins of the 10th-century Monasterio de Santa Cristina de Ribas de Síl *(open daily)* stand high above the Síl valley, in the eerie silence of an ancient chestnut grove. Set just below the dead end of a precipitous road that drops from the village of Castro, the monastery is partially sheltered by a modern wooden roof. Even when its chapel and tower are locked, visitors can follow walkways to admire what is left of its former frescoes and read explanatory placards in Spanish and English.

From the monastery, go back to Castro and drive on through Parada de Síl to turn left onto the OU0605 to **A Teixeira**. The name A Teixeira, which identifies both a specific village and a municipality, comes from the Gallego word for the abundant yew trees on the slopes of the Síl's south bank. The village houses the **Casa do Viño** (*988 207 400; open Fri–Sun in summer, phone at other times*), a museum about local wines, and is well worth a stop for the remarkable view that its terraces offer of the surrounding valleys.

🚗 *Head east from A Teixeira on the OU0607. After 5 km (3 miles) turn left onto the OU903, signposted for Monforte, to reach the Ponte do Síl.*

④ Ponte do Síl
Lugo; 27424
Very few roads access, let alone cross, the gorge of the Síl river. The drive down to the low-slung Ponte do Síl, deep in the inner canyon, is extremely beautiful. Cross the Ponte do Síl and take the OU903, which becomes the LU903 across the river, towards Monforte. Turn left onto the LU5904 to the tiny village of **Doade**. Under the grand name of the Spatium Interpretationis Riveyra Sacrata, a monument to the wine-growing traditions of the Síl gorge marks a viewpoint on the north bank of the river, just south of Doade. Depicting a female harvester weighed down by a basket of freshly picked grapes, it overlooks a remarkable stretch of vineyards. An intricate tracery of terraces and tracks laces all over the towering cliffs; everywhere vines cling to the rocky terrain and a number of toiling figures can be seen tending their individual plots.

🚗 *Stay on the OU903 from Ponte do Síl to Castro Caldenas. Turn left following a sign saying "Comarcal Comercial" and park below the castle.*

⑤ Castro Caldelas
Ourense; 32760
The old quarter of the fortified hilltop town of Castro Caldelas is dominated by the partly restored 14th-century **Castillo de Castro Caldelas** (*closed 2–4pm*). Visitors can stroll along its battlements and climb its keep to enjoy panoramic views. The castle's halls hold the **Museo Etnográfico** (*open daily*), displaying local crafts and traditions. The tourist office, opposite the main castle entrance, has displays on the region, including a relief model of the whole Síl canyon.

🚗 *Turn left and follow the OU536 from Castro Caldelas and after 23 km*

(14 miles) *turn left onto the OU636 to reach A Pobra de Trives.*

⑥ A Pobra de Trives
Ourense; 32780
Explore the pedestrian lanes of the older quarter of A Pobra de Trives and visitors will find a likeable, quietly thriving community where the bars and cafés are geared more to locals than passing tourists. East of A Pobra de Trives, the OU636 drops down to cross the Bibei river on the **Ponte Bibei**. The remote countryside east of A Pobra de Trives was once traversed by a major Roman road, the **Via Nova**, which connected Astorga with Braga. The Ponte Bibei is a relic from that era. Standing 25 m (75 ft) high and 75 m (245 ft) long, it still carries traffic across the deep valley of the Bibei. There are two Roman columns by the bridge – one commemorating its construction between AD 79 and 81 and the other honouring the Spanish-born Emperor Trajan (AD 53–117).

🚗 *Continue on the OU636, turn left onto the OU533 and right onto the N120. After 50 km (31 miles), turn left onto the A6 (direction Lugo/A Coruña) to reach Villafranca del Bierzo.*

Above left Flower-decked columbarium in Parada de Síl **Above right** Sleepy town of A Pobra de Trives **Below** Colourful and cosy restaurant in Castro Caldelas

VISITING THE PONTE DO SÍL

Catamaran Cruises
Catamaran cruises start from the Centro Turístico Ponte do Síl and cruise through parts of the river and gorge that visitors would otherwise not see.
982 254 545; www.riosil.com

EAT AND DRINK

OURENSE

A Taberna *moderate*
Dine on traditional local specialities at this charming, stone-walled restaurant.
C/ Julio Prieto, 32005; 988 243 332

A POBRA DE TRIVES

A Cepa Bar *inexpensive*
The place for tapas and a great selection of wines.
Rúa Real 6, 32780; 988 330 128; closed Tue in winter

La Viuda *inexpensive*
A centrally located restaurant, this place serves a range of fish and meat dishes.
C/ Rosalía de Castro 17, 32780; 988 330 101

Eat and Drink: inexpensive, under €20; moderate, €20–€40; expensive, over €40

Top Rugged, golden cliffs at the mines in Las Médulas **Above** Thirteenth-century Templar castle at Ponferrada

VISITING THE VALLE DEL SILENCIO

Tourist Information
C/ Gil y Carrasco 4, 24400, Ponferrada; 987 424 236; www.ponferrada.org/turismo

Parking
There is a large car park at the edge of the village of Peñalba de Santiago.

WHERE TO STAY

AROUND LAS MÉDULAS

O Palleiro *inexpensive*
This guesthouse provides attractive rooms and hearty "Roman" dinners.
C/ San Pablo, 24444, Orellán; 649 711 439; www.opalleiro.com

PONFERRADA

Hostal Virgen de la Encina *inexpensive*
Facing the Templar castle, this hotel has comfortable rooms, a bar and a café.
C/ Comendador 4, 24400; 987 409 632; http://hostallaencina.net

❼ Villafranca del Bierzo
León; 24500
Although the town of Villafranca del Bierzo has been on the beaten track for more than a thousand years – dozens of pilgrims on the Camino de Santiago still pass through this town every day – it remains unspoilt. Stretching along the east bank of the Burbia river, and up the surrounding hillsides, its slate-roofed houses are interspersed with stately squares. Its churches range from the 10th-century Romanesque **Iglesia de Santiago**, perched where the Camino enters town, to the huge 17th-century **Convento de San Nicolás el Real** down by the main square. There is also an impressive 16th-century drum-towered **castle**, which is privately owned and not open to visitors.

🚗 *Return along the N120, turning left at a sign for Carucedo. Turn left onto the N536, then right at Carucedo and follow signs to Las Médulas Then fork left and right towards Orellán, following signs to "Mirador de Orellán".*

❽ Las Médulas
León; 24444
The steep 600-m (2,000-ft) walk from the car park up to the Mirador de Orellán offers no hint of the extraordinary devastated landscape that lies beyond the ridge at the top. The green, gorse-covered mountain looks like it has been sliced in half.

Though it resembles something from the Wild West, this landscape is far from natural. This is all that remains of a colossal Roman gold mine. During the 1st and 2nd centuries AD, the mines of Las Médulas were the most important gold mines in the Roman Empire, yielding 6,500 kg (14,300 lb) of gold per year.

🚗 *Drive back to Carucedo, then head 15 km (9 miles) right on the N536 to Ponferrada.*

❾ Ponferrada
León; 24400
The town of Ponferrada, perched above the east bank of the Síl, still preserves its attractive old core. A medieval bridge reinforced with iron (*pons ferrata*), erected for the benefit of pilgrims, gave this town its name. Its main feature is a **castle**, originally fortified by the Knights Templar during the 13th century to protect pilgrims, and repeatedly enlarged thereafter. A stroll around the battlements offers a view out to the stark ridges of the surrounding mountains. Nearby, the quiet streets hold fine mansions and an interesting museum on the region, the **Museo del Bierzo** (*closed Mon*).

🚗 *From the castle, continue straight and turn right at the first roundabout onto the LE161. Head southwards following signs to Peñalba de Santiago.*

❿ Valle del Silencio
León; 24415
Early in the 10th century the Bishop of Astorga, San Genadio, established a monastery at Peñalba de Santiago. The village now centres on an exquisite little church – all that is left of the long-vanished monastery. The valley that lay beyond, known as the Valle del Silencio (Valley of Silence), was already a favoured refuge of Christian hermits, and Genadio himself spent the last 20 years of his life in meditation here. This walk is a small part of the magnificent 15-km- (9-mile-) long trail that circles the valley.

A two-hour walking tour
From the car park, enter Peñalba and take the first fork right towards the church, the **Iglesia de Santiago** ①. Turn right following the gravel road that leads down between houses. The path drops swiftly from the village, passing meadows and apple orchards. After 300 m (330 yd), turn right into the woods, along a footpath signposted "Cueva". The footpath passes beneath a heavy canopy of old chestnut, walnut and poplar trees. It is liable to be damp and muddy all year round. It soon emerges into open country, following the contours of the hillside, with mighty bare crags looming ahead

and across the valley to the right. Roughly 1 km (0.6 miles) out of Peñalba the LE14 joins the path from the right, and they continue ahead together. The only sound here is likely to be the wind in the trees and perhaps the rush of water from the Arroyo del Silencio (Stream of Silence) not far below. Cross the **wooden walkway** ② and follow the trail to a fork a short distance ahead, where the LE14 drops to the right. Take the left fork instead and climb slightly to reach the stream cascading down the hillside. Cross it on the rickety **wooden walkway** ③ that rests on the rocks – much too rudimentary to be called a bridge. Further on, the path continues to climb on the far side, although now doubling back

towards the main valley. It becomes more of a ledge than a path, roughly a third of the way up a towering cliff-face, and reaches the natural open terrace in front of the **Cueva de San Genadio** ④. The actual cave is partially walled off. On stepping through the gap, there is a small shrine to the saint with an altar carved into the stone with a simple wooden statue. The cliff is the **Peña Alba** ⑤, for which Peñalba is named. The village is clearly visible to the east from here.

To see more of the valley, visitors can take the LE14 on their walk back to Peñalba. It is a slightly longer route, with a brief stiff climb after crossing the Arroyo del Friguera, not long before reaching the southern end of the village and the car park.

Above Mountains on the way to the Valle del Silencio

EAT AND DRINK

VILLAFRANCA DEL BIERZO

Mesón Don Nacho *inexpensive*
This is a cosy, cellar-like restaurant with a wide array of tapas as well as more substantial fare.
C/ Tróqueles 1, 24500; 987 540 076; closed Wed

PONFERRADA

La Violeta *moderate*
This intimate hotel-restaurant serves local dishes such as *botillo* (pork hotpot) using fresh, seasonal produce.
Plaza del Ayuntamiento 4, 24400; 987 409 001; www.aroihoteles.com

VALLE DEL SILENCIO

La Cantina *inexpensive*
Peñalba's only restaurant, this serves rich stew and *empanada* (a meaty pie).
C/ Bajada del Silencio, 24415, Peñalba de Santiago; 987 695 370; closed Mon

DAY TRIP OPTIONS

The drive can be divided into several shorter day trips with either Ourense (on the N120) or Ponferrada (on the A6) as a base.

Romanesque monasteries

Architecture enthusiasts will enjoy the round-trip along the Síl canyon to see the medieval monasteries of Santo Estevo de Ribas de Síl ② and Santa Cristina de Ribas de Síl ③.

Leave Ourense on the N120 and follow signs for Luíntra to take the OU0508 to

Santo Estevo de Ribas de Síl. Continue on the OU0508 to Santa Cristina de Ribas de Síl. Drive eastwards, then take the LU903 to rejoin the N120 to Ourense.

Cruising along the river

For the best possible views of the Síl canyon, take a boat trip on the river. Most river cruises set off in the morning from the Ponte do Síl ④.

Head northeast from Ourense on the N120. Then turn south at Monforte de Lemos and follow the LU903 for 19 km (12 miles) to reach the Ponte do Síl.

The Roman gold mines

The extraordinary Roman gold mines at Las Médulas ⑧ are a sight worth seeing. Driving up into the hills south of the Síl river, visitors are confronted by a landscape, punctuated by rock formations and devastated by 2,000-year-old mining operations.

Follow the N536 southwest from Ponferrada. At Carucedo, 22 km (14 miles) to the west, turn left, then fork left and park 5 km (3 miles) beyond Orellán village near the viewpoint for Las Médulas.

Ocean and Mountain

Ribadesella to Llanes

Highlights

- **Awe-inspiring mountain scenery**
  Marvel at soaring peaks, precipitous gorges and lush valleys

- **Atlantic beaches**
  Jump the surf on golden ocean beaches beneath granite cliffs at Ribadesella and Llanes

- **Generous cuisine**
  Sample robust mountain dishes made with fresh produce, and washed down with fine wines or sparkling local cider

- **Remote villages**
  Discover old stone villages such as Bejes and Bulnes apparently lost in their mountain valleys, with an unbeatable tranquillity

Quiet village of Posada de Valedón, in the heart of the Picos de Europa

Ocean and Mountain

When Spanish mariners returned from their early voyages to the Americas, the first sight of land they often had from far out at sea was that of the giant summits rising up behind the Asturian and Cantabrian coasts. These summits thus gained the name "Picos de Europa". Within just 20 km (12 miles) of the Atlantic shore, rocky crags soar up over 2,000 m (6,550 ft), creating a special mix of landscapes. Each of the once-isolated valleys around the Picos has its own microclimate. This drive begins in one of the charming old ports on the Asturian coast and ends in another, passing through a breathtaking scenic display.

0 kilometres 5

0 miles 5

KEY

 Drive route

Above Immense views from the winding road below Puerto de San Glorio, *see p52*

ACTIVITIES

Splash around on the beaches of Ribadesella and Llanes

Kayak down the crystal waters of the Sella river from Cangas de Onís

Take a cable car up to the massive rock plateau above Fuente Dé for an eagle's-eye view of the Picos

Explore a fabulous range of hiking trails, from the old trail through the Desfiladero del Río Cares to the peaks above Bulnes

Spot eagles circling in the sky above mountain lakes

Relax after a walk with a glass of cool cider and fresh tapas at a traditional heavy-timbered *sidrería*

Soak up the atmosphere of ancient churches and monasteries in and around Potes

Above left Charming town centre of Ribadesella, *see p50* **Above right** Basilica of Covadonga in its mountain valley, *see p50*

PLAN YOUR DRIVE

Start/finish: Ribadesella to Llanes.

Number of days: 3–4, including half a day for a walk around Soto de Sajambre.

Distance: 350 km (220 miles).

Road conditions: Well signposted and in good condition except for narrow lanes, which can be bumpy. Roads may be closed or require chains in winter.

When to go: Weather in the Picos is very changeable, but in general skies are bright and sunny, with moderate temperatures from April to early October. Hiking trails are crowded in late July and August.

Opening hours: Most museums and monuments are closed on Mondays. On other days, they open from 10am to 2pm, and from 5 to 8pm.

Main market days: Ribadesella: Wed; Cangas de Onís: Sun; Potes: Mon; Llanes: Thu.

Shopping: The classic products of the Picos and the regions around them are cheeses, cider, honey and a wide range of hams and meats. The Liébana area around Potes is known for sweet wines and *orujo* (strong grain spirit).

Major festivals: Ribadesella: Carnaval, Feb; La Noche de San Juan, 23–24 Jun; Descenso Internacional del Sella (Kayak Race), first Sat Aug; Cangas de Onís: Shepherd's Festival, 25 Jul; Santo Toribio de Liébana: La Santuca, 2 May; Potes: Exaltación de la Santa Cruz, mid-Sep; Las Arenas de Cabrales: Fiesta del Queso, end Aug; Llanes: Vírgen de la Guía, 7–8 Sep.

DAY TRIP OPTIONS

Families will enjoy a visit to Covadonga's lakes and to Ribadesella's beachfront; **nature lovers** and **history buffs** will be drawn to driving around the valleys and mountains between Llanes and Fuente Dé, while **adventure enthusiasts** will have a great time hiking around Bulnes and then relaxing on the beaches in Llanes. For details, *see p55.*

Above Church overlooking the sea at Ribadesella **Below** Walkers heading for the Lagos de Covadonga

VISITING PARQUE NACIONAL DE LOS PICOS DE EUROPA

Information Centres
The four information centres, in Cangas de Onís, Lagos de Covadonga, Posada de Valdeón and Tama-Cillórigo (near Potes), provide maps and other information on walks and hikes in the region.
Centro de Información Casa Dago, Avda. Covadonga 43, Cangas de Onís; 985 848 614; www.magrama. gob.es/es/red-parques-nacionales

WHERE TO STAY

RIBADESELLA

Villa Rosario expensive
The grandest of Ribadesella's Indiano mansions, an ornate 1900s fantasy house, is now a hotel.
C/ Dionisio Ruizsánchez 6, 33560; 985 860 090; www.hotelvillarosario.com

AROUND RIBADESELLA

El Babú moderate
Subtle modern design is combined with an 18th-century farmhouse at this small hotel 19 km (12 miles) to the west from Ribadesella.
33343, Carrales, Caravia; 985 853 272; www.elbabu.com

AROUND CANGAS DE ONÍS

Aultre Naray moderate
A delightful, welcoming small hotel, this is in a tranquil hamlet 9 km (6 miles) north of Cangas.
33457, Peruyes; 985 840 808; www.aultrenaray.com

Where to Stay: inexpensive, under €70; moderate, €70–€120; expensive, over €120

① Ribadesella
Asturias; 33560
Ribadesella's Old Town, behind the fishermen's quays on the east side of the Sella river, is an intimate knot of narrow streets with small shops and lively restaurants. The newer town, on the west bank, is built behind a beach lined by a promenade and old Indiano mansions and hotels.

Ribadesella was founded in the 13th century, but its site has been occupied since prehistory. On the west bank is the **Cueva de Tito Bustillo** (985 861 255; open Wed–Sun in mid-Mar–Oct; reservations recommended), a system of caverns, discovered only in 1968, with Palaeolithic cave paintings dating back to around 20,000 BC. Every first Saturday in August, Ribadesella's bridge is also the finishing point for the **Descenso Internacional del Sella**, a kayak race down the Sella from Arriondas that attracts competitors from around the world.

🚗 *Follow signs to the A8 for Oviedo-Gijón-Santander on the N632. In Llovio, the road forks. Take the right fork onto the N634 to Arriondas. Turn left onto the N625 to Cangas de Onís. Follow signs to the town centre.*

② Cangas de Onís
Asturias; 33550
One of the gateways to the Picos de Europa, Cangas de Onís was the first capital of the Kingdom of Asturias. The legendary Visigothic hero of the reconquista, Don Pelayo, set up his court here after his victory over the Moors at Covadonga in AD 722. On its west side is an elegantly curving stone bridge across the Sella, the **Puente Romano**. Cangas is a friendly town, with excellent sidrerías (cider houses) and riverside restaurants to give it plenty of Asturian character.

🚗 *Follow the Avenida Covadonga out through the town to join the AS114 to Las Arenas de Cabrales. After about 4 km (2 miles), turn right on the AS262 for Covadonga.*

③ Covadonga y los Lagos
Asturias; 33589
An impressive road runs up from Cangas de Onís to the shrine of

Covadonga, which grew around the **Santa Cueva** (Holy Cave), where Don Pelayo, founder of the Kingdom of Asturias, is said to have prayed to the Virgin. The shrine also contains his tomb. Above the shrine is a huge Neo-Romanesque basilica, built between 1877 and 1901. Beyond Covadonga there is a more dramatic road, which winds up past wonderful viewpoints to the **Lagos de Covadonga** – Enol and La Ercina – over 1,000 m (3,300 ft) high. There are many well-marked walks around the lakes, from an easy circuit to hikes of a few hours. Nearby are the visitors' centre and the **Minas de Buferrera**, iron mines abandoned only in 1972.

🚗 *Drive back to Cangas de Onís, and take the last left turn before the Puente Romano bridge, signposted to the N625. Stay on this road as it runs through the Desfiladero de los Beyos.*

Virgin of Covadonga, Ribadesella

④ Desfiladero de los Beyos
Asturias–León; 33557
South of Cangas de Onís, the road follows the Sella into the Desfiladero de los Beyos, one of the most spectacular of the deep, forest-clad limestone gorges that ring the Picos de Europa. Periodically the gorge widens as side lanes lead off to hillside villages, of which **Ceneya** and **Argolibio** are among the most attractive. After 30 km (19 miles), the road enters the Valle de Sajambre, a narrow enclave within the Picos.

🚗 *Continue southwards on the N625 from Cangas de Onís. After Ribota, look for a steep left turn onto the CV80-8 for Soto and continue to the car park in the centre of the village.*

⑤ Soto de Sajambre
León; 24916

One of the most fascinating aspects of the Picos de Europa is the constant change in landscape from one valley to another, and between thickly wooded valley floors and windswept meadows up above. This walk takes visitors from the sheltered village of Soto de Sajambre, tucked into a fold in the hills, up to high mountain pastures in one of the emptiest parts of the Picos.

Above Footpath marker near Soto de Sajambre

A two–three-hour walking tour

The walk follows the PR-PNPE 9 footpath (with green signs and yellow and white markers) and is steep in parts. From the car park, follow the footpath signs for Vegabaño, to the right of the school. The path begins to climb out of the village with the sparkling Miraño river on the right, and initially runs through hay meadows typical of the Picos villages.

Go past an unusual red-painted house, **La Cubiella** ①. Rising up ahead on both sides are some of the jagged granite crags of the western Picos, Peña Beza to the left and Monte Neón to the right. Look out for eagles and other birds of prey circling the sky. About 1 km (0.6 miles) from Soto, the path enters the woods. Turn right, following the yellow and white markers to cross the Miraño river, and follow the path uphill through the forest. The path twists and turns until it meets a broader dirt track. Turn left, and follow this track round until it comes out of

the trees onto the grassy meadow of **Vegabaño** ②, which is dotted with huts built as shelters by shepherds during the weeks they spent here. To the right, the track ends at a mountain refuge. Straight ahead to the east there is a glorious view of some of the most rugged peaks of the western massif of the Picos, such as Los Moledizos (2,300 m/7,550 ft) and the Picos del Verde (2,200 m/7,200 ft). The most direct way back to Soto de Sajambre and to the car park is to retrace the same route.

🚗 *Return to the N625 and turn left. Beyond Soto, the main N625 road goes through Oseja de Sajambre, the valley's low-key main town, dominated by the mountain of Pica Ten. Past Oseja, the road winds up to the Puerto del Pontón. After the pass, turn left onto the LE244 for Posada de Valdeón. Drive towards the Valdeón valley through the Puerto de Panderrueda, with views from several miradors over the Valdeón and the peaks around it.*

La Cubiella ① Miraño vegabano ② PR-PNPE9 SOTO DE SAJAMBRE 🅿

0 metres 500
0 yards 500

Eat and Drink: inexpensive, under €20; moderate, €20–€40; expensive, over €40

Above Medieval monastery of Santo Toribio de Liébana **Below** Looking down to the Vega de Liébana from Puerto de San Glorio

WHERE TO STAY

POSADA DE VALDEÓN

Pensión Begoña *inexpensive*
This friendly little hotel houses Posada's best restaurant and has a country charm typical of the village.
Los Llanos 2, 24915; 987 740 502

AROUND POSADA DE VALDEÓN

Casa Cuevas *inexpensive*
A comfortable hotel with a traditional restaurant, this hotel is in the tiny, remote village of Caín, 7 km (4 miles) to the north of Posada de Valdeón and ringed by jagged grey crags.
24915, Caín de Valdeón; 987 740 500; www.casacuevas.es

AROUND VALLE DE CAMALEÑO

La Casona de Cosgaya *moderate*
This massive traditional *casona* (village house) has been renovated to create distinctive bedrooms and lounge areas with a luxurious feel.
Barrio Arenós, 39582, Cosgaya; 942 733 077; www.casonadecosgaya.com

Posada El Bosque *moderate*
In a modern but traditional-style house near Potes, this is a lovely small hotel with great views over the valley.
39586, Camaleño; 942 730 127; www.posadaelbosque.com

Parador de Fuente Dé *expensive*
The Parador, in the foothills of the Picos de Europa and at the base of the Fuente Dé cable car, is modern and service is excellent. The restaurant has refined versions of local cuisine.
39588, Fuente Dé; 942 736 651; www.parador.es

⑥ Posada de Valdeón

León; 24915
A green hollow ringed by massive sierras, the Valdeón is one of the most enclosed of the Picos de Europa valleys, and the largest area of the Picos within the province of León. Posada de Valdeón, its main village, is a popular hiking base with hotels and restaurants and a park information centre. A narrow road continues for 7 km (4 miles) to end at **Caín de Valdeón**, a remarkable village beneath the rocky walls of the **Desfiladero del Río Cares** gorge. It is a starting point for one of the most famous long hikes in the Picos, through the Cares ravine to the north side of the mountains at Puente Poncebos. The walk is about 11 km (7 miles) long, and takes 3 hours in each direction, on a spectacular, but safely broad path along the often sheer rock walls of the gorge. It sometimes runs through small tunnels and crosses from side to side on narrow metal bridges.

🚗 *From Posada, follow the LE243, to the right of the Pensión Begoña, out of the village. Continue on this road through Santa Marina de Valdeón and the Puerto de Pandetrave. Turn left onto the N621 at Portilla de la Reina to reach Puerto de San Glorio.*

⑦ Puerto de San Glorio

Cantabria; 39577
The differences in landscape between the northern Atlantic side of the Picos and its southern Mediterranean flanks become ever more marked as the route goes further into León. From Portilla de La Reina the N621 road runs through an almost bare rock ravine as it climbs again up to Puerto de San Glorio, perhaps the most spectacular of all the Picos passes. A side road to the left, marked Collado de Llesba, leads to the **Mirador del Oso**, a viewpoint with a bear statue and truly fabulous views over the Liébana valleys and ranks of sierras fading into the distance. The road then winds down to **Vega de Liébana**, a pleasant riverside village with relaxing restaurants.

🚗 *Continue on the N621. Enter Potes and turn left on the CA185, signposted for Espinama and Fuente Dé; this also leads to the centre of town. There is ample parking in the large squares just past the main historic buildings.*

⑧ Potes

Cantabria; 39577
The Cantabrian Liébana valleys in the southeastern Picos enjoy an unusually sheltered climate that has given them an especially lush, productive landscape. Potes is the main town and tourist centre of the Liébana and the southeast corner of the Picos de Europa, with plenty of shops offering the renowned Liébana produce – honey, sweet wines, liqueurs, sausages and cheeses. A local centre since the 9th century, Potes has a fascinating Old Town of alleys, lovely bridges and distinctive houses built precariously above the Deva river. Standing out in the middle of town, in the main square, is the **Torre del Infantado** (now the town hall), a 14th-century keep that was a stronghold of the aristocratic Mendoza clan, and the early 14th–18th-century Gothic

Where to Stay: inexpensive, under €70; moderate, €70–€120; expensive, over €120

Iglesia de San Vicente (open daily), which now hosts an exhibition on medieval manuscripts.

🚗 *Continue on the CA185 road out of Potes, and then very shortly take the left turn onto the CA885 signposted to Santo Toribio de Liébana.*

⑨ Santo Toribio de Liébana
Cantabria; 39570
The protection and fertility of the Liébana valleys made them an important centre of early Christianity, with several monasteries, of which **Santo Toribio** (open daily), above Potes, is the most important. Founded in the 6th century, it became famous for the *Lignum Crucis*, which is kept in a silver reliquary and is said to be the largest fragment of the cross on which Christ was crucified. It was also the home of the 8th-century scholar Beatus of Liébana, author of the *Commentary on the Apocalypse*. On an upper floor there is a fascinating exhibition on Beatus and medieval manuscripts. Still occupied by monks, the colossal monastery has buildings from many centuries, but retains its 13th-century church, while outside a path leads to a series of Romanesque hermitages spread about the hillside.

🚗 *Drive back to the CA185 and continue westwards on it. Follow the road through Camaleño, Cosgaya and other valley villages to Fuente Dé.*

⑩ Valle de Camaleño
Cantabria; 39588
West of Potes, the Camaleño valley has some of the most exquisite scenery in the Picos, with verdant woods and charming villages of red-roofed

old stone houses such as **Camaleño** itself, **Cosgaya** and **Espinama**, around which are attractive restaurants and small hotels in lovely *casas rurales*. **Mogrovejo**, off the main road, is a medieval village around a 13th-century tower. There are great walks around all the villages. The road ends at **Fuente Dé**, where the popular Teleférico (cable car; open daily) takes visitors 900 m (2,950 ft) up to a wild rock plateau pitted with craters. As well as a fantastic panorama over the Picos, there are many hiking routes around the plateau, including one trail down the mountain to Espinama.

🚗 *Drive back to Potes on the CA185, and continue on slightly out of town before turning left, back onto the N621, signed for Unquera and Santander. After about 5 km (3 miles) take a right turn signposted for Santa María de Lebeña. The church is located down a sharp turn on the left.*

Above left Soaring crags above Posada de Valdeón, at the base of the Desfiladero del Río Cares **Above right** Bell tower of the early medieval church in Caín **Below** Torre del Infantado in Potes

EAT AND DRINK

AROUND POSADA DE VALDEÓN
La Posada del Montañero *inexpensive*
Diners on the pretty terrace at this bar-restaurant-hotel get an imposing view of the Torre Cerredo and other peaks around Caín. Rich, meaty traditional cooking is the core of the menu.
24915, Caín de Valdeón; 987 742 711

AROUND PUERTO DE SAN GLORIO
Mesón La Vega *inexpensive*
A warm atmosphere is guaranteed at this classic timber and stone village inn by the roadside in Vega. Portions of tapas or larger dishes are generous.
39577, Vega de Liébana; 942 736 132; www.mesonlavega.com

VALLE DE CAMALEÑO
Mesón del Oso *moderate–expensive*
This giant stone inn could not be more typical of the region, and is renowned as a showcase for the traditional dishes of the Liébana, especially *cocido lebaniego*, a mountain stew with four or more meats. Booking is essential.
C/ de Potes a Fuente Dé, 39582, Cosgaya; 942 733 018; closed Jan–mid-Feb

El Urogallo *moderate–expensive*
Chef Casimiro Calleja prepares some of the region's best cuisine in his restaurant in the charming Casona hotel.
La Casona de Cosgaya, Barrio Areños, 39582, Cosgaya; 942 733 077; www.casonadecosgaya.com

Above Village of Bejes, huddled at the foot of a massive rock wall **Below left** One of the narrow cobbled streets in the isolated village of Bulnes **Below right** Mozarabic Iglesia de Santa María de Lebeña

WHERE TO STAY

AROUND DESFILADERO DE LA HERMIDA

Casona d'Alevia *moderate*
This impressive old stone house, 4 km (2 miles) to the northwest of Panes, has been renovated with antiques and tradi-tional fittings. The owners are very welcoming, and generous breakfasts feature fresh local produce.
33579, Alevia, Peñamellera Baja; 985 414 176; www.casonadalevia.com

BULNES

Casa del Chiflón *inexpensive*
To experience true mountain isolation stay over in Bulnes at this stone cottage bed-and-breakfast with snug rooms. The Casa del Chiflón is reachable only by foot or in the funicular.
33554, Bulnes; 985 845 943; www.casadelchiflon.com

AROUND LLANES

El Habana *expensive*
This country house 4 km (2 miles) south of Llanes has warm rooms and lounges, and an outdoor pool..
33509, La Pereda; 985 400 640; www. elhabana.net; closed Nov–Easter

La Posada de Babel *expensive*
This hip hotel 4 km (2 miles) south of Llanes offers a change from traditional decor with stylish rooms.
33509, La Pereda; 985 402 525; www.laposadadebabel.com; closed mid-Dec–Apr

⑪ Santa María de Lebeña
Cantabria; 39583
In a magical setting above the Deva river, Santa María de Lebeña *(tours Tue–Sun)* is the region's gem-like oldest church, built around AD 925 in the Moorish-influenced Mozarabic style. The site had probably already been used for pre-Christian Celtic religious rituals. There are Celtic symbols on the altar beneath the beautiful Romanesque figure of the Virgin of Lebeña.

🚗 *Drive back to the N621. Turn right to go through the Hermida gorge.*

Cheeses around the Picos
Manchego may be the most famous Spanish cheese, but those of Asturias and Cantabria are far more distinctive. Asturias alone has 42 different cheeses; the best known is the wonderfully powerful *cabrales*, a blue-veined "three-milk" cheese (made with milk from cows, sheep and goats). *Queso Monje Picón*, from Bejes and Tresviso, is similar, but a little more subtle, as is the highly prized *gamonedo* from around Cangas de Onís. The *quesucos* of the Liébana valleys, which are mild and soft and often used as snacks, in salads and in cakes, are very different.

⑫ Desfiladero de la Hermida
Cantabria; 39580
The Liébana valleys end at another giant gorge lined by soaring grey-rock walls, the Desfiladero de la Hermida. Part-way through the gorge, a part-concealed left turn in the village of La Hermida leads up to **Bejes**, a remote village precariously placed beneath a great grey cliff. With Tresviso on the other side of the mountain – unconnected by road, but reachable by a footpath – this is one of only two villages with a *Denominación de Origen* to produce *Queso Picón*, the oldest of all the region's cheeses, recorded since the year 926. Return to the N621 road from Bejes and turn left to travel through the rest of the gorge to **Panes**. The Hermida gorge ends here, where it meets the Cares, a densely wooded gorge that runs west to the village of **Las Arenas de Cabrales**. Drive through Panes and turn left, across a bridge, Puerto Río Cares, onto the AS114 and drive for 23 km (14 miles) to reach Las Arenas de Cabrales. This village is famed as the centre for the famous Asturian cheeses, *cabrales*, and there are shops selling cheeses, cider and other local specialities all around the town.

🚗 *In Las Arenas de Cabrales turn left on the AS264 to Puente Poncebos. Park by the funicular to take the train up to Bulnes, or turn left uphill on the CA1 to reach Sotres and Tresviso.*

⑬ Bulnes
Asturias/Cantabria; 33554, 39580
The only way to get to Bulnes is by the funicular railway at Puente Poncebos, since it is one of the very few villages in Spain still with no access by road. It is the start point for superb hikes around the awesome summit of the **Naranjo de Bulnes** (2,500 m/8,250 ft)

which is one of the highest summits in the Picos de Europa. At the bottom of the Funicular, Puente Poncebos is the northernmost point of the Desfiladero del Río Cares path from Caín. Alternatively, continuing from Puente Poncebos, drive through extraordinary landscapes to two beautiful remote villages, **Sotres** and **Tresviso**. The *Picón* blue cheese made at Tresviso and in nearby Bejes has its own *Denominación de Origen*.

🔟 *Return to Las Arenas de Cabrales and turn left on the AS114. Cross Ortiguero and turn right onto the AS115 for Posada. After Posada, turn right at the T-junction onto the AS263, passing under the A8, to reach Llanes.*

⑭ Llanes
Asturias; 33500
Rejoin the coast at the harbour town of Llanes. An important port in the Middle Ages, it has a charming Old Town of stone-walled squares, Gothic churches and noble mansions. The harbour, still a busy fishing port, has been intriguingly decorated with multicoloured painted blocks, called *The Cubes of Memory*, by contemporary artist Agustín Ibarrola (b. 1930). Llanes also has small beaches, but the best beaches nearby are just west at **Barro** and **Celorio**, framed by the dramatic Atlantic cliffs.

Asturian Cider
Cider (*sidra*), not wine, is the traditional drink of northern Spain, and above all Asturias. Asturian cider is quite sharp, with a mix of dryness and sweetness. The best place to sample it is in a traditional *sidrería* with dark timbers and barrels around the walls, along with some *cabrales* cheese or other hearty local food.

Left Lofty peaks encircle Bulnes and its lonely farms

DAY TRIP OPTIONS
The coastal towns of Ribadesella and Llanes (both near the A8) make great bases for the short trips that this drive can be divided into.

Beaches to high mountain lakes
Spend a day on Ribadesella's ① beachfront, then visit Cangas de Onís ② for a leisurely lunch, before driving to Covadonga y los Lagos ③ to see the beautiful lakes.

From Ribadesella, follow the N634, then the N625 to Cangas de Onís, then the AS114 and the AS262 to Covadonga.

History and culture
With Llanes ⑭ as base, a visit to the Liébana valleys of the Cantabrian Picos, the shops and charming old streets of Potes ⑧, the ancient churches and monasteries of Santo Toribio de Liébana ⑨ and Santa María de Lebeña ⑪, and the walks and fine restaurants along the Valle de Camaleño ⑩ to Fuente Dé, make for a great trip.

From Llanes, follow the N634 eastward and then the N621 southwest to Potes, driving through the Hermida and Liébana valleys and visiting the monastery of Santa María de Lebeña on the way. From Potes, follow the CA885 and the CA185 to Santo Toribio de Liébana and the Camaleño valley and Fuente Dé.

High peaks to the harbourside
For hiking in the Picos head for the vistas around Bulnes ⑬, or start with a hike around Bulnes, and then relax on the beautiful beaches around Llanes ⑭.

From Llanes follow the AS115 to Las Arenas de Cabrales, then take the AS264 to Bulnes and Tresviso.

Eat and Drink: inexpensive, under €20; moderate, €20–€40; expensive, over €40

The Land of Rioja

Laguardia to Quintanar de la Sierra

Highlights

- **Enchanting town**
  Dive into La Rioja's wine culture in the medieval town of Laguardia

- **Cutting edge architecture**
  Marvel at the new breed of bodegas from the world's top architects

- **Medieval monasteries**
  Discover ancient monasteries tucked in the folds of forests and mountains

- **Majestic mountains**
  Explore the little-known Sierra de la Demanda, a nature lover's paradise

Vineyards near Laguardia, capital of La Rioja Alavesa, sheltered by the hills to the north

The Land of Rioja

Famous the world over for its wine, the tiny region of La Rioja has everything visitors could want from a holiday in northern Spain. Encircled by the swooping hills of the Sierra de la Demanda, the region is rich with crystalline rivers full of fish, medieval villages and monasteries nestled in pretty valleys. The gastronomy is on a par with the neighbouring Basque region and the countryside presents no great difficulties for once-a-year walkers and cyclists. At the end of the day's sightseeing, a bottle of La Rioja's delicious eponymous product is always at hand.

Above Rows of vines around Haro, *see p63*

ACTIVITIES

Sample famous wines at the hundreds of bodegas scattered throughout La Rioja Alavesa

Learn about how wine is made at the Museo Vivanco de la Cultura del Vino in Briones

Watch storks nest in the rooftops of Haro

Trek through the forests between the Yuso and Suso monasteries

Stroll across a mountaintop to a glacial lagoon in Neila

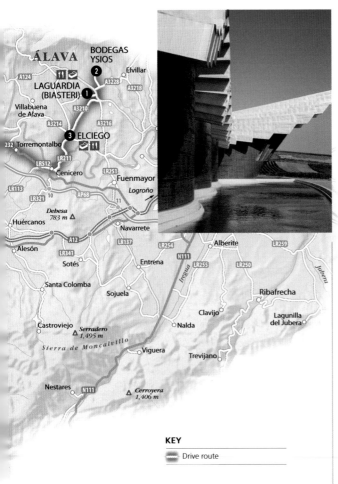

KEY

🚂 Drive route

Above Contemporary structure of the bodega in Ysios, *see p61* **Below** Rooftop view of the village of Villavelayo, *see p67*

PLAN YOUR DRIVE

Start/finish: Laguardia to Quintanar de la Sierra.

Number of days: 4–5, allowing half a day to explore the monasteries of Yuso and Suso.

Distance: 225 km (140 miles).

Road conditions: The roads are generally good around this region. There are mountain roads in the Sierra de la Demanda, with narrow stretches and lots of curves.

When to go: Spring and summer are the best times to go. The *vendimia* (harvest) takes place in October and is the best time to see the vineyards of La Rioja. Expect snow in the Sierra de la Demanda in winter.

Opening hours: Most museums and monuments are closed on Mondays. Shops are open from 9:30am to 1:30pm, and from 4 to 8pm. Restaurants are open from 2 to 4pm, and from 8 to 11pm.

Main market days: Laguardia: Tue; Haro: Tue, Sat; Santo Domingo de la Calzada: Sat; Nájera: Thu.

Shopping: Ezcaray is famous for its wine, woollen blankets and scarves. Wine-related objects (bottle-openers, glasses, etc) are available in many village shops and bodegas.

Major festivals: Haro: La Batalla de Vino, 29 Jun; San Millán de la Cogolla: Traslación de las Reliquias, 27 Sep; Anguiano: Danza de los Zancos, 21–23 Jul and last week Sep; Quintanar de la Sierra: San Cristobal, 10–12 Jul.

DAY TRIP OPTIONS

Wine lovers should visit the towns and villages of Laguardia, Elciego and Briones and taste some of their world-renowned wines at old-fashioned bodegas. **History enthusiasts** should make their way to see the ancient church at Santo Domingo de la Calzada, the twin monasteries of San Millán de la Cogolla and the Monasterio de Valvanera. For more details, *see p67*.

Above Walls around the town of Laguardia

VISITING LAGUARDIA

Tourist Information
Casa Garcetas, C/ Mayor 52, 01300; 945 600 845; www.laguardia-alava. com; open daily

Parking
Parking is available in front of Puerta de Páganos.

SHOPPING IN LAGUARDIA

Casa & Vino
Pick up tablecloths and all sorts of wine paraphernalia such as bottle-openers and decanters from this shop. It also has a range of woollen rugs and scarves from nearby Ezcaray and various grape-based beauty products.
C/ Mayor 1, 01300; 945 600 931

Enoteca Arbulu Uriarte
This shop has a wide selection of wines from the Alavesa region as well as La Rioja's famous *conservas* – jars of preserved red peppers, artichokes and asparagus.
Plaza Mayor 1, 01300; 945 621 267

WHERE TO STAY

LAGUARDIA

Hotel Villa de Laguardia *moderate*
A four-star hotel which has plush and comfortable rooms, a pool, a spa and a superb in-house restaurant with wonderful views of the area.
Paseo de San Raimundo 15, 01300; 945 600 560; www. hotelvilladelaguardia.com

Castillo El Collado *expensive*
This 10-roomed hostelry in an 18th-century palace is located just outside Laguardia's walls, and affords great views of the Cantabrian mountains. Rooms are decorated with fine period furniture, maintaining the original regal ambience of the building.
Paseo el Collado 1, 01300; 945 621 200; www.hotelcollado.com

① Laguardia (Biasteri)
Álava; 01300

The main town of La Rioja Alavesa, the part of the Rioja wine region within the province of Álava, Laguardia (Biasteri in Basque) makes a splendid start to the journey into Spain's most famous wine country. Viniculture is alive and well everywhere, from the wine shops and bars, to the fields of vineyards surrounding Laguardia's walls and finally the underground bodegas. This little medieval town's encircling ramparts, towers and fortified gateways are visible from afar. The Gothic portal of Iglesia de Santa María de los Reyes is a treat for all art enthusiasts. The following walk can be done at any time of the day.

A one-hour walking tour

Start at the car park in front of Puerta de Páganos and walk to the Plaza San Juan, also the location of the tourist office. At the centre of the plaza is the 13th-century **Capilla de la Virgen del Pilar e Iglesia de San Juan Bautista** ①. From the front of the church turn left into Calle Mayor to the small Plaza de la Cárcel. Bear left via Calle de la Cárcel and through Paseo San Juan. Turn right to **Puerta de San Juan** ② – one of Laguardia's five gates – to the other side of the walls for a fine view of the craggy Cantabrian mountain range. Turn left following the wall to the *frontón* (Basque handball or *jai alai* court) and go back into the village via the 15th-century **Puerta Nueva** ③ on the left. After 50 m (55 yd), cross Calle de Santa Engracia to come to the **Plaza Mayor** ④, where the

16th-century *ayuntamiento* (town hall) is located. A few steps further on is the current town hall with its charming carillon clock, whose dancing figurines appear at the stroke of midday and at 2, 5 and 8pm. Continue up Calle de Santa Engracia and take the first left onto Calle Traversia de Santa Engracia. Then turn right onto Calle Mayor and walk to the end of the street. This is the site of the **Iglesia de Santa María de los Reyes** ⑤ *(closed Mon)*. Built between the 12th and 15th centuries, it incorporates different styles, from Gothic to Renaissance. Its celebrated portal, with intricate figures of the apostles, was not painted until the 17th century, partly explaining its near-perfect state. To the left of the church is the **Torre Abacial** ⑥, a 13th-century defence tower that has an underground passage to the church. To the right of the church is a pretty garden on Plaza El Gaitero containing **Viajeros** ⑦, a sculpture installation of various types of shoes and bags, the work of a local culture group. Next to the garden is another small plaza with an antique water well and water basin. Cross the plaza and go down the steps. Turn left to reach the lovely garden at Paseo del Collado where there is a bust of Félix María Samaniego (1745–1801), a Laguardian writer famous for his fables (his old palatial home is now the tourist office). After stopping here for a while, go back to the car park.

🚗 *From Laguardia take the A124 northwest in the direction of Vitoria-Gasteiz. This will lead to a crossroad with a sign which says "Elvillar/Kripan". Turn right and immediately left and follow signs for Bodegas Ysios till the car park.*

Bodegas La Fabulista

The underground Bodegas La Fabulista *(Plaza San Juan s/n; 945 621 192)* is located beneath the building of the tourist office – once the ancestral home of the fable writer Félix María Samaniego, Laguardia's most illustrious son. It is a part working winery and part tourist attraction. A tour takes visitors through the extensive tunnels where the wines are created. Traditional methods are still used here: the grapes are crushed by foot, and the machine used to separate their stalks dates from 1903. At the end of the visit, guests are invited to taste some of La Fabulista's wines. Visitors can also buy some wine to take home.

❷ Bodegas Ysios
Álava; 01300

The first of a handful of spectacular contemporary bodegas now dotting La Rioja, Ysios is the work of Santiago Calatrava, the Spanish architect who designed the stadium in Athens for the 2004 Olympic Games. With the craggy Cantabrian mountains as a backdrop, it is a wonderful sight. The low-rise wooden structure is crowned with an undulating metal roof and protruding peaked "wings", lending it an articulated, church-like quality. A simple water-filled moat frames its sculptural form. The bodega can be toured, but visitors need to book in advance *(945 600 640; open daily).*

🚗 *Return to Laguardia on the A124 and follow this road around the town. At the junction with the A3216, take the A3210 signed for Elciego.*

Above left Dancing clock in the Plaza Mayor, Laguardia **Above right** Typical La Rioja landscape lined with vineyards and mountains in the background **Below** Bodega Ysios amid rows of vines near Laguardia

EAT AND DRINK

LAGUARDIA

La Muralla *moderate*
An atmospheric, bottle-lined, subterranean restaurant, serving hearty portions of regional stews and grilled meats.
C/ Paganos 42, 01300; 945 600 198

Posada Mayor de Migueloa *expensive*
This restored 17th-century palace of Viana now houses a small hotel and one of northern Spain's best restaurants. The cuisine is a Basque–La Rioja fusion, strong on fish and seafood. Try the baked hake.
C/ Mayor de Migueloa 20, 01300; 945 600 187; www.mayordemigueloa.com; closed mid-Dec–7 Jan

Eat and Drink: inexpensive, under €20; moderate, €20–€40; expensive, over €40

Above left Façade of the Hotel Marqués de Riscal, Elciego **Above right** Arcades in Plaza de la Paz, Haro **Below** Museo Vivanco de la Cultura del Vino in Briones

WHERE TO STAY

ELCIEGO

Hotel Marqués de Riscal *expensive*
As would be expected from a work by Frank Gehry, the rooms and common areas in this destination hotel are as stunning as its exterior and well worth the cost. The in-house spa specializes in vinotherapy – wellness treatments using varieties of grape-based products.
C/ Torrea 1, 01340; 945 180 880; www. hotel-marquesderiscal.com

AROUND HARO

Señorío de Casalarreina *expensive*
Located in Casalarreina, a village 7 km (4 miles) outside Haro on the road to Ezcaray, this stylish *casa rural* is situated in the old college of the Monasterio de Nuestra Señora de la Piedad. The rooms retain many of their original stone walls and wooden beams, with some bathrooms featuring Jacuzzis.
Plaza Santo Domingo De Guzmán 6, 26230, Casalarreina; 941 324 730; www.hscasalarreina.com

❸ Elciego
Álava; 01340
This pretty little village boasts one of the most acclaimed buildings in Spain, the **Hotel Marqués de Riscal** by Canadian-American architect Frank Gehry. Located on top of a natural terrace, the interesting main structure is wrapped in the architect's trademark titanium "ribbons" in glittering pink and gold colours (a metaphor for those of a wine bottle) that stand out for miles around. The interior is off limits for those who are not guests (or have at least booked for the in-house restaurant or spa), but visitors can tour the **Marqués de Riscal bodega**, which is adjacent. The original winery dates from 1858 (though modern additions

have been made) and produces some of the most renowned wine in the region. The highlight is the "Cathedral" where bottles of every vintage produced since the bodega's foundation are reverently displayed *(tours by prior reservation only)*.

🚗 *Continue on the A3210 (which becomes the LR211 after it crosses into La Rioja) until it meets the LR512 outside Cenicero. Turn right and drive through Cenicero to meet the N232. Then turn right onto this road and follow it to Briones.*

❹ Briones
La Rioja; 26330
The first thing that visitors will notice as they drive into Briones is the Baroque bell tower of the **Iglesia de Nuestra Señora de la Asunción**. As well as a handful of other buildings of note, such as the **Palacio de los Marqués de San Nicolás** (now the town hall), Briones hosts the best museum in the area. Located in a striking modern building on the main road to the village, the **Museo Vivanco de la Cultura del Vino** *(closed Mon; reservations recommended; 902 320 001)* is a fascinating trip into the world of wine – from the harvest to bottle – and shows how methods have changed over the centuries. At the end of the visit guests will be offered a glass of wine from the Vivanco bodega.

🚗 *Leave Briones, right, on the N232 and follow signs for Vitoria. After 8 km (5 miles), take the N124. Turn right and follow this road. Park on the street.*

Where to Stay: inexpensive, under €70; moderate, €70–€120; expensive, over €120

The Wines of La Rioja

La Rioja is the most internationally known Spanish wine region, with over 300 bodegas dotting the Rioja area. The region is best known for its red wines that are matured to a distinctive vanilla mellowness. Today La Rioja produces over 250 million litres (55 million gallons) of wine a year, the large majority of it red. All of it falls into three categories: *crianza* (young wine), *reserva* and *gran reserva* (matured). A DO (*Denominación de Origen* or qualified designation of origin) was decreed for La Rioja's wine in 1902 and today three exist (La Rioja Alavesa, Rioja Alta and Rioja Baja) that identify exactly where the wines are produced and their style.

⑤ Haro

La Rioja; 26200

With its romantic hanging balconies and central square featuring an elegant rotunda, Haro is a graceful town on the Ebro river. Haro became the nucleus of La Rioja's wine-making industry over 130 years ago, when a railway was built to Bilbao, facilitating exportation to the rest of Europe. The legacy is the charming **Barrio de la Estación**, a clutter of period bodegas set around the old railway station, many of which are open to the public. In the historic quarter, storks flock to the nests they have made in the florid crowns and cornices of Haro's abundant Baroque architecture. At the top of the hill is the Gothic **Iglesia de Santo Tomás**, which has a portal featuring the Way of the Cross.

Every June, Haro hosts its La Batalla del Vino festival, when boisterous crowds throw wine at each other.

🚗 *Leave Haro on the LR111/N126 on the west side of town. Continue on this road around Casalarreina to Santo Domingo de la Calzada. Park on the outskirts of the village.*

⑥ Santo Domingo de la Calzada

La Rioja; 26250

The little town of Santo Domingo de la Calzada owes its existence to the pilgrimage to Santiago de Compostela. In the Middle Ages a hermit named Domingo set up a hospice here to aid pilgrims, and out of that a town was born. His remains are buried in the 12th-century cathedral *(closed Sun)*, which also has a cage containing a pair of hens against the wall. Legend has it that Domingo resuscitated a pilgrim who had been unjustly sent to the gallows. When the townsfolk went to the judge to relate the miracle, the judge believed it to be nonsense, and explained that the condemned pilgrim could be no more alive than the roast chicken he was eating, at which point the chicken stood up and crowed. Opposite the cathedral is the 18th-century clock tower **Torre Exenta**, the tallest in La Rioja, and a hermitage with a Renaissance retable.

🚗 *Continue south on the LR111 (Avenida Alfonso Peña within Santo Domingo) and follow this road through Ojacastro for 3 km (2 miles) to Ezcaray.*

Above Tapas bars line the street to the Iglesia de Santo Tomás, Haro **Below left** The modern Marqués de Riscal wine spa at Elciego **Below right** Elaborately carved portal of the Monasterio de Nuestra Señora de la Piedad in Casalarreina near Haro

EAT AND DRINK

ELCIEGO

Hotel Marqués de Riscal *expensive*
Booking a table at this restaurant is certainly the best way to experience Frank Gehry's amazing architecture if visitors are not staying at the hotel. The cutting-edge menu has been created by the Michelin-starred Francis Paniego, of Echaurren *(see p65)* fame.
C/ Torrea 1, 01340; 945 180 880; www.restaurantemarquesderiscal. com; reservations recommended; closed Mon and Sun

HARO

El Jarrero *moderate*
Located near Haro's cathedral, El Jarrero specializes in traditional Riojan cuisine. Dishes such as potatoes flavoured with garlic, wine, peppers and *chorizo*, and lamb chops pair nicely with a *vino de Rioja* from the restaurant's impressive wine cellar.
C/ San Miguel 5, 26200; 941 303 374; closed Mon–Thu eve

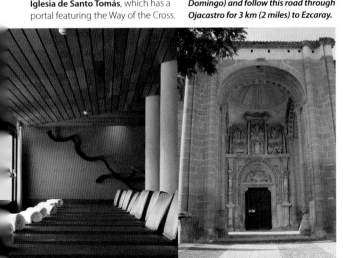

Eat and Drink: inexpensive, under €20; moderate, €20–€40; expensive, over €40

VISITING THE MONASTERIES OF SAN MILLÁN DE LA COGOLLA

Visitors need to book in advance for both monasteries through the tourist office at 941 373 082. Entry to the smaller Suso monastery is limited, so it is best to book in good time. The monasteries are located 1 km (0.6 miles) apart. Visitors can take a shuttle bus or walk, following the "Ruta de Gonzalo de Berceo".
Agustinos Recoletos, 26326; 941 373 049; www.monasteriodeyuso.org; open Tue–Sun

SHOPPING

EZCARAY

Mantas Ezcaray
Ezcaray has a long tradition of textile weaving and this factory shop sells luxurious blankets, shawls and scarves in vibrant colours and different wools, such as mohair or cashmere, at a fraction of what you would pay in high-end boutiques.
C/ González Gallarza 12, 26280; 941 354 034; open daily

WHERE TO STAY

EZCARAY

Hotel Echaurren *moderate*
Considered one of the best hotels in La Rioja, there are 21 comfortable and tasteful rooms located inside this medieval mansion. The atmospheric lounge has an open fireplace and there are two famed restaurants and a tapas bar on the ground floor.
C/ Pedro José García 19, 26280; 941 354 047; www.echaurren.com

AROUND NÁJERA

Real Casona de las Amas *expensive*
Located 8 km (5 miles) west of Nájera in the village of Azofra, this luxury hotel in a beautiful 17th-century mansion boasts genuine antique furniture. Many rooms have either a Jacuzzi or a private terrace.
C/ Mayor 5, 26323, Azofra; 941 416 103; www.realcasonadelasamas.com; closed mid-Dec to mid-Jan

SAN MILLÁN DE LA COGOLLA

La Posada de San Millán *inexpensive*
This upmarket *casa rural* is located on the grounds of the Monasterio de San Millán de Yuso and has a large garden with views over the valley.
26326, San Millán de la Cogolla; 941 373 161; www.laposadadesanmillan.es

⑦ Ezcaray
La Rioja; 26280
The gateway to **Valdezcaray** in the upper Oja valley, Ezcaray is La Rioja's only ski resort. The town is surrounded by striking verdant forests and skirted by the Oja river and it is well worth visiting in the off-season. In the centre of the town is the atmospheric Plaza de la Verdura with a pretty 1900s fountain surrounded by medieval houses with porticoes and wooden relief carvings. Ezcaray had an important woollen textile industry up until the beginning of the 1800s. Only one factory remains, the **Real Fábrica**. Built in 1752, it has been well-preserved and can be seen from the outside. Also worth a visit in Ezcaray is the 15th-century **Iglesia Santa María la Mayor**, which houses a museum of religious artifacts.

🚗 *Return to Santo Domingo de la Calzada on the LR111, and then turn right on the N120 (direction Logroño) for Nájera.*

⑧ Nájera
La Rioja; 26300
The old town of Nájera, west of Logroño, was once the capital of the Kingdom of Navarra, which at its height ruled over a huge part of northern Spain. With many shops and facilities, Nájera is a good place to stock up on anything that might be required before heading into the

Weaving from Ezcaray

Sierra de la Demanda. With the Najerilla river cutting straight through it, flanked by *paseos* and grassed areas, Nájera is a lovely place to spend an hour or so. The town's most important monument is the **Monasterio de Santa Maria la Real** *(closed Mon)*; members of the royal families of Navarra, Léon and Castille are buried here. According to legend, a statue of the Virgin was found on this site in the 11th century. The present building dates from the early 15th century and contains Gothic and Renaissance elements.

🚗 *Take the LR113 from Nájera, heading south towards Bobadilla. In Bobadilla, turn right on the LR331, following signs to San Millán de la Cogolla.*

⑨ San Millán de la Cogolla
La Rioja; 26326
The little village of San Millán de la Cogolla is known for its two monasteries. The monasteries, among the oldest in Spain, grew up around the former hermitage of San Millán, a 6th-century hermit who, over his 101-year life, attracted many scholarly disciples. Their scribes created an important collection of manuscripts, most notably the 10th-century *Glosas Emilianenses*, the first written examples of the Castilian language. Some of the manuscripts are on display in the treasury.

Located in the Cárdenas valley is the **Monasterio de San Millán de**

Yuso. The monastery was home to Gonzalo de Berceo, who in the 13th century wrote the first Castilian poetry. This has led San Millán to be dubbed "the cradle of Castilian", and Yuso is now home to Aula de la Lengua Castellana, which promotes Spanish-language studies. The monastery itself was rebuilt from the 16th to the 18th centuries in a mix of Renaissance and Baroque styles, evident in the immense plaza and monumental doors leading to the church, and a Rococo sacristy, where 17th-century paintings are hung. After visiting the monastery, follow signs on the LR421 to the Monasterio de San Millán de Suso.

Located in the depth of a pine forest on a hillside above San Millán is the **Monasterio de San Millán de Suso**. Dating from the 10th century, it is the original site of San Millán's monastic community. Etched out of pink sandstone in the Romanesque style, the saint's tomb is located inside, along with those of the "Seven Infants of Lara" who, according to legend, were beheaded by the Moors. The richly painted doors of the altarpiece depict scenes from the life of San Millán and the childhood of Jesus.

🚗 *Retrace the route to Bobadilla on the LR331, and turn right onto the LR113, following signs for Anguiano. After the village of Anguiano, drive 14 km (9 miles) and turn right onto* the LR435, following signs to the Monasterio de Valvanera. Park outside the monastery.

Anguiano Dancers
The archetypal mountain village of Anguiano is one of the prettiest in the Sierra de la Demanda. Anguiano hosts a famed tradition, celebrating its patron saint's (Mary Magdalene) day with a bizarre fiesta. Every year on 22 July nine local youths dress up in colourful, harlequin-like costumes and perform the *Danza de los Zancos*. Perched on pointed stilts, they twirl down a precarious crest, in time to music, performing an ancient rite of passage. The ritual is repeated on the last Saturday of September, when the image of Mary of Magdalene is returned to her shrine for the winter.

Above Monasterio de San Millán de Suso **Below left** Textile loom in a factory in Ezcaray **Below right** Spire of the Monasterio de San Millán de Yuso

EAT AND DRINK

EZCARAY

El Portal del Echaurren *expensive*
Local chef Francis Paniego has earned two Michelin stars for his creative take on local cuisine. Special dishes include *solomillos de rape negro sobre purrusalda* (monkfish with leeks). *C/ Pedro José García 19, 26280; 941 354 047; www.echaurren.com; closed Sun dinner and Mon and Tue in Jan–Jun*

El Rincon del Vino *expensive*
This restaurant serves delicious traditional Riojan cuisine with an emphasis on seasonal produce including mushrooms and truffles. *C/ Jesus Nazareno 2, 26280; 941 354 375*

AROUND SAN MILLÁN DE LA COGOLLA

La Cañada *inexpensive*
On the main road just north of Anguiano, 19 km (12 miles) from San Millán de la Cogolla, this is a favourite stop for hunters and walkers, so meals come hot, hearty and in large portions. *Ctra. Anguiano, Km 49; 941 745 003*

El Mirador *inexpensive*
Located 1 km (0.6 miles) outside the village of Berceo, north of San Millán de la Cogolla, this restaurant serves local dishes such as *pisto de piquillo* with cod and *patatas la riojana*. *Ctra. de San Millán s/n, 26327, Berceo; 941 373 008*

Eat and Drink: inexpensive, under €20; moderate, €20–€40; expensive, over €40

WHERE TO STAY

QUINTANAR DE LA SIERRA

Hostería de Castroviejo *inexpensive*
A cosy, stone-built inn in a pretty
village just 13 km (8 miles) east of
Quintanar, but well worth the detour,
with its traditionally decorated rooms
and delightful owners.
*C/ la Peña 12, Durelo de la Sierra,
42158; 639 645 352*

Posada Las Mayas *moderate*
A charming hotel with 10 cosy, well-
equipped rooms in a fine old stone
house in the middle of Quintanar, with
a surprisingly sophisticated restaurant
using fresh local produce.
*C/ El Cerro 5, 09670; 947 395 609;
www.lasmayas.es*

⑩ Monasterio de Valvanera
La Rioja; 26322

This impressive Gothic monastery
(open daily) located 1,000 m (3,300 ft)
above sea level on a mountaintop, is
home to the patron saint of La Rioja,
the Virgin of Valvanera. The faithful
queue up to light a candle at the feet
of the Virgin, allegedly sculpted by
Saint Lucas in AD 71 although most
historians believe the statue dates
from the 11th century. Unusually, the
feet of baby Jesus, who is seated on
the Virgin's lap, are twisted the opposite way to the direction He is facing.
Surrounded by forests and backed by
the jagged peaks of the Sierra de San
Lorenzo, the monastery has magnificent views, two restaurants and
hiking tracks, one of which winds all
the way through the mountains to
the town of Ezcaray *(see p64)*.

🚗 *Return to the LR113 and turn right
towards Mansilla de la Sierra. Park
at the lookout point for the Embalse
de Mansilla.*

⑪ Embalse de Mansilla
La Rioja; 26329

This extensive dam was constructed
in the 1950s by the regime of General
Franco. Mansilla was located at the
crossroads of two important rivers:
Najerilla and Cambrones. A dam was
required to irrigate the area, and it
was decided that the village around
it would need to be submerged. The
inhabitants were relocated to higher
ground. At low tide the remains of
the church, town hall and other buildings of the original village from the
old Ermita de Santa Caterina are
visible. The "new" Mansilla is located
further uphill, a less atmospheric
doppelgänger of its former self,
but it has spectacular views.

🚗 *Continue along the LR113 in the
same direction. In Villavelayo, turn left
onto the LR334, following signs for
Neila. Pass Neila and turn left onto the
BU822 (direction Quintanar). Drive for
4 km (2 miles) and turn right, following
signs for the Lagunas Altas de Neila.*

Above left Interior of the Monasterio de
Valvanera **Above right** Archways in the
Monasterio de Valvanera **Below left** Monasterio
de Valvanera located dramatically high up in the
hills **Below right** Typical scenery of the Sierra
de la Demanda

⑫ Lagunas Altas de Neila
La Rioja, Burgos; 09679

The four natural lagoons that make up the Lagunas Altas de Neila are enclosed in a post-glacial cirque and for many years were seen solely by shepherds and wood collectors. Now an asphalt road (a popular stretch for cycling events) leads to their threshold on the peak of La Campina, over 2,000 m (6,550 ft) above sea level and surrounded by spine-tingling views of the sierra. On ascending, a sign will direct visitors to the Larga and Negra lagoons, which are the most impressive. Visitors will then need to walk to the Larga lagoon, which goes a short way over the mountaintop. On the way, there are breathtaking views of the black water of the Negra lagoon, located on a natural terrace below. To explore the other lagoons, return to the car park and take the opposite track. The lagoons freeze over in winter; for many this is the most spectacular time to see them. There are plenty of pretty picnic spots on the road leading from Neila through a green countryside with constant views of the majestic Sierra de la Demanda.

🚗 *Return to the BU822 and turn right into the province of Burgos. Follow signs to Quintanar de la Sierra.*

⑬ Quintanar de la Sierra
Burgos; 09670

Surrounded by mountains and rivers, this sizeable town located in the province of Burgos is a popular hub for outdoor sports. Quintanar de la

Sierra's old quarter has retained some of its original architecture, such as old stone homesteads with distinctive conical chimney stacks, the 16th-century **Iglesia de San Crístobal** and an attractive Plaza Mayor with a central bandstand.

Just south of Quintanar de la Sierra, turn left onto the CL117, following signs to the **Necrópolis de Cuyacabras**. This is one of the most rewarding archaeological treasures in Spain: the remains of over 160 anthropomorphic tombs and niches carved out of rock in the midst of a pine forest. There is evidence that the site was in use in the 10th century, but historians believe the first tombs were created here 200 years earlier by Christians fleeing into the mountains from Muslim invaders.

Villages of the Sierra de la Demanda

The Sierra de la Demanda is dotted with historic villages (collectively known as Las 7 Vilas or "Seven villages") whose sheer isolation has kept their ancient homesteads and monuments incredibly well-preserved. One of the prettiest is Canales de la Sierra (reached via an exit on the LR113, 11 km/7 miles past Embalse de Mansilla), which is crisscrossed with bubbling streams and stone bridges. In Villavelayo (also on the LR113, 6 km/4 miles past Embalse de Mansilla) the Baroque Ermita de Santa Aúrea boasts a façade peppered with sculptures of saints. Visitors come to these villages to enjoy activities such as fishing and walking.

Above Façade of Ermita de Santa Aúrea in the village of Villavelayo

VISITING QUINTANAR DE LA SIERRA

Tourist Information
Plaza Mayor 1, 09670; 947 395 045; www.turismoburgos.org, www.quintanardelasierra.es/turismo-y-ocio; open daily 10am–2pm only from Jul to Sep

EAT AND DRINK

There are very few restaurants in this region. Most of the hotels listed have their own restaurants. Visitors can also take picnic supplies with them from the nearest town, as there are many pretty picnic spots en route.

DAY TRIP OPTIONS

There are two options for day trips in this region: an expedition to the wine-growing towns or a visit to the monasteries. Visitors can be based either in Laguardia or Haro to do these day trips. The N232 in the north and the LR113 in the south access most of the stops in this drive.

Wines of La Rioja Alavesa

Start the day with a walk around Laguardia ❶, soaking up the atmosphere of this splendid medieval hilltop town. Visit the bodegas around Laguardia, including Bodegas La Fabulista and Bodegas Ysios ❷.

Then head to Elciego ❸ for lunch at Frank Gehry's exclusive Hotel Marqués de Riscal. Drive to Briones ❹ to visit the excellent wine museum.

From Laguardia take the A124 northwest for Bodega Ysios. Return to Laguardia on the A124. At the junction, take the A3210, signed for Elciego. Continue on the A3210/LR211 until it meets the LR512 outside Cenicero, and turn right and drive through the village to meet the N232. Turn right for Briones.

Ancient monasteries

Visit the 12th-century cathedral in Santo Domingo de la Calzada ❻ and

head to San Millán de la Cogolla ❾ to visit the monasteries of Yuso and Suso, which are among the oldest in Spain. After this, drive to the Monasterio de Valvanera ❿, a Gothic monastery located in the mountains.

Leave Haro on the LR111/N126 to Santo Domingo de la Calzada. From Santo Domingo take the N102 to join the N120 for Nájera. In Nájera, get onto the LR113 (south). In Bobadilla turn right onto the LR331 for San Millán de la Cogolla. Return to Bobadilla on the LR331 and turn right, following signs for Anguiano. After Anguiano, turn right onto the LR435 to the Monasterio de Valvanera.

Eat and Drink: inexpensive, under €20; moderate, €20–€40; expensive, over €40

A Circuit around Navarra

Zangoza to Lizarra

Highlights

- **The pilgrim's path**
  Discover Zangoza, Roncesvalles and Lizarra, all important stopovers on the Camino de Santiago

- **Mountain scenery**
  Explore the mountains of Navarra and the breathtaking valleys that are full of wildlife

- **Caves with history**
  Visit the Zugarramurdi caves, shrouded in tales of witchcraft

- **Powerful Iruña**
  Enjoy Navarra's capital, famous for its bull-running fiesta

Way down from the witches' cave in Zugarramurdi

A Circuit around Navarra

Once a powerful, independent kingdom, Navarra is blessed with rich history and great natural beauty. Its most northerly region, bordering France, is mountainous and scantily populated, with tiny hamlets that are bastions of Basque language and culture, including the Basques' celebrated cuisine. This tour takes visitors from the *cuenca* (basin) around Iruña (Pamplona) to high country and back again. Expect enthralling scenery, ancient forests ideal for walking and inspiring medieval monasteries, hospices and churches that were built to accommodate Navarra's first tourists: the pilgrims on the Camino de Santiago.

Above High mountain road in the Navarrese Pyrenees, *see p72* **Below** Shop for pilgrims' accessories in Puente la Reina, *see p78–9*

ACTIVITIES

Listen to monks performing moving Gregorian chants in the Monasterio de Leyre

Take a walk through the remarkable Lumbier gorge

Enjoy Roncal cheese in the village of the same name

Go birdwatching in the magical Bosque de Irati

Trek through the serene Parque Natural de Señorío de Bertiz

Taste local wines and *pintxos* in Iruña

KEY

Above Pretty town of Lizarra on the banks of the Arga river, *see p79*

PLAN YOUR DRIVE

Start/finish: Zangoza to Lizarra.

Number of days: 4–5, allowing half a day to explore Iruña (Pamplona).

Distance: 425 km (265 miles).

Road conditions: There are lots of curves on the mountain roads between Erronkari and Bera. In the high mountain areas around Roncesvalles and Belagua the roads are very narrow. Some mountain roads may be closed, or require snow chains in the winter.

When to go: July and August have the most festivals and the weather will be temperate to warm. Winter is not a good time to visit, as the mountain roads may be closed.

Opening hours: Most monuments and museums are open from 10:30am to 5:30pm, while shops are open from 9:30am to 1:30pm and 4 to 8pm.

Main market days: Zangoza: Fri; Elizondo: every second Sat; Iruña: daily; Puente La Reina: Sat; Lizarra: Thu.

Shopping: The region is known for its cheeses (especially from Roncal) and charcuterie.

Major festivals: Zangoza: San Sebastián, 11–17 Sep; Otsagabia: Natividad de Nuestra Señora, 8 Sep; Iruña: San Fermín, 6–14 Jul; Lizarra: San Andrés, last week Nov.

DAY TRIP OPTIONS

Using Iruña as a base, there are many day trip options in the Navarra valley. The Valle del Baztán and the Bertiz estate are beautiful stopovers and **those interested in walking** can explore the Jardín de Señorio de Bertiz and the adjacent Parque Natural de Señorio de Bertiz. The adjoining valleys of Roncal and Salazar and the magnificent Bosque de Irati are ideal for the **lovers of countryside**. For details, *see p79.*

WHERE TO STAY

CASTILLO DE JAVIER

Hotel Xabier *moderate*
This three-star hotel, which in many ways feels like a four- or five-star, is located in the gardens of the castle complex and has a lovely outdoor restaurant with a terrace on the ground floor. The sizeable rooms are decorated with antiques, fine textiles and rugs over hardwood flooring.
31411, Castillo de Javier; 948 884 006; www.hotelxabier.com

MONASTERIO DE LEYRE

Hotel Hospedería de Leyre *moderate*
The rooms in this monastery hotel are comfortable and seem good value considering its historic setting. Guests will be well placed to listen to the monks' daily chants.
31410, Yesa; 948 884 100; www. monasteriodeleyre.com

Above Imposing battlements of the Castillo de Javier **Below** Romanesque exterior of the Monasterio de Leyre

① Zangoza (Sangüesa)
Navarra; 31400
When the Camino de Santiago gained momentum in the 12th century, so did Zangoza, which owes much of its development to the popularity of the Christian pilgrimage. Even today, *bastón*-carrying pilgrims are seen all over the town, guided by the bronze scallop-shell medallions set into the ancient streets (the *vieira* or scallop is a symbol of the route). There are two important churches here. **Santa María la Real** features a decorated portal depicting the Last Judgment. The tourist office is located opposite it. **Santiago el Mayor** was built between the 7th and 13th centuries. It has a fortified tower and a stone statue of the saint, discovered in the church foundations in 1965. For a change of style, seek out the ornately Baroque **Palacio de Ongay-Vallesantoro** and the **Casa Consistorial**, the 16th-century city hall.
🚗 *Take the NA5410 east to Castillo de Javier.*

Statue of Saint James in Zangoza

② Castillo de Javier
Navarra; 31411
The impressive structure of the Castillo de Javier *(open daily)* is surrounded by rolling green hills and forests. It dates back to the 11th century, but was added to and altered up to the 16th century and has been well-preserved.

It was the birthplace of Saint Francis Xavier, who, as well as being co-founder of the Jesuit order, has a special place in Basque religious culture as the patron saint of sportsmen. Once over the footbridge and inside, explore the castle, its paintings, medieval furniture and macabre skeleton murals in the chapel *(Mass daily at 1pm)*. The castle also houses a magnificent 13th-century crucifix. During the first two weekends of March, a pilgrimage, the Javierada, is made to here from Zangoza.
🚗 *Continue on the NA5410 to Yesa. Turn left onto the N240 towards Iruña (Pamplona), and immediately there will be signs to turn right (on the NA2113) to reach the Monasterio de Leyre. Follow signs and park.*

③ Monasterio de Leyre
Navarra; 31410
Surrounded by limestone cliffs and manicured lawns and with views of the Yesa reservoir, the Monasterio de Leyre is an impressive sight. Leyre was founded as a Benedictine monastery, but later came to be in the hands of Cistercian monks. Monks still reside here, and part of the original complex, built between the 11th and 12th centuries, has been heavily restored and now contains a hotel. Visitors are allowed access to the 11th-century church and mausoleum. The church, dedicated to Santa María, features

---

one of the most renowned portals in Navarra, an elaborate composition of strange beast, bird and human forms, though inside it is remarkably austere. The mausoleum, where the early kings of Navarra are buried, is an eerie place with a series of symmetrically placed arches. Leyre's monks are famous for their Gregorian chant, which they perform here *(open Mon–Fri, from 10:15am to 2pm, and 3.30 to 7pm, Sat–Sun, from 10:15am to 2pm, and 4 to 7pm; chants performed Mon–Fri at 7.30am, 9am and 7pm, Sat–Sun at 8am, noon and 7pm)*.

🚗 **Return to the N240, turn right in Liédena and cross the bridge. After Liédena, turn right towards Iruña (Pamplona). At the second roundabout, turn right onto the NA150. At Lumbier, follow signs for the Foz de Lumbier. Leave the car in the parking area.**

④ Foz de Lumbier
Navarra; 31440

The Foz de Lumbier, a majestic gorge surrounded by rock walls over 150 m (490 ft) high, is one of the most cele-brated beauty spots in Navarra. A train used to run through it, but this line is no longer in use and the tracks have been removed, leaving a 1,300-m (1,400-yd) path for walkers, joggers and cyclists. The gorge's craggy walls sprout thyme and lavender plants, and at its arched entrance there are abundant poplars. Visitors can spot the odd fox or *jabali* (wild boar).

🚗 **Return to Lumbier, cross the river and at the roundabout turn right onto the NA178 towards Navascués. After the village of Domeño, follow signs off this road to the Foz de Arbayún.**

⑤ Foz de Arbayún
Navarra; 31454

Unlike the Foz de Lumbier, the Arbayún gorge cannot be traversed, but a lookout point, the Mirador de Iso, has been installed directly above it. This 6-km- (4-mile-) long gorge was formed by the Salazar river eroding the rock of the Sierra de Leyre. Blessed with a microclimate, the gorge is blanketed with a diverse variety of trees, which come alive with vivid colours during autumn. It is also home to a large community of vultures.

🚗 **Return to the NA178 and continue along it as far as Navascués, where there is a right turn onto the NA214 in the direction of Burgui. At Burgui, turn left on the NA137 for Erronkari (Roncal), and park at the base of the village.**

EAT AND DRNK

ZANGOZA

Restaurante Yamaguchi *inexpensive*
Friendly, family-run hotel-restaurant, serving – despite the name – regional specialities such as *pochas de Sangüesa* (local beans served up in a rich vegetable stew), as well as game in season.
Ctra. de San Xavier, 31400; 948 870 127

Above Stone carvings at the Castillo de Javier **Below left** Breathtaking view of the Foz de Arbayún **Below right** Intricately carved portal of the Monasterio de Leyre

Above View of the picturesque hamlet of Otsagabia amid the mountains Below Old stone church in Erronkari village

WHERE TO STAY

OTSAGABIA

Camping Osate *inexpensive*
This extensive camp site has good bathroom and laundry facilities and a popular bar-restaurant on site.
NA130 s/n (follow the signs from the village), 31680; 948 890 184; www.campingosate.net

Hostal Orialde *inexpensive*
A lovely hostel, which overlooks the river, decorated with antiques and assorted bric-a-brac. The attic, which sleeps up to six, is a good option for families or friends travelling together.
Urrutia 6, 31680; 948 890 027

RONCESVALLES

Casa de los Beneficiados *moderate*
The original 18th-century pilgrims' hospice, adjacent to the Colegiata Real, now contains apartments for between two and five guests, with wooden beams and kitchenettes.
Orreaga-Roncesvalles, 31650; 948 760 105; www.casadebeneficiados.com

ELIZONDO

Hostal Trinkete Antxitonea
inexpensive
This cosy, 19th-century country house is located right in the centre of the village. Family rooms are available.
C/ Braulio Iriarte 16, 31700; 948 581 807; www.antxitonea.com

AROUND LAS CUEVAS DE ZUGARRAMURDI

Sueldegia *inexpensive*
Sueldegia, a *casa rural* in Zugarramurdi's main square, offers spacious *en suite* rooms, a comfortable common area and outdoor garden.
Lapizteguia s/n, 31710, Zugarramurdi; 948 599 088

⑥ Erronkari (Roncal)
Navarra; 31415
The valley of Roncal is famous throughout Spain for the cheese it produces with the milk of the Lacha breed of sheep that inhabit the rolling green pastures of this mountainous part of Navarra. At the heart of the valley is the sleepy village of Roncal. It is a wildly pretty place, with stone streets and houses on a curious Y-shaped layout ending at the Esca river and surrounded by forests. The shepherd-turned-opera singer Julián Gayarre (1844–90) was from here and a museum on his life and work, the **Casa-Museo Gayarre** *(open Tue–Sun)*, has been set up in Roncal.

🚗 *Leaving Erronkari, continue along the NA137 for Izaba (Isaba), and turn left on the NA140. Go through Uztarroze (Uztárroz) and through many bends until the T-junction. Turn left, on the NA140. Go through Itzaltzu (Izalzu) to reach Otsagabia (Ochagavía). Park in the village.*

The Cheese of Roncal
The celebrated cheese from the Roncal valley was the first in Spain to receive its own DO or *Denominación de Origen*: an official standard that means no other region can use its name or produce a cheese with its particular qualities. Just north of Roncal, in the village of Uztárroz, a local cheesemaking family has set up a museum on cheesemaking, Ekia *(open daily)*, where visitors can also buy their products.

⑦ Otsagabia (Ochagavía)
Navarra; 31680
The picture-perfect hamlet of Otsagabia is located in the Salazar valley, which is named after the river that runs through it. The village is renowned for its six medieval stone bridges and its white houses capped with pointed slate roofs. The lovely 12th-century **Ermita de Nuestra Señora de Muskilda** on the outskirts of the village is topped by an unusual cone-shaped tower, lending it a fairy-tale appearance. Every September, the village's famous *danzantes* (traditional dancers) perform in the honour of the Virgin of Muskilda in traditional attire.

🚗 *From Otsagabia, take the NA2012 mountain road, which ascends to the Bosque de Irati. Park at the entrance to the forest, where there is a small information office.*

⑧ Bosque de Irati
Navarra; 31670
The Irati forest occupies a special place in Basque folklore. It spreads over 170 sq km (65 sq miles) of the Aezkoa and Salazar valleys and stretches all the way into France, making it one of the largest forests in Europe. Over 23 species of birds inhabit the Irati, which is made up of surprisingly large beech and fir trees. Wildlife includes red deer, wild boar and foxes. The information centre can advise visitors on hikes through the forest and birdwatching trails. Visit the **Ermita de la Virgin de las Nieves**, a pretty hermitage, a short walk from the car park.

🚗 *Return to Otsagabia and get onto the NA140. Cross the river twice and turn right following signs for Jaurrieta and Burguete (Auritz), still on the same road. Go through Garaioa and Garralda until it meets the main N135. Turn right here for Roncesvalles.*

⑨ Roncesvalles

Navarra; 31650

This ancient mountain border village was mythologized in the medieval epic *Chanson de Roland* as the place where the heroic knight Roland died fighting against the Moors with Charlemagne's army in 778. However, history has shown that it was the Basques, not the Moors, who attacked Charlemagne's men in Roncesvalles. After the discovery of Saint James's tomb in Galicia a century later, Roncesvalles became the main point of entry for pilgrims from France into Spain on the Camino de Santiago. The **Colegiata Real** *(open daily 10am–2pm, 3:30–7pm, closed Jan)*, is where Sancho VII, the King of Navarra (r. 1194–1229), is buried.

🚗 *Return from Roncesvalles along the N135 and beyond Burguete (Auritz) continue straight on this road towards Iruña (Pamplona). At Zubiri, turn right onto the N138 towards Eugi to reach Urtasun. Turn left here onto the NA2520 for Olague. Turn right onto the N121A at Olague. Go through two tunnels and turn right onto the NA2540, through Berroeta. Follow this road to meet the N121B for Elizondo.*

⑩ Elizondo

Navarra; 31700

This village of 18th- and 19th-century town houses and red-shuttered homesteads (known as *caserios*) is the gateway to the Valle de Baztán, a breathtaking valley lined by mountains and ancient oak trees. The Baztán river runs through the valley, making it popular with walkers and watersports enthusiasts. Straddling the river, Elizondo is a pleasant place

to walk around. Visit the 20th-century **Iglesia de Santiago**, built in the Neo-Baroque style, and the 18th-century **Palacio de Arizcunera**. The town is famous for its *urrakin egina* (hazelnut chocolate) and holds a food fair in October.

🚗 *Continue on the N121B past Elizondo until the left turn for Urdax (Urdazubi), off the main road. Follow signs for Zugarramurdi on the NA4402 and then the NA4401. Park at the public car park on the outskirts of the village.*

⑪ Las Cuevas de Zugarramurdi

Navarra; 31710

The caves of Zugarramurdi, more commonly known as La Cueva de las Brujas (The Witches' Cave) *(open 11am–5:30pm Tue–Sun)*, are one of the most unusual sights in Navarra. At 120 m (130 yd) long and surrounded by thick green forest, the caves are an impressive natural wonder. In the late 1600s they were an alleged meeting place for witches. During the Inquisition, 300 women from the area were arrested and accused of witchcraft. Many were tortured and eventually executed in an act that was intended to rid Navarra of black magic. Near the caves, the **Museo de las Brujas** *(closed Mon and Tue)* puts these events in context.

🚗 *Leave on the NA4401, which then joins the N121B, to Dantxarinea on the French border. Turn left and enter France briefly and follow the local D4 wide road left to Sare. Continue on the same road to re-enter Spain and arrive at Bera (Vera de Bidasoa). Park in the Plaza Juan de Alzate at the entrance to the village.*

Above Wooden doorway of the 12th-century Ermita de Nuestra Señora de Muskilda, Otsagabia **Below** Forest around the Witches' Cave in Zugarramurdi

EAT AND DRINK

RONCESVALLES

La Posada de Roncesvalles *inexpensive*
Located in a 17th-century farmhouse, La Posada serves up hot and hearty local dishes to pilgrims. Recommended dishes are the roasted red peppers, wild mushrooms and game, including pigeon and boar.
Roncesvalles-Orreaga, 31650; 948 760 225; www. laposadaderoncesvalles.com

AROUND LAS CUEVAS DE ZUGARRAMURDI

Altzatenea *moderate*
The speciality here is large succulent steaks, which come cooked to perfection from an outdoor grill. There is a flower-filled outdoor terrace for dining on warmer evenings.
C/ Basaburua 3, 31710, Zugarramurdi; 948 599 187; closed Mon

Above Homestead with a colourful, flower-filled balcony, Bera **Below** One of the old *carboneras* in the Parque Natural de Señorío de Bertiz

VISITING PARQUE NATURAL DE SEÑORÍO DE BERTIZ

Tourist Information
The Oficina de Turismo de Señorío de Bertiz is located in the car park of the Jardín de Señorío de Bertiz. Guided visits are also available.
31720, Bertiz; 948 592 421; www. parquedebertiz.es; open 10am to 8pm in summer and 10am to 6pm in winter

WHERE TO STAY

BERA

Hotel Churrut *expensive*
An 18th-century building that the Churrut family has converted into a comfortable hotel. The gallery is an eye-catching feature with comfortable wicker armchairs and floor-to-ceiling windows that offer great views of the garden.
Plaza de los Fueros 2, 31780; 948 625 540; www.hotelchurrut.com

AROUND PARQUE NATURAL DE SEÑORÍO DE BERTIZ

Hostal Bertiz *moderate*
Located on the edge of the park, this 16th-century stone guesthouse is surrounded by a flower-filled garden and has tastefully decorated rooms.
C/ San Juan Bautista 16, Oieregi, 31720; 948 592 081; www.hostalbertiz.com

---

⑫ Bera (Vera de Bidasoa)
Navarra; 31780

Bera is the largest of the famous *cinco villas* (five towns) that dot the Valle de Bidasoa. Its close proximity to France has played an important part in Bera's prosperity, allowing it to flourish through trade. Stately *caserios* (homesteads), many bearing colourful coats of arms, flank its main street, which also has a good selection of shops. The illustrious Baroja family have their roots in Bera.

Their most famous members were the novelist Pío Baroja (1872–1956), his painter brother Ricardo and their nephew, the anthropologist Julio Caro Baroja (1914–95).

🚗 *From Bera head towards Iruña (Pamplona) on the N121A for 25 km (16 miles), and then turn left for Oronoz. Drive to the centre of the village. Turn right at the petrol station, crossing the bridge and following signs for Parque Natural de Señorío de Bertiz. Park in the car park.*

---

⑬ Parque Natural de Señorío de Bertiz
Navarra; 31720

With giant oaks, beech and chestnuts, pretty streams and waterfalls and a large community of woodpeckers, the nature reserve is a magical place to take a walk. The Jardín de Señorío de Bertiz lies on the edge of the Parque Natural de Señorío de Bertiz. The following easy to moderate 6-km (4-mile) walk consists of forest paths and tracks, all well signposted. This walk can be done any time of the day, but be sure to carry water.

A two-hour walking tour

From the car park take the tarmac road past the old guard house to the remains of the **carbonera** ①. The inhabitants of the villages surrounding the park used to collect wood in the forest to burn to charcoal in mounds such as these. Concerned about anything that might halt the regeneration of the forest, Pedro Ciga, the last lord of the manor, employed wardens to stop this practice, as he did the collection of acorns. Two paths branch out from this point. Take the Irretarazu path to

Parque Natural de Señorío de Bertiz sign

the left and walk uphill. Almost immediately there will be many oak trees. Oaks were felled here from the 16th to the 18th centuries for use in shipbuilding and since then as firewood. Since the time of Pedro Ciga, this practice too has stopped. Continue walking uphill, onto a natural elevated terrace with some great views of the Valle de Bertiz. The track leads to an area of the forest dominated by chestnut trees, some a century old. Keep walking and the oak trees will become scarcer and beech will begin to dominate. Continue to where the Irretarazu path crosses with the Iturburua path and take the latter. This goes through the valley floor where alder and ash trees can be seen, and which is crisscrossed by cascades and streams. Almost at the end of the path is the **Suspiro waterfall** ②, formed by a spring of the same name. Continue to the junction with the Suspiro path. This point lies halfway through the walk. Turn right and follow the signs to the car park. The path leads to an ancient stone **drinking fountain** ③ and bench, turning into a cobblestoned road lined with plane trees that goes back to the starting point.

Before leaving, stop at the magical **Jardín de Señorío de Bertiz** ④ at the entrance of Parque Natural de Señorio de Bertiz. This 19th-century botanical garden, one of the most beautiful in Spain, stands on land that had been gifted to the noble Ciga family by King Charles II in the 17th century. Pedro Ciga was an ardent nature lover and pioneer ecologist who, with his wife Dorotea, planted the garden and rebuilt the ancestral home, the **Palacio de Bertiz** ⑤, in Art Nouveau style before gifting it to the State in 1949. The garden's diversity is astounding, with exotic trees and

Above Giant tree in the Parque Natural de Señorío de Bertiz

plants such as cedar, gingko biloba, liquidambar, cypress, lemon and an abundance of bamboo. Flowers bloom from every nook. The manor is occasionally used for exhibitions and the old chapel has been converted into an information centre *(open daily).* After visiting the garden, go back to the car park.

🚗 *Return to the N121A and follow signs to Iruña (Pamplona). Follow "Centro Urbano" and "Todas Directions" signs to park. Use a private car park, as street parking is prohibited.*

Suspiro path

Suspiro waterfall ②

Iturburua path

③ Drinking fountain

Alzkolegi path

Ayansoro

Irretarazu path

Carbonera ①

Jardín de Señorío de Bertiz ④

Palacio de Bertiz ⑤

Baztan

0 metres 150

0 yards 150

EAT AND DRINK

BERA

Lenkonea *moderate*
High beamed ceilings and tables draped in white linen set the scene for refined yet great-value local cuisine at this restaurant, part of the Hotel Churrut.
Plaza de los Fueros 2, 31780; 948 625 540

Eat and Drink: inexpensive, under €20; moderate, €20–€40; expensive, over €40

Above Five-arched medieval pilgrim's bridge at Puente la Reina Below Romanesque structure of Palacio de los Reyes de Navarra, Lizarra

VISITING IRUÑA

Tourist Information
C/ San Saturnino 2; 948 420 700; www.turismodepamplona.es; open 9am–8pm Mon–Sat, 10am–2pm Sun in summer; 10am–5pm Mon–Fri, 10am–2pm Sat & Sun in winter.

Parking
Directions to commercial car parks are posted on all main arteries into Iruña. Centrally located car parks include the Plaza de Castillo, the Auditorio Baluarte and the bus station at the Ciudadela.

WHERE TO STAY

IRUÑA

Hotel Castillo de Javier moderate
A step up from the plethora of budget hostels in Iruña's Old Town, this hotel offers small but bright rooms.
C/ San Nicolás 50–52, 31100; 948 203 040; www.hotelcastillodejavier.com

PUENTE LA REINA

Bidean moderate
Located on Puente La Reina's main street, this casa rural offers cosy accommodation in stylish rustic surroundings. There is a good restaurant on site, which is popular with pilgrims.
C/ Mayor 20, 31100; 948 340 457; www.bidean.com

⑭ Iruña (Pamplona)
Navarra; 31110

Iruña, or Pamplona as it is more commonly known, the capital of Navarra, is said to have been founded by the Roman general, Pompey. It is probably best known for its yearly San Fermín festival, or the running of the bulls. It is a handsome town, and well worth stopping in for an afternoon or even overnight, even when the festival is not on, in order to try its famous tapas bars.

A good starting point for a quick tour is the central **Plaza de Castillo**. From here, it is easy to explore the main sights, which are signposted throughout the old city. The most important are the Gothic **Catedral de Santa María la Real** (open daily), the massive 16th-century ciudadela (citadel) built in ochre-coloured stone, and the Neo-Classical **Palacio del Gobierno de Navarra** (by appointment only), which is now the seat of Navarra's regional government. This is where Iruña's mayor heralds the beginning of San Fermín.

Once back at the Plaza de Castillo, take a break at the famous Cafe Iruña, a Belle-Époque café Ernest Hemingway frequented while writing The Sun Also Rises. A bronze life-size statue of the author sits at the entrance.

🚗 Leave Iruña (Pamplona) via the PA30 ring road, following the directions to Tarragona. Take the exit to the A12, following the directions to Logroño/Madrid. Leave the A12 at exit 18 and follow the signs to Puente La Reina. Park in the street.

San Fermín

The most famous festival in Navarra, and possibly the whole of Spain, is San Fermín, otherwise known as the running of the bulls. The whole city practically closes down for the week-long event in early July, and what may seem like madness to an outsider is actually taken quite seriously by Spaniards, with daily bull-runs (called encierros) shown live on television. In honour of Navarra's patron saint, people spill out onto the streets for spontaneous partying, a parade of gigantes (towering figures dressed in traditional costumes) and, on 7 July, the carrying of the effigy of San Fermín in procession to the cathedral amid great ceremony.

⑮ Puente la Reina
Navarra; 31100

A major stop on the Camino de Santiago, this village gets its name from the elegant humpbacked stone pedestrian bridge spanning the Arga river that was built for pilgrims in the 11th century by royal command. Visitors can reach it by walking to the end of Calle Mayor. About halfway along this street, the Plaza Julian

SHOPPING

IRUÑA
Visit the shops around the cathedral for pottery and ceramics, textiles and other paraphernalia related to the San Fermín festival.

LIZARRA
Carmelo Boneta Lopetegui
Visit Carmelo Boneta's *taller* (workshop) near the cathedral. He sells intricately carved pieces of wooden furniture and objects inspired by Basque symbolism as well as religious artifacts.
C/ La Rúa 19, 31200; 948 551 481

Mena contains a handful of bars underneath its porticoes. The 12th-century **Iglesia del Crucifijo** *(open daily)*, supposedly built by the Knights Templar, is named after the Y-shaped wooden crucifix of Christ with arms upraised, which resides inside, and is said to have been a gift from a German pilgrim in the 14th century. The **Iglesia de Santiago** *(open daily)*, located on the main narrow street of Puente la Reina, has a gilded statue showing the saint as a pilgrim.

🚗 **Return to the A12, and at exit 36 take the right onto the NA1110 to Lizarra (Estella). Pass the modern periphery and park in the street.**

🔟 Lizarra (Estella)
Navarra; 31200
In perhaps one of the earliest exercises in mass tourism, Sancho V Ramírez

(r. 1063–1094), King of Navarra, founded Lizarra in the 11th century to attract pilgrims on their way to Santiago. Lizarra has most of its major attractions across the Arga in a compact *conjunto monumental* (historic centre). Climb the dozens of steps to get to the portal of the **Iglesia de San Pedro de la Rúa** *(open Mon–Sat, from 10am–1:30pm and 6–7pm, Sun, from 9:45am–12:30pm)*. The church boasts rich 13th-century carvings of plant and figurative motifs. It has a Cistercian Mudéjar-influenced sculpted doorway. Opposite is the **Palacio de los Reyes de Navarra**, the only secular Romanesque work in Navarra and now the location of the tourist office and a **museum** *(closed Mon)* dedicated to the painter Gustavo de Maeztú (1887–1947). Next to it is the San Martín square, with its famous Fuente de Chorros, a good place to relax in the shade.

EAT AND DRINK

IRUÑA
Rodero *expensive*
This contemporary-cuisine restaurant is considered one of the best in the city. The upscale menu includes dishes such as wild pigeon with figs.
C/ Emilio Arrieta 3, 31002; 948 228 035; www.restauranterodero.com; closed Sun and 2 weeks in Aug

Tapas bars
Dozens of tapas bars line the old streets, particularly around the Calle Estafeta. Most specialize in *pintxos*, a Basque style of tapas in which small morsels are served on a round of bread.

LIZARRA
Bar-Restaurante Casanova
inexpensive–moderate
This family-run place is as popular with locals as tourists for its dishes such as roast suckling pig and red bean stew.
C/ Fray Wenceslao de Oñate 7, 31200; 948 552 809; closed Mon

DAY TRIP OPTIONS
The Navarra valley offers two day trip options. The Valle de Baztán and the Bertiz estate are both easily reached via a well-paved motorway from Iruña. Another option is to visit the valleys of Roncal and Salazar and the Bosque de Irati.

Valle de Baztán and the Bertiz estate
Drive at a leisurely pace through the enchanting Valle de Baztán in the Basque Pyrenees. Stop off and stroll around the village of Elizondo 🔟. Then head to Parque Natural de

Señorío de Bertiz ⓭ to explore this wonderful nature reserve and the Jardín de Señorío de Bertiz.

From Iruña's PA30 ring road, take exit 3 to the N121A, then the N121B to Elizondo. To reach the Bertiz estate, return along the N121B to Oronoz and drive to the centre of the village. Turn right at the petrol station, crossing the bridge and following signs for Parque Natural Señorío de Bertiz.

Erronkari, Otsagabia and the Bosque de Irati
Visit Erronkari 🟠 and Otsagabia 🟠,

which are popular Sunday destinations for Pamploneses, who come to walk and cycle around the villages that dot the valleys. Leave a few hours for walking through the dense Bosque de Irati 🟠, following signed footpaths from the car park.

From Iruña, take the A21 eastwards. Exit the motorway at the NA150 junction and follow signs to Erronkari. To reach Otsagabia from Erronkari, continue on the NA137 to Izaba (Isaba) following signs to Otsagabia. To reach the entrance to the Bosque de Irati, ascend the NA2012 road from Otsagabia.

Eat and Drink: inexpensive, under €20; moderate, €20–€40; expensive, over €40

To the Roof of Aragón

Castillo de Loarre to Hecho

Highlights

- **Castles in the air**
  Discover Loarre and Jaca, the rocky strongholds of the kings of Aragón

- **Breathtaking scenery and wildlife**
  Watch eagles, vultures and other large birds of prey glide over Los Mallos de Riglos

- **Romanesque architecture**
  Visit old churches and monasteries in San Juan de la Peña and Santa Cruz de la Serós

- **Local wines**
  Taste the little-known but surprisingly good wines of Aragón

Spectacular rock formations of Los Mallos de Riglos dominate Riglos village

To the Roof of Aragón

Forming a giant wall along the French border, the Aragonese Pyrenees dramatically cap Huesca, Aragón's northernmost province. This drive starts with the magnificent Castillo de Loarre, impressively situated overlooking the wide, flat Ebro plain and goes through tiny villages, awe-inspiring rock formations and majestic gorges. En route, visitors will see the Monasterio de San Juan de la Peña, hidden in an overhanging cliff and reputed to have been an early guardian of the Holy Grail. The tour also goes through the medieval city of Jaca, gateway to the High Pyrenees, and comes to an end in the valleys of Ansó and Hecho.

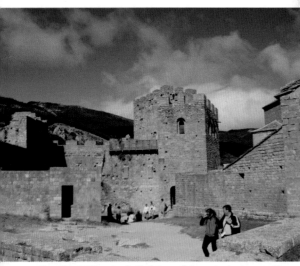

Above Majestic 11th-century Castillo de Loarre offering spectacular views, *see p84*

ACTIVITIES

Take a walk in the Pyrenees, from easy one- to two-hour strolls to more arduous hikes

Go rock climbing at the stunning rock formation of Los Mallos de Riglos

Try white-water rafting and canoeing around Biniés and Berdún

Above Thick forest around San Juan de la Peña, *see p86*
Below left Sweet shop in Jaca, *see p88* Below right
Iglesia de San Pedro in Ayerbe, *see p84*

KEY

⟨⟨⟨ Drive route

0 kilometres   5

0 miles   5

PLAN YOUR DRIVE

Start/finish: Castillo de Loarre to Hecho.

Number of days: 3–4, allowing half a day to explore San Juan de la Peña and half a day for visiting Jaca.

Distance: 180 km (110 miles).

Road conditions: Most roads are in good condition, but with lots of hairpin curves and bends, which make it slow. In winter some mountain roads may be closed, or require snow chains.

When to go: The best time to visit this region is between spring and autumn. Spring will see the rivers at their fullest for water sports enthusiasts.

Opening hours: Most museums and monuments are closed on Mondays. Shops are open from 9:30 to 11:30am, and from 4 to 8pm. Restaurants are open from 2 to 4pm, and from 8 to 11pm.

Main market days: Jaca: Fri; Hecho: Wed.

Major festivals: Murillo de Gállego: Santo Domingo, third weekend Aug; Jaca: Fiestas Patronales, last week Jun; Ansó: Fiesta del Traje, last Sun Aug; Hecho: Natividad de la Virgen, Sep.

DAY TRIP OPTIONS

Culture and **history buffs** will love the old San Juan de la Peña Romanesque sanctuary. **Nature lovers** will be enthralled by the magnificent forest of Oza and the villages of Ansó and Hecho. For details, *see p89*.

WHERE TO STAY

AROUND CASTILLO DE LOARRE

Hospedería de Loarre *moderate*
This 12-room hostelry is in a medieval mansion in the centre of Loarre, with a fine restaurant on the ground floor specializing in regional dishes. The thyme-flavoured ice cream is a must.
Plaza Miguel Moya 7, 22809, Loarre; 974 382 706; www.hospederiade loarre.com

AGÜERO

Camping Municipal Peña Sola
inexpensive
Campers wake up to the magnificent sight of the Peña Sola at this camp located at the base of Agüero village.
Ctra. 534 s/n, 22808; 974 380 533; www.campingaguero.es

MURILLO DE GÁLLEGO

Hotel Los Mallos *moderate*
Popular with outdoor sports enthusiasts, this well-kept and homey hostel offers a great-value *media-pensión*, which includes breakfast and lunch or dinner.
Ctra. de Jaca 5, 22808; 974 383 026; www.panoramicalosmallos.com

Above Hill-town of Agüero sheltered by a crag, the Peña Sola **Below** Gigantic red-hued cliffs of Los Mallos watching over the village of Riglos

① Castillo de Loarre
Huesca; 22809

The majestic 11th-century Castillo de Loarre *(open daily)* sits high above the village of the same name. It started out as a fort but was converted to a monastery during the reign of Sancho Ramírez (c.1042–94), one of the first kings of Aragón. Perched over 1,000 m (3,300 ft) above sea level, with spectacular vistas of surrounding orchards and reservoirs, much of the complex is surprisingly well-preserved. Visitors are free to wander all the rooms, passageways and turrets. Highlights of the castle include the **Iglesia de San Esteban** with its magnificent external apses; the **Royal Chapel**, a perfectly symmetrical space crowned by a large dome; and the **Queen's Balcony**, from where royals watched over their domain.

🚘 *Follow the A1206 from Loarre village to the junction with the main A132 road in Ayerbe. Turn left to park in Ayerbe village.*

② Ayerbe
Huesca; 22800

This sizeable village is a good place to stock up on necessities for the drive ahead, as many villages further up in the mountains have only one general store, with limited opening hours. Most shops, as well as the handful of restaurants, span out from a rectangular central square, dominated at its northern flank by the 17th-century **Palacio de los Marqueses**. There are some other notable buildings – the **Iglesia de San Pedro**, a 16th-century church, and the Baroque **Torre de Reloj** (clock tower). The Nobel Prize-winning physician Santiago Ramón y Cajal (1852–1934) spent his youth in Ayerbe, and there is a small museum dedicated to him in the house where he lived (*C/ Rafael Gasset 19, 22800; closed Mon, and Tue in winter*).

🚘 *Continue along the A132, signposted for Jaca, for about 6 km (4 miles), and then turn right onto the HU310/Z310 (unsigned), following signs for Riglos and Los Mallos de Riglos. Park at the entrance of Riglos.*

③ Los Mallos de Riglos
Huesca; 22808

The tiny village of Riglos is dominated by one of the most extraordinary sights in Aragón – Los Mallos de Riglos. These eight red-hued, 300-m- (985-ft-) high vertical rock formations rule over the area, which was baptized El Reino de los Mallos or "Kingdom of Mallos". They rank among the best rock-climbing territories in Europe and the views from the top are astounding. On any given day, dozens of climbers can be seen ascending over their massive surfaces. Watching the climbers is a fascinating way to spend an hour or two. The sheer number of birds of prey darting in and out of Los Mallos's jagged crevices will enthrall nature lovers.

🚘 *Return to the A132 and turn right, and then very shortly fork left again on the Z534/HU534 (unsigned) for Agüero. Park at the base of the village.*

Romanesque Architecture

Especially common throughout the Pyrenees, Romanesque is an artistic style that flourished across Europe from the 11th to the 13th centuries. Later, it morphed into the early Gothic style. Across northern Spain, Romanesque architects were most active in the building of churches, monasteries and hermitages, many on or near the route of the Christian pilgrimage route to Santiago de Compostela. Romanesque buildings stand out for their simplicity and sturdiness: thick stone walls, rounded arches and barrel vaults. Romanesque artists excelled at creating richly carved portals and highly graphic, colourful murals, designed to communicate the scriptures to a largely illiterate population.

④ Agüero

Huesca; 22808

The attractive little hill-town of Agüero, which also forms a part of the El Reino de los Mallos, is sheltered by another towering crag of stone known as the Peña Sola. The extraordinary 13th-century **Iglesia de Santiago** is located in a forest outside the village (follow signs) and is considered a stellar example of Aragonese Romanesque architecture for its exquisitely carved portal depicting scenes of Salome dancing. Most experts have attributed this work to the same sculptor who worked on the Monasterio de San Juan de la Peña *(see p86)*.

🚗 *Return to the A132 and turn left (signposted for Iruña). Park at the base of Murillo de Gállego.*

⑤ Murillo de Gállego

Zaragoza; 22808

A picturesque village of stone houses, Murillo de Gállego gets its name from the Gállego river, which runs directly through it. Walk up to the main plaza, where there is a handy children's playground and the majestic 11th-century **Iglesia de El Salvador** *(open for Mass only)*. The church was later expanded in the 16th century. Some original polychrome paintings still remain on the capitals on either side of the crypt, one of which depicts a scene of two women arguing.

🚗 *Stay on the A132 till Santa María (also indicated as Las Peñas de Riglos) and turn right onto the A1205 (Ctra. de Jaca a Santa María). After 25 km (16 miles) is Bernués, near which there is a left turn on the A1603 (unsigned) for San Juan de la Peña.*

Above left Stone portal of the 13th-century Iglesia de Santiago in Agüero **Above right** Majestic Iglesia de El Salvador in Murillo de Gállego **Below** Approach to the town of Loarre

EAT AND DRINK

AROUND CASTILLO DE LOARRE

Casa O' Caminero *inexpensive*
A popular local eatery located in a whitewashed homestead in Loarre, this restaurant serves up a hot and hearty *menu del día* (a fixed price, three-course meal). Particularly good are the *chuletas* (grilled lamb chops), game dishes and rabbit *paella*.
Ctra. Huesca–Zaragoza 8, 22809, Loarre; 974 382 696

MURILLO DE GÁLLEGO

Reino de los Mallos *moderate*
This local bodega offers wine tastings and creative cuisine in stylish surrounds overlooking their vineyards.
Ctra. A132, Km 37.2, 22808; 974 383 015; www.reinodelosmallos.es; in winter restaurant open Sat only

Eat and Drink: inexpensive, under €20; moderate, €20–€40; expensive, over €40

Above Tenth-century Real Monasterio de San Juan de la Peña

VISITING SAN JUAN DE LA PEÑA

Tourist Information
974 355 119; www.turismodearagon.com; www.monasteriosanjuan.com

Parking
Park in front of the Monasterio Nuevo, on an open field that also has picnic facilities. Parking is not permitted outside the old monastery. There is a shuttle service that runs every 20 minutes between the new and old monasteries of San Juan de la Peña (cost is included in the entry fee). Since the closure of the monastery's own hotel, the nearest places to stay are in Santa Cruz de la Serós *(see below)*.

WHERE TO STAY

SANTA CRUZ DE LA SERÓS

Hostelería Santa Cruz *inexpensive*
This traditional country inn provides simple, colourfully painted rooms, a café-bar serving tasty local cuisine, and a roaring fire in the lounge.
C/ Ordana 2, 22792; 974 361 975; www.santacruzdelaseros.com

El Mirador de Santa Cruz *expensive*
All rooms in this luxury guesthouse have pretty, antique furniture and private terraces with views over the valley. There is also an in-house spa and an outdoor pool.
Ordana 8, 22792; 974 355 593; www.elmiradordesantacruz.com

❻ Monasterio de San Juan de la Peña
Huesca; 22711

This imposing monastery complex actually consists of two sites: the incredible old Real Monasterio de San Juan de la Peña (Royal Monastery of Saint John of the Rock), a Romanesque sanctuary literally carved into the side of the cliff face; and the Monasterio Nuevo dating from the 17th century. The monasteries are located in the middle of a nature reserve of the same name. With constant views of the Pyrenees in the distance and massive rock formations bursting out of forests, the location is as exciting to explore as the medieval chambers.

A one-hour walking tour

Start the walk from the car park in front of the **Monasterio Nuevo** ① *(open daily)*. After a fire destroyed the Royal Monastery in the 17th century, a new one was built further up the hillside, on a wide field known as Llano de San Indalecio. Although the new monastery contains none of the dramatic stony carvings of the original San Juan de la Peña, it is noted for being a fine piece of monastic architecture and has maintained its elegant Baroque façade. The interior has been heavily altered and restored, with much of it given over to a four-star hotel and temporary exhibitions on art and history. To the right of the new monastery is a well-marked path stretching northwards. This goes through a thick forest of pine, holly, beech and maple to the **Balcón de Pirineo** ②, a panoramic lookout point across the valleys of Ansó and Ordesa with the mountains framing the horizon. An indicator will help visitors identify each one, including France's Midi d'Ossau. Return to the new monastery and go past the Centro de Interpretación located next to it. The visitors' centre, housed in the **Ermita de San Homónimo** ③, provides information on the mountains and countryside that surround the complex. Take the south-leading track directly in front of the visitor centre. This zigzagging track will lead to a hermitage and *mirador* (lookout point), the **Ermita**

Stone capital in the old monastery cloister

Real Monasterio de San Juan de la Peña
❻

Ermita de San Voto ⑤

Balcón de Pirineo ②

Monasterio Nuevo ①

Ermita de San Homónimo ③

Ermita de Santa Teresa ④

A1603

0 metres 500
0 yards 500

de Santa Teresa ④. The hermitage itself lies in ruins, but it has fine views of the valleys and mountains of the pre-Pyrenees, including the village of Loarre *(see p84)*.

Return to the Ermita de San Homónimo. Follow the main tarmac road to the west that leads to the old monastery. About 50 m (165 ft) after the turn-off to the Tozal de San Salvador, take the route, marked by a stone indicator, to the **Ermita de San Voto** ⑤, a simple stone structure with another *mirador* with further views of the Pyrenees. From here, join up again with the main road that goes to the **Real Monasterio de San Juan de la Peña** ⑥.

The Real Monasterio de San Juan de la Peña, or royal monastery, was founded in the 10th century by a group of hermit monks fleeing the Moorish invasion. Seeking sanctuary in the folds of an overhanging rock, they chiselled out a church in Mozarabic style on the ground floor. The church later expanded to an important holy site under the order of the Benedictines. Legend has it that the Holy Grail – the chalice that was used in the Last Supper – was hidden here from the Moors; a replica is on display in the central apse in the upper church. The monastery was a customary stop for pilgrims on the Camino de Santiago. In the 18th century, a Neo-Classical pantheon featuring some exquisite relief carvings was built on the site of a medieval necropolis. The highlight of the structure is the Romanesque cloister. Conceived to represent New

Jerusalem, this space features 20 Romanesque capitals with carved scenes from the scriptures by an anonymous artist known simply as El Maestro.

After visiting the old monastery, either walk or take the shuttle service back to the car park in front of the Monasterio Nuevo.

🚗 *Continue on the A1603 to Santa Cruz de la Serós. Park in the street at the entrance to the village.*

⑦ Santa Cruz de la Serós
Huesca; 22792

A wonderfully intact little village, Santa Cruz de la Serós is made up of typical mountain houses. Built entirely of stone, they feature cylindrical chimney stacks nicknamed *espantabrujas* (something that is believed to scare off witches). There are two important Romanesque monuments here. The first, on the main road to the entrance of the village, is the tiny 11th-century **Iglesia de San Caprasio**, whose simple interior can be viewed from behind a grid at the entrance. The second, in the middle of the village, is the 11th-century **Iglesia de Santa María**. Carved in the centre of its portal is a *crimsón*, a compass-type symbol common in Romanesque imagery that depicts the beginning and end of the universe. The town also has some good bed-and-breakfasts and high-quality restaurants.

🚗 *Leave Santa Cruz de la Séros on the A1603 and follow it until it meets the N240. Turn right and follow signs to the citadel in Jaca.*

Top Intricately carved exterior of the Real Monasterio de San Juan de la Peña **Above** Sturdy exterior of the 11th-century Iglesia de Santa María, Santa Cruz de la Serós **Below** View of the elegant and simple Monasterio Nuevo in San Juan de la Peña

---

SHOPPING IN SANTA CRUZ DE LA SERÓS

Embarrarte
A wide range of ceramicware and pottery is on display from local artists, with modern designs in vibrant blue and gold. There is also a range of traditional designs.
La Fuente 3, 22792; 974 363 106

EAT AND DRINK

SANTA CRUZ DE LA SERÓS

O' Fogaril *moderate*
This restaurant serves delicious food. Try local dishes such as *pochas* (white beans in a thick soup).
C/ Baja 6, 22792; 974 361 737; closed Mon–Fri in winter

Above Ornate altar in the 16th-century Iglesia de San Pedro in Ansó **Below left** Eleventh-century castle in Biniés **Below right** Sign for the *casa rural* Hotel Barosse near Jaca **Bottom right** Exterior of the excellent Restaurante Gaby, Hecho

VISITING JACA

Tourist Information
Plaza de San Pedro 11, 22700; 974 360 098; www.jaca.es

Parking
Private car parks are located in the Paseo Manuel Gímenez Abad behind the Ciudadela and on Calle Tierra de Biescas on the western flank.

Water sports
UR Pirineos offer rafting, canoeing, kayaking and canyoning on the Veral and Gállego rivers.
Ctra. A132, Km 38, 22808, Murillo de Gállego; 974 383 048; www.urpirineos.es

WHERE TO STAY

AROUND JACA

Hotel Barosse *expensive*
Hosts Jose and Gonzalo make guests feel thoroughly at home at their bed-and-breakfast, 4 km (2 miles) south of Jaca, where every detail has been meticulously conceived for comfort.
C/ Estiras 4, 22712, Barós; 974 360 582; www.barosse.com

ANSÓ

Posada Magoria *inexpensive*
This is the best place to stay in the village, with a rear garden overlooking the river. The restaurant serves home-grown, organic, vegetarian fare.
A1602 s/n, 22700; 974 370 049; www.posadamagoria.com

⑧ Jaca

Huesca; 22700
Founded in the 2nd century, Jaca was the first capital of the kingdom of Aragón and is the gateway to the High Pyrenees. The town is home to the **Ciudadela de Jaca** *(open Tue–Sun)*, a massive pentagonal citadel built in the 16th century, and one of only two of its kind remaining in Europe. It has remained perfectly intact and can be visited despite it still having a military role.

Cross the Avenida Primer Viernes de Mayo into the Old Town, the site of the town's 11th-century **Catedral de San Pedro** *(open daily)*, one of Spain's oldest and the first in the country to be built in the Romanesque style. Its cloisters contain the **Museo Diocesano** *(open daily; guided tours available)*, which holds many fine examples of Gothic and Romanesque frescoes and sculpture. The picturesque pedestrianized streets surrounding the cathedral contain an eclectic range of cafés and bars, as well as shops specializing in cakes, sweet delicacies and unique local wines.

🚗 **Return to the N240 and retrace the route back to the junction with the A1603. Continue through Puente la Reina as far as Berdún (34 km/**

21 miles). At Berdún, turn right on the A1602 (Carretera de Berdún) and follow signs for Biniés. Park at the entrance to the village.

⑨ Biniés

Huesca; 22773
The picturesque Valle de Ansó is considered the most beautiful valley in the region. Its bucolic villages are typically made up of red-roofed stone houses, and Biniés is no exception. Located 680 m (2,250 ft) above sea level, Biniés is home to the Baroque **Iglesia de San Salvador** *(open for Mass only)*, which sits on the village's main square. At the rear of the village is an 11th-century castle, now privately owned. There is a walking track around its perimeter, which affords some magnificent views and a couple of picnic spots.

The Hecho coat of arms

Continue along the same road to the dramatic **Foz de Biniés**, which is signposted, but also easily recognizable by two natural stone overhanging arches. This majestic gorge is over 50 m (165 ft) long and enclosed by rocky crags over 200 m (655 ft) high. Running through it is the Veral river, a popular spot for fishing, white-water rafting and canoeing.

🚗 **Continue along the A1602 and fork left on the A176 to Ansó. Park in the car park in the outskirts of the village.**

EAT AND DRINK

JACA
Casa Fau *moderate*
Underneath ancient stone arches,
this popular place serves mounds of
mouth-watering tapas and *pintxos*
such as prawns in béchamel sauce,
stuffed red peppers and wild
mushrooms with *foie gras.*
Plaza Catedral 3, 22700; 974 361 594

HECHO
Restaurante Gaby *moderate*
Chef Pepo continues the legacy of
Gaby, his aunt and a renowned cook
who turned her mountain home into a
tiny but famed restaurant and hotel, and
has added a creative touch all his own.
*Plaza Palacio 1, 22720; 974 375 007;
www.casablasquico.es; book ahead;
closed Sun eve and 2 weeks in Sep*

10 Ansó
Huesca; 22728
An archetypal mountain village
located in the Pyrenean foothills,
Ansó is made up of stone chalets
with hanging balconies, intricately
carved shutters and doors, cobble-
stoned streets and steep tiled roofs.
Ansó remained very isolated for
centuries due to poor road links,
which lead to a strong sense of
tradition and even its own dialect,
called *Cheso,* passed down the generations. On the first floor of the
16th-century Gothic **Iglesia de
San Pedro** is the **Museo del Traje
Ansotano**, which displays medieval
traditional costumes. On the last
Sunday of August, the villagers dress
in traditional costume and parade
through the streets, a spectacle that
draws a sizeable crowd. For those
who feel like a dip, there is a lovely
municipal pool in the village.

📷 *Return to the junction with the
A1602 and turn left, still on the A176
for Hecho. Park on the outskirts of
the village.*

11 Hecho
Huesca; 22720
The village of Hecho rivals Ansó for
sheer atmosphere, with a cluster of
yet more charming old houses with
hanging balconies brimming with
pots of red geraniums. One of them
contains the Restaurante Gaby, considered the best place in the Valle
de Hecho for traditional local dishes.
The impressive 18th-century **Iglesia
de San Martín** was probably built on
the site of an original Romanesque
structure. On the outskirts of the city
there is an open-air sculpture garden,
the work of noted French artist Pedro
Tramullas (b. 1937). The garden also
includes the works of several other
artists of the region.

Just north of Hecho in the village
of **Siresa** is the Romanesque **Iglesia
de San Pedro**. Further north, the **Selva
de Oza** is a great place to take a walk,
with giant oak and pine trees and a
thick vegetation of ferns. Just before
the entrance to the forest, there are
signs to the **Boca del Infierno** (Hell's
Mouth), an impressive gorge.

Above Isolated and picturesque mountain
village of Ansó **Below** Breathtaking view
over the mountains with the town of Jaca
in the distance

DAY TRIP OPTIONS
With a base in Jaca visitors have the
option of two day trips: a day in San
Juan de la Peña, and another day
exploring the Aragonese villages,
Ansó and Hecho. Jaca is best
approached by the N240.

Culture and history buffs
Visit the Monasterio Nuevo in San
Juan de la Peña 6 in the morning,
then have a picnic lunch in its

gardens. Go down to the nearby
Real Monasterio de San Juan de la
Peña, and then return in the shuttle
bus that runs between the two.

*Return to Jaca on the same route,
via the A1603, then the N240.*

Villages and forests
Visit Ansó 10 first, taking the
incredible drive along the A1602.
After visiting the neighbouring

village of Hecho 11, head to the Selva
de Oza to take a walk in this forest of
ferns, giant oak and pine trees.

*From Jaca take the N240 to Berdún.
Turn right onto the A1602 to Ansó.
From Ansó take the A176 to Hecho. To
visit the Selva de Oza take the HUV2131
from Hecho northwards in the direction of Siresa. Return to Hecho, then
take the A176 back to Puente la Reina,
then the N240 back to Jaca.*

Mountains and Valleys

La Seu d'Urgell to La Pobla de Segur

Highlights

- **Stunning scenery**
  Lose yourself in the idyllic blend of peaks, lush forests and glittering lakes in the Parc Nacional d'Aigüestortes i Estany de Sant Maurici

- **Romanesque marvels**
  Discover gems of early medieval art in the remote villages of Barruera, Durro, Erill la Vall and Boí

- **Valley villages**
  Experience the calm, clear air of the tiny, picturesque villages around the high mountains

Church spire stands tall above the mountain village of Llessui

Mountains and Valleys

Each part of the Pyrenees has its own distinctive character. The eastern Pyrenees in Catalonia have a special beauty, with a centrepiece in Parc Nacional d'Aigüestortes i Estany de Sant Maurici, where soaring rock pinnacles over 2,000 m (6,550 ft) high are offset against gem-like lakes left by the last Ice Age. This magnificent hiking country is easily accessible from the main roads. The once-isolated valleys between the mountains have a long human history too, and their importance 1,000 years ago is reflected in the Romanesque churches found even in remote villages. Just a brief circuit around the mountains goes through a fascinating variety of landscapes and ancient grey-stone towns.

Above Medieval church in the mountain town of Sort, *see p94*

ACTIVITIES

Hike through Parc Nacional d'Aigüestortes i Estany de Sant Maurici to look down over glittering mountain lakes

Go white-water rafting through the rapids of the Noguera Palleresa

Ride a mountain bike through the woods and villages of Val d'Aran

KEY

 Drive route

Above Colourful façades in La Seu d'Urgell, *see p94*
Below left Picturesque mountain town of La Seu
d'Urgell, *see p94* **Below right** Snowcapped granite
crags in Parc Nacional d'Aigüestortes i Estany de Sant
Maurici, *see p95*

PLAN YOUR DRIVE

Start/finish: La Seu d'Urgell to La
Pobla de Segur.

Number of days: 3–4, allowing half
a day for the walk in Parc Nacional
d'Aigüestortes i Estany de Sant Maurici.

Distance: 370 km (230 miles).

Road conditions: Roads are well
signposted and in good condition, but
can be slow. Snow chains are required
in winter.

When to go: April to October is hiking
season in Aigüestortes. Normal hiking
is dangerous during winter.

Opening hours: Most monuments
and museums are open from 10:30am
to 5:30pm, while shops are open from
9:30am to 1:30pm, and from 4 to 8pm.

Main market days: La Seu d'Urgell:
Tue, Sat; **Sort:** Tue; **Vielha:** Thu; **La
Pobla de Segur:** Wed.

Shopping: Val d'Aran produces
various local specialities: liqueurs,
mushroom pâtés, cheeses and honey.

Major festivals: La Seu d'Urgell:
Carnaval, Feb; **Sort:** Sant Feliu,
1 Aug; **Llavorsí:** Festa Major, late
Jul; **Vielha:** Carnaval, Feb; **Vall
de Boí:** Las Fallas, mid-Jun in
Durro; **La Pobla de Segur:** Diada
dels Raiers, first weekend in Jul.

DAY TRIP OPTIONS

Adventure buffs will enjoy hiking
up to the peaks of Aigüestortes, while
nature lovers should explore the villages in the Val d'Aran and the contrasting Vall de Boí. For details, *see p97.*

Top Romanesque cathedral in La Seu d'Urgell
Above Peak of Pui Pla, above the Estany de la
Ratera Below Hikers by the pristine Estany de
Sant Maurici

WHERE TO STAY

LA SEU D'URGELL

Hotel Andria *moderate*
This charming hotel has been a
landmark on La Seu's main promenade
since the 19th century. With a lovely
terrace and garden, the hotel is exceptional value.
Passeig Joan Brudieu 24, 25700;
973 350 300; www.hotelandria.com

Parador de La Seu d'Urgell *expensive*
A luxurious parador around the
remains of a Dominican friary in
La Seu, with the former cloister as
an impressive centrepiece.
C/ Sant Domènec 6, 25700; 973 352
000; www.parador.es

ESPOT

Hotel Els Encantats *moderate*
This hotel in the middle of Espot has
different, imaginative decor in each of
its 14 well-equipped bedrooms. Guests
can take advantage of a range of
guided hikes and the hotel's small spa.
Ctra. de Espot s/n, 25597; 973 624 138;
www.hotelencantats.com

1 La Seu d'Urgell
Lleida; 25700
An important Pyrenean crossroads
since Roman times, La Seu d'Urgell
has a charming Old Town of narrow
streets and stone arcades around
the Romanesque **Catedral de Santa
Maria d'Urgell** (*seu* is an old Catalan
word for "cathedral"). Beside the
Segre river there is a "waterpark",
the **Parc Olímpic del Segre**, built
for the kayaking events of the 1992
Olympics. A typically Catalan *rambla*
(promenade), **Passeig Joan Brudieu**,
bonds the Old and New Towns.
    Southwest of La Seu d'Urgell the
road soon climbs into dramatic
mountain scenery as it leaves the
Segre valley to cross over to the
Noguera Pallaresa valley through
the pass of **Coll de Cantó**. There are
many twists and turns on the way.
🚗 *From the town centre follow signs
south for Lleida onto the N260. In Adrall,
turn right to continue on the N260 (a
steep climb) for Sort (47 km/29 miles).*

2 Sort
Lleida; 25560
Sort was the stronghold of the
medieval Counts of Pallars, and the
remains of their castle – little more
than a tower and some walls – now
form the centrepiece of the old
town. Modern Sort is a centre for
hiking, rafting and other mountain
sports. Its tiny former prison is now a
museum, **El Camí de la Llibertat** (open
daily Aug, Sat and Sun rest of the year)
commemorating the role of the

Pyrenean valleys as an escape route
from Nazi-occupied Europe during
World War II. Exit Sort on the C13
and, just north of town, look out for
a left turn onto the LV5233. This road
goes into the Vall d'Assua and to the
gorgeous mountain village of **Llessui**
(park at the entrance to the village),
with a winter sports centre nearby.
From Llessui, rejoin the C13 and turn
left, signed for Vielha, continuing
through the rugged Noguera gorge
to **Llavorsí**, a riverside town that is a
popular adventure sports centre.
🚗 *Go through Llavorsí on the C13 and
after 12 km (7 miles) turn left on the
LV5004 for Parc Nacional d'Aigüestortes
i Estany de Sant Maurici and Espot.
In Espot, park by the visitor centre.*

3 Espot
Lleida; 25597
The main gateway to the Parc
Nacional d'Aigüestortes i Estany de
Sant Maurici, Espot is a charming
grey-stone mountain village in a deep
valley with a watchtower and a bridge
from the early Middle Ages. It makes
an excellent base for exploring the
park. Staff at the visitors' centre (Casa
del Parc) provide maps and ideas for
longer or shorter walks. A 4WD taxi
service runs from the village to the
park entrance (4 km/2 miles) and then
up to the Sant Maurici lake (another
1 km/0.6 miles). Driving to the park
entrance then walking up to the lakes
will add over an hour to the walk.
🚗 *Take one of the 4WD taxis to
Estany de Sant Maurici for the walk.*

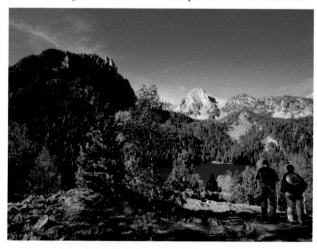

④ Parc Nacional d'Aigüestortes i Estany de Sant Maurici

Lleida; 25597

Extending over 140 sq km (55 sq miles), the Parc Nacional d'Aigüestortes i Estany de Sant Maurici contains some of the most exquisite scenery in the entire Pyrenees, dotted with towering, snow-capped granite peaks and over 200 sparkling-blue glacial lakes, fed by countless mountain streams. This circuit around the most celebrated of the lakes, Estany de Sant Maurici, goes into the heart of a breathtaking alpine landscape. The walk is best done in the morning.

Above Tiled stone streets in medieval Llessui

A two–three-hour walking tour

The 4WD stops at the **taxi stop** ① by the park warden's hut. The panorama from here is dazzling, with the lake or *estany* of Sant Maurici backed by a ring of mountains. Take the footpath signposted "Cascada de la Ratera" to the left of the park warden's hut (for an easier walk, follow the broader track right of the hut). The footpath runs through a fir forest right beside the lake until it meets the **Cascada de la Ratera** ② stream and turns right to climb up beside it. The path then veers right, slightly away from the stream, as it climbs to meet the main track, where a sign points left to the **Estany de la Ratera** ③, a little pool in an alpine meadow and a fine place to spot birds. To get here takes a little over an hour. This is the best place to turn back on a shorter walk, and return to the Estany de Sant Maurici by the main track. To continue, follow the red-and-white GR11 footpath signs around the tributary lake, **Estanyola de la Ratera** ④, and turn left, under a massive tree trunk, back across the

ridge toward Sant Maurici. At a crossing of paths, where the GR11 goes off to the right, take the path left, signed **"Mirador de l'Estany"** ⑤, a viewpoint far above Sant Maurici. Beyond the mirador, take the path signed "Volta de l'Estany–Portarró de l'Espot". It narrows to run across a giant bank of rocky scree, before climbing again to another crossing, where a path right leads to the Portarró pass. Turn left instead (following "Volta de l'Estany") for the descent back to Sant Maurici. The path becomes smoother, crossing the flower-filled meadow of **Subenuix** ⑥. It then crosses the **Barranc de Subenuix** ⑦ stream. For the quickest way back, find the path left across the dam; otherwise, follow the main track past the **Refugi Mallafré** ⑧ mountain refuge, then turn left on the Espot track and follow this back to the taxi stop.

🚗 *From Espot, return to the C13 and turn left. Near Esterri d'Àneu, follow the C13 (which becomes the C28) left. The road climbs up over Port de la Bonaigua into the Val d'Aran.*

Above Thirteenth-century church and a typical house in the Aranese village of Salardú
Below Congost dels Collegats gorge between La Pobla de Segur and Gerri de la Sal

WHERE TO STAY

VAL D'ARAN

Hotel deth Pais
inexpensive–moderate
This traditional 18-room hotel is located by the main square in the old village of Salardú. The rooms are attractively decorated.
Placa dera Pica, 25598, Salardú; 973 645 836; www.hoteldethpais.com

Hotel Albares *inexpensive*
In a typical Aranese town house in the old part of Vielha, this friendly hotel has 15 comfortable rooms.
Passeig dera Llibertat 11, 25530, Vielha; 973 640 081; www.hotelalbares.com

VALL DE BOÍ

Ca de Corral *inexpensive*
Bright colours and quirky fittings are common features of this relaxed *casa de pages*, with a pretty garden.
C/ Pradet, 25528, Taüll; 660 196 678; www.cadecorral.com

AROUND LA POBLA DE SEGUR

Casa Leonardo *moderate*
Located in the village of Senterada, 10 km (6 miles) from La Pobla de Segur, this charming café and bed-and-breakfast is full of an extraordinary range of antiques. It also makes a great base for exploring the mountains.
C/ la Begoda, 25514, Senterada; 973 661 787; www.casaleonardo.net

⑤ Val d'Aran
Lleida; 25598, 25530

The C28 climbs into **Port de la Bonaigua**, which at 2,050 m (6,800 ft) is one of the highest and most dramatic passes in the Pyrenees and the gateway to the Val d'Aran. The C28 continues up to a broad, windswept plateau, before descending into the lush valley to the west. The Val d'Aran is a major winter sports area. There is a ski station at Bonaigua, and a little further on is **Baqueira-Beret**, one of Spain's most fashionable ski resorts. Baqueira boasts more than 150 km (93 miles) of skiing slopes. The C28 then goes on to **Salardú**, a lovely Aranese village with a fine 13th-century church, which has murals dating from the 16th century. Follow the same road, the C28, into Vielha. There is a car park to the right before the main river bridge.

Capital of the Val d'Aran, **Vielha** boasts distinctive architecture in its tiny old town, with chalet-style houses flanking the Nere river. The **Església de Sant Miquèu** has a fine Gothic altarpiece and, its greatest treasure, the *Crist de Mijaran*, a 12th-century painted figure of Christ. Another tower tops a 17th-century house that is now the **Museu dera Val d'Aran** *(closed Mon except Jul–Aug)*, a museum of Aranese history and customs.

🚗 *At the roundabout on the west side of Vielha turn left (south) on the N230, signed for Lleida and Vilaller. Follow this road through the tunnel into the Vall del Noguera Ribagorçana, and after 24 km (15 miles) take the left*

turn onto the L500 Vall de Boí road. The L501 turn-off leads to Boí.

⑥ Vall de Boí
Lleida; 25526, 25527, 25528

The Vall de Boí is an idyllic closed side valley that became a centre for art in the early Middle Ages. The 11th–12th-century churches in its villages of **Barruera**, **Durro**, **Erill la Vall** and **Boí** are gems of Romanesque architecture, and since 2000 have collectively been a UNESCO World Heritage Site. Several had magnificent fresco paintings, the originals of which are now in the Museu Nacional d'Art de Catalunya in Barcelona. There are, however, copies of the original paintings in most of the churches. The valley is also the western entrance to the Aigüestortes and Sant Maurici national park, with a park information centre in Boí. There is also a multilingual information centre on the valley's history (which runs tours of the churches) in Erill la Vall, the **Centre Romànic de la Vall de Boí** *(open daily)*. From Erill la Vall, carry on up to Boí, then stay on the L501 road to Taüll.

Taüll deserves special attention as the most beautiful of all the Vall de Boí villages. It has two spectacular churches, the **Església de Santa Maria** within the maze-like village and the **Església de Sant Climent** just outside it, with a six-storey tower that visitors can climb. Sant Climent's mural of Christ, the *Crist de Taüll* (now in Barcelona, although there is a copy in the church) is one of the finest early medieval European paintings.

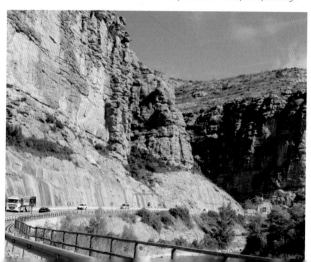

Retrace the route to the N230 and turn left for Pont de Suert.

Rafters of the Pyrenees

For centuries one of the traditional occupations in the Noguera Pallaresa valley was cutting timber in the mountains and transporting it downriver in log rafts (or *rais*). This dangerous trade died out in the early 20th century. However, since the 1970s, the craft of the loggers has been revived, and this ancient way of life evoked with an annual festival, the Diada dels Raiers, in the first weekend of each July. The festival invites log-rafters from around the world.

Above Bell tower in the idyllic village of Boí

7 Pont de Suert

Lleida; 25520

Pont de Suert has a fascinating old quarter of secluded squares and tunnel-like alleys leading down to the Noguera Ribagorçana river. Leave Pont de Suert and turn left onto the N260 (signed) for La Pobla de Segur via the pass at **Coll de la Creu de Perves** (1,350 m/4,450 ft). The road winds up into dramatic scenery again as it leaves the valley to climb the mountain ridge up to the pass. There are stunning views all along this road, especially at the pass itself and at the remarkable villages of **Viu de Llevata** and **Sarroca de Bellera**. The road descends down to laid-back **Senterada** at the entrance to the **Vall Fosca**, another lovely valley leading towards Aigüestortes from the south.

Keep following the N260 through Senterada. Take a left turn signed for Sort to enter La Pobla de Segur.

8 La Pobla de Segur

Lleida; 25500

A historic Pyrenean crossroads, La Pobla de Segur has a Romanesque hermitage and the impressive **Casa Maurí**, a complex combining a mansion and olive oil mill built in the Catalan Modernist (Art Nouveau) style in 1907. Its mosaics have been finely restored. The building now serves as the town hall and tourist office. Also in La Pobla is the **Museu dels Raiers** *(open Tue–Sat)*, commemorating the skilled timber raftsmen of the Noguera Pallaresa valley. The heart of the Old Town, Carrer Major, has several stately medieval houses.

Northeast of La Pobla the road passes through a red-walled gorge, the **Congost dels Collegats**, very different from the high-mountain scenery further north, to a valley village, **Gerri de la Sal**. The village has a medieval bridge and *salines*, stone pans once used for drying salt.

DAY TRIP OPTIONS

Driving along mountain roads takes time, and there are no fast short cuts between the main valleys, so to retrace the same routes to the initial start will take a lot out of a day. Visitors can be based either in La Seu d'Urgell or Vielha, in the north, to do the following day trips.

Mountain towns

Experience the varied Pyrenean landscape by beginning at La Seu d'Urgell 1 and following the main route to Sort 2 and Espot 3, although there may not be time for a long walk in Parc Nacional d'Aigüestortes i Estany de Sant Maurici 4 if visitors are returning to La Seu d'Urgell the same day. Alternatively, from Sort head down to La Pobla de Segur 8 on the road south to Lleida.

Return from Espot to Sort and then take the N260 east back to La Seu d'Urgell, or the same road to La Pobla de Segur.

Explore the Val d'Aran

The Val d'Aran 5 is a natural area to explore in a day – especially if entering on the quicker road, the N230, from the northern, French end. Take a look around Vielha, capital of the Val d'Aran, before going up to the ski towns of Salardú and Baqueira. If time permits, visitors can leave the valley by the tunnel from Vielha and turn into the beautiful Vall de Boí 6. Stop by picturesque valley villages such as Barruera, Durro, Erill la Vall and Boí to visit their magnificent 11th–12th-century churches.

From Vielha, take the C28 road, signed for La Seu d'Urgell, as far as Salardú and Baqueira. Return to Vielha and then take the N230 south to reach Vall de Boí.

The Catalan Heartland

Girona to Cadaqués

Highlights

- **Girona's old quarter**
  Get lost in the stone warren of El Call, Girona's alluring Jewish quarter

- **Volcanic scenery**
  Traverse a landscape of long-extinct volcanoes, now covered in forest and dotted with pretty villages

- **Romanesque gems**
  Admire the spectacular Romanesque monasteries of Ripoll and Sant Joan de les Abadesses

- **Surrealism at its best**
  Be dazzled by the originality and playfulness of Salvador Dalí at his museum in Figueres

- **Whitewashed Cadaqués**
  Relax in the charming fishing village of Cadaqués

Harbour at Cadaqués, a favourite with artists

The Catalan Heartland

According to tradition, Guifré el Pilós (Wilfred the Hairy) founded Catalonia from his strongholds in the eastern Pyrenees in the 9th century. This drive explores the magnificent monasteries he founded at Ripoll and Sant Joan de les Abadesses, as well as the glorious mountain scenery that surrounds them. The ancient city of Girona retains its enchanting medieval core, and the nearby lake of Banyoles has become a serene summer retreat, with parks and natural swimming pools. One of the most famous Catalans of all time, Salvador Dalí, created a spectacular museum at Figueres, and his exquisite home can be found near the utterly delightful fishing village of Cadaqués.

ACTIVITIES

Take a dip in the giant natural swimming pool at Banyoles lake

Go up, up and away in a hot-air balloon over the volcanic hills around Olot

Hike up volcanoes, through Pyrenean valleys, or around the dramatic Cap de Creus

Rent a boat at Cadaqués to explore the tiny coves around the cape

Tuck into hearty mountain dishes in local restaurants all over this region

Left Tiny medieval village of Mieres near Santa Pau, *see p103*

KEY

🚗 Drive route

Above Narrow lane in the historic centre of Banyoles, *see p103* **Below** Pont Vell in Sant Joan de les Abadesses, *see p105*

PLAN YOUR DRIVE

Start/finish: Girona to Cadaqués.

Number of days: 3–4, allowing half a day to explore Girona.

Distance: 265 km (165 miles).

Road conditions: Most of the roads are well paved and signposted. There are a few stretches of steep terrain with hairpin bends. In the winter, there can be snow in the Ripoll/Sant Joan de les Abadesses region.

When to go: May and June are ideal, not too hot or crowded. Girona is wonderful year-round, but Cadaqués is best avoided in July and August as it is too crowded then.

Opening hours: Museums are open from 10am to 1pm, and from 4 to 6pm. Shops are open from 9:30am to 1:30pm and from 4 to 8pm. However, most museums in this region are closed on Mondays.

Main market days: Girona: Tue, Sat; Olot: Mon; Ripoll: Sat; Figueres: Thu; Cadaqués: Mon.

Shopping: The Catalan heartland is famous for its cured sausages (including *fuet*) and wines.

Major festivals: Girona: Sant Narcís, late Oct–early Nov; Olot: Corpus Christi, Jun; Festa del Tura, 8 Sep; Ripoll: Festa Major, mid-May; **Sant Joan de les Abadesses:** Festa Major, second Sun of Sep; Besalú: Sant Vicenç, 22 Jan; Festa Major, last weekend Sep; Figueres: Santa Creu, around 3 May; Cadaqués: Festa Major d'Estiu, first week Sep.

DAY TRIP OPTIONS

Visitors interested in walks and **hiking trails** can explore Olot and the volcanoes as a day trip. **Art enthusiasts** should head to Figueres to visit the Dalí Museum and then on to Cadaqués to see his charming home. **Families** will enjoy the resort of Banyoles, where kids can play in the lake. For details, *see p107*.

Above Steps leading up to Girona's impressive Gothic cathedral

VISITING GIRONA

Tourist Information
Rambla de la Llibertat 1, 17004; 972
226 575; www.girona.cat/turisme

Parking
Parking is available in Plaça de
Catalunya, in the pay-and-display car
park near the train station (follow signs
for RENFE) and near Pont de Sant Feliu.

WHERE TO STAY

GIRONA

Pensión Bellmirall *inexpensive*
The charming little Bellmirall occupies
a historic town house right in the heart
of Girona's atmospheric old quarter.
C/ Bellmirall 3, 17004; 972 204 009

AROUND GIRONA

Hotel Masferran *expensive*
Located in a 17th-century farmhouse,
this is a lovely Rusticae hotel just 7 km
(4 miles) west of Girona.
C/ Cami de la Bruguera, 17150, Sant
Gregori; 972 428 890; www.
masferran.com

BANYOLES

Ca La Flora *inexpensive*
A little charmer in the old quarter of
the town, with simple, tasteful rooms
and a lovely café with tables on a
flower-filled patio.
C/ Llibertat 91, 17820: 972 582 480

① Girona
Girona; 17004

The prosperous and elegant little city of Girona is handsomely set
on the banks of the Onyar river. At its heart is El Call, the former
Jewish quarter, a warren of narrow streets and tiny passages
crowned by a magnificent Gothic cathedral. The city is well-known
for its fine traditional cuisine, which can be sampled in numerous
restaurants, cafés and bars. The best time to do this walk is late
afternoon, as the city is particularly pretty at dusk.

A two-hour walking tour
Park in Plaça de Catalunya and cross
the bridge to see the tourist office on
the left, on the Rambla de la Llibertat,
an elegant, bustling boulevard with
plenty of delightful terrace cafés.
Stroll up to the Plaça del Vi,
which is overlooked by the
ajuntament ① and the
Teatre Municipal ②.
Continue along Carrer
Ciutadans to reach another
charming little square, the
Plaça de l'Oli, with a
diminutive fountain.

Tapestry of the Creation,
Catedral de Girona

From here, plunge into
the Jewish quarter, taking Carrer B.
Carreras Peralta, which leads into
Carrer de la Força. This street, one of
the most atmospheric in the city, was
the very heart of the Jewish ghetto.
The history of the Jews of Girona,
once famous throughout Europe for
their great learning, is documented
in the **Museu dels Jueus** ③ *(open*

Tue–Sun) in the Centre Bonastruc Ça
Porta at No. 8 Carrer de la Força. As
the narrow street climbs, visitors will
see the interesting **Museu d'Història
de la Ciutat** ④ *(open Tue–Sun)* on the
left at No. 27. Carrer de la Força
opens out into a beautiful
square, the Plaça de la
Catedral, dominated by a
flank of steps leading to
the **Catedral de Girona** ⑤.
Although the façade is
Baroque, the rest of the
cathedral is Catalan Gothic
at its purest. The cathedral's
museum contains several
fine treasures, including a celebrated
11th-century tapestry depicting the
Creation. There is more wonderful
medieval art, as well as later works, in
the excellent **Museu d'Art** ⑥ *(open
Tue–Sun)*, housed in the nearby Palau
Episcopal. Return to the Plaça de la
Catedral and take the gateway near
the curiously truncated **Església de**

*(map labels:)*
BELLAIRE
Església de San Pere
⑨ de Galligants
Església de
PONT DE Sant Feliu
SANT FELIU
⑦ ⑧ Banys Àrabs
Jardins de
⑩ la Francesa
⑤ Catedral de Girona
PLAÇA
DE LA CATEDRAL
④ ⑥ Museu d'Art
Museu d'Història
de la Ciutat
③
Museu dels
Jueus
PLAÇA
DE L'OLI
① Ajuntament
PLAÇA
DEL VI ②
Teatre
Municipal
PLAÇA DE
CATALUNYA

Onyar
PASSING DE LA DEVESA
FIGUEROLA
BONASTRUC CAPORTA
JAUME I
ANSELM CLAVE
P RENFE
20 DE JUNY
SEQUIA
GRAN VIA JAUME I
CROSER
NOU
PONT DE
PEDRA
AV. SANT FRANCESC
PLAÇA POMPEU FABRA

Passeig Arqueològic

0 metres   250
0 yards   250

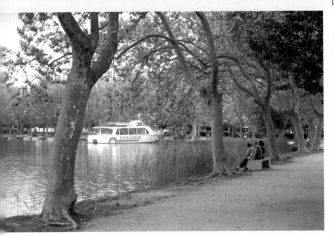

Sant Feliu ⑦. On the left are the 12th-century Arabic-style baths **Banys Àrabs** ⑧ *(open daily)*. Beyond the little bridge is the Romanesque **Església de San Pere de Galligants** ⑨, now converted into a beautiful archaeological museum *(closed Mon)*. Return to the Banys Àrabs and bear to the left to get to the **Jardins de la Francesa** ⑩, small gardens that are one of several access points to the Passeig Arqueològic, a panoramic walkway atop the old city walls. Bear right to find the walls and then walk southwards along them all the way to Plaça General Mendoza. From here walk back along the river to the car park.

🚗 *Leaving Girona, follow signs for Banyoles onto the NIIa (Avinguda de França), and then turn left onto the C66. At Banyoles, follow signs for the "Estany" (Lake). Park next to the lake.*

❷ Banyoles
Girona; 17820

Banyoles has a charming medieval core and a lake. The lake has been a favourite summer vacationing spot since the 19th century, and its shores are still dotted with small *pesqueres* – fishing huts built right onto the water. There are a couple of natural bathing spots, a footpath and cycle track right around the lake. Visitors can rent bikes here. A short stroll around the Old Town throws up a handful of pretty Romanesque and Gothic churches, arcaded streets and several delightful squares to relax in.

🚗 *Leave Banyoles by the southern end of the lake, following signs for the GI524 towards Mieres and Santa Pau. Park outside the village.*

Parc Natural de la Zona Volcànica de la Garrotxa

The GI524 is a stunning stretch of road twisting through the Parc Natural de la Zona Volcànica de la Garrotxa towards the distant, violet shadows of the pre-Pyrenean mountain ranges. The boundary of the nature reserve starts at Mieres, a tiny stone village wrapped around a church. The Parc Natural de la Zona Volcànica de la Garrotxa encompasses a beautiful landscape of long-extinct volcanoes, now thickly covered with forest and scattered with tiny villages, including Santa Pau. Some of the best walking trails start at the park information office in the midst of a beech forest.

Above People relaxing around the lake at Banyoles **Below** Arcades framing the Plaça Major in Banyoles

Eat and Drink: inexpensive, under €20; moderate, €20–€40; expensive, over €40

Above Seven-arched bridge at Besalú **Below left** Ornate window in a Modernista mansion in Olot **Below right** Twelfth-century church in Sant Joan de les Abadesses

❸ Santa Pau
Girona; 17811
A perfectly preserved medieval village perched on a low hilltop, Santa Pau is the jewel of the Garrotxa region. The village grew up around a 12th-century castle, with thick stone walls and crenellated towers, which still dominates the centre. Densely wooded hills spread out in every direction, sheltering some of the loveliest walking paths in all of Catalonia. Many of them go up to the craters of extinct volcanoes: the best are Santa Margarida and the Croscat.

🚗 *Continue on the GI524 towards Olot. After about 10 km (6 miles), the road will lead directly to Olot's town centre where there is pay-and-display parking next to the Mercat Municipal.*

❹ Olot
Girona; 17800
The prosperous market town of Olot is beautifully set in the gentle wooded hills of the extinct volcanic zone of La Garrotxa. The soft light inspired a generation of 19th-century artists, known as the Olot School, whose works are on view at the **Museu Comarcal** *(closed Mon)*. The museum is housed in an 18th-century hospice. The narrow streets, with their winsome, early 20th-century Modernista mansions, old-fashioned shops and bakeries, are a delight to explore.

🚗 *Take the ring road out of Olot, following "Totes Direccions" signs across two roundabouts until there are signs for the N260 for Vallfogona de Ripollès. Continue past Vallfogona into Ripoll and follow signs for "Centre". Park in the main square.*

❺ Ripoll
Girona; 17500
Ripoll contains one of the great jewels of Catalan Romanesque architecture: at the very centre of town is the 10th-century **Monestir de Santa Maria** *(open daily)*, established by Guifré el Pilós, legendary founder of Catalonia. The magnificent portal miraculously survived the destruction of the church following the dissolution of the monastery in 1835. It is carved with biblical scenes and a menagerie of beasts.

🚗 *From Ripoll head north along the C26 and turn right on the N260, following signs for Sant Joan de les*

WHERE TO STAY

SANTA PAU

Cal Sastre *inexpensive*
This is a sweet little inn in a restored stone house.
C/ Cases Noves 1, 17811; 972 680 049; www.calsastre.com

AROUND OLOT

Mas Garganta *moderate*
Located 5 km (3 miles) from Olot, this lovely bed-and-breakfast has a pool.
Ctra. A Riudaura, 17179, La Pinya; 972 271 289; www.masgarganta.com

RIPOLL

El Trobador *inexpensive*
Centrally located on the edge of the Old Town, this has comfy rooms and a good traditional restaurant.
Passeig del Compositor Honorat Vilamanyà 4, 17500; 975 702 353

SANT JOAN DE LES ABADESSES

El Reixac *inexpensive*
Housed in a beautiful farmhouse, this hotel has rooms with kitchenettes.
El Reixac, 17860; 972 720 373; www.elreixac.com

BESALÚ

Casa Marcial *inexpensive*
This B&B has immaculate little rooms in a stone town house in the old quarter.
C/ Conde Tallaferro 15, 17850; 608 029 427; www.casa-marcial.com

Where to Stay: inexpensive, under €70; moderate, €70–€120; expensive, over €120

Abadesses. Follow signs for the "Estacionament Gratuït" to find the car park on the left, next to the bridge.

Burial ground of the Count-Kings of Catalonia

Numerous early Catalan rulers, including Guifré el Pilós, were buried in the crypt of the Monestir de Santa Maria in Ripoll, but their tombs were desecrated after the monastery was closed in the 1830s. After the church was rebuilt in the late 19th century, plaques were erected in their memory on either side of the main altar. The small sarcophagi of Catalan counts still line the nave.

⑥ Sant Joan de les Abadesses

Girona; 17860

Now a sleepy country town, Sant Joan de les Abadesses grew up around an important abbey, founded by Guifré el Pilós in the 9th century for his daughter, Emma. Dim and austere, it is easy for visitors to imagine themselves back in the Middle Ages while visiting this church. Behind the main altar is a 12th-century sculpture depicting the Descent from the Cross, composed of curiously modern articulated figures. The town is another excellent base for walkers, with a host of good walking trails. To the east is Vall de Bianya, a valley with a sprinkling of farms and a clutch of Romanesque churches.

🚗 Follow the N260 out of Sant Joan de les Abadesses through the Vall de Bianya. Turn left at the big roundabout at La Canya, following signs for the GI522 for Sant Joan les Fonts and Castellfollit de la Roca. At Castellfollit, park in the municipal car park on the left at the entrance to the village.

⑦ Castellfollit de la Roca

Girona; 17856

Castellfollit de la Roca is perched alarmingly on a sheer lava cliff which plunges dramatically to the river below. From the riverside, visitors can gaze up at the medieval village, its stone houses strung vertiginously along the cliff edge. Castellfollit's sleepy streets are perfect for an aimless stroll, and offer more splendid views of the rolling landscape.

🚗 Continue through the village, following signs for the N260/A26, towards Figueres and Girona. Fork right at exit 67 onto the Carretera d'Olot straight to Besalú. Park at the entrance of the village; the centre is closed to tourist traffic.

⑧ Besalú

Girona; 17850

A picture-postcard medieval walled town, Besalú is firmly on the tourist trail. However, even the crowds of day-trippers from the nearby Costa Brava cannot dim its ancient charm. A splendid medieval seven-arched bridge, punctuated with towers, spans the river and leads into the cobbled streets of the Old Town. The **Plaça de la Llibertat** is handsomely fringed with 16th-century arcades, and the village boasts the only surviving *mikveh*, a Jewish ritual bathhouse, in Spain.

🚗 From Besalú, return to the N260/A26 (no longer an autovía highway from this point), and follow signs for Figueres. In the city centre, roadside parking is fairly easy to find, but there is a large pay-and-display car park near the RENFE train station. From here, it is a 10-minute walk to the Dalí Museum.

Above Graceful Església de Sant Esteve in Olot **Below** Cloister of the Monestir de Santa Maria in Ripoll

ACTIVITIES IN THE GARROTXA

Walking in the Fageda d'en Jordà
Walking trails in this beech forest start at the Can Jordà park information office, down a forest road 4 km (2 miles) west of Santa Pau. Maps and leaflets are available in local tourist offices.

Hot-air balloon rides in Olot
Several companies offer hot-air balloon rides in the Garrotxa region. *www.voldecoloms.cat*

EAT AND DRINK

SANTA PAU

Portal del Mar *moderate*
The restaurant serves Mediterranean cuisine prepared with local produce. C/ Vila Vella 16, 17811; 972 680 442; *www.portaldelmar.es*

OLOT

Les Cols *expensive*
This award-winning restaurant serves superb cuisine using local ingredients – from wild trout to wild mushrooms. C/ de la Canya s/n, 17800; 972 269 209; *www.lescols.com*; closed Sun, Mon eve, and 3 weeks in late Jul–mid-Aug

SANT JOAN DE LES ABADESSES

Casa Rudes *inexpensive*
A good place to try Catalan mountain dishes, such as *trinxat* (mashed potatoes and vegetables topped with bacon). Ctra. Major 10, 17860; 972 720 115; *www.santjoandelesabadesses.com*

BESALÚ

Cúria Reial *moderate*
A traditional restaurant serving local cuisine and specializing in *carns a la brasa* (meat cooked over hot coals). Plaça de la Llibertat 14, 17850; 972 590 263; *www.curiareial.com*

Eat and Drink: inexpensive, under €20; moderate, €20–€40; expensive, over €40

Top Beach in the resort town of Roses
Above Surrealistic towers of the Dalí Museum in Figueres **Below** Sixteenth-century fortress in Roses

WHERE TO STAY

AROUND FIGUERES

Mas Falgarona *expensive*
A beautiful country-house hotel, Mas Falgarona is located in a village just 5 km (3 miles) west of Figueres.
Avinyonet de Puigventós, 17600; 972 546 628; www.masfalgarona.com

CADAQUÉS

Hotel Blaumar *moderate*
The family-run Blaumar is just a few minutes' walk from the town centre.
C/ Massa d'Or 21, 17488; 972 159 020; www.hotelblaumar.com; closed Nov–mid-Mar

L'Hostalet de Cadaqués *moderate*
Conveniently located in the town centre, this trendy hotel has eight double rooms.
C/ Miquel Rosset 13, 17488; 972 258 206; www.hostaletcadaques.com

Rural accommodation
This region boasts a range of rural accommodation – from farmhouses to renovated *finques* (country houses).
www.ruralcatalunya.com, www.rusticae.es

⑨ Figueres
Girona; 17600

The Old Town in Figueres and its busy *rambla* (promenade) have an understated charm, but there is only one big reason to visit the city: the fabulous **Teatre-Museu Dalí** *(closed Mon Oct–May; www.salvador-dali.org)*. This occupies an old theatre, converted by the celebrated artist himself, surreally topped with diving figures and enormous eggs. Within, the museum is equally eccentric, with galleries leading off a central patio in which a car with a warbling diva is the main exhibit. In the Mae West room, visitors are invited to climb a ladder and view the furnishings morph into the features of the celebrated actress.

🚗 *To leave the city, follow "Totes Direccions" signs, which will lead to the NII ring road. Take the exit for the C260, following signs for Roses. Near Castelló d'Empúries, take the bridge on the left to cross the La Muga river to reach the centre of the town, where parking can be found.*

⑩ Castelló d'Empúries
Girona; 17486

This pretty stone town still retains the vestiges of its medieval walls, along with a cluster of fine churches and medieval mansions gathered around delightful squares. The beautiful **Basílica de Santa Maria** is one of the jewels of Catalan Gothic architecture, its sublime arches succeeding elegantly in the airy nave. An amble around the historic centre, now largely pedestrianized, reveals handsome

convents and arcaded squares. The town is also the starting point for the Parc Natural dels Aiguamolls de l'Emporda, protected wetlands which shelter numerous bird species.

🚗 *Return to the C260, and turn right for Roses. There is free parking next to the market on Carrer Doctor Ferran.*

Parc Natural dels Aiguamolls de l'Emporda

The wetlands of the Parc Natural dels Aiguamolls de l'Emporda extend for much of the Bay of Roses. Wooden trails wind between lakes and marshes to scattered observation points, where there are flamingos, herons and the extraordinary jewel-coloured purple swamphen. The park also has rarer species such as the endangered bittern and the Garganay duck. From Castelló d'Empúries, follow signs for the Parc Natural dels Aiguamolls de l'Emporda and park near the information office *(El Cortalet, 17486; 972 454 222).*

⑪ Roses
Girona; 17480

The largest resort town on this stretch of coast, Roses is big and blowsy, with just a few scattered remnants to remind visitors of its ancient history. The oldest of these is the **Conjunt Megalític**, a collection of magnificent dolmens which date back 5,000 years. The massive, squat **Ciutadella** is a Renaissance fortress, erected in 1543 over the ruins of an 8th-century Arabic citadel. Within are scattered remains attesting to the numerous ancient civilizations, from the Greeks to the Romans, who have settled here. Most people come to Roses for the glorious golden beaches. Visitors can rent a small boat to explore the surrounding *cales* – tiny, pebbly bays which, if they are lucky, they might even have to themselves.

🚗 *From Roses, return in the direction of Figueres, following signs for the GI614. Just before Cadaqués, follow signs to Cap de Creus on the left, on a tiny road which twists up over the wild and beautiful natural park.*

⑫ Parc Natural del Cap de Creus
Girona; 17489

The Cap de Creus is a magnificent headland formed by the last gasp of the Pyrenees as it plunges into the Mediterranean. Wind-whipped and craggy, it is one of the most beautiful corners of Catalonia, and now protected as a nature park. The wild terrain still bears vestiges of the terraces laid out by the monks of the austere **Monestir de Sant Pere de Rodes**, near the town of Port de la Selva. The monastery houses the tourist information office *(open daily; 972 193 191)* of the nature park.

🚗 *Continue on the GI614 to Cadaqués. It is best to park on the outskirts and walk to the centre, as parking can be difficult in the high season.*

⑬ Cadaqués
Girona; 17488

Cadaqués is an exquisite fishing village curved around a perfect bay and crowned with a simple church. Its extraordinary light has drawn artists including Picasso and Dalí since the

Above Lighthouse at the tip of the wild Cap de Creus

early 20th century. Dalí's intimate home *(visits must be booked in advance; 972 251 015)*, which he converted from a cluster of whitewashed cottages, overlooks the adjoining bay at Port Lligat. The views from the little square in front of the church at the top of Cadaqués are sublime, stretching out across the huddled rooftops to the shimmering sea beyond.

The Dalí Triangle
The Dalí Museum in Figueres, the artist's private home near Cadaqués and a converted medieval castle in Púbol make up the Dalí Triangle. The tiny village of Púbol is a short excursion from Girona. This is where Dalí's wife and muse, Gala, lived in queenly splendour in the Castell Gala Dalí, an 11th-century baronial palace *(Plaça Gala Dalí, Púbol-la-Pera; 972 488 655)*. Her husband was required to make appointments in advance, and Gala would receive him while seated on her throne

ACTIVITIES ON CAP DE CREUS

Hiking
Two long-distance footpaths meet at Cadaqués: the GR11 across the Pyrenees, and the GR92 along the Mediterranean coast.

EAT AND DRINK

FIGUERES

Hotel Empordà *expensive*
Try the *paella* with lentils and crayfish at this restaurant which serves the finest cuisine in the region.
Avda. Salvador Dalí i Domènech 170, 17600; 972 500 562; http://hotel emporda.com

CADAQUÉS

Casa Nun *moderate*
This restaurant occupies a thin house on the seafront. Locally caught fish is the highlight of the menu here.
C/ Port-dixos 6, 17488; 972 258 856

DAY TRIP OPTIONS
With a base in Girona, there are many places in this drive that are easily accessible as a day trip. The AP7 motorway (toll) is a useful north–south route, which links Girona with Figueres, but most destinations are reached on the smaller roads.

Olot and the volcanoes
The relaxed country town of Olot ④ is surrounded by the surreal, flattened peaks of long-extinct volcanoes. The nearby Garrotxa Volcanic Zone is a

nature park with hiking trails and pretty little villages.

Follow the C66 from Girona to Banyoles, then take the GI524 to Olot through the stunning volcanic zone. Return via the fast A26 and then down the C66.

On the Dalí trail
Head to Figueres ⑨ to visit the Teatre-Museu Dalí, before heading to the wild coast of the Cap de Creus ⑫ and the white fishing village of Cadaqués ⑬.

Take the AP7-E15 to Figueres, then head east along the C260. Just before

reaching Roses, turn inland on the GI614 to reach Cadaqués.

Lakes and bridges
Families will enjoy the pretty, verdant resort of Banyoles ② , where kids can splash around in the clear natural lake, or take hikes around its lovely shores. Beyond Banyoles, the village of Besalú ⑧ with its perfectly preserved old bridge is a delight to explore on foot.

Take the C66 directly from Girona to Banyoles, and then on to Besalú.

Eat and Drink: inexpensive, under €20; moderate, €20–€40; expensive, over €40

Vineyards and Gothic Treasures

Sant Sadurní d'Anoia to Delta de l'Ebre

Highlights

- **Home of cava**
  Visit the renowned vineyards and cava cellars of the Penedès

- **Monasteries and walled town**
  Experience a medieval world in three great Gothic monasteries and the walled town of Montblanc

- **Compact paradise**
  Explore the twisting valleys and soaring crags of the Priorat, and sample fine wines from its vineyards

- **Delta perspectives**
  Spot flamingos and experience a dramatic change of landscape in the vast wetlands of Delta de l'Ebre

Twelfth-century monastery at Santes Creus

Vineyards and Gothic Treasures

Between Barcelona and the mouth of the Ebre river lies an astonishing variety of landscapes: the broad vine-clad hills of the Penedès, the steep narrow valleys and massive yellow-stone *mesas* of the Priorat and Montsant, the wide Ebre valley and finally the vast flatness of the Delta de l'Ebre. A thousand years ago this region was the frontier between Christian and Muslim lands. Its rich history can be traced in magnificent Gothic monasteries and walled towns, and in the Moorish fortress of Tortosa. This is also a land of superb food and fine wines – from the famous labels of the Penedès to the characterful vintages of the Priorat – that make its discovery a catalogue of pleasures.

Above Olive trees, cultivated widely in the Priorat, *see p115*

ACTIVITIES

Discover how cava gets its sparkle at a winery in Sant Sadurní d'Anoia

Pick out the symbols in the stunning Gothic carvings in the monasteries of Santes Creus and Poblet

Look down at the world from the heights of Siurana

Hike up into the hills of Montsant, richly scented with Mediterranean herbs

Taste and compare wines on a slow tour around the Priorat's hillside vineyards

Ride a bike through the Delta de l'Ebre, scanning the horizon for flamingos and other wild birds

KEY

🚌 Drive route

Above Gothic cloister of the monastery at Santes Creus, *see p112*
Below Rugged landscape of the Priorat, *see p115*

PLAN YOUR DRIVE

Start/finish: Sant Sadurní d'Anoia to Delta de l'Ebre.

Number of days: 3–4, including half a day in Montblanc and Tortosa.

Distance: 340 km (210 miles).

Road conditions: Mostly well-signed roads, although signs can be unclear in rural areas. The Priorat's winding roads make travel slower.

When to go: April to October is the best time, but July and August can be very hot and crowded with tourists. The smaller vineyards may be too busy for visitors during the grape harvest in September and October.

Opening times: The opening hours of the major attractions vary between seasons, but in general the major monasteries and museums are closed on Mondays. Wine cellars are often closed on Mondays and Tuesdays.

Main market days: Sant Sadurní d'Anoia: Thu; Vilafranca del Penedès: Sat; Montblanc: Fri; Prades: Tue; Falset: Tue; Móra d'Ebre: Fri; Tortosa: Mon.

Shopping: Wine is the region's top buy and is sold at most vineyards. Sant Sadurní, Vilafranca, Escaladei, Gratallops and Falset have shops with good stocks of local vintages.

Major festivals: Sant Sadurní d'Anoia: Festa de la Fil·loxera, early Sep; Semana del Cava, second week, Oct; Vilafranca del Penedès: Carnaval, Feb; Fira de Santa Llúcia, Dec; Montblanc: Sant Antoni Abat i Tres Tombs, Jan; Carnaval, Feb; Festes de Sant Maties, May; Prades: Festa del Cava, Jul; Falset: L'Encamisada, 17 Jan; Fira del Vi, early May; Tortosa: La Festa del Renaixement de Tortosa, end Jul.

DAY TRIP OPTIONS

For **wine** and **culture lovers**, a day of cava and culture in Sant Sadurní and Vilafranca make an easy trip from Barcelona. **History enthusiasts** can combine Santes Creus, Vallbona and Poblet. The Priorat is a mecca for **wine buffs**, while **fans of birdlife** might explore Tortosa and the Delta. For details, *see p117*.

Left Thirteenth-century Església de Sant Miquel, Montblanc **Right** Caves Cordoniu, Sant Sadurní d'Anoia

VISITING CAVES CODORNIU

Avda. Jaume Codorniu s/n, 08770, Sant Sadurní d'Anoia; 938 913 342; www.visitascodorniu.com

VISITING BODEGUES TORRES

The winery offers exclusive tours with professional guides.
M. Torres 6, 08720, Vilafranca del Penedès; 938 177 400; www.torres.es

WHERE TO STAY

SANT SADURNÍ D'ANOIA

Fonda Neus *moderate*
In Sant Sadurní itself, the renovated Fonda Neus is a reliable traditional hotel, with an old-fashioned restaurant.
C/ Marc Mir 14–16, 08770; 938 910 365; www.fondaneus.com

AROUND SANT SADURNÍ D'ANOIA

Can Bonastre Wine Resort *expensive*
A 16th-century estate, 19 km (12 miles) north of Sant Sadurní, it has its own vineyard and gourmet restaurant.
Ctra. B-224, Km 13, 21, 08783; Masquefa; 937 728 767; www.canbonastre.com

AROUND VILAFRANCA DEL PENEDÈS

Arianel·la de Can Coral *moderate*
Housed in an old farmhouse, 13 km (8 miles) north of Vilafranca, this charming rural hotel has a pretty garden and pool.
Avda. Can Coral, 08787, Torrelles de Foix; 938 971 579; www.arianella.com

AROUND SANTES CREUS

Ca La Nuri *expensive*
Friendly, rural B&B located about 3 km (1.9 miles) from Santes Creus, with just four en suite rooms and a pretty courtyard.
C/ Sant Antoni 10, Vila-Rodona, 43814; 665 455 752

MONTBLANC

Fonda Cal Blasi *moderate*
A comfortable, friendly hotel in the Old Town, it serves generous breakfasts.
C/ Alenyà 11, 43400; 977 861 336; www.fondacalblasi.com

Mas Carlons *moderate*
An imposing country house in its own vineyard, just outside Montblanc, Mas Carlons has spacious rooms and a swimming pool.
43400, Montblanc; 977 860 045; www.mascarlons.com

① Sant Sadurní d'Anoia
Barcelona; 08770

Sant Sadurní is the capital of cava, Catalan sparkling wine, with over 80 producers in and around the town. Many cellars are in the town centre, but the largest ones are on the outskirts. Most spectacular is the huge **Caves Codorniu** (book visits online at www.visitascodorniu.com), with graceful buildings built in 1902–15, designed by the great Catalan architect Josep Puig i Cadafalch (1867–1956). There are several other engaging Modernista buildings in Sadurní, including the town hall built in 1900.

🚌 *From the centre of Sant Sadurní d'Anoia follow signs for Vilafranca onto the C243a. Turn left when this road joins the C15 to enter the town of Vilafranca del Penedès.*

Historic advertising at Caves Cordoniu, Sant Sadurní d'Anoia

② Vilafranca del Penedès
Barcelona; 08720

Historic capital of the Alt Penedès comarca (district), Vilafranca is known more for its still wines and brandy than for cava. There are cellars and vineyards all around the town, including the famous **Bodegues Torres** (daily tours), 4 km (2 miles) north on the road to Pacs del Penedès. Vilafranca was an important town in the Middle Ages, still evident from the distinguished Gothic **Basílica de Santa María**, beside which is a 14th-century mansion, the Palau Baltà. The 13th-century Palau Reial or royal palace now hosts a

wine museum, the **Vinseum** (open Tue–Sun).

🚌 *Follow the Avinguda Tarragona through Vilafranca and at the first large roundabout turn right onto the Carretera de Sant Jaume dels Domenys (B212). This becomes the TP2125. Before Sant Jaume dels Domenys, turn right onto the TP2442 for El Pla de Manlleu. Follow the road, which becomes the T244, and at the next junction turn left onto the TV2441 for Santes Creus.*

③ Santes Creus
Tarragona; 43815

The majestic **Monestir de Santes Creus** (open Tue–Sun) that dominates this village was founded in 1158. It no longer houses a religious community, but is almost completely intact. The delicately decorated 17th-century Bishops' Palace now serves as a town hall. Visitors enter the monastery through its magnificent Gothic cloister, with an intricate variety of beasts, figures and symbols carved on its columns. The 13th-century church contains the tombs of several kings of Aragón. Other parts worth visiting include the monks' dormitory, with its wonderfully elegant arches.

🚌 *From the village, stay on the same road to meet the TP2002. Turn left to Vila-Rodona, pass through this town and go under the motorway to meet the C51. Turn right for Valls. Follow signs onto the N240 towards Montblanc. Go left around the city walls to park behind the tourist office.*

Where to Stay: inexpensive, under €70; moderate, €70–€120; expensive, over €120

❹ Montblanc

Tarragona; 43400

Montblanc is a medieval jewel. It stands within a ring of fortified walls and 31 towers that were begun in 1366 on the orders of King Pere III "the Ceremonious", at a time when this town was already an important military stronghold and merchant centre.

Above City walls of the medieval town of Montblanc

A two-hour walking tour

Head left from the car park towards the 13th-century **Antiga Església de Sant Francesc** ①. Start the tour by walking around the walls. Go past the small gate of Portal de Sant Jordi to the 14th-century **Església de Sant Marçal** ②, which is partly set into the wall. Keep right, passing below battlements at Baluard de Santa Anna, close to the Pont Vell (Old Bridge) over the Francolí river. On the east side of the Old Town, the walls past the striking **Torre dels Cinc Cantons** ③ are partly obscured by newer buildings, but re-emerge near the **Portal de Bové** ④. From here, walk back towards Sant Francesc.

Turn right into the Carrer Major to pass inside the walls. On the right is the 15th-century **Palau-Fortalesa del Castlà** ⑤, built for Montblanc's military governors, and the 13th-century **Església de Sant Miquel** ⑥. Go up and turn left into Pere Berenguer de Vilafranca to **Plaça Major** ⑦, site of a Friday market and the 13th-century Casa de la Vila (town hall). Head up Carrer Hortolans to reach **Església de Santa Maria la Major** ⑧, a striking example of a 14th-century Catalan Gothic church with a 17th-century Baroque façade. Exit the square to the left of the church and continue uphill to **Pla de Santa Bàrbara** ⑨, from where there are great views. Descend via Travessera de la Pedrera back to Carrer Major, and turn right. Opposite Pere Berenguer, turn left into **Plaça dels Àngels** ⑩, then left down Carrer dels Jueus, the remains of a Jewish ghetto. Pass the 14th-century Gothic mansion **Palau Alenyà** ⑪ and turn right into Carrer Font de la Vila, then left into Carrer River to come to Portal de Bové. Go right along Muralla de Jaume II to Carrer Major and turn left to return to the car park.

📷 *Go back to the N240. At the first roundabout take the C14 for Tàrrega. After Solivella turn left onto the TP2335/LP2335 for Vallbona.*

VISITING MONTBLANC

Tourist Information
Antiga Església de Sant Francesc, 43400; 977 861 733; www.montblancmedieval.org

Parking
Approaching from Valls on the N240, follow the road left around the town walls to find the tourist office in the Antiga Església de Sant Francesc. Behind it there is a free car park.

EAT AND DRINK

SANT SADURNÍ D'ANOIA

Cal Blay Vinticinc *expensive*
An elegant modern restaurant in an old wine cellar, combining adventurous cuisine with Penedès wine traditions.
C/ Josep Rovira 27, 08770; 938 910 032; www.calblay.com; open Wed–Mon for lunch, Fri and Sat dinner

AROUND SANT SADURNÍ D'ANOIA

Cal Xim *expensive*
Located in a village, 5 km (3 miles) from Sant Sadurní d'Anoia, this restaurant serves Catalan fare.
Plaça Subirats 5, 08739; Sant Pau d'Ordal; 938 993 092; www.calxim.com; open Mon–Sun for lunch, Fri and Sat dinner

SANTES CREUS

Cal Mosso *inexpensive*
This convivial restaurant has *calçotades* in season, salads and Catalan snacks.
Plaça Santa Llúcia 1, 43815; 977 638 484; closed Mon in summer

MONTBLANC

El Call de Montblanc *moderate*
Located in a 14th-century house near the old Jewish quarter of Montblanc, the restaurant serves Catalan, Basque and international dishes.
C/ Sant Josep 15, 43400; 977 860 120; www.elcalldemontblanc.com; open Tue–Sun lunch, Fri and Sat dinner

Eat and Drink: inexpensive, under €20; moderate, €20–€40; expensive, over €40

Right Cistercian monastery in Vallbona de les Monges **Below** Romanesque church of Siurana with the hills in the north

⑤ Vallbona de les Monges
Lérida; 25268

The road north leads through very different, more arid and empty countryside to the region's smallest royal monastery, **Monestir de Santa Maria de Vallbona** *(closed Mon, except Aug)*, with an impressively remote feel. While Poblet and Santes Creus were men's monasteries, from 1175 Vallbona was a women's convent (*de les Monges* means "of the nuns"). It received endowments from Catalan queens, especially the wife of Jaume I Violant of Hungary (1216–51), who is buried here. It is still home to a community of nuns, but visitors can see the main parts of the building, including the intimate **cloister** and its rare Gothic domes.

🚗 *Continue along the LP2335 from Vallbona to Maldà, turn left, and then almost immediately left again onto the L220 through Els Omells de na Gaia. Just past this village, drive onto the L232/T232 for Senan and L'Espluga de Francolí. Approaching L'Espluga, follow signs for Poblet.*

⑥ Monestir de Poblet
Tarragona; 43448

Grandest of the region's three great monasteries, the Monestir de Poblet *(open daily)* looks more like a castle than a monastery. It was also the most treasured by the medieval Catalan monarchs, many of whom were buried here. Founded in 1150, it was closed in 1835, but since 1940 Cistercian monks have again been its resident, giving it a special atmosphere. Many parts of the complex can be visited, beginning with the cloister and early

Gothic chapterhouse. The royal tombs in the massive church are unique, with effigies of the monarchs in rows on shared sarcophagi raised on columns beside the altar. Above the cloister are the spectacular arched scriptorium, where the monks once copied manuscripts, and the snug 14th-century palace built for King Martí I (1356–1410).

🚗 *Turning to the left from the Monestir de Poblet entrance, take the T700, which is well signposted for Riudabella and Prades.*

⑦ Prades
Tarragona; 43364

Past Poblet, the landscape changes radically as the road winds up through thick plantations of Mediterranean pines on the slopes of the Muntanyes de Prades range, with superb views on either side. Prades itself is a unique town, known as the *Vila Vermella* or "Red Town", thanks to the strange colour of the local stone used in its tightly packed buildings, which include a Gothic-Baroque church and a Renaissance fountain. The lovely arcaded Plaça Major has enjoyable bars and restaurants. The drive to the west from Prades towards Albarca, the great flat slab of the Serra de Montsant looms ever larger ahead, a spectacularly rugged backdrop to the winding road.

🚗 *Follow the main road out of Prades, now the T701, signed for Cornudella de Montsant and Reus. At Albarca, turn left onto the C242. Just before Cornudella, turn left onto the TV3225 for Siurana.*

8 Siurana
Tarragona; 43362
The scenery becomes ever more rugged beyond Albarca on entering the **Priorat**, an area of steep, vine-clad hills, ravine-like valleys and dramatic crags, where it is impossible to travel fast. A side road twists and turns up to the extraordinary village of Siurana. A natural fortress, on a crag 735 m (2,400 ft) above the valley floor, with sheer drops on three sides, this was the last Muslim stronghold in Catalonia, taken in 1154. Remains of a Muslim cemetery can still be seen near the Romanesque church in the village. There are spectacular walks around Siurana, and the views on all sides are unforgettable. Return to Cornudella and head 9 km (6 miles) west on the TV7021. Just off the road, to the right, is La Morera de Montsant, the starting point for hikes up into the Serra de Montsant Nature Park.

🚗 *From La Morera de Montsant, turn right back onto the TV7021, which then becomes the TV7022, for Escaladei.*

9 Escaladei
Tarragona; 43379
The delightful little village of Escaladei is surrounded by vineyards and has great little wine shops. A road from the village leads to the Carthusian monastery, **Cartoixa d'Escaladei** *(open Tue–Sun)*, which once had

Above Village of Siurana, high up on a crag
Below Entrance to the monastery in Escaladei

authority over the area. Founded in 1194, it was rebuilt in Baroque style in the 17th and 18th centuries, but is now an atmospheric ruin.

🚗 *Return to Escaladei village and turn right to join the T702. Turn right again at the fork for Vilella Baixa.*

10 Vilella Baixa
Tarragona; 43379
A gorgeous drive leads on to Vilella Baixa, one of the most extraordinary Priorat villages. Set along a steep rocky ridge, it has created its own vertical style of architecture, with such tall houses that it has been labelled "the New York of the Priorat". Continuing on the road through Vilella Baixa then turning right onto the T710 leads to **Gratallops**, another striking hilltop village, again surrounded by fine vineyards.

🚗 *Continue south on the T710 from Gratallops to reach Falset.*

Wines of the Priorat
Until the late 1980s, the red wines of the Priorat were a Catalan secret. Conditions in its vineyards are almost unique – a combination of staircase-steep terraces and special soils that produces distinctive wines that are robust but very subtle. Winemaking had gone on here for centuries, but a big change came in 1989, when winemakers such as Alvaro Palacios (with labels such as *Les Terrisses*) and Carles Pastrana *(Clos de l'Obac)* began to combine new techniques with the Priorat's long traditions. Since then, Priorat wines have won worldwide acclaim, and many more small wineries have opened up, although production on the terrace-vineyards is necessarily small. The Montsant wine region, which surrounds the core of the Priorat, is less known but also enjoys a growing reputation.

EAT AND DRINK

PRADES

L'Estanc *moderate*
A charming restaurant on Prades' lovely main square, L'Estanc has rustic decor which goes well with Catalan country cooking, including a rich *escudella* (meat and vegetable stew) and delicious home-made desserts.
Plaça Major 9, 43364; 977 868 167; www.restaurantlestanc.cat; closed Wed and mid-Jan–mid-Feb

AROUND SIURANA

El Balcó del Priorat *inexpensive*
This large, modern restaurant, 17 km (11 miles) from Siurana, serves Catalan country dishes and excellent, all-local wines. It has stunning views of the Montsant and the valleys below.
C/ Bonrepós, 43361, La Morera de Montsant; 977 827 211; www.balcodelpriorat.com; open lunch Wed–Mon, dinner Sat only

VILELLA BAIXA

El Racó del Priorat *inexpensive–moderate*
A friendly, relaxed village restaurant with attractive traditional menus, featuring fresh seasonal ingredients, including strictly local game such as wild boar and an impressive selection of fine local wines.
C/ Priorat 9, 43374; 977 839 065; open lunch Tue–Sun

Eat and Drink: inexpensive, under €20; moderate, €20–€40; expensive, over €40

Above Roadside bar in Gandesa's town centre

VISITING TORTOSA

Tourist Information
Rambla Felip Pedrell 3, 43500; 977 449 648; www.turismetortosa.com; open Tue–Sun

Parking
Parking is very limited in the old city. It is usually easier to cross the Mil·lenari bridge and park in the newer part of the city, and then walk up.

WHERE TO STAY

AROUND FALSET

Mas Ardèvol moderate
This bed-and-breakfast, located 1 km (0.6 miles) outside Falset, has lovely rooms and serves meals prepared from garden produce.
Ctra. de Falset a Porrera, 43730; 630 324 578; www.masardevol.net

Mas Figueres moderate
Comfortable rooms and great views are offered at this eccentric house just 3 km (2 miles) south of Falset.
Ctra. de Falset, Km 2, 43775, Marçà; 977 178 011; www.masfigueres.com

TORTOSA

Parador de Tortosa – Castell de la Zuda expensive
Housed in the castle high above the city, this parador's modern rooms blend well into the medieval architecture.
43500, Castell de la Zuda; 977 444 450; www.parador.es

AROUND TORTOSA

Villa Retiro expensive
An extravagant fantasy-palace of a country house 15 km (9 miles) north of Tortosa, this is now a luxury hotel.
C/ dels Molins 2, 43592, Xerta; 977 473 003; www.hotelvillaretiro.com

AROUND DELTA DE L'EBRE

Delta Hotel moderate
This is a modern hotel on an "island" beside the town of Deltebre.
Avda. del Canal, 43580, Deltebre; 977 480 046; www.deltahotel.net

⑪ Falset
Tarragona; 43730

Although it is the capital of the Priorat comarca, Falset lies within another wine Denominación de Origen, Montsant. At the top of its hill are the remains of a 12th-century castle, below which is a placid old town with distinguished Renaissance and Neo-Classical buildings, such as the 17th-century palace that is now the town hall. Falset's most impressive structure, though, is the Modernista **Cooperativa Agrícola** (977 830 105) built by architect Cèsar Martinell in 1919. The building can be visited – telephone or enquire at the tourist office for details. Falset also has excellent wine shops.

🚗 **Leave Falset on the N420 towards Móra la Nova and Alcañiz. West of Falset the road emerges from mountains into more open, rolling country, moving much faster down to the great Ebre river and cross it at Mòra d'Ebre. The N420 climbs up again to reach the next stop at Gandesa.**

⑫ Gandesa
Tarragona; 43780

The centre of the Terra Alta wine region, Gandesa is home to another great Martinell wine cellar, the **Cooperativa Agrícola** (for tours, contact the tourist office; 977 420 910). The town was also the hub of the 1938 Battle of the Ebro in the Civil War, commemorated in a museum, the **Centre d'Estudis de la Batalla de l'Ebre** (open Tue–Sun).

South from Gandesa, the C43 leads to one of the finest Cèsar Martinell wine cellars at **El Pinell de Brai** (open daily), fronted by a marvellous mosaic frieze by Xavier Nogués. Continuing south there are more fine views and another sudden change of landscape as the road drops back to run beside the Ebre river through orange groves.

🚗 **Keep on the C43 to meet the C12 and turn right for Tortosa. Stay on the road past the town, then turn left and cross the Ebre by the Pont del Mil·lenari (C42). Turn left following "Centre Ciutat" signs to the old city.**

⑬ Tortosa
Baix Ebre; 43500

The main city of southern Catalonia, Tortosa was already a key crossing point over the Ebre in Roman times. It was also a stronghold of Andalusia's Muslim rulers until it was taken by the armies of Ramon Berenguer IV of Catalonia in 1148. With summer temperatures often over 30° C (86° F), it is a city with a very southern feel.

The Moorish **Castell de la Zuda**, built on a steep crag with a commanding position above the Ebre, was captured and incorporated into a later Christian castle, part of which is now a parador hotel. Views from the castle are superb, and allow visitors to see many more fragments of the city's old walls and fortifications.

On the east of the castle away from the river, narrow streets and stone steps lead down into the old city. The **Reials Col·legis** (Royal Colleges) on Carrer Sant Domènec, now a historical archive, have a 16th-century patio carved with a remarkable collection of often strange faces and figures. Below the castle is the rather bizarre

Portico of the Catedral de Tortosa

Catedral de Tortosa, which was begun in the 14th century and has a massive 17th-century Baroque façade. The building was never quite finished, and has been left with only a simple flat roof. Many more smaller details can also be seen around the old city, including Muslim inscriptions and relics of the medieval Jewish quarter. Outside the narrow streets, there is a pleasant riverside walk.

🚗 **Recross the Ebre on the Mil·lenari bridge and turn left onto the C12 for Roquetes, then left again for Amposta. Cross the river again on the southernmost bridge (on the N340) and immediately turn right onto the TV3454 for Deltebre.**

The Wine Cathedrals

Around 1910, Mancomunitat, one of Catalonia's regional authorities, set about an ambitious programme to support small local vineyards by setting up cooperatives to make and sell their wine. To give these institutions the dignity they deserved, they were housed in extraordinary Modernista-style cellars, many designed by the architect Cèsar Martinell, a student of Gaudí. They were dubbed *catedrals del vi*, wine cathedrals, because of their grandeur, but many also resemble the great cathedrals of the Middle Ages in both their structure and style.

⓮ Delta de l'Ebre

Tarragona; 43870, 43580

Beyond Amposta, with the last bridge over the river, there is yet another utterly different world in the Ebre delta, of flat fields of rice stretching off as far as the eye can see towards broad misty horizons. At the centre of this vast stretch of land is the sleepy municipality of **Deltebre**, where there is a river ferry to **Parc Natural del Delta L'Ebre**. It also has the information centre of the park *(C/ Martí Buera 48, 43870; 977 489 679; open daily)*.

The delta wetlands make an ideal habitat for all kinds of wild birds, including flamingos, which are a common sight around the lagoons. The flat delta is also a perfect spot for cycling, and bicycles are available for hire in Deltebre. Boat trips from Deltebre are also popular.

Beyond Deltebre, the road winds down to **Ríumar**, where there are beaches with good seafood restaurants beside the river.

EAT AND DRINK

FALSET

Hostal Sport *moderate*
The dining room at Falset's foremost traditional hotel has a reputation as a showcase for local food and wines.
C/ Miquel Barceló 4–6, 43730; 977 830 078; www.hotelpriorat-hostalsport.com

AROUND GANDESA

Cal Pelegrí *moderate*
Local gourmets make a detour to this restaurant in Corbera d'Ebre, 5 km (3 miles) north of Gandesa. Specialities include roast goat and seafood.
Avda. Casal s/n, Corbera d'Ebre, 43787; 977 055 022; www.cal-pelegri.com

TORTOSA

Sidrería Amets *moderate*
This Basque-style *sidrería* (cider house) offers excellent wines and the food runs from tapas to meat and seafood dishes.
Passeig Joan Moreira 13, 43500; 977 446 699; www.sidreriaamets.com; closed Sun dinner, Sun all day Jun–Aug

El Celler D'En Panxampla *moderate*
Enjoy *calçots* and other traditional local specialities at this welcoming country inn, 8 km (5 miles) from Tortosa.
C/ d'Alfara, 43527, Els Reguers; 977 474 135

AROUND DELTA DE L'EBRE

Restaurant Casa Nuri *moderate*
With tables overlooking the riverbank, this is one of the best places to enjoy local rice dishes and fresh seafood.
Ctra. final Goles de l'Ebre s/n (Pas de Illa de Buda), 43580, Deltebre (Ríumar); 977 480 128; www.restaurantnuri.com

Left Rooftops of Tortosa, with a view of the unique flat roof of the cathedral

---

DAY TRIP OPTIONS

The AP7 and the AP2 offer quick and easy access to every part of this route. The AP7 runs from Barcelona through the Penedès and down to Amposta; the AP2 turns off west of Vilafranca.

Cava and Gothic treasures

Visit some cava houses in Sant Sadurní d'Anoia ❶ and Vilafranca del Penedès' ❷ wine museum. Then wander into the countryside to the Monestir de Santes Creus ❸.

Take the AP7 from Barcelona to Sant Sadurní and Vilafranca. Go south on the B212; turn right onto the TP2442, which becomes the TP244, and then left onto the TV2441 for Santes Creus.

The Cistercian trail

Get immersed in splendid medieval monasticism amid the Gothic glories of Santes Creus ❸, Vallbona de les Monges ❺ and Poblet ❻, and wander around the impressive walls of Montblanc ❹.

Drive to Santes Creus from Barcelona on the AP7 and AP2. Follow the itinerary from here. Join the AP2 at junction 9, near Montblanc, to return.

Wines and lost valleys

Lovers of wines and rural calm can spend a perfect day on a slow drive around Siurana ❽, Escaladei ❾, Vilella Baixa ❿ and Falset ⓫, dropping in on vineyards and marvelling at the extraordinary clifftop locations of its villages.

From Barcelona, take the AP7 to junction 34, then take the N420 Gandesa road and turn right on the C242 to Siurana. Return from Falset on the N420.

Moorish castles and birding spots

For a varied trip, explore old Tortosa ⓭ and its Moorish Castell de la Zuda in the morning, then head to the Delta de l'Ebre's ⓮ beaches and bird-filled lagoons.

Take the AP7 south to Amposta, turning right on the C12 for Tortosa and left on the TV3454 for the Delta.

Eat and Drink: inexpensive, under €20; moderate, €20–€40; expensive, over €40

From the Mountains to the Plains

Alcañiz to Albarracín

Highlights

- **Breathtaking scenery**
  Visit ancient villages tucked away in the Matarraña National Park

- **Majestic birds of prey**
  Witness the rare sight of hundreds of vultures swooping down from the mountains at feeding time in Mas de Bunyol, near Valderrobres

- **Amazing architecture**
  Marvel at the engaging mix of Moorish and Modernista architecture in Teruel

- **Fortified village**
  Get lost amongst the ancient stone monuments and edifices of Albarracín

View of the towers and rooftops of the Mudéjar Iglesia de San Pedro in Teruel

From the Mountains to the Plains

The largely undiscovered area of Matarraña is one of abundant wildlife, medieval villages, waterfalls, rivers and constant views of Els Ports (the gates), an ancient mountain range. From the mountains, this drive takes visitors across the plains of lower Aragón to Teruel, another little-known gem with an intriguing Moorish past. The drive finishes in Albarracín, one of the most beautiful of Spain's fortified towns.

0 kilometres   10

0 miles   10

Above View of the village of La Fresneda in the distance, *see p122* **Below** Turret of the cathedral in Albarracín, *see p127*

KEY

⟪⟫ Drive route

ACTIVITIES

Hike through the olive and almond orchards of Matarraña

Cool off in the natural swimming pool in the village of Beceite

Taste Aragonese wines in Teruel

PLAN YOUR DRIVE

Start/finish: Alcañiz to Albarracín.

Number of days: 3–4, allowing half a day to explore Teruel.

Distance: 290 km (180 miles).

Road conditions: Roads are generally well paved and signposted; there is some steep terrain and hairpin bends in Matarraña.

When to go: Matarraña can get cold in winter and in summer the water-falls and streams can be dry. Autumn and spring are the best times to visit the region.

Opening hours: Shops are open from 9:30am to 2pm, and from 4 to 8pm. Restaurants are open from 2 to 4pm, and from 8 to 11pm. Most museums and monuments are closed on Mondays.

Main market days: Alcañiz: Tue; La Fresneda: Wed, Sat; Cretas: Mon; Beceite: Fri; Teruel: Thu; Albarracín: Wed.

Shopping: *Jamón* (ham) and beautiful Mudéjar-style green and bronze tiles are available in Teruel. Pick up cheese, *embutidos* (charcuterie), olive oil and almonds from Matarraña.

Major festivals: Alcañiz: Fiestas Patronales, 8–13 Sep; **Teruel:** Fiestas del Ángel, second Sun Jul; **Albarracín:** Fiestas Patronales, 8–17 Sep.

Above Houses in Albarracín perching on a lofty cleft, *see p127* **Below** Arches framing an alley in Beceite, *see p124*

DAY TRIP OPTIONS

Nature lovers will enjoy driving through the northern part of this drive and visiting the charming villages of Alcañiz, La Fresneda, Valderrobres and Beceite. **Architecture enthusiasts** and **history buffs** will be enthralled by the towns of Teruel and Albarracín. For details, *see p127*.

Above left Plaza Mayor in La Fresneda
Above right Ornate altarpiece of the Ermita de San Antonio Abad **Below** Courtyard of El Castillo in Alcañiz

WHERE TO STAY

ALCAÑIZ

Hotel Guadalupe *moderate*
Located right opposite the cathedral in Alcañiz, this three-star hotel has rooms that are functionally comfortable. There is a great bar downstairs specializing in *pintxos* or local tapas.
Plaza España 8, 44600; 978 830 750

LA FRESNEDA

Camping La Fresneda *inexpensive*
This is a small camp site surrounded by almond trees and overlooking the Les Ports mountain range. A small bar-restaurant serves simple fare.
Partida Vall de Pi, 44596; 978 854 085; www.campinglafresneda.com; closed Oct–Mar

El Convent 1613 *expensive*
As the name suggests, this high-end hostelry is located in an old convent dating from 1613.
C/ Convento 1, 44596; 978 854 850; www.hotelelconvent.com

TORRE DEL COMPTE

La Parada del Compte *expensive*
A wonderful *casa rural* with cosy wood-lined bungalows in lovely verdant surroundings.
Finca la Antigua Estación del Ferrocarril, 44597; 978 079 025; www.hotelparadadelcompte.com; closed Jan

AROUND ACRÓPOLIS IBÉRICA

Lo Raconet de la Plaça *inexpensive*
This simple and comfortable rustic-style villa in the heart of Calaceite offers exceptional value.
Plaza Espanya 9–19, 44610, Calaceite; 978 851 519; www.casaruralcalaceite.com

① Alcañiz
Teruel; 44600

An archetypal Aragonese castle-town located by the Guadalope river, Alcañiz has a splendid array of monuments for its size, all neatly tucked around the central Plaza de España. The largest is the **Iglesia de Santa María Mayor** *(open daily)* with its soaring Gothic tower and ornate Baroque portal, a work of Basque sculptor Juan Bengoechea. Next to it is **La Lonja** *(closed to the public)*, another Gothic treasure that once served as a commodities exchange. Follow signs to the 13th–14th century castle, **El Castillo**, once a stronghold of the Knights of the Order of Calatrava. Though it is now a hotel, visitors can wander around the grounds. Across the river, the **Atrivm** *(closed Mon)*, a visitors' centre, tells the history of the region through multimedia and expositions.

🚗 *Take the N232 in the direction of Tarragona. Bear left on the A231, signposted for Valjunquera and Valderrobres, to reach La Fresneda.*

② La Fresneda
Teruel; 44596

With its pretty 16th-century porticoes along the Calle Mayor and cobble-stoned squares, La Fresneda is one of Matarraña's most colourful villages. Highlights include the gargoyle-dotted *ayuntamiento* (town hall), the **Iglesia de Santa María la Mayor** and the remains of the castle at the very top of the village's steep streets. Also worth a visit are a couple of ancient dungeon-like jails on the Plaza Mayor. Ask at the tourist office (on the Plaza Mayor) for opening times, which tend to vary for all sights in the village.

🚗 *Continue along the A231. After 1 km (0.6 miles) take the turn-off on the left onto the narrow TEV3001 (unmarked) for Torre del Compte. Continue on this road for 4 km (2.5 miles).*

③ Torre del Compte
Teruel; 44597

A small village, Torre del Compte has a fine 14th-century church, a town hall, a museum and a stylish rural hotel, the **Parada del Compte**. The **Centro Etnográfico** *(open daily 11am–1pm, ring the doorbell)* contains a collection of everyday items and ephemera from the region's fiestas, industries, workshops and farms. All around Torre del Compte there are magnificent views of the olive and almond orchards that blanket Matarraña, with the majestic Els Ports mountain range providing a beautiful backdrop.

🚗 *Continue on the TEV3001 till the N420 again. Turn right and follow signs to Calaceite. On approaching the town, turn right onto the A1413 for the Acrópolis Ibérica, signposted "Poblado Ibérico de San Antonio".*

④ Acrópolis Ibérica
Teruel; 44610

The fascinating Acrópolis Ibérica is the remains of an Iberian village which had reached its height in the third century BC; the ancient streets and homes' foundations can be clearly imagined from what one can see today. Juan Cabre discovered them in 1903, and a museum dedicated to his work is located in neighbouring Calaceite *(open Fri–Sun)*. At the high point of the Iberian site is the tiny **Ermita de San Antonio Abad** dating from 1798. The larger building on the opposite hill is the 18th-century **Ermita de San Cristóbal**. Its interior was ransacked during the Civil War. All that remains of the saint's original statue is a severed hand, which has been laid at the base of a replacement statue.

🚗 *Continue on the A1413, following the signs to Cretas.*

The Iberians

The Iberians were the original Spaniards. They populated the peninsula between the 6th and 1st centuries BC and flourished in agriculture and the arts before the Roman conquest. Archaeologists, on excavating in the Bajo Aragón, have discovered vestiges of this ancient culture. There have been initiatives to present them to the public with multilingual signages and exhibition spaces for artifacts. In Cretas an information centre has been set up with a small museum on the Iberian language. Visitors can pick up a map of Bajo Aragón's *Ruta de los Iberos*, an itinerary that contains over 20 sites.

⑤ Cretas
Teruel; 44623

This once-walled village has preserved three of its original gates: Valderrobres, San Roque and San Antonio. The late Gothic **Iglesia de la Asunción** *(open for Mass only)* was ransacked during the Civil War; when the war ended, the village's inhabitants donated a percentage of their olive crops until enough funds were gathered to commission a new retable. Just in front of the church is the majestic arch of the **Casa Sapera**, the threshold to the **Plaza de España**. Noble stone mansions dating from the 15th and 16th centuries flank the village's main square. In the square's centre is a curious column, brought here in 1962. Its origins are unclear, bar the decorative cross – a sign of the Order of Calatrava, *patrones* of the village until the 12th century.

🚗 *Leave Cretas on the A1413 and continue along it until the A231. Turn right here and follow signs to the village of Valderrobres.*

Above left Bell tower of the Iglesia de Santa María la Mayor in La Fresneda **Above right** Richly decorated doorway of the cathedral in Alcañiz **Below** El Castillo looks over the town of Alcañiz

EAT AND DRINK

ALCAÑIZ

La Oficina *moderate*
This excellent value *mesón* (inn) specializes in traditional, home-made food using local produce, including the area's famed olive oil. Highlights include meat dishes with options such as steak with Roquefort sauce.
Avda. de Aragón 12, 44600; 978 870 801

La Parilla *moderate*
Enjoy succulent grilled meats and vegetables at this simply decorated *mesón*, which prides itself on sourcing the best local ingredients.
C/ Calanda 35, 44600; 978 832 389

TORRE DEL COMPTE

La Parada del Compte *expensive*
Creative cuisine using locally sourced ingredients is complemented by wine from the restaurant's own bodega. The menu is small, but generally includes a variety of salads for starters and meat, pork or fish dishes for mains. Leave room for the delicious panna cotta and fig dessert.
Finca la Antigua Estación del Ferrocarril, 44597; 978 769 072; www.hotelparadadelcompte.com; closed Jan

Eat and Drink: inexpensive, under €20; moderate, €20–€40; expensive, over €40

Above View of the village of Valderrobres with its castle **Below** Façade of the old church in Beceite

⑥ Valderrobres

Teruel; 44580

Located on the banks of the Matarraña river, Valderrobres is the grandest of the villages here. Ancient stone town houses flank the banks of the river. Cross over the medieval bridge and through the grand **Torre San Roque** into the Old Town to come directly into the main square and the **Casa Consistorial**, a 16th-century building conceived in the Aragonese Mannerist style. At the top of the Old Town is the Catalan Gothic **Iglesia de Santa María del Mar Mayor** (open for guided visits only when visiting the castle), which has a huge rose window. Next door is the 13th-century **castle** (open winter: Fri–Sun, summer: Tue–Sun), which was commissioned by the archbishops of Zaragoza. It still has a large swath of its original ramparts.

🚗 *Take the A 2412 (unsigned) to reach Beceite.*

Feeding the Vultures

One of the most remarkable experiences in Matarraña is to be had just outside of Valderrobres in the tiny locality of Mas de Bunyol. Since the 1990s, a local couple has been coaxing a population of magnificent leopard vultures to swoop down and feed off butchers' cast-offs. Today, over 300 of these astounding creatures have been known to descend from the mountains and feed. A special observatory has been built for visitors to watch the spectacle, one of only two of its kind in Spain.

⑦ Beceite

Teruel; 44588

Dramatically perched in a valley surrounded by mountains and striking ridges, this sleepy little village is blessed with views that take the breath away. In its narrow streets exposed brick *casas* with hanging wooden balconies jostle for space with more modern structures. Highlights include the 18th-century **Ermita de Santa Ana** with an arched entrance and a belfry, and the Baroque **Iglesia de San Bartolomé** (open for Mass only). Cross the old stone bridge down Arrabel del Puente to **Antigua Fábrica Noguera**, an old paper mill now turned into an arts and craft gallery. Visitors who feel like a dip, or even a lovely walk, should follow signs from here to **El Parrizal**, a natural park that traces the course of the Matarraña river and crosses dozens of waterfalls and natural pools. About 1 km (0.6 miles) along this unmarked road is the **Piscina Natural de L'Assut**, a man-made pool of water diverted from the river. The walk is simple and suitable for all age groups.

🚗 *Drive back along the A2412 to Valderrobres, then the A231, passing La Fresneda till the N232. Head for Alcañiz. At Alcañiz take the N211 at the roundabout on the western side of town, following signs to Teruel. Continue for 47 km (29 miles) on this road and then take the TEV8215 towards the Grutas de Cristal and Molinos. Park on the outskirts of Molinos.*

WHERE TO STAY

MOLINOS

Hostal de la Villa *inexpensive*
A comfortable old-world hostel located inside an 18th-century building offering basic rooms and hearty, home-cooked meals in its first-floor dining room.
Plaza Mayor 5, 44556; 978 849 234

Where to Stay: inexpensive, under €70; moderate, €70–€120; expensive, over €120

8 Molinos
Teruel; 44556

This picturesque little hamlet, nestled in a valley, is bereft of the housing developments that blight many villages in the area, and is home to a surprising museum. Eleuterio Blasco Ferrer (1907–93) was a noted Spanish Expressionist whose work hangs in major museums around the world. Although born in Teruel, his mother lived in Molinos and for this reason the village's town hall houses a small, light-filled gallery of his works *(open Apr–Oct: 2pm and 4–8pm; Nov–Mar: guided tours only)*. Most of the notable buildings here can be viewed by guided tours only. Tours of the village start in front of the church on Plaza Mayor, where the Tourist Office is located *(978 849 085; daily tours at 12:30, 4, 5:30 and 7pm during high season; ring ahead for other times)*.

🚗 *Follow the TEV8215 and signs for the Grutas de Cristal.*

9 Grutas de Cristal
Teruel; 44556

Discovered in 1961, these crystal caves extend over 620 m (680 yd) and are noted for their large variety of formations, especially vertical stalactites, and fossils. They are also home to a large community of bats *(978 849 085; open summer: 11am to 1pm and 4 to 6–7pm; winter: Sat & Sun and for tours Mon–Fri)*.

🚗 *Go back to Molinos on the TEV8215 and turn left onto the TE41 to reach the N211. Continue towards Montalbán. After Montalbán, take the N420 towards Teruel. After about 20 km (12 miles) turn left onto the A1403 in the direction of Aliaga to Hinojosa de Jarque.*

10 Parque Escultórico de Hinojosa de Jarque
Teruel; 44157

The sweeping plains and sculptured cornfields of this agricultural swath of Aragón are home to one of its most special sites: the Parque Escultórico, a sculpture park in and around the tiny village of Hinojosa de Jarque. Dozens of Spanish artists took part in the project, dedicated to the "memory, myth and legend" of Aragonese villages, over four years in the mid-1990s, creating the 36 abstract pieces that now dot the landscape. Locals fed and accommodated the artists as they worked, making it a community achievement.

🚗 *Return to the N420 via the A1403 and turn left. Continue for about 50 km (31 miles) to Teruel. On the way you pass Calanda, the birthplace of film director Luis Buñuel, where there is a museum dedicated to him.*

Figure in the church of Molinos

EAT AND DRINK

BECEITE

Antigua Posada Roda *inexpensive*
This traditional, stone-built inn has a cosy restaurant where you can tuck into generous portions of local fare, including game in season. They also have rooms.
C/ Villanueva 25, 44588; 978 850 254; www.antiguaposadaroda.com

Bar-Terraza Pont Nou *moderate*
On the main road just outside Beceite is this fabulous little outdoor bar which serves drinks, cocktails and snacks on a lawn overlooking a dramatic gorge. *Paella* is served at lunchtime, but needs to be ordered by mid-morning.
A2412 Beceite-Valderrobres, 44588; 978 850 251

VALDERROBRES

Cervecería El Castellano *inexpensive*
This buzzing little wood-lined tapas bar serves up *raciones* of melt-in-your-mouth *calamares*, fluffy *croquetas* and spicy *chorizo*, all of which go down extremely well with their tap beer.
C/ Santiago Hernández 3, 44580; 978 890 552

Above Portal of the church in Molinos
Below left Carved balcony door in Beceite
Below right Main town square in the village of Valderrobres

Left Remains of an abandoned castle in Albarracín **Right** Interior of the Mausoleo de Los Amantes, Teruel **Below** Arabic exterior of the Iglesia de San Pedro in Teruel

VISITING TERUEL

Tourist Information
C/ San Francisco 1, 44001; 978 641 461; www.turismodearagon.com, www.teruelversionoriginal.es

Parking
Park in the private car park at the Estación de Autobuses (bus station). The largest car park is located at the Estación de Ferrocarril (train station) from where it is a five-minute walk into the Old Town. Another one is located inside the Old Town on Plaza San Juan. Parking on the street is not recommended.

WHERE TO STAY

TERUEL

Hospedería El Seminario *inexpensive*
The modest rooms in this 18th-century religious building in the centre of Teruel offer exceptional value.
Plaza Pérez Prado nº 2, 44001; 978 619 970; www.hospederiaelseminario.com

Spa Hotel *moderate*
Located on the outskirts of town, rooms here are modern and family-friendly.
Avda. de los Hostales (Polígono de la Paz), 44001; 978 618 618; www.spahotel.es

ALBARRACÍN

Hotel Albarracín *moderate*
This three-star hotel belongs to the small Gargallo chain, and is located in a brick palace in the historical centre.
C/ Azagra s/n, 44100; 978 710 011; www.hotelalbarracinteruel.com

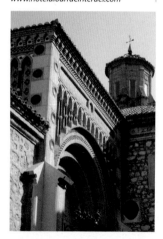

⑪ Teruel
Teruel; 44001

The city of Teruel is one of the last of Spain's undiscovered secrets. Free of mass tourism, Teruel is an enchanting place located on a naturally elevated terrace. On approach, its most distinctive feature is its four ornate Mudéjar towers. These reign over even more UNESCO-classified Baroque, Gothic and Modernista architectural gems in Teruel's compact and easy-to-navigate Old Town. A large university ensures a vibrant nightlife in the city.

A one-hour walking tour
From the car park walk down the busy Ronda de Ambeles to the cylindrical **Torreón de San Esteban** ①, the entrance to the old Jewish quarter. Turn right up Calle Abadia to get to the Plaza Breton; the **Casa Bayo** ②, an elegant blue apartment block in a restrained Art Nouveau style, is on the right. Turn right into Matias Abad, a tiny lane that leads to the tourist office and two of Teruel's most extraordinary sights – the **Mausoleo de Los Amantes** *(open daily)* and the stunning **Iglesia de San Pedro** ④. The mausoleum encloses the mummified cadavers of Diego and Isabel, who, legend has it, literally died of broken hearts but are preserved here for eternity clutching each other's hands in an exquisitely carved piece of marble by sculptor Juan de Ávalos (1911–2006). Adjacent to the mausoleum is the dazzling Iglesia de San Pedro built in the 14th century. The building was constructed by the city's Mudéjar population, who offered their skills to the city's authorities in exchange for special privileges after Teruel was taken by the Christians. Every surface of the church has been embellished with the most vivid Arab-inspired motifs, in deep gold and jewel colours to stunning effect. The adjacent San Pedro tower *(open daily)*, the oldest in the city, is equally rich, featuring intricate tiles and glazed bricks on its columns and borders.

Where to Stay: inexpensive, under €70; moderate, €70–€120; expensive, over €120

Walk back to the tourist office, turn right and then right again into the Plaza del Torico with its central fountain sporting bronze bulls' heads. The pretty **Casa del Torico** ⑤, on the right, is the city's most emblematic Art Nouveau building. Go to the top of the plaza and turn left into the Plaza de la Catedral. The **Catedral de Santa María** ⑥ is a complex structure, spanning eight centuries of different styles. Its most striking feature is an intricately carved wooden ceiling, covering the entire central nave, a magnificent piece of work with Islamic and Gothic influences. The retable, by French artist Gabriel Joly, dates from the 16th century and depicts the life of Christ in Renaissance style. On the opposite side of the plaza, turn right into Calle Yagüe de Salas and walk to the end. Here are three important monuments. On the right is the **Torre de San Martín** ⑦, which is richly embellished in decorative brickwork and Islamic motif. In front is the **Casa de Cultura** ⑧, now the city's public library, and to the left is the **Seminario Conciliar** ⑨, an 18th-century Jesuit College converted into a hotel. Turn right past the Torre de San Martín into Calle San Martín and follow it as it veers to the right. Turn left and then fork right on Calle San Miguel. On the right is **Los Arcos** ⑩, a 16th-century aqueduct. Retrace the route on Calle San

Detail of Iglesia de San Pedro

Miguel and continue down to the Plaza Fray Anselmo Polanco. This is the site of the **Museo Provincial** ⑪ *(open Tue–Sun)*, which is worth perusing for its eclectic collection of artifacts and antique toys. Continue straight ahead on Calle Rubio and Calle Ainsas to Plaza Judería. From here take a left to reach the Ronda de Ambeles and the Estación de Autobuses, back to the car park.

🚗 **Exit Teruel northbound via the N234. Go past the large roundabout. Take the A1512 in the direction of Albarracín. Park at the bottom of the village.**

⑫ Albarracín
Teruel; 44100
The gateway to the Montes Universales mountain range, this pink-hued medieval city literally spills out over a lofty crest, with its awesome ramparts snaking even further up into the sierra. Park at the base of the village and walk up to its small yet atmospheric **Plaza Mayor** where there are a handful of bars and restaurants. The peak of the village is the location of the 16th-century **cathedral** *(open daily)*, which contains a small museum of tapestries, and the **Palacio Episcopal** *(open daily)* with its Baroque portal. For breathtaking views, ascend further to the remains of the **castle**, carved into the rock in the 11th century by a powerful Berber family.

TERUEL

Aquí Teruel *inexpensive*
This tapas bar specializes in local produce such as Jamón de Teruel and cheeses and wine from Aragón.
C/ Yagüe de Salas 4, 44001; 978 612 365

Cafetería Sarto *moderate*
Start the day at this buzzing cafeteria with hot egg and ham rolls, fluffy *tortilla de patatas*, fresh orange juice and great coffee.
C/ Joaquin Costa 12, 44001; 978 602 039

Yain *moderate*
Creative, expertly crafted dishes are served here in a modern setting. A three-course menu with wine is offered for both lunch and dinner.
Plaza de la Judería 9, 44001; 978 624 076; www.yain.es; closed Mon, and Sun and Tue dinner

Below Vibrant Plaza del Torico in Teruel

DAY TRIP OPTIONS

This drive can clearly be divided into two shorter day trips. The A221 accesses all the stops in the north; and the A23, in the south. Visitors can base themselves in either Alcañiz or Teruel to do the following day trips.

Charming villages
Start the day from the castle town of Alcañiz ① and visit its church and castle. Then drive to the colourful village of La Fresneda ②. Head to Valderrobres ③, located on the banks of the Matarraña river, to watch a local couple feed leopard vultures as they swoop down in

hundreds. Then drive to Beceite ④ for lunch, after which take a relaxing walk to El Parrizal, a natural park by the Matarraña river. The walk is approximately four hours long and can be done by anyone.

Leave Alcañiz on the N232 following signs to Tortosa. At the junction of the N420, take the A231 to La Fresneda. From La Fresneda, drive south on the same road straight to the town of Valderrobres. At Valderrobres, take the A2412 to Beceite. Return to Alcañiz the same way.

History and architecture
Spend the morning taking in the

fabulous architecture and visiting the many sights in Teruel ⑪. After a lazy lunch at one of its many restaurants, drive to the mountain town of Albarracín ⑫, where the setting sun washes the ancient stone buildings with incredible pinkish hues. There are some gorgeous views from the remains of the castle. Visit the cathedral and Palacio Episcopal and spend the evening in the Plaza Mayor, which has a handful of restaurants and bars.

Exit Teruel via the N234 on the western side of the town. Go past the large roundabout, then take the A1512 in the direction of Albarracín.

The Land of the Templars
Morella to Ares del Maestre

Highlights

- **Enchanting walled town**
  Explore Morella – bordered by medieval walls and crowned by a magnificent castle

- **Medieval Mirambel**
  Take a stroll back into the Middle Ages in this perfectly restored village

- **Limestone landscapes and dry-stone architecture**
  Take in the endless views of crags, valleys and plateaux

- **Stunning panoramas**
  Climb up to the Maestrazgo's most spectacular viewpoint, Ares del Maestre

Small hilltop village of Ares del Maestre

The Land of the Templars

During the centuries of war against the Muslim rulers of southern Spain, the Grand Masters (*maestres*) of the Knights Templar and other military orders were put in control of the austerely beautiful upland region straddling the borders of Aragón and Valencia. This thus became known as the Maestrazgo (or the *Maestrat* in Valencian). This route sets out from the "capital", Morella, and traverses the mountains north to south to visit two handsome, historic seigneurial towns, taking visitors across landscapes characterized by their dry-stone wall architecture. There are few main roads and no cities in the Maestrazgo, making this back roads country *par excellence*.

Top right Cloister wall below the castle in Morella, *see p132* **Above** Dry valley en route to the chapel of the Virgen del Cid, Iglesuela del Cid, *see pp134–5*

ACTIVITIES

Taste the gourmet specialities of the Maestrazgo, including lamb, pork, cheeses and truffles

Go rambling around Iglesuela del Cid, known for its spectacular dry-stone architecture

Experience the colourful fiestas of the region

0 kilometres 5

0 miles 5

KEY

Drive route

PLAN YOUR DRIVE

Start/finish: Morella to Ares del Maestre.

Number of days: 2–3, allowing for half a day in Morella.

Distance: 250 km (155 miles).

Road conditions: Generally reasonable, but parts of the road between Mosqueruela and Iglesuela del Cid are in poor condition.

When to go: Spring to autumn are ideal. In winter, the Valdelinares section may be blocked by snow.

Opening hours: Most churches are open for Mass only, but if visitors are interested, they can find the person who has the keys to open them. Monuments and museums are closed on Mondays.

Main market days: Morella: Thu, Sun.

Shopping: This region is famous for its traditional textiles, ham, charcuterie, cheese and pastries.

Major festivals: Morella: Sexenni, Aug, every six years, next in 2018; **Mirambel**: Fiestas Patronales en Honor a San Lamberto y San Roque, Aug; **Mora de Rubielos**: Fiestas de San Miguel, Sep.

DAY TRIP OPTIONS

Nature lovers will find Morella an ideal base for exploring the northern mountains, while **families** and **history buffs** will enjoy a visit to the churches of Rubielos de Mora and Mora de Rubielos. For details, see p135.

Above right Façade of the church at Cinctorres near Morella, see p132 **Below** Ares del Maestre located beneath a rocky crag, see p135

Right Typical timber-framed house in Morella
Far right Gothic monastery of Convent de Sant Francesc, Morella

VISITING MORELLA

Tourist Information
Plaçeta de Sant Miquel s/n, 12300; 964 173 032; www.morella.net; closed Mon

Parking
It is best to use the public parking above Portal de Sant Miquel. There is very restricted access for cars into Morella because streets are narrow.

WHERE TO STAY

MORELLA

El Hotel del Pastor *moderate*
El Hotel has traditional decor with modern amenities and spacious rooms with balconies. Price includes breakfast.
San Julián 12, 12300; 964 161 016; www.hoteldelpastor.com

CANTAVIEJA

Balfagon *moderate*
The Balfagon has 46 rooms on three floors. The attic rooms have more character and are quieter than the rest.
Avda. Maestrazgo 20, 44140; 964 185 076; www.hotelbalfagon.com

MORA DE RUBIELOS

Jaime I *inexpensive*
All the rooms of this hotel are individually styled and some have terraces or balconies.
Plaza de la Villa, 44400; 978 800 184; www.hoteljaime.com

La Trufa Negra *expensive*
La Trufa Negra is a slick, contemporary hotel with spa facilities.
Avda. Ibañez Martín 8–10, 44400; 978 807 144; www.latrufanegra.com

❶ Morella
Castelló; 12300

A first view of Morella, the main town of the Maestrazgo, never fails to impress. Raised up dramatically from the surrounding landscape, it consists of a fan-shaped labyrinth draped around a rock outcrop on which stands a ruined castle.

A 90-minute walking tour

This walk can be done any time but it is wise to avoid midday in summer. From the car park, walk to the tourist information office and turn right onto the Plaçeta de Sant Miquel. Across this square is the **Portal de Sant Miquel** ❶, one of the old gates through the medieval walls. Turn left at the corner, go uphill a few steps and turn left by the souvenir shop into Carrer de Don Juan Giner. Bear right on the upper fork into Carrer Mare de Déu del Pilar. After passing the **ajuntament** ❷, a 14th–15th-century mansion, the street becomes Carrer Segura

A medieval sundial in Forcall

Barreda, then Carrer Marquesa Fuente del Sol before feeding into the porticoed Carrer Blasco d'Alagó. The town's main restaurants are all on or just off this street. When the porticoes end, take the flight of steps on the right. Turn right at the top of this first flight up a second, broad flight of steps into a square, Plaça Sant Francesc. Across the square is the 13th-century Gothic monastery, the **Convent de Sant Francesc** ❸, which has a beautiful cloister. Climb up the slope to the **Castillo de Morella** ❹ (open daily), a 13th-century Moorish fortification which includes a courtyard, governor's quarters, dungeons and a tower.

Once back from the castle, turn left from the monastery and walk downhill to the **Basilica Arxiprestal de Santa Maria** ⑤. This church has a magnificently decorated carved spiral staircase leading to the choir loft.

Take the steps opposite the church and continue down Carrer Colomer to meet the porticoed main street, Carrer Blasco d'Alagó. Almost directly across the street, between a souvenir shop and a bar, is a narrow, dark flight of roofed steps. Go down these and turn left into the **Juderia** ⑥, Morella's medieval Jewish quarter. Go through the arch and follow the street downhill. Turn right down the stepped street at the end and take the first left, Carrer de Noguer/Sant Julià (it has two names). This leads to a fork by a shrine to St Julià, patron saint of Morella. Take the upper road, which runs behind the town hall. This road merges with Carrer Juan Giner. Carry straight on to the souvenir shop on the corner. Turn right onto the Plaçeta de Sant Miquel and to the car park.

🚗 *Take the CV14 northwest from the town. After 10 km (6 miles), turn left onto the CV124 to Forcall. Turn right onto the CV120 at Forcall and follow it past La Mata de Morella. Turn left onto the A226 (TE810) to reach Mirambel.*

② Mirambel
Teruel; 44141
Partly preserved, partly restored, Mirambel seems frozen in the Middle Ages. Upon entering through the Portal de las Monjas Agustinas, look up to see the intricate carving above. Do not miss looking into the shop (behind the ruined castle), El Horno, which is a 13th-century baker's, now stocked with regional Maestrazgo produce including cheeses and hams.

🚗 *Continue southwest on the A226 to reach Cantavieja. Park in the Plaza de España, just outside the Old Town.*

③ Cantavieja
Teruel; 44140
The Old Town of Cantavieja is stretched along a ridge high above a river valley. Its main point of interest is the Plaza Mayor, the square which contains the town hall and is enclosed on three sides by beautiful buildings of golden stone. Off the main street, Calle Mayor, are several large houses

built by the rural nobility in the 17th and 18th centuries.

🚗 *Leave Cantavieja for Mora de Rubielos on the A226, a dramatic road, signed for Fortanete and Teruel, to reach the Puerto de Cuarto Pelado (1,650 m/5,450 ft). Turn left onto the VF-TE-22 before Fortanete for Valdelinares. Drive over the Puerto de Fortanete (1,800 m/5,950 ft) and, at the T-junction, turn left onto the TEV3 towards Valdelinares. Turn right onto the VF-TE-01 at the next junction, signposted "Estación de Esqui", which goes through the ski resort (rather than the town) of Valdelinares. At the roundabout at the bottom of the hill, turn left for Mora de Rubielos onto the A228, which passes through La Virgen de la Vega and Puerto de San Rafael (1,550 m/5,100 ft) and leads to Mora de Rubielos.*

④ Mora de Rubielos
Teruel; 44400
The main road into Mora de Rubielos from the north is deflected around the great square 14th-century Castillo de Mora de Rubielos. Behind this, across a pretty square, is the former collegiate **Església de Santa Maria la Mayor**, built in Gothic style. The rest of the town, which includes some atmospheric streets and squares, and four old gateways, shelters beneath these two monumental buildings.

🚗 *Take the A232 southeast from the town to Rubielos de Mora.*

Top Església de Santa Maria la Mayor, Mora de Rubielos **Above** Intricate latticework in Mirambel **Below** Main gate to the 14th-century castle in Mora de Rubielos

EAT AND DRINK

MORELLA

Fonda Moreno *moderate*
A simple, stylish place, this serves the staples of Morella's cuisine: lamb, pork, sausages, ham and truffles.
Sant Nicolau 12, 12300; 964 160 105; www.lafondamoreno.com

Meson El Pastor *moderate*
This is a centrally located restaurant serving the specialities of Morella, including meat cooked with truffles.
Cuesta Jovani 5 y 7, 12300; 964 160 249; www.mesondelpastor.com; open for lunch only, except Fri & Sat; closed Wed

MORA DE RUBIELOS

El Rinconcico *moderate*
Traditional Mediterranean cuisine with Aragonese influences is served at this wheelchair-accessible eatery.
Santa Lucía 4, 44400; 978 806 063; www.elrinconcico.com; closed Tue

Eat and Drink: inexpensive, under €20; moderate, €20–€40; expensive, over €40

Above left Puerto de Linares on the road to Mosqueruela **Above right** Intricately carved wooden window in Rubielos de Mora **Below** Looking over the rooftops of Rubielos de Mora

WHERE TO STAY

RUBIELOS DE MORA

La Villa *moderate*
Housed in a castle-like 16th-century house, La Villa has a fine restaurant.
Plaza del Carmen 2, 44415; 978 804 640; www.delavillahotel.es

IGLESUELA DEL CID

Hospederia de La Iglesuela del Cid *moderate*
More plush than the Maestrazgo's other hotels, this is an 18th-century mansion with a great restaurant.
Ondevilla 4, 44142; 964 107 207; www.hospederiasdearagon.com

ARES DEL MAESTRE

Hotel d'Ares *inexpensive*
Located on the town square, this is a 12-room hotel with a restaurant.
Plaza Mayor 4, 12165; 964 443 007; www.hotelaresdelmaestrat.com

Dry-Stone Architecture

The natural abundance of limestone blocks littering the landscape, coupled with the need to control flocks of sheep, has left the Maestrazgo a legacy of dry-stone architecture, which UNESCO is considering adding to its World Heritage list. Around Iglesuela del Cid and Vilafranca del Cid, lengthy strings of walls, all without mortar, divide up the pastureland and enclosed droving lanes. Most ingenious of all are the circular shepherds' cabins with their domed rooms formed out of delicately balanced stones.

5 Rubielos de Mora
Teruel; 44415

That Rubielos was a well-to-do place between the 15th and 17th centuries can be seen in the opulence of its grand seigneurial mansions. One of the best of them, a beautiful Renaissance building, serves as

the town hall. Be sure to stop at the church, **Ex-Colegiata de Santa Maria la Mayor** *(open for Mass; the tourist office can arrange access at other times)*, which has the second-widest Gothic nave in Spain. On a walk around the village, visitors will find many more well-preserved historic stone and timber buildings. Enjoy the view over the rooftops of Rubielos de Mora from the road towards Castelló.

Leave Rubielos de Mora and head northwards on the A1701. Along the road are two venerable villages, **Nogueruelas** and **Linares de Mora**. The latter has an ancient castle, vestiges of its walls and gateways, and an 18th-century clock tower.

🚗 *Continue on the same road, the A1701, as it goes through the Puerto de Linares (1,700 m/5,650 ft) to reach the next stop, Mosqueruela.*

6 Mosqueruela
Teruel; 44410

The charm of this town lies in the fact that it has not yet been gentrified or restored, and so gives a glimpse of the Maestrazgo before modernity arrived. There are some porticoes off the square beside the beautiful 13th- and 14th-century church and stretches of the town wall, together with five gateways, which are still intact.

Leave Mosqueruela on the A1701. There are many dry-stone walls and cabins on the stretch of road over the Puerto de Mosqueruela pass (1,500 m/4,850 ft).

🚗 *Continue on the A1701, which becomes the CV173 across the provincial border. The road is now narrower and rougher. Follow signs for the Camino del Cid (a tourist route that links places associated with the medieval hero El Cid) near the chapel on the outskirts of the town; do not take the road which turns off to the left for Cantavieja. At the T-junction for Iglesuela del Cid, turn left onto the A227 for the town, or stop to see the Puente de la Pobleta de San Miguel, a 14th–16th-century humpbacked bridge, on the right.*

7 Iglesuela del Cid
Teruel; 44142

This small town has a nucleus of fine civic buildings around the church and town hall dating from its heyday

Where to Stay: inexpensive, under €70; moderate, €70–€120; expensive, over €120

between the 16th and 18th centuries. From the "back" of town (through the Portal San Pablo), there is a good walk or drive (3 km/2 miles each way) across a bridge over a dry valley to the isolated **Capilla de la Virgen del Cid**. From Iglesuela del Cid, retrace the route on the A227 to the junction by the bridge and turn left onto the CV15 for **Vilafranca del Cid**. The town has a museum explaining the dry-stone architecture of the region. After Vilafranca del Cid continue on the CV15 towards the Col de Ares pass (1,500 m/4,950 ft).

🚘 *Continue on the CV15 and turn left at the Col de Ares pass onto the CV1260 for Ares del Maestre.*

⑧ Ares del Maestre
Castelló; 12165
The approach on the CV1260 to Ares del Maestre offers a breathtaking view of the village. It is spectacularly situated beneath a 1,300-m- (4,300-ft-) high rock of the Mola d'Ares mountain. Sights of interest include the Gothic *ayuntamiento* (town hall), the

Neo-Classical parish church, and the remains of a castle. Once at the village, an option is to climb up to the castle, from where there is a great view of a massive sweep of uplands. To get there, take the narrow street to the left of the church, near the town hall. The path setting out from the right of the church is longer.

Above left Church spire in the town of Iglesuela del Cid **Above middle** Statue of a knight in Ares del Maestre **Above right** Classic medieval chapel just outside Mosqueruela **Below** Shepherds' cabins built into dry-stone walls beside the road near Iglesuela del Cid

EAT AND DRINK
There are very few restaurants in this region. Most of the hotels listed have their own restaurants.

DAY TRIP OPTIONS
For those who can only spend a night in the region, the itinerary can be divided into two parts, with either Morella (on the N232) and Rubielos de Mora (on the A1701) as base.

Explore the northern mountains
Use Morella ① as a base and take a couple of hours to explore this old town before setting off. Drive to Mirambel ② and Cantavieja ③, Iglesuela del Cid ⑦ and finally to

Ares del Maestre ⑧, the village sited beneath a spectacular high rock.

Follow the route to Mirambel and Cantavieja, then take the A227 to Iglesuela del Cid. Either return to Morella via Cinctorres on the CV125 or take the CV15 (as per the route) to Ares del Maestre and return on the CV12.

Two southern towns
Explore the beautiful Renaissance town of Rubielos de Mora ⑤ to see

the church, and then head north on the A1701 road to Linares de Mora. From here, pick up the route to the town of Valdelinares and head through La Virgen de la Vega on the VF-TE-01 and then the A228 to arrive in Mora de Rubielos ④. Visit the church, then the castle, or just wander around its atmospheric streets and stop for a lazy lunch break.

Return along the A232 to Rubielos de Mora.

Eat and Drink: inexpensive, under €20; moderate, €20–€40; expensive, over €40

Behind the Costa Blanca

Xàtiva to Xàbia

Highlights

- **The Borgia dynasty**
  Discover the history of the infamous popes of Xàtiva

- **Mysterious caves**
  Explore a man-made labyrinth of caves chiselled into the side of a mountain in Bocairent

- **Secluded coves**
  Unwind on the secluded beaches of the Costa Blanca

- **Valencian cuisine**
  Enjoy delicious *paella* in its birthplace – the Valencian region

View of Bocairent from the Covetes dels Moros

Behind the Costa Blanca

The Costa Blanca is one of Spain's most popular tourist destinations, but the lush mountain terrain that lies in its interior is virtually unexplored. Those who do venture into its interior will discover sweeping plains dotted with mountaintop villages, castles and forts from centuries of Moorish rule. They will also stumble upon Baroque churches and town houses characteristic of Valencia and Alicante. This drive starts in the rugged rural interior and sees the rocky, pine-covered mountains and gorges of the Sierra de Aitana open out onto the breathtaking blue of the Mediterranean Sea.

KEY

Drive route

ACTIVITIES

Walk up to Xàtiva's famous castle

Explore the ancient caves in Bocairent

Hike or cycle through the Parc Natural de la Serra de Mariola

Go shopping in Gata de Gorgos, the "bazaar of the Costa Blanca"

Bask in a secluded cove in Xàbia

Left Entrance to the Gothic Església de Sant Bartomeu in Xàbia, *see p143* **Above** Steeple of the Església de l'Assumpció de Nostra Senyora overlooking Albaida, *see p141* **Below right** Steps leading to the prison in the castle in Xàtiva, *see pp140–41* **Below left** Colourful flamenco dresses and headdresses at a stand in Xàbia, *see p143*

PLAN YOUR DRIVE

Start/finish: Xàtiva to Xàbia.

Number of days: 2–3, allowing half a day to explore Xàtiva.

Distance: 175 km (110 miles).

Road conditions: Mostly well paved and signposted with some steep terrain and hairpin bends. There are many roundabouts and one-way streets in villages.

When to go: July and August can be very hot. April to June and September to late November are good times to visit this region.

Opening hours: Shops are open from 9:30am to 1:30pm, and from 4 to 8pm; restaurants open from 2 to 4pm, and from 8 to 11pm.

Main market days: Xàtiva: Tue; Xàbia: Thu.

Shopping: Look out for handmade jewellery and other local crafts in Xàbia, and locally crafted hats, bamboo furniture, basketware and local *moscatel* wine in Gata de Gorgos.

Major festivals: Xàtiva: Las Fallas, 16–19 Mar; Fira de agosto, 14–20 Aug; Xàbia: San Juan, 24 Jun; Moros y Cristianos, third weekend Jul.

DAY TRIP OPTIONS

Nature lovers and **adventure enthusiasts** will enjoy exploring the labyrinth of caves in Bocairent and a visit to the Parc Natural de la Serra de Mariola, while **families** will have a great time on the beaches on the outskirts of Xàbia. For details, *see p143*.

Above Façade of the 15th-century Església de Sant Francesc, Xàtiva

VISITING XÀTIVA

Tourist Information
Alameda Jaume I, 50, 46800; 962 273 346; www.xativaturismo.es; open Tue–Sun

Parking
Parking is available on Avinguda de la República Argentina, below the Old Town.

WHERE TO STAY

XÀTIVA

La Maga inexpensive
This guesthouse has stylish rooms decorated in neutral tones, and a Mediterranean cuisine restaurant.
C/ Almas 56, 46800; 695 796 587; www.lamagarooms.com

Hotel Mont Sant moderate
Xàtiva's best hotel is located at the base of the castle.
Subida al Castillo s/n, 46800; 962 275 081; www.mont-sant.com

ONTINYENT

Kazar expensive
This grandiose hotel, inspired by a Moorish palace and visited by the King of Spain, has lush and regal interiors.
C/ Dos de Mayo 117, 46870; 962 382 443; www.hotelkazar.com

BOCAIRENT

L'Agora moderate
This hotel is housed in a pretty Art Nouveau building and has period furniture to match.
Sor Piedad de la Cruz 3, 46880; 962 355 039; www.lagorahotel.com

L'Estació moderate
Once a train station, this charming 13-room hotel has smartly decorated rooms and enchanting gardens.
Parc de L' Estació s/n, 46880; 962 350 000; www.hotelestacio.com

Where to Stay: inexpensive, under €70; moderate, €70–€120; expensive, over €120

① Xàtiva
Valencia; 46800

Dominated by the ruins of a Moorish-Gothic castle, Xàtiva is a place steeped in history. The town is famed for its association with the region's most notorious family, the Borjas, better known by their Italian name as the Borgias. The two Borgia popes Calixtus III (1378–1458) and the famously corrupt Alexander VI (1431–1503), father of Lucrezia and Cesare Borgia, were both born here.

A one-hour walking tour

Mid-morning is the best time to start this walk. From the car park walk south on Carrer Baixada del Carme and then on Portal de Lleó to **La Seu** ①, Xàtiva's massive Mannerist-style cathedral with bronze sculptures of the two Borgia popes at its main entrance. Across the square is the 15th-century **Hospital Real** ②. Turn left into Carrer Noguera to arrive at the **Plaça del Mercat** ③, Xàtiva's main square. Exit via Carrer de les Botigues, and turn left into Calle del Peso to reach the **Museo de l'Almodí** ④, the municipal museum (closed Mon), located in a mid-16th-century Renaissance-style building. Return to Carrer de les Botigues and walk downhill on Carrer Font d'Alós to a small square with a Baroque-style fountain. Across the square is the **Església de Sant Francesc** ⑤, a 15th-century church (open for Mass only). The square is a pleasant place to take a break, perhaps sampling a horchata, a drink made from crushed tiger nuts, at one of the cafés. Turn right into Carrer Montcada to see the **Palau del Marqués de Montortal** ⑥,

a medieval palace. Continue along the street to reach the **Plaça de la Trinitat** ⑦, a small square with a Gothic fountain bearing the Kingdom of Valencia's coat of arms. Continue in the same direction to reach three pleasant squares. The first is Plaça Alexandre VI, named after the Borgia pope Alexander VI, whose casa natal (childhood home) is the austere 14th-century mansion on the right. Adjacent is the Plaça Benlloch with the **Font d'Almodar** ⑧, a fountain dating from the 18th century. Lastly, there is the Plaça Sant Pere, which contains two important sites – the **Església de Sant Pere** ⑨ (open daily for Mass), an impressive 15th-century church, and the **Ex-Convento de Sant Onofre el Nou** ⑩, an attractive 18th-century building topped by a fetching Baroque bell tower. The walk can be extended by a visit to Xàtiva's famous castle (closed Mon). Turn right on Carrer Fuente and right again into Carrer de San Cristòbal. Turn left and then right onto Carrer de San José. Bear to the left to emerge onto Carrer Rinconada Collar de la Paloma, then take the first left and walk up to the **castle** *(closed Mon)*. It is a fairly steep climb on foot. This lofty location, first fortified by the Iberians and Romans, bears evidence of Moorish occupation and the Gothic period. Divided into the upper and lower wings and spread over a precarious U-shaped peak, this site contains chapels and prisons, turrets and ramparts, grottoes and gardens; it also has superb views of the surrounding countryside. Don't miss the **Capilla de Santa Maria**, where the 11th Count of Urgell is buried. After exploring the castle, go back to Carrer de Sant Pere, and to the car park.

🚗 *Follow the signs from the Plaza Espanya (the busy roundabout next to the bullring) to the N340 towards Gandia. Just before Montaverner, follow signs onto the CV60 towards Gandia, then back onto the N340 to Albaida.*

② Albaida
Valencia; 46860
The village of Albaida has an interesting *casco antiguo* (Old Town) for its size. Walk up the stairs to Carrer Sant Miguel to the workshop of local artist **Rafael Amorós**. Further up is the Plaça Major and the Gothic **Església de l'Assumpció de Nostra Senyora** *(open daily)*. Behind it, the Plaça Pintor Segrelles features a couple of eclectic museums: the **Museu José Segrelles** *(open Tue–Sun, closed mid-Jun–mid-Sep: Sun & afternoons)*, the ceramic-embellished *casa natal* of a local painter famous for his watercolours; and the **Museu Internacional de Titelles** *(open daily)*, a puppet museum.

🚗 *From the roundabout at the town's base, follow signs onto the A7, then turn left onto the CV81 to Ontinyent.*

③ Ontinyent
Valencia; 46870
Ontinyent is famous for its festival of *Moros y Cristianos*, during which the town hall dons a faux-fortress-like façade in commemoration of the *reconquista*. This sizeable town has an intriguing *casco antiguo* with ancient stone portals, maze-like streets and winding stairways laid out over different levels, which give way to small plazas shaded by clusters of palm trees. The oldest part of the town, La Vila, dates back to the 14th century and is

dominated by the majestic **Església de Santa Maria**, which opens for Mass only.

🚗 *From Plaza Major, follow signs onto the CV81 to reach Bocairent.*

④ Bocairent
Valencia; 46880
This atmospheric hilltop town is home to two of the region's most fascinating sites. The first is the **Covetes dels Moros** (Moors' Caves) *(closed Mon; guided tours only)*, a labyrinthine network of man-made caves chiselled into a cliff face, connected to each other on various levels and with windows looking out over the valley. The intention with which this awe-inspiring structure was constructed is still being debated, although the general consensus is that the town's original Arabian inhabitants used the caves for storing harvested grain. The second is the **Cava de Sant Blai** *(closed Mon in winter)*, an underground ice cave where snow was sold for food preservation.

🚗 *Continue along the same road, the CV81. After 9 km (6 miles), turn left onto the CV795 and drive through Banyeres de Mariola, the entry point for the Parc Natural de la Serra de Mariola, a nature reserve, en route to Alcoy.*

Above Ontinyent skyline punctuated with church spires **Below** Ceiling of the Cava de Sant Blai in Bocairent

EAT AND DRINK

XÀTIVA
El Túnel *moderate*
Behind a heavy wooden door in the old quarter, you'll find tasty tapas and classic oven-cooked rice dishes. *C/ Portal Valencia 22, 46800; 962 288 237; www.eltuneltapas.com; closed Mon & Tue, and Wed dinner, 1st week of Sep and 2nd week of Jan*

Pebre Negre *moderate*
This restaurant specializes in rice dishes – from the ubiquitous *paella* to *arroz negre* (rice cooked in squid ink) and *arroz a banda* (rice in fish stock). *Alameda Jaume I, 46, 46800; 962 280 723; www.pebrenegre.com*

Carpanel *expensive*
A reputable restaurant, this place has an exposed-brick interior courtyard and an extensive range of local wines. *C/ Sant Francesc 38, 46800; 962 281 585; www.tavernacarpanel. com; closed Sun in summer and Mon during the rest of the year*

BOCAIRENT
Restaurant L'Estació *moderate*
Fresh salads, pastas and soups complement heartier meat and fish dishes in this lovely hotel-restaurant. *Parc de L' Estació s/n, 46880; 962 350 000; www.hotelestacio.com*

Verdant Wilderness

The village of Banyeres de Mariola,
through which the route passes, is
the gateway to the Parc Natural de
la Serra de Mariola. The park has
majestic mountains and valleys with
fields of wild flowers, archaeological
finds, ancient hermitages and bubbling streams. Information on walks
and cycling in the park can be
obtained in Banyeres at the Centre
d'Interpretació Ull de Canals (965 566
531; www.llardemariola.com). Located
in a historic farmhouse, the centre
also has a restaurant, bicycles for
hire and accommodation.

5 Alcoy
Alicante; 03801

Straddling two rivers and known as
the "city of bridges", Alcoy (Alcoi in
Valencian) is the largest town in the
region and a good spot for picking
up supplies, with a good selection
of shops and corporate-type hotels.
Alcoy has a handful of sights worth
seeking out. The gigantic **Església
de Santa Maria** (open daily) dominates
the cityscape with its glittering blue
dome, while the **Plaça de Dins** features
elegant porticoes and outdoor cafés.

🚗 *Leave via the CV70 to the east of
the city, following signs straight to
Benasau and Guadalest. It changes to
CV755 near Benimantell. Park in the
main plaza on the outskirts.*

6 Guadalest
Alicante; 03517

The approach to the dramatic clifftop
village of Guadalest is spectacular. The
old part of this village is accessible
only on foot through a single entry:
a sloping tunnel cut into the rock on
which the ruins of a Wagnerian castle

and the belfry of the church, the
Nuestra Señora de la Asunción, are
precariously perched. The **Castell de
Guadalest** (open daily), originally a
Moorish fort, was partially destroyed
by an earthquake in the 17th century.
After exploring the castle, access to
which is through the Casa Orduña,
wander around the plaza on the
village's upper plateau and take in
the views of the gorges and rocky
mountains, some of which are the
highest in the sierra. The **Museo de
Micro-Miniaturas** (open daily) displays
copies of Goya's Le Maja Desnuda
(The Nude Maja), painted on the
wing of a fly, and Los Fusilamiento
del 3 de Mayo (The Shootings of May
Third), painted on a grain of rice.

🚗 *Follow the CV755 out of Guadalest
through the Sierra de Aitana mountain
range to turn left onto the AP7 motorway. Follow signs for Xàbia and leave
the highway at exit 63 (right) to turn
left onto the N332 to Gata de Gorgos.*

7 Gata de Gorgos
Alicante; 03740

The little whitewashed village of Gata
de Gorgos is known as the "bazaar of
the Costa Blanca" for its strong artisan
heritage. Shops line its streets selling
hats, bamboo furniture, colourful
basketware and local moscatel wine.
At the end of September, during the
festival of **San Miguel**, the town hosts
an artisan fair.

🚗 *Leave on the N332 and turn right
onto the CV734, following signs to
Xàbia. Parking is available at the Plaza
de la Constitución Española.*

Above Pristine beach in Xàbia **Below left**
Belfry of the Església de Nuestra Senyora de
Asunción, Guadalest **Below right** Sunflower
field near the picturesque village of Mariola,
en route to Alcoy

⑧ Xàbia

Alicante; 03730

Although, like many of Spain's coastal destinations, Xàbia (Jàvea in Castilian) has been urbanized, its Old Town, pebble beaches and hidden coves make for a wonderful stop along the Costa Blanca.

Recently given a major face-lift, Xàbia's Old Town, originally a walled village, has been steam-cleaned and peeled back to its former glory. The town centre is perched on a hill, a short way inland, on the site of a 17th-century Iberian walled settlement. Steep streets, with whitewashed buildings and handsome brick town houses, lead to the **Església de Sant Bartomeu** *(open daily)*, which dates back to the 16th century and was fortified to serve its congregation as a refuge in times of invasion. It has openings in the doors through which missiles could be aimed at attackers. Next to this is the *ajuntament* (town hall), with a range of architectural elements from the medieval to the Neo-Classical. Close by, the **Museo Soler Blasco** *(closed Mon)* is an elegant edifice containing ethnological artifacts pertaining to the region.

Xàbia's port curves around the glorious **Platja de la Grava**, a picture-postcard pebble beach skirted by a promenade and lined with dozens of outdoor cafés. At its northern end is a marina and the **Duanes del Mar**, where local fishermen sell their daily catch. Dazzling views of the bay of Xàbia, whose beaches are free of high-rise buildings, can be seen from its highest point, the **Cap de Sant Antoni**. Walking tracks sprawl out all over this small cape through a nature park known as the **Parc Natural de El Montgó**, after the mountain peak at its centre. A popular route is the one-hour, mid-level **Ruta de Sant Antoni-Molins**, which takes visitors to one of the town's many landmarks, a cluster of abandoned windmills, most of which date back to the 14th century. The remains of 12 windmills, 11 of which are within the Parc Natural de El Montgó, overlook the cape. With a decline in wheat production by the end of the 18th century, these windmills went out of use and their iron mechanisms and fans were dismantled, leaving only the massive brick bases guarding the bay of Xàbia. Given their proximity to each other, they are a striking sight.

Above Boats moored at the northern end of the port in Xàbia **Below** Locally crafted basketware on display in Gata de Gorgos

VISITING XÀBIA

Tourist Information
Plaza Presidente Adolfo Suárez 11, 03730; 965 790 736; www.xabia.org

EAT AND DRINK

XÀBIA

Posit Restaurant *moderate*
This seafood restaurant serves up succulent *paella* and other rice dishes local to this part of the coast.
Plaza Almirante Bastarreche 11, 03730; 965 793 063; closed Wed

Restaurant El Rodat *expensive*
Try the *menú de desgustación*, at this restaurant housed in the Hotel El Rodat, for a full taste of the highly creative cuisine.
C/ La Murciana 9, 03730; 966 470 710; www.elrodat.com

DAY TRIP OPTIONS

This route can be easily divided into two distinct day excursions: the first covering the inland countryside behind the Costa Blanca; and the second a visit to the coast itself, combined with a visit to the famous castle of Guadalest. The main access road for Xàtiva is the A7, while Xàbia is served by two main roads: the paying AP7 and the toll-free N332.

Caves and parkland
Using Xàtiva ① as a base, head to Bocairent ④ to see the astounding labyrinthine Covetes del Moros.

Continue to Banyeres de Mariola, the gateway to the Parc Natural de la Serra de Mariola, which offers several walking and cycling routes.

From Xàtiva follow signs to the A7/CV645 from the roundabout at the Avinguda de les Corts Catalans. Continue along the A7/CV645, turn right onto the CV81 to pass Ontinyent and follow the signs to Bocairent. After visiting Bocairent, continue on the same road, then turn off into the CV795 and follow signs to Banyeres de Mariola, the gateway to the Parc Natural de la Serra de Mariola.

Castle and beaches
With Xàbia ⑧ as a base, visit the many beaches and coves that are located on its outskirts. Guadalest ⑥ is a popular excursion from Xàbia. It is best to go in the afternoon, when it is quieter and there are fewer bus tours.

From Xàbia, follow the Carretera de la Granadella to its southernmost point to reach the Cala de la Granadella. To reach Guadalest, take the CV734 then the N332 to the AP7 in the direction of Benidorm. Take exit 64, then follow the CV755 mountain road to the Castell de Guadalest.

Eat and Drink: inexpensive, under €20; moderate, €20–€40; expensive, over €40

Along the Duero

Peñafiel to Clunia

Highlights

- **Charming town**
  Wander around the streets of Peñafiel and visit the impressive castle perched high above the town

- **The wine route**
  Stop by the bodegas of La Ribera del Duero for a taste of their world-renowned wines

- **Gastronomic delights**
  Excite your tastebuds in Aranda del Duero with great *asadores* or restaurants specializing in local delicacies

- **Ancient ruins**
  Explore the ruins of the city of Clunia, which date back to the pre-Roman occupation of the Iberian Peninsula

Medieval Castillo de Peñafiel in the lush Duero valley

Along the Duero

Located in the southerly swath of the regions of Burgos and Valladolid, La Ribera del Duero gets its name from the Duero river that snakes through it. The river runs all the way to Oporto in neighbouring Portugal, and throughout history has been the lifeblood of the agriculture and the crafts around it. High-quality wine is produced in this region and its production started here over 2,000 years ago. With its blankets of vineyards and hundreds of bodegas hugging the river's edge, La Ribera del Duero is a popular destination for day-tripping Madrileños, who come here for a Sunday lunch of *lechazo* (slow-roasted lamb) in one of the many famed *asadores* (restaurants that specialize in Castilian-style roast meats) that dot the region. Afterwards, there are forests and valleys to stroll through, castles to explore and ancient villages to discover.

Above Timber-framed Plaza de los Duques in Peñaranda de Duero, *see p150* **Below** Renaissance façade of Iglesia de Santa María in Gumiel de Izán, *see p150*

KEY

Drive route

0 kilometres 5

0 miles 5

ACTIVITIES

Drive up to the hilltop castle in Peñafiel

Go wine tasting in La Ribera del Duero's many bodegas

Take a walk around Curiel, located in the verdant Valle del Cuco

Enjoy a lazy picnic beside the Duero river

Wander the grounds at the ancient Monasterio de Santa María de la Vid

Above left Site of Roman ruins in Clunia, *see p151* **Above right** Old-fashioned bodega in Aranda de Duero, *see p150* **Below** Traditional stone bodegas in Peñafiel, *see p148*

PLAN YOUR DRIVE

Start/finish: Peñafiel to Clunia.

Number of days: 2–3, allowing half a day to explore Peñafiel.

Distance: 175 km (110 miles).

Road conditions: The roads here are very good. There is some heavy traffic along the N122.

When to go: September is when the grapes ripen. The warmest months are from May to Jul.

Market days: Peñafiel: Thu; Roa: Tue; Aranda de Duero: Sat; Peñaranda de Duero: Fri.

Shopping: Wine is available from the bodegas to speciality shops in the villages. The tourist offices in Peñafiel and Aranda de Duero have information on which bodegas are open to the public for tours and tastings.

Opening hours: Shops are open from 9:30am to 1:30pm, and from 4 to 8pm. Restaurants are open from 2 to 4pm, and from 8 to 11pm.

Major festivals: Peñafiel: Fiestas de Nuestra Señora y San Roque, 14–18 Aug; **Roa:** Romería de la Virgen de la Vega, 8 Sep; **Aranda de Duero:** Fiestas Patronales, 8–16 Sep.

DAY TRIP OPTIONS

Wine lovers can drive along La Milla de Oro, the golden route for wine, and visit the many bodegas that dot the area. **History buffs** should head to Aranda de Duero, Peñandra de Duero, the Monasterio de Santa María de la Vid and Clunia to see their castles, churches and Roman ruins. For details, *see p151.*

Above Castillo de Peñafiel in the Duero valley

VISITING PEÑAFIEL

Tourist Information
Plaza del Coso 31–32, 47300; 983 881 526; www.turismopenafiel.com; closed Mon

Parking
Visitors can park in the public car park at the base of castle.

WHERE TO STAY

PEÑAFIEL

Hotel Convento Las Claras *moderate*
Set in the historic heart of Peñafiel, this hotel is housed in a converted convent.
Plaza de los Comuneros 1, 47300; 983 878 168; www.hotelconvento lasclaras.com

AROUND PEÑAFIEL

La Vida *expensive*
Once a 17th-century rustic house, this comfortable hotel boasts a charming restaurant and wine spa.
Plaza Mayor 1, 47313, Aldeyuso; 983 881 559; www.lavida.es

AROUND LA MILLA DE ORO

Posada Fuente de la Aceña
moderate
This contemporary hotel is beautifully set in a 300-year-old watermill.
C/ Molino, 47350, Quintanilla de Onésimo; 938 680 910; www.fuenteacena.es

Hotel Arzuaga *expensive*
Surrounded by vineyards, this five-star hotel has a wine-therapy spa and lets guests participate in the grape harvest and hunting deer in the hotel grounds.
Ctra. N122, Km 325, 47350, Quintanilla de Onésimo; 983 681 146; www.hotelarzuaga.com

CURIEL DE DUERO

Residencia Real Castillo de Curiel
moderate
The old castle overlooking Curiel has been converted to a luxury hotel.
Trascastillo, 47316; 983 880 401; www.castillodecuriel.com

❶ Peñafiel
Valladolid; 47300

Built along the verdant banks of the Duero river, dominated by an ancient castle and with a surprisingly eclectic clutch of specialist museums, Peñafiel is the best introduction to the region of La Ribera del Duero.

A two-hour walking tour
Start at the car park and ascend on the marked track to the **Castillo de Peñafiel** ① *(closed Mon)*. Dating from the 15th century, it offers impressive views over the entire region. The structure of the castle has often been compared with that of a huge boat. The castle also houses the Museo Provincial del Vino in its patio.

Go back down to the car park and follow the perimeter of the Parque de San Vicente to the left. Walk down Calle Varquilla and then take a left to enter **Plaza del Coso** ②. This wide, sand-covered plaza is often used for bullfighting and festive events and is flanked by traditional housing, with decorative hanging balconies. The tourist office on Plaza del Coso organizes guided tours (Tue–Sun) to the Gothic–Moorish **Convento de San Pablo** ③, a 14th-century convent. Backtrack along Calle Derecha al Coso, passing the medieval **Casas Hidalgas** ④ on the left and the quaint chimney-like ventilation shafts of ancient

underground **bodegas** ⑤ on the right. Continue on this road till the **Iglesia de Santa María** ⑥, a 17th-century church with a Baroque bell tower. The church houses a Museo Comarcal de Arte Sacro *(open Fri–Sun)*, with a collection of 12th–15th-century religious objects made from precious metals. Turn left up Calle Episcopal and walk down Calle Reoyo to the Plaza de San Miguel Reoyo. On the right is the 16th-century **Iglesia de San Miguel** ⑦ *(open for Mass only)*, whose austere Romanesque walls hide a rich interior with Baroque retables. Cross the Duero via the Puente de la Judería. Under the bridge is a parkland where visitors can have a picnic. Cross the bridge to reach the 17th-century **Convento de Santa Clara** ⑧, which has now been converted into a hotel. Retrace the route to the car park.

🚗 *Head northwest on Calle de Subida al Castillo and turn right on the N122. At 1 km (0.6 miles) towards Aranda de Duero, turn right to reach Bodegas Pago de Carraovejas.*

② La Milla de Oro

Valladolid; 47340
This stretch of road, locally known as La Milla de Oro (Golden Mile), offers a good insight into the region's wine culture. The first vineyard that comes up just outside Peñafiel is **Bodegas Pago de Carraovejas**. After a stop here, return to the N122 and turn left toward Valladolid. After about 20 km (12 miles) you'll find the **Finca Villacreces** on the right, beautifully set in pine forest: it has produced some very fine wines, notably under its Pruno label. Be sure to prebook your tasting before a visit here. Returning to the N122, turn right towards Quintanilla de Onésimo. You'll soon be passing the famed vinyeards of Vega Sicilia *(not open to the public)*; another 2 km (1 mile) further on is the renowned **Bodegas Arzuaga**, which offers wine tastings and visits to the vineyards and production facilities, and has a good hotel and restaurant. Just before Sardón de Duero is **Abadía Retuerta**, a vineyard located in a beautiful 12th-century abbey.

🚗 *Return to the N122 and head back to Peñafiel. On approach, follow signs for the VA101. Then turn right onto the VP3017/VP3018 to the village of Curiel de Duero. Park near the Iglesia de Santa María at the entrance of the village.*

③ Curiel de Duero

Valladolid; 47316
The tiny village of Curiel de Duero is one of the prettiest in the Valle del Cuco, a picturesque valley of forests, wheat and sunflower fields, and home to foxes, rabbits and partridges. The valley is popular with locals for walking and hunting. Curiel's most striking building is the Gothic-Mudéjar **Iglesia de Santa María** *(open for Mass only or ask at the tourist office during the summer months)*. On the highest point of Curiel and perched on a rocky platform is the 12th-century fortress-like castle, now converted into a hotel.

🚗 *Leave Curiel on the VP3018 and turn left onto VP3017. At Valdearcos de la Vega, take the VA134, which becomes the BU134. Get onto the BU133 after Mambrilla de Castrejón and follow signs to Roa. Park on the village outskirts.*

④ Roa

Burgos; 09300
The bustling, largely industrial little village of Roa has a secret gem: the **Colegiata de Nuestra Señora de la Asunción** *(open Jul–Aug, rest of the year open for Mass only)*. Situated on Roa's Plaza Mayor, this imposing 16th-century building exudes typical Castilian sobriety from the exterior, with its massive stone walls and rectangular bell tower. In contrast, the church's interior of bare ivory-coloured walls, soaring columns and elegant, carved vaults is simple and uplifting. Some noted decorative pieces here are attributed to a celebrated sculptor of the period, Gil de Siloé.

🚗 *Exit Roa on the BU120. When it joins the N122, turn left, following signs to Aranda de Duero. Park on the outskirts of the old city by the river.*

Above left Magnificent Monasterio de Santa María de la Vid **Above right** Bodega in Peñaranda de Duero **Below** Roman amphitheatre in Clunia

WHERE TO STAY

ARANDA DE DUERO

Aranda *moderate*
Charming, central hotel, with warmly decorated rooms and a 16th-century wine cellar.
C/ San Francisco 51, 09400; 947 501 600; www.hotelaranda.com

AROUND ARANDA DE DUERO

Hotel Tudanca-Aranda II *inexpensive*
One of the best near the city, the Tudanca-Aranda II is located 6 km (4 miles) south of Aranda de Duero. The rooms in this hotel are spacious and comfortable, and the in-house restaurant is highly recommended.
N1 (Autovía del Norte), Km 153, 09470; Fuentespina–Aranda de Duero; 947 506 011; www.tudancaaranda2.com

AROUND GUMIEL DE IZÁN

El Rincón de la Tía Elena *inexpensive*
This cheerful *casa rural*, located in Oquillas, 7 km (4 miles) north of Gumiel de Izán, offers homespun comfort and wholesome home-cooked meals.
C/ Real 31, 09350, Oquillas; 654 909 294; www.elrincondelatiaelena.com

PEÑARANDA DE DUERO

Posada Ducal *moderate*
A 12th-century building, this hotel is decorated in regal style. It also has an excellent in-house restaurant and offers guests a free tour to a winery.
Plaza Mayor 1, 09410; 947 552 347; www.laposadaducal.com

MONASTERIO DE SANTA MARÍA DE LA VID

Hospedería La Vid *moderate*
The residence inside the Monasterio de Santa María de la Vid is a good place for a simple and quiet stay.
Ctra. Soria La Vid de Aranda, 09471; 947 530 510; www.monasteriodelavid. org; minimum stay 1 week Jul–Aug

⑤ Aranda de Duero
Burgos; 09400

Although small in size, the capital of La Ribera del Duero has much to offer, with its good selection of shops, restaurants and a maze of ancient underground bodegas. The town's main sight is the imposing 15th-century **Iglesia de Santa María** *(open for Mass only)*, with a richly rendered threshold. Behind the church is another important religious edifice, the **Iglesia de San Juan Bautista** *(closed Mon in Jan and Feb)*, which houses a **Museo de Arte Sacro** *(closed Mon)*. Opposite this is the **Casa de las Bolas** *(closed Mon)*, which has a collection of paintings from the 15th to the 20th centuries. Walking in the opposite direction will lead to Aranda's main square, which is a good place to relax.

🚗 *Leave town northbound on the N1A and turn right onto the A1 heading northwards towards Burgos. Take exit 168 and follow signs to Gumiel de Izán.*

⑥ Gumiel de Izán
Burgos; 09370

Santo Domingo de Guzman (1175–1221), the monk who founded the order of Dominicans, is Gumiel de

Izán's most famous resident. He spent his infancy in a medieval home that still stands in the village's main square. It is one of a handful of well-preserved whitewashed structures with column-like supports which form arcades. Opposite is the **Iglesia de Santa María** *(open daily Jul–mid-Sep, and open for Mass only for the rest of the year or by request; 947 544 018)*, an imposing structure, considering the size of this tiny village, built between the 14th and 17th centuries with an elaborate Renaissance portal.

🚗 *Leave Gumiel de Izán southbound on the BU922 and turn left on the BU912. Go through Villanueva de Gumiel on the BU912 following signs to Peñaranda de Duero. Go through Quemada and turn left onto the BU925 towards Peñaranda de Duero.*

⑦ Peñaranda de Duero
Burgos; 09410

Behind the remains of the ancient stone walls of this little village lies a real surprise: the elegant **Plaza de los Duques** (Plaza Mayor) which is lined with porticoed timber-framed buildings. Set among the traditional medieval homes is the **Iglesia de Santa**

Ana (closed Mon), which features Roman busts, transferred here from the digs at nearby Clunia, and heavy Baroque detailing on the portal. Opposite is the superb Renaissance **Palacio de los Zuñiga y Avellanda** (open Fri), once home of the noble family of Zuñiga y Avellanda. Stroll up to the castle (car access is difficult) overlooking Peñaranda de Duero which affords great views of the area.

🚗 *Take the BU923 when coming out of the Plaza Mayor, signposted to La Vid. Once there, park outside the monastery.*

⑧ Monasterio de Santa María de la Vid
Burgos; 09471
The impressive monastery, located on the banks of the Duero, is home to one of the oldest monastic orders in Spain. The monastery was inspired by a group of French monks devoted to San Norberto, though today it is run by the Order of Augustines. The edifice spans from the 12th to the 18th centuries, and has a variety of styles from Romanesque to Gothic, Renaissance and Neo-Classical. Visitors can wander around the lovely gardens that surround the monastery. To see the library (one of the largest for religious manuscripts in Spain), cloister and museum (closed Mon), visitors will need to take a tour, which lasts about an hour.

🚗 *Leave on the BU923 north from the monastery. At Peñaranda de Duero turn right onto the BU925 and keep on this road. After Coruña del Conde, look out for a sign indicating Clunia.*

⑨ Clunia
Burgos; 09454
The site of Clunia, on a ridge 1,000 m (3,300 ft) above sea level, had first been occupied by the Iberians. Many centuries later, when the Romans took over, it became one of the most important strongholds in Hispania Tarraconensis. Forty thousand people lived there between the 1st and 3rd centuries AD. The Romans' logical urban planning of Clunia is evident from what remains today, especially the surprisingly intact **amphitheatre**, which was cleverly placed in order to incorporate a view of the Sierra de la Demanda as a backdrop, and **Los Arcos** (closed Mon), the expansive thermal baths. Three impressive mosaic works, which once graced the floors of private homes, still stand.

Above View of the valley below from the castle in Peñaranda de Duero **Below** Façade of the Iglesia Colegio in Peñaranda de Duero

EAT AND DRINK

ARANDA DE DUERO

Tapas in Aranda de Duero *inexpensive*
The old city in Aranda de Duero is swarming with good tapas bars. Try *morcilla* (a local sausage similar to English black pudding) or *pimientos del piquillo* (roasted red peppers).

El Lagar de Isilla *moderate*
An eatery that offers great tapas in the front bar, a formal rear dining room and an ancient underground bodega. *C/ Isilla 18, 09400; 947 510 683; www.lagarisilla.es; closed Sun dinner*

GUMIEL DE IZÁN

Bodegas Portia *moderate*
Enjoy sophisticated regional fare in this elegant restaurant, located in the Portia winery on the edge of town. *Ctra. N1, Km 170, 09370; 947 102 700; open lunch only*

PEÑARANDA DE DUERO

Señorio de Velez *moderate*
The Señorio de Velez serves comfort food favourites such as grilled lamb chops, fish soup and rice pudding. *Plaza Duques de Alba 5, 09410; 947 552 201*

DAY TRIP OPTIONS
This drive can be divided into two day trips, with visitors being based either in Peñafiel or in Aranda de Duero. The *autovía* (A1) and the N122 easily access all the sights in this area.

Wine tasting
Start the day at the ancient town of Peñafiel ① and explore its many museums and the castle. Then spend the rest of the day visiting, tasting and buying wine at the many bodegas along La Milla de Oro ②.

Leave Peñafiel on the N122 west towards Valladolid to visit the bodegas, and return the same way.

Churches, monastery and Roman ruins
Visit the churches in the capital of La Ribera del Duero, Aranda de Duero ⑤, and stop by its many restaurants and bodegas. Head to the Monasterio de Santa Maria de la Vid ⑧, located on the banks of the Duero river. Take a stroll around its lovely grounds. Visit Peñaranda de Duero ⑦, a tiny village crowned by a castle with great views

of one of the most charming villages in Burgos. Then head north to Clunia ⑨ to see the ancient Roman ruins, and the amphitheatre which is still in spectacular condition.

Take the N122 from Aranda de Duero to the Monasterio de Santa María de la Vid. Then head north on the BU923 for Peñaranda de Duero. From Peñaranda, take the BU925. After Coruña del Conde, look out for a left for Clunia. To return to Aranda de Duero, keep on the BU925, which goes back to the town.

The Spine of Castile
Toros de Guisando to Ciudad Rodrigo

Highlights

- **Mountain landscapes**
  Explore some of the least visited parts of Spain around Valle del Alberche, with stunning views

- **Regional architecture**
  Stop in remote mountain villages, where traditional half-timbered houses lean over cobbled streets

- **Charcuterie and honey**
  Enjoy one of Spain's most noted culinary regions, Castilla y León

- **Historic Ciudad Rodrigo**
  Visit the fortified town that challenged French, Spanish and British soldiers

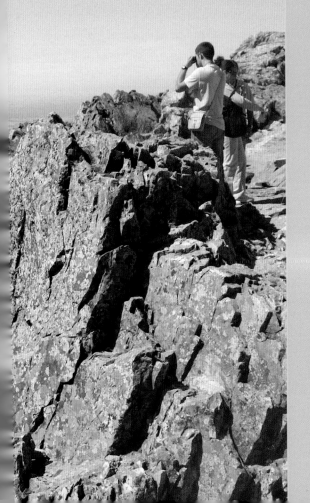

Peak of Peña de Francia overlooking the surrounding plains and rolling hills

The Spine of Castile

West of Madrid, the craggy heights of the spectacular Sierra de Gredos, the Sierra de la Peña de Francia and several smaller mountain ranges offer a wonderful contrast to the more familiar plains of central Spain. Between the mountains, this drive winds through traditional farming country cut by valleys and streams. En route are villages dotted with medieval houses and cobbled streets, high-altitude pastures above the tree line and fine old towns full of historical sites.

KEY

Drive route

Above Portal of Catedral de Ciudad Rodrigo, see p160 **Below** Medieval church in Ramacastañas in the Valle del Alberche, see p156

0 kilometres 10

0 miles 10

ACTIVITIES

Hike on a Roman road to the pass of Puerto del Pico

Take a walk between the lakes and peaks at Hoyos del Espino

Relax in Candelario, lulled by the calming sound of rushing water in the town's canals

Walk in the footsteps of Wellington on the ramparts of Ciudad Rodrigo

Above City walls of Ciudad Rodrigo in Salamanca, *see p160* Below Ibex grazing in the Valle del Tormes, *see p158*

PLAN YOUR DRIVE

Start/finish: Toros de Guisando to Ciudad Rodrigo.

Number of days: 4, allowing a day to explore Ciudad Rodrigo.

Distance: 465 km (290 miles).

Road conditions: Mostly well surfaced; occasionally narrow and winding. Higher roads may be affected by snow closures during winter.

When to go: In summer, the mountains can be crowded, but the weather is perfect. Spring and autumn are sometimes wet, but quieter.

Opening hours: Most museums and monuments are closed on Mondays. On other days, they open from 10am to 2pm, and in some cases, reopen from 5 to 8pm.

Main market days: Arenas de San Pedro: Wed; Béjar: Thu; La Alberca: Fri; Ciudad Rodrigo: Tue, Sat.

Shopping: Dry-cured ham and honey are the regional specialities.

Major festivals: Arenas de San Pedro: Virgen del Pilar, 8 Sep; La Alberca: Fiestas de la Asunción, 15 Aug; Ciudad Rodrigo: Carnaval del Toro, Feb.

DAY TRIP OPTIONS

History buffs will enjoy a visit to the castles in the villages of Arenas de San Pedro and Mombeltrán, while **architecture enthusiasts** should head to Ciudad Rodrigo and La Peña de Francia. For details, *see p161*.

Top Stone bulls of Guisando **Above left** Hiking up to Puerto del Pico pass **Above right** Castillo de Don Álvaro de Luna, Arenas de San Pedro

VISITING TOROS DE GUISANDO

From Madrid, take the A5–E90 Carretera de Extremadura as far as Navalcarnero (exit 32). At the roundabout, take the M507 and continue on it (direction Villamanta) until Aldea del Fresno. At the next roundabout, turn left towards Méntrida and then right onto the M507 towards Villa del Prado. Turn right onto the N403 (direction Ávila). After San Martin de Valdeiglesias, turn left onto the AV904 for Toros de Guisando.

WHERE TO STAY

AROUND TOROS DE GUISANDO

Hotel Toros de Guisando *moderate*
This good-value hotel with large rooms is 10 km (6 miles) north of El Tiemblo.
Avda. de Madrid, 05270, El Tiemblo; 918 627 082; www.torosdeguisando.com

ARENAS DE SAN PEDRO

Hosteria El Bodegón de Gredos *moderate*
A decently maintained hotel, this place also has a restaurant.
Plaza Condestable Dávalos 2, 05400; 920 371 379; www.elbodegondegredos.com

AROUND CASTILLO DE LOS DUQUES DE ALBURQUERQUE

Hotel Marji *inexpensive*
Located to the south of Mombeltrán, this hotel has great views of the castle.
C/ Calvo Sotelo 64, 05410, Mombeltrán; 920 386 031

Where to Stay: inexpensive, under €70; moderate, €70–€120; expensive, over €120

① Toros de Guisando
Ávila; 05270

The ancient stone carvings of four life-size bulls face the hill of Guisando in the eastern foothills of the Sierra de Gredos. The bulls are examples of *verracos*, granite megalithic sculptures of animals, found in a few provinces in Spain and Portugal. Although the origins of the Bulls of Guisando are uncertain, it is believed they were carved by a pre-Celtic people called the Vettones around the 2nd century BC.

🚗 *Drive north to the N403 and turn left (direction Ávila) to follow the highway past the slip road for El Tiemblo and, on the left, the Embalse del Burguillo reservoir. Just past El Barraco, look out for the small sign for the AV905 to Béjar.*

② Valle del Alberche
Ávila; 05134

After Navarredondilla, the AV905 descends into the Alberche valley, offering a scenic route west, zigzagging over the ridges to the village of Navatalgordo. Stop at the viewpoint 7 km (4 miles) after the village. Shortly after, the route cuts sharply left onto the AVP419, crossing the Alberche river on a modern bridge that stands next to an old, pretty one. Look out for the traditional, conical haystacks typical of the region. From here onward, there are several fine

viewpoints, including a superb vista from a rocky bluff on the left. At Navarrevisca, turn right onto the AV913 and drive up to the Collado de Serranillos pass (1,600 m/5,200 ft), from where are more good views. At San Esteban del Valle, turn left onto the AVP706 and descend into Santa Cruz del Valle, passing several shady picnic spots en route; the last of these has excellent views across the valley to the castle in Mombeltrán.

🚗 *Drive through Santa Cruz del Valle to meet the N502. Turn left and drive into Ramacastañas. At the main roundabout, exit onto the AVP708 for the Cuevas del Águila.*

③ Cuevas del Águila
Ávila; 05400

Also known as the Grutas del Águila, these interesting "eagle caves" *(open daily; 920 377 107)*, discovered in 1963, consist of a water-formed limestone cavern. Guided tours run mornings and afternoons throughout the year, offering views of the multihued formations, coloured by mineral deposits and organic material mixing with the limestone accretions. There is a lovely picnic area, bar and restaurant outside.

🚗 *Return to Ramacastañas, take the second exit from the roundabout onto the AV923, and follow signs for Arenas de San Pedro. Park by the castle.*

④ Arenas de San Pedro
Ávila; 05400

The small town of Arenas is the commercial hub for the southern Gredos and acts as a base for visits to the Parque Regional de la Sierra de Gredos. The town is dominated by the 15th-century **Castillo de Don Álvaro de Luna** *(open to the public; 969 346 001)*. The riverside decking overlooking the Arenal and its medieval bridge is a pleasant spot to relax.

Take the AVP713 west out of Arenas to **Guisando**, a picturesque village well worth a visit. From Guisando take the AVP712 to **El Hornillo**, which has a *piscina natural*, a lovely semi-natural swimming pool, on the Cantos river. Then take the AVP711 to **El Arenal**; an easily accessible hiking route to the Gredos park starts just out of the town.

🚗 *From El Arenal, follow the cobbled street. At the end of it, turn right onto the unsigned Carretera Forestal de las Majadas. In Mombeltrán, turn right onto the N502, and then left.*

⑤ Castillo de los Duques de Alburquerque
Ávila; 05410

With its lofty round towers hidden by plane trees, the 15th-century Castillo de los Duques de Alburquerque rises from the south side of Mombeltrán. The tourist office on the main road can organize short tours.

🚗 *Rejoin the N502 that runs through Mombeltrán and head north towards*

Ávila and the Puerto del Pico pass, via Cuevas del Valle. Be careful of the tight hairpin bends while leaving Cuevas del Valle.

⑥ Puerto del Pico
Ávila; 05413

At 1,352 m (4,436 ft), Puerto del Pico is the most important road pass in the Sierra de Gredos. The Romans constructed a robust stone road over the mountains here, linking the basin of the Tiétar river to the south with that of the Tormes to the north. The road, the Calzada Romana, has been restored and makes for a good, if steep, 6-km (4-mile) hike up to the pass. Park by the church in Cuevas del Valle and then walk up to the pass.

🚗 *From the pass, continue down the N502 into the northern Gredos, turning left onto the AV941 for San Martín del Pimpollar and Hoyos del Espino.*

Above At the top of the Puerto del Pico pass in the Sierra de Gredos **Below left** Looking down from the Puerto del Pico pass to Mombeltrán **Below right** Towering ramparts of the Castillo de los Duques de Alburquerque in Mombeltrán

EAT AND DRINK

CUEVAS DEL ÁGUILA
Cuevas del Águila *inexpensive*
A restaurant that serves original, Spanish cuisine. Highlights of the menu are dishes such as roasts and *chuletón* (grilled meats seasoned with sea salt).
Ctra. Cuevas del Águila, 05418; 920 377 106; closed Dec–Feb: Mon–Fri

ARENAS DE SAN PEDRO
El Bodegón de Gredos *moderate*
This hotel in Arenas de San Pedro also has a restaurant.
Plaza Condestable Dávalos 2, 05400; 920 371 379; www.elbodegonde gredos.com

Eat and Drink: inexpensive, under €20; moderate, €20–€40; expensive, over €40

Above El Barco de Ávila by the banks of the Tormes river **Below** Medieval town of Miranda de Castañar

WHERE TO STAY

AROUND VALLE DEL TORMES

El Milano Real *moderate*
Located in Hoyos del Espino, this Rusticae hotel, with a spa, is exceptionally stylish and welcoming.
C/ Toleo 2, 05634, Hoyos del Espino; 920 349 108; www.elmilanoreal.com

La Casa de Arriba *moderate*
This is a 17th-century stone house in Navarredonda de Gredos, which has spectacular views of the mountains.
La Cruz 19, 05635, Navarredonda de Gredos; 920 348 024; www.casadearriba.com

Parador de Gredos *moderate*
The oldest parador in the state-run group, this hotel, located near Navarredonda, is recommended for cosy stays in autumn or winter.
Ctra. AV941, Km 10, 05635 Navarredonda de Gredos; 920 348 048; www.parador.es

CANDELARIO

Centro Turismo Rural Artesa *moderate*
There are very comfortable rooms in this mid-18th-century house.
C/ Mayor 57, 37710; 923 413 111; www.artesa.es

MIRANDA DEL CASTAÑAR

Condado de Miranda *inexpensive*
Modest, comfortable, clean rooms, and the price includes breakfast.
C/ de La Perdiza 13, 37660; 923 432 026; www.hotelcondado demiranda.com

LA ALBERCA

Hotel Antiguas Eras *moderate*
This hotel has idiosyncratic decor and a popular bar-café in the basement.
Avda. Batuecas 29, 37624; 923 415 113; www.antiguaseras.com

Where to Stay: inexpensive, under €70; moderate, €70–€120; expensive, over €120

7 Valle del Tormes
Ávila; 05634

Enter the upper Tormes valley on the AV941 through **Navarredonda de Gredos** and stop in the next village, **Barajas**, to look at the old forge, now an occasionally open tourist office. Further down the road, **Hoyos del Espino** has several riding and activity centres, and small restaurants and modest hotels along the main road. To hike in the Gredos, turn south onto the AV931, just east of Hoyos, up to the end of the road (called La Plataforma). Either do the three-hour round-trip walk to the Los Barrerones col and viewpoint, or the five-and-a-half-hour round-trip hike to the spectacular Laguna Grande. Park at La Plataforma and set off before midday, equipped with good footwear and waterproofs.

Returning from La Plataforma, turn left after 4 km (2 miles) and cross a cattle grid to follow the valley of the Garganta del Barbellido on the Camino Panorámico el Polvoroso (signed). There is a good swimming spot by an old bridge at 11 km (7 miles). To rejoin

the AV941, cross the next cattle grid on the outskirts of Navacepeda de Tormes and turn left, following the road uphill. At El Barco, proceed into the Old Town and park to the right of the castle.

8 El Barco
Ávila; 05600

Dominating the riverbank in the old quarter of El Barco, the massive, round-towered **Castillo de Valdecorneja** was founded in the 12th century and rebuilt in the 14th century. The castle is well worth exploring, as is taking a stroll around its perimeter, a short promenade with good views across the Tormes river to the west. The town's 14th-century parish church, the **Iglesia de Nuestra Señora de la Asunción**, which blends Gothic, Romanesque and Renaissance styles, is open for visits on weekends (Sat noon, 1pm, 5pm, 6pm & Sun 11am).

Drive west out of El Barco on the AV100/SA100, following signs for Béjar. On the outskirts of Béjar, turn left at the traffic lights onto SA515 for Candelario (signposted). Park in the Plaza Mayor.

9 Candelario
Ávila; 37710

A pretty mountain village full of traditional architecture – wooden-framed houses with balconies – Candelario makes for a very pleasant overnight stay. Stroll through the narrow alleys that echo with the sound of running water through a network of small canals, called *regaderas*. These canals that traditionally coped with the blood from the winter slaughter of thousands of pigs, now deal with rain and the spring snow melt. From the Plaza Mayor, head uphill and take a right after 1 km (0.6 mile) to drive to a fine viewpoint over the Embalse de las Angosturas.

🚗 *Take the DSA192 to the village of La Garganta. Once there, take a sharp right, signposted Puerto de Béjar, soon joining a country road through groves of sweet chestnut. On the south side of Puerto de Béjar, join the N630/A66 for Béjar. Follow signs right into Béjar and left into the "Centro Urbano". Drive to the western end of town to the old quarter. Park by the square between the church and the palace.*

⑩ Béjar
Salamanca; 37700

Built in a dramatic location on a narrow ridge between two valleys, the old textile town of Béjar is made up of a tight grid of streets. A few old mills still stand in the adjacent valley to the north, a 10-minute walk from the town centre, where a *ruta textil* (textile route) follows the river under the bridges. The Plaza Mayor is dominated by the 12th-century **Iglesia de Santa María la Mayor** and the Renaissance **Palacio Ducal**. Drive or walk to the western end of Béjar, where a well-presented **Museo Judío David Melul** *(open Thu–Sat)* tells the story of the town's Jewish community.

🚗 *Drive west, around the back of the Iglesia de Santiago, and then north, to reach the SA220. Turn left towards Ciudad Rodrigo. After 25 km (16 miles), there is a snack bar and a petrol station – useful, as the countryside is virtually uninhabited. At the confusing junction before Miranda del Castañar, Ciudad Rodrigo is signposted right (SA220). Stay on the main road (SA225), and take the sudden left for Miranda.*

⑪ Miranda del Castañar
Salamanca; 37660

Miranda del Castañar's crumbling 15th-century castle is emblematic of this medieval, walled bastion's flaking appeal. The village is perched on a hill with panoramic views, and the entrance road is the only access. Its streets are lined with ancient houses with wide eaves. Walk up the narrow high street to the 13th-century Gothic church, calling at shops selling hams and other local produce.

🚗 *Return to the SA225 and turn left for Cepeda; 2 km (1 mile) later, turn right onto the DSA260 (CV111) after the bridge towards Mogarraz. About 5 km (3 miles) later, the road leads to the Mirador Peña de Cabra viewpoint on a tight right-hand bend. Continue to La Alberca; follow the main road around the Old Town centre to park.*

⑫ La Alberca
Salamanca; 37624

The genteel capital of the Sierra de la Peña de Francia, La Alberca is a much-visited Spanish national monument. Its narrow streets are lined with wood-framed houses, and its flower-bedecked Plaza Mayor, with its arcades and rows of granite columns, boasts a fine cross. The terraced gardens and old Moorish irrigation system that underpin the town are the subject of a popular walk – the *Senda de Los Cortinales* – details of which are on the board near the office of the Parque Nacional de las Batuecas on the west side of the town.

🚗 *Leave La Alberca on the SA201 towards Ciudad Rodrigo, turning left after 5 km (3 miles) onto the DSA342 (CV134), and left again onto the SA203 for the Peña de Francia monastery.*

Top left Hikers going up one of the many trails in the Sierra de Gredos **Top right** Stone archway in the town of Miranda del Castañar **Above** Charming mountain village of Candelario

EAT AND DRINK

CANDELARIO
Taberna El Ruedo *moderate*
A popular traditional restaurant just off Candelario's lovely Plaza Mayor, El Ruedo is an excellent place to find well-prepared, hearty cuisine served with style. Game and mushrooms are specialities here.
Avda. del Humilladero 2, 37710; 923 413 422; www.posadapuerta grande.com; closed Mon

MIRANDA DEL CASTAÑAR
Bar Restaurante Las Petronilas *moderate*
This is a much-loved local establishment serving home-style mountain cooking, especially beans, *patatas menéas* (potatoes with bacon), lamb, pork and various stews.
Avenida de la Constitución, 37660 (on the way into town); 923 432 483; closed Tue and in Aug & Sep

Eat and Drink: inexpensive, under €20; moderate, €20–€40; expensive, over €40

Above Roman bridge crossing the Agueda river in Ciudad Rodrigo

VISITING CIUDAD RODRIGO

Tourist Information
Avda. de Sefarad, 37500; 627 453 424; http://turismociudadrodrigo.com

Parking
Car parks are outside the old city walls on the northeast side and by the Puerto del Conde. Alternatively, drive in and park in the Plaza Mayor.

WHERE TO STAY

CIUDAD RODRIGO

Conde Rodrigo I *inexpensive*
Set in a fine old house, this hotel offers well-priced rooms.
Plaza San Salvador 9, 37500; 923 461 404; www.hotelesciudadrodrigo.com

Parador Enrique II *expensive*
This hotel enjoys a beautiful castle setting in the highest location in town.
Plaza del Castillo 1, 37500; 923 460 150; www.parador.es

⓭ La Peña de Francia
Salamanca; 37532
Visible for miles around, the peak of La Peña de Francia (1,700 m/5,650 ft) is surmounted by a huge telecom tower and a venerable Dominican monastery – although only one friar still lives here as church warden. The peak is the site of a vision of the

black Madonna on 18 May 1434, one of dozens in Spain. A tiny grotto, into which visitors can descend, marks the site of the vision.

Drive back down, but turn right after 3.5 km (2 miles) onto the DSA352 at the Los Lobos pass, signposted to the valley town of **Monsagro**. A long, sweeping descent, with dramatic views back to La Peña, becomes a narrow road that leads to the Plaza Mayor. In the first week of September, the town hosts the Fiestas de Monsagro, a local festival, when contestants vie to climb a greasy pole and grab the ham tied to the top.

🚗 *From the Plaza Mayor, take a sharp right onto the DSA352. At Serradilla take the DSA350 for Ciudad Rodrigo, then the DSA354, then turn left onto the SA220. Arriving at Ciudad Rodrigo, drive into the old city via the Puerta de la Colada; turn right immediately. Park beside the walls of the castle.*

⓮ Ciudad Rodrigo
Salamanca; 37500
A short drive from the Portuguese border, the fortified town of Ciudad Rodrigo played a significant role in the early 19th-century Peninsular Wars, when it was a key bastion of defence against Napoleon's ambitions. As well as being replete with Napoleonic-era sites and references, the town contains some magnificent Renaissance mansions.

A two-hour walking tour
Start at the car park and walk to the **Catedral de Santa Maria** ① *(open daily)* on Avenida de Yurramendi,

opposite the tourist information office. The cathedral, founded in the 12th century, is a mix of styles, and the cloister features a series of grotesque miniature figures on the columns. A 30-minute guided visit to the 18th-century Torre de las Campanas or bell tower *(Spanish only; closed Mon)* offers great views from the belfry. Across the square the **Museo del Orinal** ② *(closed Thu)*, housed in the Casa de los Miranda, has a collection of chamber pots from all around the world. Go down Calle de los Cáceres, opposite the cathedral, to get to the Plaza del Conde. The first building of note, to the left, is the Renaissance **Palacio de los Ávila y Tiedra** ③ (also known as the Palacio de los Castro), a mansion built on monumental scale. Like the **Palacio del Conde de Alba de Yeltes** ④ (now a bank), across the square on the right, it was built in the 16th century and is privately owned. The third mansion is the **Palacio de Moctezuma** ⑤ *(open Mon–Fri)*, now the town's Casa de Cultura, with a changing programme of events.

Go back to the cathedral, turn right to climb up to the boardwalk and start walking clockwise around the city walls. For wheelchair access, start from the ramp in the Plaza de Herrasti, named for the general who was the governor of the town when it was besieged by Napoleon. On strolling down the boardwalk, visitors will come to the Romanesque **Iglesia de San Pedro y San Isidoro** ⑥ down on the Campo del Pozo. Return to the walls and stroll around the southeast corner, from where the panoramic view is particularly impressive, and walk down to street level to visit the 14th-century **Castillo de Enrique II** ⑦, now the town's parador.

Approaching the northwestern part of the wall, where the fiercest action took place when Wellington recaptured the city from Napoleon's forces, look out towards the bullring to see **four large guns** ⑧. Plaques mark the Great Breach where the walls were finally stormed. Note the pockmarks of cannon damage on the façade of the Catedral de Santa María. Descend to street level, and relax in the Plaza del Buen Alcalde, or head to the Plaza Mayor for a lunch stop. Then walk back to the car park.

Above Dominican monastery at Peña de Francia **Below** Twelfth-century Catedral de Santa María in Ciudad Rodrigo

EAT AND DRINK

CIUDAD RODRIGO

Bar Arcos *inexpensive*
Work through a variety of *raciones* in this bar and watch the world go by on the Plaza Mayor. This is also a good breakfast venue, with good *churros*.
Plaza Mayor 18, 37500; 923 480 749

Mesón El Charro *inexpensive*
This atmospheric old tavern is a reliable local favourite, with a wide choice of tapas and *raciones* on offer.
C/ Diez Taravilla 9, 37500; 923 460 005

Restaurante Mayton *moderate*
This is a cool and elegant retreat featuring exposed stonework, and serves superb fish and meat dishes. Try the *tostón* (suckling pig) with baked potatoes.
C/ Colada 7, 37500; 923 460 720; closed for dinner Sun and Mon in winter

DAY TRIP OPTIONS

Start from either Ciudad Rodrigo or Madrid to do the following day trips. The A5–E90 Carretera de Extremadura easily accesses Madrid and most other stops in this drive.

Castles in the eastern Sierra Gredos
Start the drive from Toros de Guisando ❶ through the scenic Valle del Alberche ❷ with many fine viewpoints and little villages dotting the way. Then stop by the small town of Arenas de San Pedro ❹ to see the 15th-century Castillo de Don Álvaro de Luna. From here, head to visit the castle in Mombeltrán ❺.

Follow the driving instructions in the text and bear in mind that some sections of the route are very narrow.

Monastery and walled city
The other alternative would be to drive to La Peña de Francia ⓭ to visit the Dominican monastery. Then head to Ciudad Rodrigo ⓮ for a lazy stroll, and lunch, around this Napoleonic-era site. The town is rich in architecture, with beautiful mansions scattered around it.

Return to Madrid via the A5–E90.

Eat and Drink: inexpensive, under €20; moderate, €20–€40; expensive, over €40

Roman Ruins and Unspoilt Landscapes

Trujillo to Las Hurdes

Highlights

- **Historic cities**
  Walk through the well-preserved medieval centres of Trujillo, Plasencia and Coria

- **Virgin meadows and Mediterranean forests**
  Explore the Parque Nacional de Monfragüe and see rare mammals and birds of prey

- **Rural idylls**
  Drive from village to village through rows of oak and olive trees

- **Old-world Spain**
  Visit the peaceful, pretty hamlets of Las Hurdes, a reminder of how life used to be in Spain

Panoramic view of the golden-brown city of Plasencia

Roman Ruins and Unspoilt Landscapes

Despite the baking heat and low rainfall throughout the long summer, northern Extremadura boasts regions that are wild, untamed and green, as well as rolling farmlands and mountain villages. The drive starts at Trujillo and takes visitors through the Parque Nacional de Monfragüe, which protects rare species like the European lynx and Eurasian black vulture. The tour ends at the remote villages of Las Hurdes, which lie on the steep southern flank of the Sierra de la Peña de Francia, the mountain range that separates Cáceres from Salamanca.

Above Romanesque Catedral Nueva in Plasencia, *see p168* **Top right** Salto del Gitano on the outskirts of the Parque Nacional de Monfragüe, *see p166* **Below** Ancient stone walls built by the Moors in Plasencia, *see p166*

KEY

Drive route

ACTIVITIES

Climb up to Trujillo's Moorish fortress for panoramic views of farmlands and mountains

Go hiking or biking in the Parque Nacional de Monfragüe and catch a glimpse of its rare flora and fauna

Stop for a lunch of *migas* – the regional dish of day-old bread, garlic, *pimentón* (paprika), olive oil, alfalfa and pan-fried pork ribs – in Jarandilla de la Vera

Visit the Catedral Nueva, the stunning Romanesque cathedral in Plasencia

Drive up high mountain roads to the lost world of Las Hurdes

PLAN YOUR DRIVE

Start/finish: Trujillo to Las Hurdes.

Number of days: 2–3, allowing half a day to explore Plasencia.

Distance: 310 km (190 miles).

Road conditions: Well paved and generally fairly well signposted; there are steep inclines and switch-backs around the Monasterio de Yuste and Las Hurdes.

When to go: Autumn and spring are the loveliest seasons, with notable highlights such as the cherry tree blossoms in late March in the Valle del Jerte near Plasencia; winter is often sunny and the oak-tree groves are at their greenest.

Opening hours: Shops, bars and cafés, monuments and museums are generally open from 10am to 6 or 7pm in the towns and cities; in small villages and hamlets, many shops and tourist attractions close for siesta from 3 to 5pm.

Main market days: Trujillo: Thu; Plasencia: Tue; **Coria:** Thu.

Shopping: There are several small workshops producing ceramics, silverware, gold ornaments, wooden handicrafts and local costumes in Trujillo. Cherry liqueurs and traditional Montehermoseña caps are available in Plasencia. Home-made jams and desserts are available in Coria.

Major festivals: Jarandilla de la Vera: Las Escobazos y la Encamisá, 7 Dec; **Plasencia:** Fiesta de Árbol, first Sun after Easter Sun; Martes Mayor, first Tue Aug.

DAY TRIP OPTIONS

Nature lovers will enjoy spending a day walking around Parque Nacional de Monfragüe, observing its lush flora and abundant fauna. **Families** will be enthralled by Coria and the villages of Las Hurdes, which are steeped in history. For details, *see p169.*

Above View of the Tajo as it flows through the Parque Nacional de Monfragüe **Below** Reliefs on the corner of the Palacio de los Marqueses de la Conquista *(see p174)*, Trujillo

② Torrejón el Rubio
Cáceres; 10694

This tiny hamlet has been a way station since the 13th century. It has an impressive 16th-century church, the **Iglesia de San Miguel Arcángel** *(open daily)*. As the gateway to the Parque Nacional de Monfragüe, Torrejón el Rubio gets many visitors and is a good place to stop for a snack or coffee.

🚗 *Continue on the EX208 towards Villarreal de San Carlos, which marks the entrance to the Parque Nacional de Monfragüe. Visitors can stop at the Mirador del Salto del Gitano for spectacular views of the Tajo river and of an impressive rocky pinnacle. From the viewpoint, continue on the EX208 through the national park.*

③ Parque Nacional de Monfragüe
Cáceres; 10530

Designated a national park in 2007, Monfragüe is a 200-sq-km (75-sq-mile) patch of wilderness in an otherwise intensively farmed agricultural region. The Tajo and Tiétar rivers cut in from the east with their confluence inside the park. The banks of the rivers create a deep green swathe through the heart of Extremadura. The area is noted for its importance as a breeding area for some rare and protected birds, including the black vulture, black stork, Imperial eagle and Bonelli's eagle. Monfragüe is also a habitat for one of the world's most endangered wild cats, the lynx, and it is this that led to it being upgraded from "parque natural" to "parque nacional".

Continue on the EX208 to reach Villarreal de San Carlos where there is an information centre *(open daily; 927 199 134)* for the Parque Nacional de Monfragüe. Founded in 1784, Villarreal de San Carlos is young by Extremedura standards. It is a convivial hamlet with a small church, the **Iglesia de Nuestra Señora de la Merced** *(open only for the Festividad de Mercedes on 24 Sep)* and several restaurants.

For those interested in spending a few hours exploring the park, the information centre provides walking maps, field guides and information about the weather and trail conditions. Head south on the EX208 to the **Puente del Cardenal**, constructed

① Trujillo
Cáceres; 10200

The Old Town in Trujillo *(see pp174–5)*, with its steep cobbled streets, walls and citadels, is evocative of the *reconquista*, when the Moors fought in vain against Christian attempts to recapture the town. From the Moorish fortress, at the very top of the hill on which the city is built, visitors can walk down between several medieval churches, palaces and houses dating from the 15th and 16th centuries. One of these was the home of the Pizarro family, which produced four infamous conquistadors, including Francisco Pizarro, conqueror of Peru, whose statue stands in the main plaza.

🚗 *Trujillo's traffic is controlled by a one-way system (the scheme changes at weekends) clearly marked with arrows and bollards. Follow the arrows and signs for the EX208, out of the Old Town, towards Plasencia. Follow the road for 40 km (25 miles) to reach Torrejón el Rubio.*

WHERE TO STAY

TRUJILLO

NH Palacio de Santa Marta *expensive*
Trujillo's most beautiful and best-run hotel, this boutique hotel has 50 spacious bedrooms, all stylishly modern, with king-size beds. The suites have some of the best views of the plaza.
C/ Ballesteros 6, 10200; 927 659 190; www.nh-hotels.com

Parador de Trujillo *expensive*
This charming 43-room hotel occupies part of what used to be a 16th-century convent, with breakfast served in the chapel. Rooms overlook patios and, while the main square is within easy walking distance, the parador is located up a quiet back street, so peace and quiet are assured.
Santa Beatriz de Silva 1, 10200; 927 321 350; www.parador.es

AROUND PARQUE NACIONAL DE MONFRAGÜE

Casa Rural Al-Mofrag *inexpensive*
Though built in 2006, this handsome six-bedroom property is built from local stone near the park's information office and in a style in keeping with the traditions of rural Monfragüe.
C/ Villarreal 19, 10530, Villarreal de San Carlos; 686 454 393; www. casaruralalmofrag.com

Where to Stay: inexpensive, under €70; moderate, €70–€120; expensive, over €120

in 1450 at the behest of the Bishop of Plasencia to link the towns of Trujillo and Plasencia. After crossing the bridge, the trail follows the Tajo to the main road bridge and then veers away from the riverbank to climb steeply up to the **Ermita y Castillo de Monfragüe** (open only for local festivities). The castle was built in 811 by the Moors, and the monastery was added after the Reconquest led by Alfonso VIII in 1180. Continue, following the line of the EX208 road, on to the Salto del Gitano. There are sweeping views of the Tajo river from here.

🚗 *Immediately north of Villarreal de San Carlos is a right turn onto the EX389 signposted "Saltos de Torrejón", which exits the national park. This is the back road to La Bazagona, going across the Torrejón-Tiétar dam and past many panoramic viewpoints. Ignore the right turn after La Herguijuela for Serrejón and to soon arrive at La Bazagona, a main junction for both railway and road systems. Follow the EX389 to Jaraíz de la Vera for 11 km (7 miles) before turning right onto the EX203 towards Jaraíz de la Vera and Jarandilla de la Vera.*

④ Jarandilla de la Vera

Cáceres; 10450
This charming little village is a popular stopover for lunch for those visiting the Monasterio de Yuste or setting off on walks in the nearby countryside. It merits a stroll to see a few buildings, including the grand 12th-century **Señora de la Torre** and the house of Don Luis de Quijada, tutor of Don Juan de Austria, Charles V's illegitimate son. Visitors can see remnants of the Roman presence

in a bridge and a mausoleum just outside the village. The village's one imposing building, the 15th-century **Castillo de los Condes de Oropesa**, used by Charles V for several months prior to his taking up residence in the Monasterio de Yuste, is now a parador.

🚗 *Retrace the route on the EX203 to Cuacos de Yuste and turn right onto the EX391 for the Monasterio de Yuste.*

⑤ Monasterio de Yuste

Cáceres; 10412
In 1556 Charles V retired from public life and took refuge in the Hieronymite **Monasterio de Yuste** (closed Mon). He died here two years later. The monastery's location, in the wooded Valle de la Vera, is peaceful and idyllic. The church's Gothic and Plateresque cloisters are open to the public, as is the austere palace, but some areas, including the cloisters adjacent to the mansion, are closed, as there are still a handful of monks in residence.

🚗 *Continue on the steep EX391 following signs for Garganta la Olla.*

⑥ Garganta la Olla

Cáceres; 10412
This area of Extremadura is characterized by gorges and ravines. Garganta la Olla is a tiny hamlet but is better known as the name of the neighbouring wide gorge, a popular spot for families, who picnic in the woodlands at the side of the Tiétar river and bathe in its cool waters.

🚗 *The EX391 ends in a T-junction. Turn right here. Take the left fork after Garganta onto the CC17, which goes back to the EX203. Turn right and follow the road towards Plasencia.*

Above Terrace café in Jarandilla de la Vera
Below left Gardens in Monasterio de Yuste
Below right Estatua de la Madre in Trujillo

EAT AND DRINK

TRUJILLO

Mesón La Troya *inexpensive*
The Mesón La Troya is well liked by local residents and visitors alike. Housed in a classic and very charming 16th-century *mesón* (inn), it serves hearty meals, including good *solomillos* (steaks), *migas* (the local fry-up) with pork and a range of tapas.
Plaza Mayor 10, 10200; 927 321 364

Nuria *inexpensive*
Opt for tapas or main meals from the à la carte menu on this restaurant's outdoor terrace.
Plaza Mayor 27, 10200; 927 320 907; www.hostal-nuria.com

JARANDILLA DE LA VERA

Puta Parió II *moderate*
Set in the back streets, this little restaurant is in what used to be the residence of Don Luis de Quijada, and is full of history. Downstairs is a busy little tapas bar where locals watch TV while eating tasty *tortilla*, fish and sausages. Upstairs is an intimate restaurant specializing in regional dishes, such as *migas* (breadcrumbs toasted in olive oil, garlic and paprika), exceptional tomato soup and bull's tail.
C/ Francisco Pizarro 8, 10450; 927 560 392; closed Mon

Above Ornate balcony of a house in Plasencia

VISITING PLASENCIA

Tourist Information
Oficina de Turismo, C/ Santa Clara 2,
10600; 927 423 843; www.plasencia.es

Parking
Parking is available at two locations on
Avenida del Valle.

WHERE TO STAY

PLASENCIA

Hotel Exe Alfonso VIII moderate
This modern 56-room hotel is
decorated in a contemporary style.
Avda. Alfonso VIII, 32, 10600; 927 410
250; www.hotelexealfonsoviii.com

CORIA

Hotel Sumaiya El Palacio moderate
This hotel in the old town is housed in
the 17th-century Palacio Episcopal.
Plaza de la Catedral s/n, 10800; 927
508 117; www.hotelsumaiyaelpalacio.
com

AROUND LAS HURDES

Hospedería Hurdes Reales moderate
This is a four-star, 30-room hotel, 10 km
(6 miles) from Vegas de Coria, with a
restaurant that serves typical hurdana
goat- and pork-based dishes.
Ctra. Factoria s/n, 10625; Las Mestas;
927 434 139; www.hospederiasde
extremadura.com

⑦ Plasencia
Cáceres; 10600

Plasencia was founded by King Alfonso VIII as a city-fortress in 1186, when the Jerte river was the southwestern frontier of Castile. The imposing city walls date from the end of the 12th century, and there was originally a huge Alcázar (or keep) in the northern quarter which was demolished in the 1940s. Plasencia has been an important trading hub since Roman times, due to its position on the Ruta de la Plata (Silver Route) between Seville and Gijón.

A two-hour walking tour

From the car park, walk up Calle Talavera to the **Plaza Mayor** ①, the city's main square. Many of the grand palaces, stately ancestral homes and churches are around this square. Walk across the plaza and up Calle del Rey to see the shortened tower of **La Casa de las Argollas** ②. Go back to the Plaza Mayor and up Rúa Zapatería, through the medieval quarter, till the narrow Plaza de San Vicente Ferrer. At one end of this plaza is the 15th-century **Iglesia de San Vicente Ferrer** ③, with an adjoining convent that now houses the city's beautiful parador. The north side of the square is dominated by the Renaissance **Palacio de Mirabel** ④. Try ringing the bell; if it's convenient, the owners will show you around. From the plaza, turn right into Plaza de San Nicolás. Walk across the plaza and turn left, then right into Calle Blanca. Turn right into Calle Trujillo till Plaza del Marqués de la Puebla, which houses the **Museo Etnográfico y Textil** ⑤ (closed summer: Mon & Tue; winter: Sun), in a building

that served as a hospital in the 14th century. It now has displays of local crafts and traditional costume. Continue down Calle del Obispado to reach the two cathedrals. The **Catedral Nueva** ⑥ (closed Mon), built in the 15th–16th-century, has two Plateresque façades, a Baroque organ and beautifully carved wooden choir stalls. The Romanesque **Catedral Vieja** ⑦ (closed Mon), built between the 13th and 14th centuries, houses a museum with works by the Spanish painter José de Ribera (1591–1652) and a 14th-century Bible. It acquired over the intervening centuries a Gothic nave and rose window, as well as Renaissance elements. Walk under the arch on the eastern side of the cathedral square and turn left into Avenida de Calvo Sotelo and then almost immediately right into Calle de Juan Gómez Pasajero. Walk across the crossroads into Calle de San Marcos. Continue on this road till the right turn into Paseo Caño Soso, which gives access to the **Parque de la Isla** ⑧, formed naturally by the Jerte river as it divides near the city. Perhaps the most popular of the city's green spaces, it offers good panoramic views of the cathedrals and other monuments. Retrace the route on Paseo Caño Soso till the car park.

Follow the N630 southwest from Plasencia towards Cáceres. Follow signs to Cáceres on the A66; take exit 479. Follow the EX108 until Coria, passing through farmland. Look out for the walled town of Galisteo on the right and continue westwards towards Coria.

8 Coria
Cáceres; 10800

Surrounding the old part of Coria are impressive Roman walls. Inside these is a compact labyrinth of a city, ideal for walking. At the heart of the city is the Gothic-Romanesque **Catedral de Santa María de la Asunción** *(open daily)*, built between the 15th and 18th centuries. Other key buildings are the 15th-century Convento de Madre de Dios; the Palacio Episcopal, built in 1626; the Iglesia de Santiago, dating from the 16th century; the Royal Prison, site of the **Museo de la Cárcel Real** *(closed Mon & Tue)* and, on the outskirts of town, a **Jardín Botánico** *(closed Sat & Sun)*. Coria's Castillo de los Duques de Alba, also from the 15th century, still has its keep standing.

Continue northwest on the EX109. When the road forks, turn right onto the EX204, which is the "Ruta a Las Hurdes". On the left, to the northwest, are the hills of the Sierra de Gata. Continue on the EX204 to Pinofranqueado, the gateway to Las Hurdes.

9 Las Hurdes
Cáceres; 10628

Las Hurdes' black slate mountains and lonely hamlets have a mythic quality for many Spaniards. The area was very poor, depending on goat herding and terrace farming for subsistence. In the 1950s paved roads opened up Las Hurdes on both sides of the Sierra de Gata and it is now easily accessible from Salamanca and Extremadura.

Pinofranqueado is the gateway to the region and has a camp site, several small hotels and a public swimming pool. Fifteen kilometres (9 miles) along the EX204 is Vegas de Coria, from where there is a left turn onto the CC55 for **Nuñomoral**, a popular base for walks up to Fragosa and El Gasco – also accessible by car. Eight kilometres (5 miles) to the northwest of Nuñomoral is **Casares de las Hurdes**, where visitors can see the slate from the mountains used on the roofs of many local houses.

Above View of the village wall in Galisteo

EAT AND DRINK

PLASENCIA

Succo *moderate*
Choose between two different spaces and menus: one for tapas at the front; and, for regional dishes with a modern twist, a small dining room at the back.
C/ Vidrieras 7, 10600; 927 412 932; www. restaurantesucco.es; closed Sun dinner

CORIA

Don Pedro *moderate*
This family-friendly restaurant in the Sumaiya El Palacio hotel is the place to come to explore updated *extremeño* classics and other Mediterranean fare.
Plaza de la Catedral, 10800; 927 508 117

AROUND LAS HURDES

La Posada del Casar *moderate*
In the south of Las Hurdes, this rural hotel has a cosy stone dining room where they serve traditional dishes.
C/ Mayor 36, Casar de Palomero, 10640; 927 436 410; www. laposadadelcasar.es

---

DAY TRIP OPTIONS

This drive in northern Extremadura can be broken down into two day trips, with either Trujillo (on the A5) or Coria (near the EXA1) as base.

Natural parkland

After breakfast and a morning stroll around Trujillo ➊, drive to Torrejón el Rubio ➋ to see the 16th-century Iglesia de San Miguel Arcángel. Continue to Villarreal de San Carlos, where there is an information centre for Parque Nacional de Monfragüe ➌. Spend the afternoon exploring the national park on foot; look out

for birds such as black storks, herons, European bee eaters and Azure-winged magpies, as well as deer and lizards.

From Trujillo, head northwards towards Torrejón el Rubio on the EX208. Continue to Villarreal de San Carlos and turn right onto the EX389 just north of the town to drive through the Parque Nacional de Monfragüe.

Historical villages

Start the day at the historic city of Coria ➑, and visit the imposing cathedral. Northwest of the city is a

road to Villanueva de la Sierra, where visitors can take a back road to El Bronco, Cerezo and Mohedas, before rejoining the main road at Caminomorisco. Head northeast towards Vegas de Coria, Nuñomoral and Casares de las Hurdes, villages typical of Las Hurdes ➒.

Leave Coria on the EX108. When the road forks, take the right fork onto the EX204. At Villanueva de la Sierra, turn right onto the EX205 to reach El Bronco, then join the EX204 in Vegas de Coria and the CC55 to Nuñomoral and Casares de las Hurdes.

Eat and Drink: inexpensive, under €20; moderate, €20–€40; expensive, over €40

Cities of the Conquistadors

Cáceres to Jerez de los Caballeros

Highlights

- **Medieval cities**
  Explore Cáceres, Trujillo and Guadalupe
  from where the conquistadors set out
  to explore the Americas

- **Palaces and mansions**
  Visit Trujillo's many stately mansions,
  built over centuries by Moorish and
  Christian nobles

- **Roman Lusitania**
  Walk through the impressive Roman
  ruins at Mérida, once the capital of an
  ancient Roman province

- **Little Andalusia**
  Stop by Zafra, the architectural and
  spiritual twin of Seville

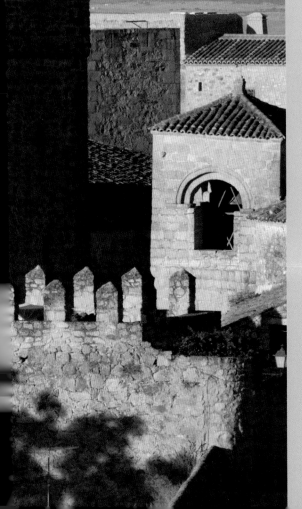

Panoramic view of the castle and walls
of Trujillo

Cities of the Conquistadors

Of all Spanish regions, Extremadura, which means "the land beyond the Duero river", is the most remote from the modern world. It was the birthplace of many conquistadors and emigrants to the New World, and some of Spain's finest Roman architecture can be seen in this region. This winding drive takes visitors from medieval Cáceres through Trujillo to Guadalupe. After a couple of hours in real backcountry, during which visitors will drive along the valley of the Guadiana river, they will arrive in Mérida, the ancient capital of the Roman province of Lusitania. Visitors will also pass through Zafra, where they can relax in one of the plazas, surrounded by Andalusian-style buildings, and then finally arrive in Jerez de los Caballeros, with its beautiful churches.

KEY

Drive route

0 kilometres 20

0 miles 20

Above View of Trujillo on the approach from Cáceres, *see p174*

ACTIVITIES

Stroll around the stunning back streets of Cáceres

Take a tour of Trujillo and see where the Pizarro brothers, the conquistadors of Peru, lived

Enjoy drinking an ice-cold sugarcane juice in Guadalupe's busy plaza

Explore the medieval town of Mérida and its impressive Roman ruins

Taste the acclaimed wines of the Guadiana region

Above left Main shopping street in Zafra, *see p177* **Above right** Façade of the Monasterio de Guadalupe, *see p175* **Below** Panoramic view of the Guadalupe valley, *see p175*

PLAN YOUR DRIVE

Start/finish: Cáceres to Jerez de los Caballeros.

Number of days: 3, allowing half a day each to explore Trujillo and Mérida.

Distance: 450 km (280 miles).

Road conditions: Well paved and generally well signposted; beyond Guadalupe, the road is somewhat narrower until it joins the N430.

When to go: Autumn and spring are very pleasant; winter is often sunny.

Opening hours: Shops, monuments and museums are generally open from 10am to 6 or 7pm in the towns and cities; in small villages and hamlets many shops and tourist attractions close for siesta between 3 and 5pm. Many attractions have shorter hours at weekends, and in winter.

Main market days: Cáceres: Wed; Trujillo: Thu; Mérida: Tue; Zafra: Sun.

Shopping: Buy high-quality Spanish shoes and cured ham from Cáceres; local cheese, honey and copper and *tilatón* (copper-zinc) ornaments from Guadalupe; Bellota ham and cheese from Zafra.

Major festivals: Cáceres: Extremúsika (Music Festival), Mar–Apr; Festival de San Jorge, 22–23 April; WOMAD (World of Music and Dance), May; Mérida: Festival de Teatro Clásico (Classical Drama Festival), Jul–Aug; Zafra: Feria de Ganado (Livestock Fair), first week Oct; Jerez de los Caballeros: La Feria del Jamón (Ham Fair), first week May.

DAY TRIP OPTIONS

History buffs will enjoy visiting Cáceres, Trujillo and Guadalupe, while **architecture lovers** will be amazed by the heritage buildings, palaces and monuments in the towns of Mérida and Zafra. For details, *see p177*.

Top View of the old city and its battlements in Cáceres **Above** Plaza in Trujillo, with Pizarro's statue in the forefront

VISITING TRUJILLO

Tourist Information
Plaza Mayor, 10200; 927 322 677;
www.turismotrujillo.com

Parking
Parking is available at Paseo Ruiz de Mendoza.

WHERE TO STAY

CÁCERES

Parador de Cáceres *expensive*
This parador is a labyrinth of patios, gardens and corridors, with tasteful decor.
C/ Ancha 6, 10003; 927 211 759;
www.parador.es

GUADALUPE

Hospedería del Real Monasterio
moderate
Guests can enjoy the Gothic courtyard and Franciscan monks' home cooking.
Plaza Juan Carlos I, 10140; 927 367 000;
www.hotelhospederiamonasterioguad
alupe.com; closed mid-Jan–mid-Feb

① Cáceres

Cáceres; 10001
The medieval town of Cáceres grew to prominence after 1227 when Alfonso IX of León conquered the region and established trade routes through northern and central Extremadura. Cáceres became a UNESCO World Heritage Site in 1986.

The Old Town is surrounded by walls built by the Almohad, 12th-century Muslim rulers and has perfectly preserved palaces, churches and residential buildings. The architecture here reflects a blend of Roman, Islamic, Northern Gothic and Renaissance styles. Old Cáceres is almost devoid of the taint of modern society and, as many of its streets are too narrow even for small cars, a morning stroll here is a tranquil affair. Most of today's serene Renaissance town dates back to the late 15th and 16th centuries, after which economic decline set in. There are several older parts, including the **Casa y Torre Carvajal**, a typical Renaissance mansion with a peaceful garden and topped by a 13th-century Arab tower, and the **Torre del Bujaco**, also a beautiful Moorish construction, dating from the 12th century. Other sights include the 15th-century **Casa y Torre de las Cigüeñas** (House and Tower of the Storks), with its crenellated tower; the **Convento de Santa Clara**, built between the 14th and 17th centuries; the **Museo Provincial** *(closed Mon)*, housed in the atmospheric Casa de las Veletas; and the **Palacio de los Golfines de Abajo**, which melds Gothic, Mudéjar and the ornate Plateresque styles and features a battlemented façade. The **Plaza de Santa María**, framed by beautiful palaces and the Iglesia de Santa María, is the hub of Old Town life.

🚗 *Leave town heading eastwards on the N521 and the A58 following signs to Trujillo. Parking is available at Paseo Ruiz de Mendoza.*

② Trujillo

Cáceres; 10200
Trujillo is an elegant, tranquil medieval city with some impressive architecture. It was the birthplace of several conquistadors, most notably Francisco Pizarro, who conquered Peru; Francisco de Orellana, the first European to sail up the Amazon river; and Gaspar de Rodas, the first governor of Antioquia, Colombia. Grandiose statues, quirky museums and fascinating bas-reliefs remind visitors of the town's connection to the Americas.

A 90-minute walking tour

From the car park walk northeast and turn left into Calle de los Herreros and then straight into Calle de las Tiendas into the **Plaza Mayor** ①, a beautiful sight in the morning, when there is likely to be no traffic and very few pedestrians, or at night, when floodlights illuminate the surrounding buildings. On all four sides, and on several of the adjoining streets, are escutcheoned palaces and mansions, some of which have been converted into restaurants and shops.

Overlooking the plaza is the **Iglesia de San Martín** ②, built in the 16th century, with its two lichen-covered bell towers. In front of the main door of the church stands an imposing

Bell tower in Iglesia de San Martín

equestrian bronze statue of Pizarro, the work of the American sculptor Charles Rumsey. Walk clockwise around the plaza from the base of the statue, taking in the Renaissance-style **Palacio de San Carlos** ③ *(closed to the public)* on the northeast corner. The **Palacio de los Marqueses de Piedras Albas** ④, a Gothic mansion with a Renaissance gallery, is at the southeast corner of the plaza. However, the most impressive building is the Plateresque **Palacio de la Conquista** ⑤, located towards the southwest corner. It has the magnificent coat of arms of the Pizarro family over the window. Directly opposite is the **Casa de las Cadenas** ⑥, seat of the Chaves-Orellana family. Head for the stairs between the statue of Pizarro and the church and turn left onto Calle de los Ballesteros to reach the **Torre del Alfiler** ⑦ (Needle Tower), decorated with tiles from the town of Talavera de la Reina. Continue on Calle de los Ballesteros, heading past the NH hotel, another beautiful palace now converted into a stylish boutique hotel, to reach the **Puerta de Santiago** ⑧, a gate into the oldest part of the city. Straight ahead, on Calle de Santa María, is a stonewalled church, the **Iglesia de Santa María la Mayor** ⑨, facing the **Palacio de Pizarro-Hinojosa** ⑩.

Turn left, then right into Calle de Santa María and then right into Calle de la Puerta de Coria to reach the **Museo de la Coria** ⑪ *(open Sat & Sun mornings)*, a former convent full of didactic but lively displays on the archaeology, history, cuisine and culture of the New World. Turn left to reach the **Casa Museo de Pizarro** ⑫, full of artifacts relating to the life of the conquistador and to everyday life in the 15th and 16th centuries. From here take the inclined Calle del Castillo to the **Castillo y Murallas** ⑬, built in Moorish times on the remains of a Roman fort. Retrace the route back to the car park in Paseo Ruiz de Mendoza.

🖬 *Take the EX208 southeast out of Trujillo. At Zorita, turn left onto the EX102 and then left again onto the EX380 to Guadalupe.*

❸ Guadalupe
Cáceres; 10140
The village of Guadalupe grew around the Hieronymite **Monasterio de Guadalupe**, founded in 1340, which harbours an image of the Virgin Mary, discovered here in the early 14th century. The exterior of the main building is a mix of Gothic, Mudéjar and Plateresque styles. In the main square there are shops that sell traditional monastic crafts.

🖬 *Retrace the route to the EX102 and follow it eastwards past Alía. Turn right onto the CC151, which becomes the BA49 across the provincial border. Turn right at Castilblanco onto the N502 and follow the road as it veers southwards. Turn right into Herrera del Duque town centre, and follow the brown signs indicating "Peloche" onto the BA138. Fork right and then turn left after the dam. Follow Mérida signs on the N430 and A5.*

Above left Beautiful interior of the monastery in Guadalupe **Above right** Ruins of the Castillo y Murallas in Trujillo

EAT AND DRINK

CÁCERES
Atrio expensive
A contemporary take on Spanish cuisine has won Atrio two Michelin stars.
Plaza de San Mateo, 10002; 927 242 928; www.restauranteatrio.com

TRUJILLO
La Cadena inexpensive
This typical *mesón* on the main square of Trujillo serves up hearty portions of regional food.
Plaza Mayor 5, 10200; 927 321 463; www.mesonhostallacadena.es

GUADALUPE
Posada del Rincón moderate
Find traditional cuisine with creative touches here, right by the monastery.
Plaza de Santa Maria de Guadalupe 11, 10140; 927 367 114; www.posadadel rincon.com; closed Tue

Above Teatro Romano in Mérida **Below left** Puerta de Jerez in Zafra **Below right** Road approaching the Old Wall in Mérida

VISITING MÉRIDA

Tourist Information
Paseo José Álvarez de Buruaga, 06800; 924 330 722; www.turismomerida.org

Parking
Parking is in Calle de las Atarazanas and in Calle Cabo Verde.

WHERE TO STAY

MÉRIDA

Bluecity Mérida Palace moderate
Housed in a pair of elegant palaces, this hotel maintains a regal atmosphere and has all modern conveniences.
Plaza España 19, 06800; 924 383 800; www.bluebayresorts.com

ZAFRA

Huerta Honda moderate
The Huerta Honda is stylish, yet traditional, and has chic rooms that are extremely comfortable.
Avda. López Asme 30, 06300; 924 554 100; www.hotelhuertahonda.com

Parador de Zafra expensive
Also known as the Hotel Duque de Feria, this parador occupies a majestic 15th-century castle. The rooms here are elegant and spacious.
Plaza Corazón de María 7, 06300; 924 554 540; www.parador.es

❹ Mérida
Badajoz; 06800

Founded by Augustus in 25 BC, Mérida, then known as Emerita Augusta, grew into the cultural and economic capital of Lusitania, Rome's westernmost province. The city, however, lost its eminence under the Moors. Though a small city, Mérida has many fine Roman monuments. Now the capital of Extremadura and a UNESCO World Heritage Site, it has a Roman amphitheatre and theatre, aqueduct, circus and temples. The best approach to the town is via the Puente de Guadiana that leads to the original entrance of the Roman city.

The most concentrated set of ruins is to the west of the city, where a tiny gateway provides access to the huge **Teatro Romano** and **Anfiteatro**. The amphitheatre was used mainly for displays of gladiatorial combat with condemned prisoners, servants and paid soldiers taking on each other as well as wild animals, but the fossa arenaia (the depression at the centre of the arena) could also be water-proofed or flooded with water for spectacles. The theatre was built in 16–15 BC and is one of the best preserved Roman theatres in the world. Seating in this venue was determined by one's status in society – the orchestra pit was reserved for those of the highest class, senators and officials, while the top rows were for slaves and the poor. The theatre is still used for performances and is at its most magnificent when hosting the Festival de Teatro Clásico de Mérida, an annual classical theatre festival, in June and July.

Mérida's **Museo Nacional de Arte Romano** (closed Mon), just north of the theatre, is one of the most stunning museums in Europe, boasting

Bronze statue at Mérida's theatre

large collections of coins, sculptures, ceramics and mosaics. Opened in 1986 and designed by renowned Spanish architect Rafael Moneo (b. 1937), the museum building is a marvel in itself – the low lights and plain decor create a calming environ-ment, enhancing the displays.

In the city centre are the 1st-century-BC **Templo de Diana** at Romero Leal and the beautiful **Arco de Trajano** at the northern end of Calle Trajano. The **Museo de Arte Visigodo** (closed Mon) is in the Convento de Santa Clara, which is situated off the main square. The **Iglesia de Santa Eulalia**, built in the 5th century during the reign of Constantine in honour of the city's patron saint, is located on the north side of the city. St Eulalia, martyred during the Roman era, is believed to have been buried here along with several clerics.

Spain's oldest Moorish building, the **Alcazaba de Mérida** (open daily), which has towers, a cistern and Roman ruins, overlooks the Guadiana river and the Roman bridge over it. One in a series of fortresses along the

Christian border with Islamic Spain, it served both the Moors and the Christians as a stronghold.

🚗 *Leave town heading southwards on the A66. Turn left on the N630 at exit 675 towards Los Santos de Maimona. Just before entering the town, fork right onto the EX101 to Zafra.*

❺ Zafra
Badajoz; 06300
Just west of the main highway in the south, Zafra is a white-walled town of pastel-coloured houses, decorated with window boxes brimming over with flowers. At the heart of this convivial town, nickamed "little Seville" because of its Moorish character, are two arcaded squares. The large central square, the 16th-century **Plaza Grande**, is located near the Iglesia Nuestra Señora de la Candelaria. On its far corner is the **Plaza Chica**, the old square. Once a bustling marketplace, it is now a calm, intimate square with a handful of small restaurants around it.

The largest church in town is the Gothic-Renaissance Iglesia Nuestra Señora de la Candelaria. It has nine panels painted by Francisco Zurbarán (1598–1664) on the retable in a chapel designed by the Spanish architect and sculptor José Benito de Churriguera (1665–1725). The 1457 **Alcázar de los Duques de Feria**, which boasts a spectacular façade, beautiful coffered ceilings and a 16th-century Herreran patio, is now a government-run parador.

🚗 *Exit the town on the EX320 following signs to Salvatierra de los Barros and Barcarrota. At Barcarrota, turn left onto the N435 which leads straight to Jerez de los Caballeros.*

❻ Jerez de los Caballeros
Badajoz; 06380
Set on a hillside, with its profile broken by three Baroque church towers, Jerez de los Caballeros is one of Extremadura's most picturesque towns. This small town is also historically important – Vasco Núñez de Balboa, who "discovered" the Pacific, was born here in 1475. The old quarters of the town are centred around the three churches – **San Bartolomé, San Miguel** and the **Santa María de la Encarnación**. Social life in Jerez de los Caballeros, however, revolves around the plaza and the bullring.

Above View of the Alcázar de los Duques de Feria in Zafra **Below** Arched Plaza Chica in Zafra

VISITING ZAFRA

Parking
Parking in the old city of Zafra is difficult unless visitors are staying at the parador, so park in one of the bays around the edges of the wall.

EAT AND DRINK

MÉRIDA

Tabula Calda *moderate*
Elegant Slow Food restaurant that uses its own home-grown organic produce to create Extremaduran dishes with a Sephardic Jewish influence.
C/ Romero Leal 11, 06800; 924 304 950; www.tabulacalda.com

ZAFRA

La Rebotica *moderate*
A romantic restaurant with each table inside an arched alcove, specializing in local dishes like *rabo de toro* (oxtail stew) and *higos en salsa de coñac* (figs in cognac sauce), and desserts.
C/ Boticas 12, 06300; 924 554 289; closed Sun dinner and Mon

DAY TRIP OPTIONS
The drive can be divided into two short trips, with either Cáceres (on the N521) or Mérida (on the A66) as a base.

Heritage cities
Start the day with breakfast and a slow walk around Cáceres ❶, a UNESCO World Heritage Site and a beautiful city, famous for its storks. Head east to Trujillo ❷, another impressive historic town that is the birthplace of Francisco Pizarro,

Francisco de Orellana and other famous conquistadors. End the day at Guadalupe ❸, famous for its Monasterio de Guadalupe which houses a 14th-century image of the Virgin Mary. The town is also home to some excellent restaurants.

Take the N521 from Cáceres following signs for Trujillo. Park in Trujillo's new town as the historic centre is a labyrinth and there is very limited parking with narrow roads lined by high walls. From Trujillo, take the

quiet EX208 southeast, then the EX102 northeast to Guadalupe.

Roman roads
Mérida ❹ was once the capital of Lusitania and is now a UNESCO World Heritage Site worth a morning's exploration. In the afternoon, head to Zafra ❺, where Extremeño and Andaluz cultures are blended in the architecture and local cuisine.

From Mérida, take the A66 southwards to Zafra.

Don Quixote's La Mancha

Puerto Lápice to Consuegra

Highlights

- **Gem-like towns**
  Visit some of Spain's most beautiful old towns, immortalized by Cervantes

- **Unusual discoveries**
  Surprise yourself in La Mancha's hills and woods

- **Wetland habitats**
  Pack a pair of binoculars to catch the rich birdlife of the Parque Natural de Lagunas de Ruidera

- **Castle-monastery**
  Explore the Castillo de Calatrava la Nueva, perched on a craggy summit

A spectacular view of the windmills of Consuegra in La Mancha

Don Quixote's La Mancha

South of Madrid, La Mancha (from *manza*, meaning "parched earth" in Arabic) seems arid and inhospitable from the motorway. Get off the *autovía* and onto the best regional roads in Spain to discover the reality of the Manchegan countryside – rolling wheat fields and stunning sunsets, white windmills and jewel-like lakes. Try wines from the biggest vineyard in the world, and look out for reminders, everywhere, of Spain's most famous literary creations, Don Quixote and Sancho Panza.

Above Fifteenth-century Santuario de Nuestra Señora de Las Virtudes, *see p184*

ACTIVITIES

Explore the windmills at Campo de Criptana before lazing over lunch

Go birdwatching at dawn and have a late breakfast followed by a swim in Laguna Concejo

Park the car and go walking to Castillo de Rochafrida and Don Quixote's Cueva de Montesinos

Have a night out at the theatre in Almagro's Corral de Comedias

KEY

🟦 Drive route

Top Church of San Carlos del Valle, near Villanueva de los Infantes, *see p184*
Right Vineyards rolling across the Manchegan landscape, *see p184*

PLAN YOUR DRIVE

Start/finish: Puerto Lápice to Consuegra.

Number of days: 3–4, allowing half a day to explore the Parque Natural de las Lagunas de Ruidera.

Distance: 400 km (250 miles).

Road conditions: Nearly all the roads are excellent in the region. Some ice is possible in winter.

When to go: Summer is extremely hot. Spring and autumn can be delightful, with warm, sunny days and cool nights.

Opening hours: Most monuments are open from 9:30am to 2pm and from 5pm to 8pm. Many of them are closed on Mondays.

Main market days: Campo de Criptana: Tue; Villanueva de los Infantes: Fri; Almagro: Wed; Consuegra: Sat.

Major festivals: Campo de Criptana: Virgen de Criptana, Easter Mon; Almagro: Festival Internacional de Teatro Clasico, Jul.

DAY TRIP OPTIONS

Don Quixote enthusiasts should visit Puerto Lápice, after which they can head to Campo de Criptana to see the windmills. **History buffs** could spend a day visiting a bullring, a Renaissance palace and a medieval castle in Las Virtudes, Viso del Marqués and Calzada de Calatrava. For details, *see p187*.

VISITING PUERTO LÁPICE

Start the tour through Quixotic Spain by taking the Madrid–Seville highway (Autovía del Sur), A4-E5 and leaving at Puerto Lápice (exit 134).

WHERE TO STAY

PUERTO LÁPICE

Hotel El Puerto *inexpensive*
This is a very decent, motel-style accommodation with a bar-restaurant.
Avda. Juan Carlos I, 59, 13650; 926 583 050; www.hotelpuertolapice.es

PARQUE NATURAL DE LAS LAGUNAS DE RUIDERA

Hotel Albamanjón *expensive*
Opened in the late 1970s, this delightful boutique hotel nestled on the shore of Laguna San Pedro offers a range of rooms, each with its own patio, terraced on the hillside behind the main house. It has an excellent restaurant and café.
Lagunas de San Pedro 16, 02611, Ossa de Montiel; 926 699 048; www.albamanjon.net

AROUND PARQUE NATURAL DE LAS LAGUNAS DE RUIDERA

Hotel Restaurante Entrelagos *inexpensive*
A lakefront hotel, (1 km/0.6 miles south of Ruidera along the lakeshore road) catering mostly to weekending Madrileños and bird-watchers. The rooms here are reasonably spacious and comfortable.
Ctra. de las Lagunas, Km 1, Entrelagos, 13249, Ruidera; 926 528 022; www. entrelagos.com

Top left Statue of Don Quixote in Puerto Lápice **Top right** Lake Concejo in Parque Natural de las Lagunas de Ruidera **Above** Windmills scattered across the rocky hillside of Campo de Criptana **Below** Fishing in the crystal-clear lakes in Ruidera

❶ Puerto Lápice
Ciudad Real; 13650

Sleepy Puerto Lápice was immortalized by Cervantes' novel. The **Venta del Quijote**, the sprawling inn at this one-street farming town below the low hills of the Montes de Toledo, claims to have been the model for the inn mistaken by Don Quixote for a castle at the very beginning of his adventures. The cobbled courtyard where Quixote was "knighted" by the landlord is always busy with tour groups, but the inn's terraces and basement make for a cool hideaway.

🚗 *From the Venta del Quijote, drive to the town's colonnaded Plaza Mayor, then turn right, signposted "Cuenca N420". Follow this road around Alcázar de San Juan to Campo de Criptana. Entering the town, follow signs for "Molinos". Go straight at the Don Quixote roundabout. Turn left before the Repsol station and left again at the sign for Sierra de los Molinos. Follow the blue signs. Park by the windmills.*

❷ Campo de Criptana
Ciudad Real; 13610

The prettily whitewashed old Moorish quarter of town, the Albaicín Criptano, spreads out beneath 13 windmills on the rocky hillside, of which 10 have been restored (out of an original group of 32, the largest concentration in the region). This is the site of Don Quixote's "terrifying and never-to-be-imagined Adventure of the Windmills", in which the knight jousts with a whirling sail and is flung off his horse. Visit the tourist office *(open daily, am only Sun & Mon)*, located in Molino Poyatos, for information on visits to the restored **Molino Infante** and **Molino Culebro** *(irregular opening hours)*.

🚗 *From the town centre, follow signs for Ciudad Real, then at the lights on the Don Quixote roundabout get onto the CR1222, signposted to Arenales de San Gregorio. At the railway crossing turn left before the tracks. Go over the railway bridge, through Arenales, and turn right for Tomelloso on the CM3103. Join the CM3102 and bypass Tomelloso for Argamasilla de Alba on the N310. On the outskirts of Argamasilla, turn left, signed "CM3115 Lagunas de Ruidera". At the T-junction in Ruidera town, turn right and climb the hill and turn left, following signs for Lagunas de Ruidera. Follow the lakeshore road and turn left at the Hotel Albamanjon sign. Past the hotel there is a picnic spot under a stand of Lombardy poplars. About 1 km (0.6 miles) beyond the poplars there is a tiny church. Park here.*

❸ Parque Natural de las Lagunas de Ruidera
Ciudad Real; 13249 and Albacete; 02611

The Parque Natural de las Lagunas de Ruidera is one of the largest natural wetland areas in central Spain. Comprising a chain of 15 lakes, the area is naturally wooded and a significant refuge for a large number of birds, as well as other fauna and flora. Start the walk early to avoid crowds and see the lakes and wildlife at their best.

A three-hour walking tour
From the parking near **Ermita de San Pedro de Verona** ①, walk down to a Y-junction with wooden signs. Take the Pie de Enmedio trail on the left and follow the green arrows, leading across the valley and up over the hill, southwards. The footpath winds to the crest of the ridge, from where there are panoramic views, and then loops down to the shore of **Laguna Concejo** ②. Concejo is considered the best faunal area in the lake chain. Spend some time pottering along the marshy shoreline trail – here an unmade road – and observing the birds and other wildlife. Look out for ospreys fishing over the lake, harmless viperine snakes at the water's edge, azure-winged magpies in colourful flocks (brought to Spain from China by sailors in the16th century) and, if lucky at dawn, a wild boar or a genet.

After 2 km (1 mile) of following the shore of the lake, turn east and follow the trail a further 2 km (1 mile)

through fields towards the hills. At the T-junction signposted "Ruta de Don Quijote", turn left along the trail. Then, before the small bridge, turn left and walk down the track into the poplars. Follow the footpath round to the left until the signpost indicating "Subida al Castillo", which leads up to the ruins of the medieval **Castillo de Rochafrida** ③. Retrace the path to the main trail and turn left to walk back to the car. Visitors with time can walk, 2 km (1 mile) up the road from the church, to the **Cueva de Montesinos** ④ – the limestone cave that features in Book II of *Don Quixote* – up on the plateau. Look out for great and little bustards in the scrub.

🚗 *Take the CR650/AB650 back to the N430 in the direction of Manzanares, turning left after 15 km (9 miles) for Villanueva de los Infantes (CM3129). In town, follow "Centro Urbano" signs and turn left in Plaza Santisima Trinidad. Drive up, then turn left into Plaza Mayor. Park outside the square.*

Top Ruins of a medieval castle in Ruidera **Above** Renowned Venta del Quijote in Puerto Lápice

VISITING PARQUE NATURAL DE LAS LAGUNAS DE RUIDERA

Tourist Information
Centro de Recepción, Avda. Castilla–La Mancha, 13249; 926 528 116; www.lagunasderuidera.es; closed Mon & Tue and Dec–Feb: Mon–Fri

Parking
Park near the Ermita de San Pedro de Verona.

EAT AND DRINK

PUERTO LÁPICE

Venta del Quijote *inexpensive*
A popular and busy pub, tapas bar and full-blown restaurant, this place offers a good choice of *raciones* and full meals.
El Molino 4, 13650; 926 576 110, www.ventadelquijote.com

CAMPO DE CRIPTANA

Las Musas *moderate*
This top-notch restaurant on the hillside by the windmills has fine views of the old quarter of town. Try the cod or roast lamb.
C/ Barbero 3, 13610; 926 589 191; www.lasmusasrestaurante.com

PARQUE NATURAL DE LAS LAGUNAS DE RUIDERA

Restaurante Albamanjón *moderate*
With its idyllic setting, the Albamanjón is a wonderful lunch or dinner venue. Try their game stews or slow roast lamb.
Lagunas de San Pedro 16, 02611, Ossa de Montiel; 926 699 048; www.albamanjon.net

Eat and Drink: inexpensive, under €20; moderate, €20–€40; expensive, over €40

Above Patio in the Santa Cruz palace at Viso del Marqués **Below** Bronze statues of Don Quixote and Sancho Panza in the square in Villanueva de los Infantes

WHERE TO STAY

VISO DEL MARQUÉS

Hospedería la Almazara del Marqués *moderate*
Palatial style in keeping with its location, this hotel has an austere exterior but a very pleasant interior, with cool public areas and 18 large rooms.
C/ Almagro s/n, 13770; 926 337 154; www.hospederialaalmazara.com

AROUND CASTILLO DE CALATRAVA DE LA NUEVA

Hostal las Palomas I *inexpensive*
Friendly enough, with very reasonable, clean, air-conditioned rooms above the busy bar, this place is located on one of Calzada de Calatrava's two main streets. Seafood-based *comedor* (dining room) at the back.
C/ Cervantes 10, 13370, Calzada de Calatrava; 926 876 852; www.hostallaspalomas.com

④ Villanueva de los Infantes
Ciudad Real; 13320
This small Manchegan town has a magnificent Neo-Classical arcaded Plaza Mayor, with the splendid **Iglesia de San Andrés** on its north side and wooden-balconied houses lining its south. Villanueva has a strong claim to be Cervantes' model for the hometown of Don Quixote and there are evocative modern bronzes of Don Quixote and Sancho Panza, with their animals, in the square. Just off the square, west of the church is the 16th-century **Alhóndiga**, the old corn exchange, now the Casa de Cultura. The town is full of beautiful architecture – details are available at the tourist office *(closed Sun pm)*, off the east side of the square.

🚗 *Exit Plaza Mayor on the one-way street and, at the roundabout, take the exit signposted Montiel on the CM3127. Turn right at the crossroads, signposted Cózar on the CM3129. Follow the CM3129 to Torre de Juan Abad. Turn sharp right for Castellar de Santiago on the CM3200. After 11 km (7 miles) from Castellar, turn right on the rough CR6102 towards Las Virtudes. In Las Virtudes, park outside the bullring on the left.*

⑤ Las Virtudes
Ciudad Real; 13730
The extraordinary 17th-century **Plaza de Toros** and the adjoining 15th-century **Santuario de Nuestra Señora de las Virtudes** *(no official opening hours)* are the only sights in tiny Las Virtudes. The square **Plaza de Toros** (bullring), which dates from 1645, is vibrant, with red-painted woodwork, stone walls and orange sand. Bullfights are very occasionally staged here between late April and early September. The Santuario de Nuestra Señora de las Virtudes contains some of the finest Baroque frescoes in the region, many of them bearing influences from those in the palace in Viso del Marqués *(see p185)*.

🚗 *Leave Las Virtudes on the CR6102 until it meets the A4-E5 highway. Turn right (towards Madrid) and take exit 217 to head for Santa Cruz de Mudela. Go straight on the main street until it forks. Take the left fork and turn right twice. Get onto Calle Gloria to find Bodegas Antonio Cañaveras.*

⑥ Bodegas Antonio Cañaveras
Ciudad Real; 13730
The vineyards of La Mancha, centred on the region's wine capital, Valdepeñas, amount to more than 2,000 sq km (775 sq miles) and produce half the country's output of wine. They are locally known as "the world's biggest vineyard". Although historically viewed as a source for blending both white and red grapes, wines from *Denominación de Origens* La Mancha and D.O. Valdepeñas have been well reviewed since the 1980s. Stop to taste and buy wine at the Bodega Antonio Cañaveras *(C/ Gloria 42, Santa Cruz de Mudela; 629 739 298)*.

🚗 *Return to the A4-E5 and head south. Exit at junction 223 for Bazán and fork right. At Bazán, turn left on the CR5226 to Viso del Marqués. In the village, park outside the main square.*

⑦ Viso del Marqués

Ciudad Real; 13770

The Renaissance palace of Viso del Marqués completely dominates this little town. Everything about the palace *(closed Mon, Sun pm; open mornings only Jul–Aug)* is built on a huge scale. Commissioned by the Marquis of Santa Cruz in 1564 and constructed by Italian architects and artists between 1574 and 1588, it contains many vivid frescoes and a Classical patio. The palace is also home to Spain's national maritime archives. Facing the palace is the exceptionally pretty Plaza Mayor, full of greenery, a splashing fountain and noisy birdlife. For visitors without picnic supplies, the **Los Leones** restaurant is a good place to stop by.

🚗 *Follow the CM4111 to Calzada de Calatrava and turn left after 26 km (16 miles). The road leads to the centre of Calzada de Calatrava, one block south of Plaza Mayor. Follow signs to Guardia Civil and Parque Reina Sofia (public gardens) and after passing them, leave town on a road signposted to Villanueva de San Carlos. At the huge Junction, take the direction signposted CR504 for Puertollano. The castle will be on the horizon.*

⑧ Castillo de Calatrava la Nueva

Ciudad Real; 13370

This brooding castle-monastery *(closed Mon, also Sun afternoon Oct–Mar; be careful of steep stairs and unguarded drops)*, perched on a craggy summit, was founded in 1217 by an order of Cistercian soldier-monks in the vanguard of the Reconquest of Spain. These monks, the Knights of Calatrava, were Spain's first military-religious order. Particularly impressive is the Cistercian church; in this

remote and hostile location, its construction was a remarkable feat and, although empty inside, it is still beautiful. The ruins of **Salvatierra**, the Muslim castle captured by the Calatrava knights in the 12th century, is visible across the valley, but not accessible by road. Visitors can walk to the site, but it has no facilities. The drive from the castle towards Almagro is a good opportunity to see waterfowl, and there are usually lots of storks here, especially near the bridge over the Jabalon river.

🚗 *From the castle, return towards Calzada de Calatrava, but use the bypass, towards Ciudad Real. At the roundabout, turn right into Calzada, then left at the petrol station, signposted "Almagro" on the CM4129, which becomes the CM413. In Almagro, the parador (with free parking) is signposted left. Otherwise, turn right (signed) to the car park behind the church, Iglesia Madre de Dios.*

Above left Seventeenth-century square bullring of Las Virtudes **Above right** Rose window above the entrance to the church in the Castillo de Calatrava **Below** View from the remote Castillo de Calatrava, perched on a mighty crag

EAT AND DRINK

VISO DEL MARQUÉS

Restaurante Los Leones *moderate*
This informal, family-run restaurant on Plaza Mayor offers good Castillian cuisine, big on local meat and vegetables. Eat at tables in the square, or in the dining room at the back.
Plaza del Pradillo 7, 13770; 926 336 098; www.mesonlosleones.es; closed Wed

WHERE TO STAY

ALMAGRO

La Casa del Rector *expensive*
Adjoining an 18th-century courtyard
with a ceramic-tiled floor, this avant-
garde hotel offers spacious rooms,
terraces, a spa and a restaurant serving
delicious regional dishes.
*C/Pedro Oviedo 8, 13270; 926 261 259;
www.lacasadelrector.com; closed 24 Dec*

Parador de Almagro *expensive*
A converted 16th-century convent in
the old town, this is a good example of
the Parador group. It is full of antique
furniture, with 54 large rooms.
*Ronda de San Francisco 31, 13270;
926 860 100; www.parador.es*

CONSUEGRA

La Vida de Antes *moderate*
A perennially popular, small, family-run
hotel, mixing old-style decor with
modern comforts and offering an
exceptionally restful ambience.
*C/ Colón 2, 45700; 925 480 609;
www.lavidadeantes.com*

Above Shady colonnades in Plaza Mayor in
Almagro **Below** Raised wooden boardwalk
through the scenic wetlands of Daimiel

⑨ Almagro
Ciudad Real; 13270

This pretty town, one of the richest
in Spain in the 16th century, has the
largest and finest Plaza Mayor in La
Mancha, featuring green window
frames above the colonnades. On
its south side, the fascinating
16th-century open-air theatre, the
Corral de Comedias *(open daily,
closed 1 or 2–5pm)*, is the focus
of Almagro's annual, major
theatre festival. Most of the
town's other notable sites are
a five-minute walk from here,
including some superb
Renaissance mansions. Visit
the **Almacén de los Fúcares**,
the 16th-century home and
business house of the Fugger
family of Germany – bankers to

**Ornate knocker of a
mansion in Almagro**

Charles V (1500–58). The **Museo Etnográfico** *(closed Mon)* displays traditional
local crafts and practices. The tourist
office is on Ejido de Calatrava, next to
the bus station *(closed Mon)*.

🚗 *Leave the Old Town car park and
drive around the ring road until the
major roundabout on the east side of
town by the Hospedería de
Almagro convent. Exit on the
road signposted "CM4124
Daimiel". In Bolaños de
Calatrava, follow the
CM4107, which makes a
sharp left. At the round-
about on the Daimiel
bypass, turn right and
drive 3 km (2 miles) before
turning left again onto the
CR201, which becomes the
CR2012, for Villarrubia de los Ojos.*

The Dry Marshes of Daimiel

The town of Daimiel is the access
point for the Parque Nacional de las
Tablas de Daimiel *(926 693 118;
www.lastablasdedaimiel.com)*,
whose marshlands were formed by
the confluence of the Cigüela and
upper Guadiana rivers. Parts of the
marshlands that had been dry since
the late 1980s have completely
recovered in the last few years. In
winter, the marshes attract some
migrant birds. For the best birdwatching opportunities, arrive early
in the morning. The park has trails
incorporating attractive wooden
boardwalks linking the islands via
dry reedbeds and stretches of
shallow water; a good stop for
drivers. Allow 90 minutes for the
2-km (1-mile) Isla del Pan trail,
marked in yellow.

Where to Stay: inexpensive, under €70; moderate, €70–€120; expensive, over €120

Spain's Golden Age of Theatre

Almagro's Corral de Comedias survives in its original form from the early 17th century, a period when public theatre first flourished in Castille, fed by the prolific output of Spain's Shakespeare, Félix Lope de Vega, and his successor, Pedro Calderón de la Barca. Both playwrights put their plots centre stage, and brought new relevance to old tales by creating characters that their enthusiastic audiences could believe in.

⑩ Villarrubia de los Ojos

Ciudad Real; 13670

A small agricultural centre, well off the tourist track, Villarrubia de los Ojos lies at the foot of the Sierra de Villarrubia, part of the Montes de Toledo. It is worth stopping to see the sculptures of vineyard workers, at two roundabouts, movingly executed in rough wood by local carpenter and artist Valentín Rodríguez Camacho (www.carpinteria-rustica. com). The inscription on the town centre sculpture translates: "To the workers of Villarrubia and all those who have left their land to bring dignity to their lives elsewhere".

To the north of the town, the road twists into the hills over the pass of **Puerto de los Santos** (970 m/3,200 ft), where lynx are said to survive, and then drops through a beautiful rolling rural landscape of wheatfields, oak and thistle.

🚗 *From the town centre sculpture roundabout, take the CR200/CM3268 north, direction Urda, then take the CM4116 to Consuegra. On the way into Consuegra, past the bullring, turn right to climb the hill of windmills. Park outside the tourist office.*

⑪ Consuegra

Toledo; 45700

Consuegra, founded by the Romans, is famous for its photogenic ridge of 12 windmills, one of which serves as the town's tourist office (open daily). It is an easy 15-minute walk to the southern end of the ridge for wonderful panoramic views. En route is the originally Moorish castle (open daily), which makes a perfect short visit, with plenty of rooms and walkways to explore and views (beware of unguarded drops). The same ticket gives access to the museum located on the town's Plaza Mayor in the 17th-century **Corredores** (former town hall). Just outside town, the dead-straight 700-m (2,300-ft) stone wall across the fields is the **Presa Romana**, a Roman dam. To get to the dam, take the road to Urda past the bullring, then turn left at the blue house with the tyres and follow the track for 2 km (1 mile).

Above Moorish castle in Consuegra **Below** Façade of a superb Renaissance mansion in Almagro

SHOPPING

ALMAGRO

Manzano Gracia
Stop here for lacework made on the premises or locally, including embroidered items, bedspreads and curtains. *C/ Gran Maestre 3 (ring the bell), 13270; 926 882 487; www. encajesalmagro.com*

EAT AND DRINK

ALMAGRO

Bar Donde Sea *moderate*
A variety of generous free tapas, served with beers and wines, makes Donde Sea a reliable standby. Try the *queso manchego* (Spanish sheep cheese). *Plaza Mayor (south side, near the Corral de Comedias), 13270*

Méson El Corregidor *expensive*
This restaurant is located in a smart 19th-century family house with a variety of dining areas, and serves dishes which innovate on local traditions. Try the spinach and garlic cod, or one of the aubergine dishes. *C/ Jerónimo Ceballos 2, 13270; 926 860 648; www.elcorregidor.com; closed Mon and Tue*

DAY TRIP OPTIONS

With a base in Puerto Lápice and using the N420 and the A4E5, one day could be spent visiting the windmills and another day at the palace at Viso del Marqués and the bullring in Las Virtudes.

Quixotic Spain and windmills
Start the day in the sleepy town of Puerto Lápice ①, visiting the cobbled courtyard where Quixote was "knighted" by the landlord. Then head to the whitewashed old Moorish quarter of Campo de Criptana ②, before taking a stroll among the windmills.

Follow directions in the itinerary starting from Puerto Lápice and return on the same route.

Bullrings, palaces and castles
Visit the 15th-century Sanctuary of Las Virtudes ⑤ in Santa Cruz de Mudela, which contains some of the finest frescoes in the region, and the 17th-century bullring. Then head to the palace of Viso del Marqués ⑦. If visitors have time, they can go a little further to the Castillo de Calatrava la Nueva ⑧.

Drive 80 km (50 miles) south of Puerto Lápice at junction 220 of the A4-E5, and from there visit Las Virtudes. Follow instructions in the itinerary to Viso del Marqués and to Calatrava la Nueva before driving back to the A4-E5.

Eat and Drink: inexpensive, under €20; moderate, €20–€40; expensive, over €40

White Pueblos

Arcos de la Frontera to Jimena de la Frontera

Highlights

- **Classic Andalusia**
  Drive through the land of rolling fields, with Moorish whitewashed villages perched on dramatic cliff tops

- **Green Grazalema**
  Enjoy picnics and trekking in the Parque Natural de la Sierra de Grazalema

- **Wonderful architecture**
  Take in the dramatic setting and the Moorish and Renaissance architecture of Ronda, beside a spectacular gorge

- **Fiestas, ferias and romerías**
  Watch flamenco and bullfights, and enjoy the cuisine at celebrations throughout the region

Puente Nuevo across the El Tajo gorge in Ronda

White Pueblos

One of the classic images of Andalusia is that of its *pueblos blancos* – fortified hillside towns which are whitewashed in traditional Moorish style. The "frontera" in the names of some settlements refers to the fact that this was once the border between Christian and Muslim kingdoms. This drive starts from the handsome town of Arcos de la Frontera, through less-visited and smaller settlements, to Grazalema, which lies at the centre of one of Spain's most popular hiking areas. The tour also weaves through dramatically located white villages such as Gaucín and Jimena de la Frontera and ends in one of the region's most atmospheric towns, Ronda.

Above Picturesque Gaucín in the Sierra del Hacho, see *p197* **Above right** Parador de Ronda, beside the El Tajo gorge, see *p196* **Below** Gate in Ronda's city walls, see *p196*

ACTIVITIES

See wonderful architecture – Gothic, Mudéjar and Renaissance – in Arcos de la Frontera

Hike around the foothills of the Sierra del Pinar in Grazalema

Watch a bullfight in Ronda

Eat classic Andalusian tapas with chilled sherry all over this region

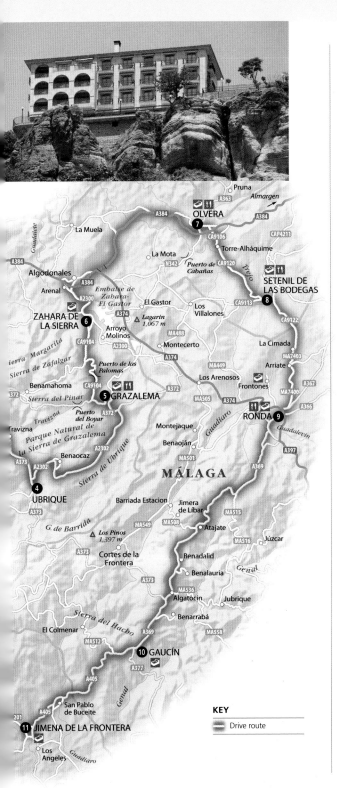

PLAN YOUR DRIVE

Start/finish: Arcos de la Frontera to Jimena de la Frontera.

Number of days: 3–4, allowing half a day each to explore Arcos de la Frontera and Ronda.

Distance: 225 km (140 miles).

Road conditions: Roads are well signposted and smoothly paved. Many parts of the route are winding hill roads; there are no barriers in some sections of the road.

When to go: The region is great to visit all year round, but July and August can be very hot, and many places are crowded.

Opening hours: Shops are generally open from 10am to 9pm (smaller shops may close for lunch, reopening around 5pm). Many attractions have shorter hours on weekends.

Main market days: Arcos de la Frontera: Fri; Grazalema: Tue; Ronda: Sun; Jimena de la Frontera: Fri.

Shopping: There are many shops selling leather goods in the lively shopping district in Ronda.

Major festivals: Arcos de la Frontera: Toro del Aleluya, Easter Sun; Ronda: Corrida Goyesca (traditional bullfight), first or second Sat in Sep; Jimena de la Frontera: Festival Internacional de Música, mid-Jul.

DAY TRIP OPTIONS

History buffs and **nature lovers** will enjoy visits to Ronda, Guacín and Jimena de la Frontera, while **adventure lovers** will enjoy walking the hill trails around Zahara de la Sierra, Grazalema and Ubrique. For details, see p197.

Above View of Arcos de la Frontera and its hilltop castle **Below** Courtyard of the Hotel Casa Grande in Arcos de la Frontera

VISITING ARCOS DE LA FRONTERA

Tourist Information
C/ Cuesta de Belén 5, 11630; 956 702 264; www.turismoarcos.es

Parking
There is limited parking around the Plaza del Cabildo and only a couple of hotels have their own parking areas – it may be wise to park in the New Town and walk into the Old Town of Arcos.

WHERE TO STAY

ARCOS DE LA FRONTERA

Casa Grande *moderate*
Elegant and intimate, Casa Grande offers the best accommodation in Arcos. There are just four doubles and two suites in this 18th-century mansion, all decorated with a fusion of Moroccan and local design.
C/ Maldonado 10, 11630; 956 703 930; www.lacasagrande.net

El Convento *moderate*
This 17th-century convent has only 13 rooms, most with amazing views. There is a rooftop terrace for basking in the evening sun.
C/ Maldonado 2, 11630; 956 702 333; www.hotelelconvento.es

Parador de Arcos de la Frontera *moderate*
Housed in the Casa del Corregidor, the parador has views of the Guadalete river and the plains surrounding it. The parador's restaurant offers traditional dishes such as *corvina a la roteña* (sea bass in red pepper sauce).
Plaza del Cabildo s/n, 11630; 956 700 500; www.parador.es

❶ Arcos de la Frontera
Cádiz; 11630

A whitewashed town typical of the region, Arcos de la Frontera is one of the most spectacular of the *pueblos blancos*, positioned along a sheer cliff that overlooks the valley of the Guadalete river. Although legend has it that a son of Noah founded Arcos, it is more probable that it was the Iberians. Known as Arcobriga during Roman times, the town grew considerably under the Moors who built a labyrinthine quarter that twists up to the town's castle.

The **Plaza del Cabildo**, the pretty main square, is at the heart of Arcos de la Frontera and easily found by following the signs for the parador that occupies the east side of it. The opposite side is occupied by a lovely 11th-century Moorish castle, rebuilt by the Christians after the *reconquista*. The third side is dominated by the impressive late Gothic-Mudéjar **Iglesia de Santa María de la Asunción** *(closed Sat and Sun pm, except for Mass)*, noted for its choir stalls and altarpiece. The church has different styles as various generations have added to, improved or repaired the building, originally built in the 13th century.

The final side of the square is most remarkable for not being there at all – the sheer walls of the *peña nueva* (new rock) plunge down from here. Stand on the edge to take in sweeping views of the river valley below and of the rolling hills.

A string of narrow streets, Calle Escribanos, Calle Boticos and Calle Nuñez de Prado, lead to the 17th-century **Convento de las Mercedarias Descalzas**, home to a closed order of nuns who sell cakes and biscuits. Ring the bell, give the order through a grille and the baked goodies will be delivered on a revolving lantern, all without any face-to-face contact. Find the entrance on the right-hand side of the narrow passageway leading from the parador to the Hotel El Convento.

For some down-to-earth delights, stroll to the **Galería de Arte Arx-Arcis** *(closed Sun)* on Calle Marqués de Torresoto near Plaza Boticos. A crafts museum and shop, housed in a labyrinthine building, it displays locally fashioned carpets, blankets, artwork

Iglesia de Santa María de la Asunción

and ceramics. Near Plaza Boticos is the unfinished church that was started in the 18th century by the Jesuits, who were forced to abandon it on their expulsion from Spain. Further along the road is the precariously perched Gothic **Iglesia de San Pedro**, built between the 16th and 18th centuries. Its thick-set tower provides stunning views over the sheer drop down to the Guadalete river.

For more breathtaking views of the Guadalete river, go to the **Mirador de Abades** on Calle Abades. On Calle Almirante are two palaces, the **Casa Palacio de Cuenca** on the left and the **Antigua Casa Palacio del Marqués de Torresoto**, now a hotel, a 17th-century Renaissance palace which has a richly decorated exterior and beautiful interior patios.

🚗 *Leave Arcos heading northwards on the A393. Then join the A384 and follow it northeast towards Bornos.*

Where to Stay: inexpensive, under €70; moderate, €70–€120; expensive, over €120

956 709 733; open daily). El Bosque is also a popular site for hunting and fishing and houses a trout farm.

🚗 **Drive back to the A373 and continue southwards on it. At the fork after Travizna, bear right, still on the A373, to Ubrique.**

④ Ubrique
Cádiz; 11600

A picturesque *pueblo blanco* in the Serrania de Ronda mountains, Ubrique has a long, interesting history which stretches over many empires and centuries. Its origins can be traced back to Palaeolithic times or earlier. Much of the area's finest architecture was burned down during Napoleon's invasion but **Ocuri**, a Roman city 1 km (0.6 miles) from Ubrique, is still remarkably preserved and excavations have unearthed a 1st-century-BC crematorium and irrigation aquifers. The town is well-known for its flourishing leather industry. Leather handbags and shoe shops along the streets in the centre hark back to the 18th century, when immigrants from southern Italy brought the leather trade with them.

This beautiful and tranquil town is also known for its flamboyant bullfighter, Jesulín de Ubrique, now retired, who has an estate nearby.

🚗 **Drive back to where the road forks and turn right onto the A2302 towards Grazalema. When the road forks again, just before the town, bear left onto the A372 to Grazalema.**

Left Iglesia de San Pedro in Arcos de la Frontera **Below** Ubrique at the foot of the Sierra de Ubrique

EAT AND DRINK

ARCOS DE LA FRONTERA
Peña Flamenca de Arcos *moderate*
Put on your dancing shoes and head on down to Arcos' flamenco club. There are shows occasionally.
Plaza de la Caridad s/n, 11630; 956 701 251

EL BOSQUE
Enrique Calvillo *moderate*
Fresh trout with ham, bull's tail, game and classic Spanish ham are some of the standards at this lively, friendly restaurant housed in a *hotel rural*.
Avda. Diputación 5, 11630; 956 716 105; www.hotelenriquecalvillo.com

② Bornos
Cádiz; 11640

Sprawled across a wide open valley, Bornos is primarily an agricultural town. The centre of this small town is filled with stately houses and small, manicured gardens. The dam on the Guadalete river makes it look like a lake here and the well-watered fields surrounding the town produce a range of fruits and vegetables. Bornos is famous for its cabbage stews as well as its basket-making.

🚗 **Continue on the A384 following signs for Villamartin, 12 km (7 miles) to the northeast. At Villamartín turn right onto the A373 and then, after crossing the road to Prado del Rey, turn left onto the A372 to El Bosque.**

③ El Bosque
Cádiz; 11670

This picturesque village has a few noteworthy 18th-century buildings, including the Ermita del Calvario, the Iglesia de Nuestra Senora de Guadalupe and the Molino del Duque mill. However, El Bosque is better known to travellers as one of the main gateways to the **Parque Natural de la Sierra de Grazalema**, a nature reserve covering 535 sq km (205 sq miles). Walking permits are required for some areas of the park because some species of flora found here, such as the millenarian *Abies pinsapo* (Spanish fir) tree, are rare. Information and permits for the walks are available at the park's visitor centre *(Avenida de la Diputación;*

Eat and Drink: inexpensive, under €20; moderate, €20–€40; expensive, over €40

Above Panoramic view from the Puerto de las Palomas pass *Below* Quiet village of Zahara de la Sierra dominated by its ruined castle

WHERE TO STAY

GRAZALEMA

Hotel Peñón Grande *inexpensive*
This friendly, family-run hotel on a pretty square has traditionally decorated rooms.
Plaza Pequeña 7, 11610; 956 132 434

Hotel Fuerte Grazalema *moderate*
An eco- and family-friendly hotel, with a swimming pool, farm animals, an organic vegetable garden and various organized activities. Lovely views, too.
Baldío de los Alamillos, Ctra. A372, Km 53, 11610; 956 133 000; www.fuertehoteles.com

ZAHARA DE LA SIERRA

Hotel Arco de la Villa *inexpensive*
On the edge of the Parque Natural de la Sierra de Grazalema, this quiet hotel has just 17 rooms, all with views of the nearby lake. Breakfast, of bread, oil and jams, is included.
Paseo Nazarí, 11688; 956 123 230; www.tugasa.com

OLVERA

Sierra y Cal *inexpensive*
This 34-room hotel has a large terrace with a swimming pool and a tea lounge. Its restaurant is acclaimed for its local cuisine.
Avda. Nuestra Señora de los Remedios 2, 11690; 956 130 303; www.tugasa.com

SETENIL DE LAS BODEGAS

El Almendral *moderate*
A friendly, typically Andalusian hotel, this place has an outdoor pool, a tennis court and a manicured lawn.
C/ Setenil-Ronda, 11692; 956 134 029; www.tugasa.com

⑤ Grazalema
Cádiz; 11610

The village of Grazalema is set in the centre of the **Parque Natural de la Sierra de Grazalema**. It was very prosperous between the 17th and 19th centuries, when it became so famous for its textile manufacturing industry that it was called *Cádiz el Chico* (Little Cádiz). A number of grand houses and churches are testimony to this wealthy era. The village's Artesanía Textil de Grazalema guild is busy reviving the traditional methods of cloth-making and blanket-weaving.

The Parque Natural de la Sierra de Grazalema has some of the highest rainfall in Spain and a walk around Grazalema offers impressive views over the green hills that surround the village on all sides. There are a number of walking and horse riding trails from here, as well as an array of mountain sports, including bungee jumping, potholing and abseiling. The influx of visitors to the village from Cádiz and Seville means that restaurants and other facilities are sometimes overstretched at weekends and in the peak summer season.

🚗 *Continue westwards on the A372 from Grazalema, then turn right onto the CA9104 (still signed as the CA531 in some stretches) towards Zahara de la Sierra. Rising through a series of switchbacks to the pass at Puerto de las Palomas (1,360 m/4,450 ft), the road offers outstanding panoramic vistas. Visitors can park up at the pass and marvel at the impressive bit of road construction. At the junction after the pass, bear right, still on the CA9104, to Zahara de la Sierra.*

The White Towns

Western Andalusia is instantly recognizable by its classic white villages and towns. The houses are painted in traditional Moorish style. Many of these fortified hillside villages were founded by Berber tribes who settled in the area during the eight centuries of Moorish presence. These flat-roofed houses, often built of baked clay, are usually whitewashed in spring mainly for a practical reason: to deflect the sun's harsh rays. They also have few windows to help keep the interiors cool. The Andalusian Moorish legacy is also evident in the exquisite ubiquitous glazed tiles, patios and wrought ironwork.

⑥ Zahara de la Sierra
Cádiz; 11688

The houses of Zahara de la Sierra are scattered on a hillside beneath the ruins of a castle that sit high above on the mountain peak. The Moorish castle *(open daily)* gives spectacular views over this village and the artificial lake that spans the foot of the hill. Declared a historic monument in 1983, the town has many attractive sights such as the **Torre del Homenaje**, a 16th-century watchtower, the **Iglesia de Santa María de la Meza** with its Baroque altarpiece and the **Arco de la Villa**. There is a restored olive mill, **Molino El Vínculo** *(696 404 368; open Fri–Sun, phone ahead to arrange tour)*, just outside Zahara de la Sierra, where visitors are shown how olive oil is traditionally produced. The reservoir just outside the town provides the option of water sports.

🚗 *Leave Zahara on the A2300 and follow signs for Algodonales. Turn right onto the eastbound A384 and*

when the road forks, bear left, still on the A384, for Olvera. At the cross-roads near the town, turn left onto the A363 to reach Olvera.

⑦ Olvera
Cádiz; 11690

In the early 20th century this town's economy received a boost as Olvera became a key station on a new rail link between Almargen and prosperous Jerez de la Frontera. Today this abandoned track bed still nourishes the town's economy, providing visitors with an interesting hiking and biking route to Puerto Serrano. Other interesting sights in Olvera include its castle and the **Iglesia de la Encarnación** with its small but fascinating museum *(closed Mon)*. Also worth a visit is the **Ermita de Nuestra Senora de los Remedios** *(open daily)*, just 2 km (1 mile) from Olvera. It has a room displaying interesting offerings such as photographs, trophies and wedding dresses, all dedicated to the Virgen de los Remedios to thank her for her "miracles".

🚗 *Leave the town centre following signs for Ronda. Turn right southwards, onto the CA9106, a quiet country road, which becomes the CA9120 after the small white village of Torre-Alháquime. On the outskirts of Setenil de las Bodegas, turn left onto the CA9113 which will take visitors into the town.*

⑧ Setenil de las Bodegas
Cádiz; 11692

Setenil de las Bodegas is a *pueblo blanco* with a difference, with many of its streets carved into the side of an overhanging gorge of volcanic tufa rock formed by the Trejo river. Depending on the time of year, this town's tourist office *(open daily)*, housed in a medieval building, can arrange visits to some local cave homes. The town's ruined Moorish castle has a vestigial tower that is worth a careful climb. The "bodegas" in the town's name hark back to the town's wine trade, which flourished from the 15th century onwards but was wiped out in the 1860s by phylloxera (insects that destroy vines). Olives and almonds are still important local industries. Setenil also produces quality meat products and is known for its fine pastries.

🚗 *Leave town on the CA9113 eastwards and almost immediately turn right onto the CA9122, which becomes the MA7403 when entering the Málaga province. Continue on the MA7403 to Arriate, a tiny, quiet town overlooking the Ronda mountain range. Just south of Arriate the road becomes the MA7400, which joins the A367 to Ronda.*

Above Picturesque walking trail in the Sierra de Grazalema **Below left** Sign at the entrance to Setenil de las Bodegas **Below right** Church in the white village of Olvera

SETENIL DE LAS BODEGAS

Above El Tajo gorge within Ronda

VISITING RONDA

Tourist information
Paseo de Blas Infante, 29400; 952 187
119; www.turismoderonda.es

Parking
Parking is available on the Plaza
del Socorro.

WHERE TO STAY

RONDA

Parador de Ronda *expensive*
Book in advance to get a room here.
The views are amazing, the decor inno-
vative and the experience palatial.
Plaza de Espana s/n, 29400; 952 877
500; www.parador.es

AROUND RONDA

Hotel La Fuente de la Higuera
expensive
This luxurious hotel, 10 km (6 miles)
north of Ronda, is cool and chic. The
Mediterranean cuisine served here
using organic produce is top-class too.
Partido de los Frontones s/n, 29400,
Frontones; 952 165 608; www.
hotellafuente.com

GAUCÍN

La Fructuosa *moderate*
Warm and inviting, this upscale country
house offers a comfortable base.
Luis de Armiñan 67, 29480; 617 692
784; www.lafructuosa.com

JIMENA DE LA FRONTERA

Posada La Casa Grande *inexpensive*
This small hotel is run by a Norwegian
expat. Rooms are spacious and bright.
C/ Fuentenueva 42, 11330; 956 641
120; www.posadalacasagrande.es

⑨ Ronda
Málaga; 29400

Rainer Maria Rilke (1875–1926), the great German poet, called Ronda
the "dream city". Ronda's clifftop buildings sit astride a high limestone
cleft, parted by the Guadalevín river and surrounded by mountains.
The town's adopted symbol is the 18th-century Puente Nuevo (New
Bridge) that spans the gorge and links the old Moorish citadel in the
south (La Ciudad) to the newer town (the Mercadillo quarter), home
to one of Spain's oldest bullrings. It is here that the walking tour begins.

A three-hour walking tour

From the car park walk down Calle
de Espinel to Calle Virgen de la Paz.
Turn left into it to reach the **Puente
Nuevo** ①, which spans the jaw-
dropping El Tajo gorge created by
the Guadalevín river. It links the old
Moorish citadel in the south to the
newer town in the north and was
completed in 1793 after four decades
of impressive work by stonemasons
and labourers. Civil War prisoners were
forced to jump to their deaths from
the bridge and the pre-jump jail,
above one of the arches, has now
been converted into a museum.

Turn left into Calle de Santo
Domingo to reach the inaccurately
named **Casa del Rey Moro** ② (House
of the Moorish King), actually built in
1709. Beneath the house is a rock-cut
stairway, which does date back to
Moorish times, leading to beautiful
French landscaped gardens. Continue
down Calle de Santo Domingo and
then turn right into Calle Marqués de
Salvatierra to see the 18th-century

Palacio del Marqués de Salvatierra ③.
The palace is closed to the public
but look for the figurines on the
façade which were inspired by Latin
American native art. Beside the palace is a stone cross marking the spot
where Don Vasco Martín de Salvatierra
camped after the Reconquest of
Ronda in June 1485. Take in views of
the Puente de San Miguel, Ronda's
oldest bridge, and the 13th-century
Baños Árabes (Arab Baths) from here.

Continue along Calle Marqués de
Salvatierra and turn left down Calle
de Armiñán to arrive at the picturesque orange-tree-lined **Plaza de la
Duquesa de Parcent** ④. Stroll in the
shade towards the northern end
of the square to visit the **Iglesia de
Santa María la Mayor** ⑤, once a
Roman temple, then a mosque and
now the town's main church. The
local archaeology museum is housed
in the **Palacio de Mondragón** ⑥,
a fine building to the west of the
church on Calle de Manuel Montero.
From here, walk across the Plaza de

María Auxiliadora to the narrow, winding Calle Tenorio and follow it back to Calle de Armiñán and the Puente Nuevo.

Walk back down Calle Virgen de la Paz to the **Plaza de Toros** ⑦, one of the oldest and most beautiful bullrings in Spain, inaugurated in 1785. It is here that the classic Ronda style of bullfighting was developed by Pedro Romero, one of the fathers of bullfighting. Walk back down Calle de Espinel, to the right of the bullring, to reach the car park.

🚗 *Leave Ronda on the A369 which heads to Gaucín, 37 km (23 miles) to the southwest.*

⑩ Gaucín
Málaga; 29480
Located more than 600 m (2,000 ft) high in the Serrania, Gaucín offers views over the Mediterranean, the Atlantic, the Rock of Gibraltar and the Rif mountains of North Africa on clear days. Gaucín takes its name from the Arab word *guazan* (strong rock), a reference to the Sierra del Hacho on which it is perched. The

Romans made use of its unique strategic position and built the **Castillo del Águila** (Eagle's Castle) which also has later Moorish additions.

The heart of the village is a tangle of narrow, twisting streets and was once a haven for brandy and tobacco smugglers who travelled through the surrounding hills.

Gaucín was popular with British officers in the 19th century, who used to stop here on the way to Gibraltar. Today, many wealthy expats reside here, served by an ample choice of bars, restaurants and art shops.

🚗 *Leave Gaucín on the A405. In San Pablo de Buceite take the road to the right, still the A405, and head westwards on it to Jimena de la Frontera, re-entering the province of Cádiz.*

⑪ Jimena de la Frontera
Cádiz; 11330
Jimena de la Frontera is set beneath an extensive ruined Moorish castle, amid hills where wild bulls graze in the shade of olive and cork trees. The Moors used the village as a strategic military point. Jimena de la Frontera is also popular with expats, and approximately one in nine of its residents is foreign. However, it still retains its local whitewashed charm and steep cobbled streets.

Beneath the village is the Hozgarganta river valley, which is a spectacular place for hiking and swimming if the weather is favourable. The surrounding countryside also has several game reserves and rich forest land.

EAT AND DRINK

RONDA
Almócabar *moderate*
This is one of the best places in Ronda for tapas, served in the front bar, or a full meal in the restaurant. The latter has interesting Arab-Andalusian dishes. Drink the excellent local red wine, Cortijo de las Monjas.
Plaza Ruedo Alameda 5, 29400; 952 875 977; closed Tue

La Gota de Vino *moderate*
Serving a large range of great wine, this restaurant also has an excellent menu with dishes made with ingredients from the local market.
C/ Sevilla 13, 29400; 952 875 716; closed Sun

Azahar *moderate*
Sophisticated renditions of regional favourites with a touch of international flair are on the menu here.
Calle Jerez 25, 29400; 952 871 240; www.restaurante-azahar.com

Asador Casa Santa Pola *moderate*
This traditional restaurant offers delicious local cuisine with a creative touch, and is set in a historic building with beamed ceilings and balconies offering wonderful views.
C/ Santo Domingo 2, 29400; 953 879 208

Above Field of flowers on the outskirts of Jimena de la Frontera

---

DAY TRIP OPTIONS
This drive can be divided into two shorter day trips for those who do not have the time to attempt the full drive. Visitors can use either Ronda (near the A397) or Zahara de la Sierra (near the A2300) as a base for these trips.

Beautiful white villages
Start at Ronda ⑨, the city of bridges and the most popular of the *pueblos blancos*. The town is a great place to walk around in. Head south to Gaucín ⑩ for views of the Costa del Sol and, on a clear day, Morocco. Continue to Jimena de la Frontera ⑪,

a pretty hilltop hamlet with an impressive Moorish castle.

Leave Ronda on the A369, which heads southwest to Gaucín. Continue on the A369 till the road forks. Take the A405, the road to the right, and head westwards on it to Jimena de la Frontera.

High roads and hiking
Start off at Zahara de la Sierra ⑥, a striking white village on a steep hillside topped by a Moorish castle, from which there are spectacular views over the town and the lake on the outskirts of the town. Head south to Grazalema ⑤, a lively town known

for its carpet-weaving and textile industry and the hub of arguably the best hillwalking region in the whole of Andalusia. Head south towards Ubrique ④, which provides access to other hill trails in the Parque Natural de la Sierra de Grazalema.

Take the CA9104 southwards from Zahara de la Sierra towards Grazalema and then turn left onto the A372 to reach Grazalema. From Grazalema continue on the A372 to the southwest and then turn right onto the A2302 towards Ubrique. Turn left when the road forks onto the A373 to reach the hillside town of Ubrique.

Eat and Drink: inexpensive, under €20; moderate, €20–€40; expensive, over €40

Coast of Light

Jerez de la Frontera to Tarifa

Highlights

- **Sherry stops**
  Explore old bodegas all over this
  region and sample *fino* and
  manzanilla sherry

- **Europe's oldest city**
  Discover the secret alleyways and
  laid-back ambience of old Cádiz

- **Secret beaches**
  Enjoy the long ocean beaches
  between Rota and Zahara de
  los Atunes

- **Windsurfer's paradise**
  Take a boat trip to see whales or go
  windsurfing and kitesurfing in Tarifa

Catedral Nueva by the waterfront in Cádiz

Coast of Light

The Costa de la Luz is the western stretch of the Andalusian coastline facing the Atlantic Ocean. The beaches here are wide and long and the sand is finer and more golden than on the neighbouring Costa del Sol – the special light makes it extraordinarily beautiful. Strong Atlantic winds and waves attract windsurfers and surfboarders from all over Europe to this region. This drive goes through some lovely seaside towns and, just inland, sleepy white *pueblos*, starting with the sherry-making city of Jerez. The tour ends at Tarifa, the windsurfing capital of Europe.

Above Enjoying the beach at Rota, *see p204* **Below** Domes of the Catedral Nueva in Cádiz, *see p205*

KEY

Drive route

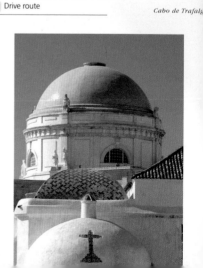

ACTIVITIES

Watch and hear flamenco in Jerez de la Frontera during the Festival de Flamenco

Go sherry tasting and bodega-hopping in Sanlúcar de Barrameda

Explore Cádiz and its Old Town

Wander through the pretty white villages of Medina-Sidonia and Vejer de la Frontera

Swim, surf, windsurf or kitesurf on the beach at Tarifa

Above Ornate façade of Catedral de San Salvador in Jerez de la Frontera, see p202

PLAN YOUR DRIVE

Start/finish: Jerez de la Frontera to Tarifa.

Number of days: 3–4, allowing half a day each to explore Jerez de le Frontera and Cádiz.

Distance: 220 km (140 miles).

Road conditions: Well paved and signposted throughout; some busy roads around Jerez and Cádiz.

When to go: The ideal time to visit the Costa de la Luz is March to June and mid-September to October when it is not too hot and there are not too many visitors. July to mid-September is the peak season and can be very hot, especially inland.

Opening hours: Shops, monuments and museums are generally open from 10am to 8 or 9pm (some close for lunch). Many attractions have shorter hours at weekends, and in winter.

Main market days: Jerez de la Frontera: Mon; Sanlúcar de Barrameda: Wed; Cádiz: Mon; Tarifa: Tue.

Shopping: Antiques and antiquarian books, jewellery and handicrafts can be purchased in Cádiz.

Major festivals: Jerez de la Frontera: Festival de Flamenco, Feb/Mar; Feria de Jerez, May; Fiesta de Vendimia (grape harvest festival), early Sep; Sanlúcar de Barrameda: Exaltación del Río Guadalquivir (horse racing on the beach), mid-Jul to mid-Aug; Cádiz: Carnaval de Cádiz, Feb/Mar; Tarifa: Romería de la Virgen de la Luz (traditional pilgrimage on horseback), first Sun Sep.

DAY TRIP OPTIONS

Wine lovers will enjoy driving the sherry circuit from Jerez de la Frontera to El Puerto de Santa María through Sanlúcar de Barrameda, Chipiona and Rota. **Families** and **adventure enthusiasts** will enjoy a drive to the beaches at Zahara de los Atunes and Tarifa. For details, see p207.

Above Tio Pepe vineyard on the road from Jerez de la Frontera to Arcos

VISITING JEREZ DE LA FRONTERA

Tourist Information
Plaza del Arenal s/n - Edificio Los Arcos, 11403; 956 338 874; www. turismojerez.com

Parking
Parking is available in Los Cisnes on Calle Larga.

SHERRY BODEGAS

Bodegas Gonzáles-Byass
C/ Manuel Maria González 12, 11403; 956 357 016; www.gonzalezbyass.com; open daily

Bodegas Fundador-Pedro Domecq
C/ San Ildefonso 3, 11403; 956 151 500; www.bodegasfundadorpedrodomecq. com; closed Sun; booking advisable

EQUESTRIAN DISPLAYS

Real Escuela Andaluza de Arte Ecuestre
Avda. Duque de Abrantes, 11407; 956 319 635; www.realescuela.org; tours Mon, Wed & Fri; shows Tue, Thu & one Sat per month, plus Fri in Aug & Sep

WHERE TO STAY

JEREZ DE LA FRONTERA

La Fonda Barranco *moderate*
An old house in the heart of Jerez has been carefully restored to house this elegant and comfortable small hotel.
C/ Barranco 12, 11403; 956 332 141; http://lafondabarranco.com

Casa Viña de Alcántara *expensive*
Housed in a stately mansion 21 km (13 miles) from Jerez, Casa Viña has extensive grounds and sherry vineyards.
Ctra. Jerez-Arcos; 956 393 010; www.vinadealcantara.com

SANLÚCAR DE BARRAMEDA

Hotel Posada de Palacio *moderate*
Comfort and a traditional Andaluz ambience are combined in this mansion in Sanlúcar's Old Town.
C/ Caballeros 9, 11540; 956 364 840; www.posadadepalacio.com

Where to Stay: *inexpensive, under €70; moderate, €70–€120; expensive, over €120*

❶ Jerez de la Frontera
Cádiz; 11407

Jerez first rose to prominence under the Moors who ruled it until 1264. Their greatest architectural achievement in the city is the 11th-century Alcázar which encompasses a well-preserved mosque, now a church. The capital of sherry production, Jerez is surrounded by a countryside blanketed with rows of vines. The city has several world-famous sherry bodegas. It is also famous for its flamenco and there are flamenco venues to suit all budgets. The city is the regional centre for equestrian skills and horse-lovers from all over come to see the performances at the Real Escuela Andaluza de Arte Ecuestre, the Royal Riding School.

A two-hour walking tour

From the car park walk northwards on Calle Larga, the main shopping artery. Turn right into Alameda Cristina to reach the **Palacio Domecq** ① which is typical of the 18th-century late Baroque sherry barons' homes. Next to the palace, on Calle Rosario, is the **Convento de Santo Domingo** ② *(open for Mass only)*. The Baroque altar here is worth seeing. Go back to Calle Larga and continue southwards on it to a distinctive circular building, the popular **Gallo Azul Café** ③. From Plaza Esteve, the square in front of the café, head southwest down Calle Lanceria to the **Plaza del Arenal** ④ where horse races are sometimes held. Head up Calle Consistorio, to the north of the plaza, to reach the **Plaza de la Asunción** ⑤, home to Jerez's *ayuntamiento viejo* (old town hall). From the plaza turn left to walk down Calle de José Luis Díez, which

becomes Calle Cruces, to visit the **Catedral de San Salvador** ⑥ *(open daily; Sun Mass only)*, which is built on the site of an old mosque and is a mix of Gothic, Renaissance and Baroque styles. The towers of the cathedral offer views of the surrounding area. Southwest of the cathedral, down Plaza del Arroyo, is the **Puerta del Arroyo** ⑦, a 16th-century city gate. Two of the town's largest sherry bodegas, González-Byass and Fundador-Pedro Domecq, are on either side of the gate and both offer tours. Go back towards the cathedral and turn right on Calle Encarnación to the 12th-century **Alcázar de Jerez** ⑧ *(open daily)*. The fortress has a camera obscura, a small round darkened room with a rotating angled mirror at the apex of the roof, projecting images of the landscape onto a flat surface inside. From the Alcázar, walk eastwards down Calle de Manuel María

González to the Plaza de Arenal. Walk across the plaza and to the car park.

🚌 *From central Jerez follow signs for the NIVa Cádiz road and in the outskirts of the city turn right onto the A480, which becomes the A471 near Sanlúcar de Barrameda.*

2 Sanlúcar de Barrameda

Cádiz; 11540

The city of Sanlúcar is famous as the departure port for Columbus's third voyage in 1498 and for Magellan's 1519 expedition – during which his lieutenant, Juan Sebastián de Elcano, completed the first circumnavigation of the globe.

The town is divided into two main districts: the Barrio Alto, the old part of the town up on the hill, and the Barrio Bajo beneath it. The centre proper is in the Barrio Bajo, and has elegant pedestrian thoroughfares and a series of pretty plazas. There is a long promenade, Bajo de Guía, beside the Guadalquivir river, lined with outdoor seafood restaurants that are great places for an atmospheric feast.

Sanlúcar has a number of impressive churches, including the 16th-century **Iglesia de Santo Domingo** and 17th-century **Iglesia de San Francisco**, both in the Barrio Alto. The Old Town also has two palaces – the **Palacio de los Duques de Medina-Sidonia** and the **Palacio de Orleans y Borbon** (the town hall). Next door to the latter is the town's oldest church, the 16th-century **Iglesia de Nuestra Senora de la O** (closed Mon), which features a richly decorated Mudéjar

doorway. A short walk away, on Calle Caballeros, is the **Castillo de Santiago**, the 15th-century Moorish castle, flanked on two sides by *manzanilla* sherry bodegas, including the town's largest sherry-maker, **Barbadillo**, founded in 1821. *Manzanilla*, a light, dry sherry, is said to owe its salty tang to the local sea breeze.

Sanlúcar is also home to some of the oldest horse races in Europe. The 1,500 m (1,650 yd) and 1,800 m (2,000 yd) races take place just before sunset, along the beach at the mouth of the Guadalquivir river, every August, with thousands of spectators in attendance.

Across the Guadalquiver river to the west of Sanlúcar is the vast Parque Nacional de Doñana. Boat trips run at regular intervals from the Sanlúcar waterfront to the park.

🚌 *Return to the A480 and follow signs to Chipiona, 9 km (6 miles) to the west.*

The Rules of Sherry

Real sherry can only be produced in the triangle formed by Sanlúcar de Barrameda, El Puerto de Santa María and Jerez de la Frontera, and gets its name from Jerez. It is made from two main varieties of grapes, Palomino and Pedro Ximénez, and also gets its special qualities from the region's white *albariza* soils. Andalusians drink the light, pale *fino* and *manzanilla* styles of sherry, which are 15.5 per cent alcohol (only a little stronger than many table wines), with tapas. The longer-aged, richer, yet still dry styles of *amontillado* and *oloroso* sherry, with a higher percentage of alcohol, are traditionally made mainly for export.

Left Mudéjar doorway of the Iglesia de Nuestra Senora de la O, Sanlúcar **Below** Catedral de San Salvador in Jerez de la Frontera

VISITING SANLÚCAR DE BARRAMEDA

Tourist Information
C/ Calzada del Ejército, 11540; 956 388 001; www.sanlucarturismo.com

Parking
There is convenient underground parking at La Calzada, just opposite the Hotel Guadalquivir.
Avda. la Calzada del Ejército, 11540; 956 385 408

SHERRY BODEGAS

Bodegas Barbadillo
C/ Luis de Eguilaz, 11, 11540; 956 385 521; www.barbadillo.com

EAT AND DRINK

JEREZ DE LA FRONTERA

Cafetería La Vega moderate
This is the place to come to soak up some real local atmosphere, and the tapas and traditional fish dishes can all be recommended.
Plaza Estéve, 11540; 956 337 748

Bar Juanito moderate
An atmospheric tapas bar and restaurant, this place has a reputation for its exceptionally large portions.
C/ Pescardería Vieja 8; 956 334 838; www.bar-juanito.com; closed Sun dinner

SANLÚCAR DE BARRAMEDA

Casa Bigote moderate
This is a former sailor's tavern that is the most famous of the terrace restaurants on the Bajo de Guía, with a fine view of the mouth of the Guadalquivir.
C/ Bajo de Guía 10; 956 362 696; www.restaurantecasabigote.com

Above Wooded park near Playa de la Castilla in Rota **Below** Statue at the Catedral Neuva in Cádiz

VISITING BODEGAS IN EL PUERTO DE SANTA MARÍA

Bodegas Osborne
C/ de los Moros, 11500; 956 869 000; www.osborne.es; open Mon–Sat; advance booking required

Bodegas Terry
C/ Toneleros s/n, 11500; 956 151 500; www.bodegasterry.com; closed Sun

WHERE TO STAY

CHIPIONA

Hotel Brasilia *moderate*
With its pleasant garden, swimming pool and solarium, this is one of Chipiona's most enjoyable hotels.
Avda. del Faro 17, 11550; 956 371 054; www.brasiliahotel.net

ROTA

Hotel Caribe *moderate*
This hotel is a peaceful refuge after a day of swimming and sunbathing.
Avda. de la Marina 60, 11550; 956 810 700; www.hotel-caribe.com

CÁDIZ

Hotel Argantonio *moderate*
Mosaic floors and warm stone interiors make this elegant boutique hotel one of the most romantic refuges in Cádiz.
C/ Argantonio 3, 11002; 956 211 640; www.hotelargantonio.com

Pension Centro-Sol *inexpensive*
A tiny pension housed in a refurbished Neo-Classical building, this hotel is situated in one of Cádiz's lovely alleyways.
Manzanares 7, 11004; 956 283 103; www.hostalcentrosolcadiz.com

Where to Stay: inexpensive, under €70; moderate, €70–€120; expensive, over €120

③ Chipiona
Cádiz; 11550

Situated on one of the quieter stretches of the Costa de la Luz, Chipiona offers 12 km (7 miles) of golden beaches. Playa de Regla is one of the best beaches, but for a quieter experience Playa Cruz del Mar or Las Canteras are worth a try. Popular with Spanish tourists, Chipiona is known for its bracing waters along its beaches and good seafood restaurants: white crabs and lobster are two popular local products. This seaside town is home to the **Faro de Chipiona** *(guided visits; 956 922 627)*, Spain's tallest lighthouse and the third highest in the world. It dates from 1867, but a lighthouse was first built on this spot by the Romans in 140 BC to guide ships to the entrance of the Guadalquivir. The town has attractive buildings such as the 16th-century **Parroquia de Nuestra Senora de la O** and the 14th-century former **Monasterio de Nuestra Senora de la Regla**.

🚗 *Take the A491 southwards out of Chipiona. After 12 km (7 miles), follow signs onto the A2075 to Rota.*

④ Rota
Cádiz; 11520

Founded by the Phoenicians, Rota derived its name from the Moorish *Rabita Rutta* (watchtower of Rota). This attractive seaside resort has some lovely beaches including the Playa de la Costilla, an EU Blue-Flagged beach and a conservation area for

dune landscapes and pine forests. The town also has a 13th-century Moorish castle, the **Castillo de la Luna** *(open daily; guided visits 1pm and 5pm Sat & Sun; 956 846 345)*. The 16th-century **Iglesia de Nuestra Senora de la O** illustrates a mix of architectural styles – Gothic/Renaissance, the ornate Plateresque and Baroque. The local wine, *tintilla*, is made from dark, ripe grapes in local bodegas, such as El Gato.

🚗 *Return to the A491 via the A2075 and turn right. When the road forks, turn right onto the CA603, which leads to El Puerto de Santa María.*

⑤ El Puerto de Santa María
Cádiz; 11500

Situated on the bay of Cádiz, at the mouth of the Guadalete, El Puerto de Santa María is surrounded by picturesque beaches such as Vistahermosa, La Puntilla and Valdelagrana. The town is well-known for the excellent seafood and tapas served at the restaurants along the **Avenida de la Bajamar**, the main promenade. El Puerto de Santa María exports large quantities of sherry and was once the most important sherry exporting town in Spain. It is home to many bodegas such as Terry and Osborne, which produce *fino*, a dry, pale sherry, as well as *moscatel*, *oloroso* and *amontillado* and are open to the public.

The town is famous for its bullring, **Plaza de Toros**, built in 1880 and one of the largest in Spain. Bullfights are organized during the Feria season in August and the Feria de la Primavera (Spring Fair) in May, which is dedicated to sherry. The town also has an 18th-century fountain, **La Fuente de las Galeras**, which used to supply water to ships bound for the Americas. A few archaeological remains from the Palaeolithic era can be found in the **Museo Arqueológico Municipal** *(closed Mon)*. A short distance from the museum is the 13th-century **Castillo de San Marcos** *(open Tue if prebooked by phone, and for guided visits 10:30am–1:30pm Thu & Sat; 627 569 335)*, built on the site of a mosque and watchtower.

🚗 *Take the CA32 out of the town and drive towards the Parque Natural Bahia de Cádiz. Follow signs for the N443 and on crossing the Puente de José León de Carranza, turn right onto the CA33 to Cádiz.*

6 Cádiz

Cádiz; 11002

Almost entirely surrounded by water, jutting into the Bay of Cádiz, Cádiz lays claims to being Europe's oldest city. While legend names Hercules as its founder, history credits the Phoenicians with establishing the town of *Gadir* (walled city) in 1100 BC. Archaeologists have found remnants of almost every major maritime culture since then in the Old Town.

Modern Cádiz is made up of two parts – the compact Old Town and the sprawling New Town. Most of the Old Town's architecture dates back to the 18th and early 19th centuries, when Cádiz rose to prominence as a cargo port. From the seawall there are views of the surrounding regions – the **Torre de Telefonica** stands high above everything else – and also of the sweeping bulge of the peninsula. Cádiz briefly became Spain's capital in 1812 when the nation's first constitution was drafted here.

Wandering along the waterfront is a good preamble to viewing Cádiz's sites. The **Catedral Nueva** was conceived as a Baroque masterpiece by the Spanish architect Vicente Acero; the building project was curtailed several times as funds ran out. A smaller cathedral, the **Catedral Vieja**, was originally built in the 13th century but was badly damaged during the English assault on Cádiz in 1596. On Calle del Marqués del Real Tesoro is the **Torre Tavira** *(open daily)*, the city's watchtower; there are splendid views over Cádiz through its camera obscura. The 19th-century church, **Oratorio de San Felipe Neri**, and the **Museo de Cádiz**

(open Tue–Sun), which maps the city's history, are other sites worth visiting in the city. The museum is in Plaza de Mina and houses exhibits dating back to Phoenician, ancient Greek and Roman times, and also has one of the largest art collections in Andalusia.

Head up Calle Compañia to the Plaza Topete, which is locally known as the Plaza de las Flores, for all the florists that have stalls here. There is a handsome Correos (post office) here too. The Carnaval *(Feb–Mar)* in the city is one of the largest and the most colourful in Europe, with much singing, dancing and all-night partying.

📷 *Exit on the wide Avenida de Andalusia, which becomes the well-signposted CA33. This will lead past the junction for the Puente de José León de Carranza and on to San Fernando. Take the A48 from the junction after San Fernando and then turn right onto the A390 for Chiclana de la Frontera. Pass through this town and turn left at the next junction, still on the A390, for Medina-Sidonia.*

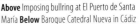

Above Imposing bullring at El Puerto de Santa María **Below** Baroque Catedral Nueva in Cádiz

VISITING CÁDIZ

Tourist Information
Avda. Ramón de Carranza, 11006; 956 285 601; www.andalucia.org; www. cadizturismo.com

Parking
Parking is available in San Jose in Avenida Ana de Viya.

EAT AND DRINK

CHIPIONA

La Cuba *moderate*
Fish, seafood and meat share an ever-changing menu here. Try the taster's menu, a sampling of several platters at a very reasonable price. *Avda. de la Laguna s/n, 11550; 956 370 572*

ROTA

Restaurante El Fresquito *moderate*
The blood sausage, the seafood and fish tapas and *piriñacas* (pepper, tomato and onion salads) here are all delicious. *Plaza de las Canteras 13, 11520; 956 840 832*

CÁDIZ

Freiduría Cervecería Las Flores *moderate*
This friendly neighbourhood bar-restaurant serves up the Andalusian dish of *pescaito frito* (fried fish). *Plaza Topete 4, 11001; 956 241 001*

Ventorrillo del Chato *expensive*
A picturesque inn in an 18th-century staging post by the sea, this restaurant specializes in authentic Andalusian cuisine. Recipes use fresh fish from the bay and local meat and vegetables. *Via Augusta Julia, 11011; 956 250 025; www.ventorrilloelchato.com*

Above left Castilo de Guzmán el Bueno, Tarifa **Above right** Vejer de la Frontera atop its mountain crag **Below left** Decorated porch in Medina-Sidonia **Below right** Iglesia de Santa María la Coronada in Medina-Sidonia

WHERE TO STAY

VEJER DE LA FRONTERA

Hotel Casa del Califa *moderate*
Set in a complex of eight historic houses, this stylish hotel has rooms with Moorish influences and a highly recommended restaurant.
Plaza de Espana 16, 11150; 956 447 730; www.lacasadelcalifa.com

ZAHARA DE LOS ATUNES

El Varadero *expensive*
The 10 rooms at this original, hip hotel are right on the beach, with an innovative restaurant and balconies for watching the superb sunsets.
Urbanización Atlanterra, 11393; 956 439 038; www.el-varadero.com

TARIFA

Posada La Sacristia *expensive*
This 17th-century inn has individually styled rooms, many with a distinct Moorish and Oriental touch in the decor. It also has an in-house restaurant.
San Donato 8, 11380; 956 681 759; www.lasacristia.net

Hotel Misiana *expensive*
The rooms of this chic boutique property feature modern art and Moroccan furnishings. The hotel also has a bar and a café.
C/ Sancho IV El Bravo 16, 11380; 956 681 759; www.misiana.com

AROUND TARIFA

Mesón de Sancho *moderate*
This is a classic, family-friendly roadside inn-cum-restaurant, 8 km (5 miles) from Tarifa, serving hearty Andalusian meat and fish dishes.
Ctra. Cádiz-Málaga, Km 94, 11380; 956 684 900; www.mesondesancho.com

⑦ Medina-Sidonia
Cádiz; 11170

This peaceful, small town is situated off the main *pueblos blancos* trail, on a hill overlooking rolling fields. The Guzman family, who took the town from the Moors, were granted the dukedom of Medina-Sidonia in the 15th century. The town then became one of the most important ducal seats in Spain. The town is surrounded by medieval walls within which there are narrow, cobbled streets of whitewashed houses with traditional iron *rejas* or grills on their windows.

Medina-Sidonia contains some interesting buildings, including a ruined **Castillo** *(open daily)* and Roman sewers. The Gothic **Iglesia de Santa Maria la Coronada** is the town's most notable and important building. Inside it is a collection of religious works of art dating from the Renaissance, including paintings and a spectacular retable with beautifully carved panels.

🚗 *Take the CA2032, then the CA203, out of the town and head southwards onto the A396. Turn left onto the N340 and when the road forks, right onto the A393/A314 for Vejer de la Frontera.*

⑧ Vejer de la Frontera
Cádiz; 11150

High up on a hill above the steep gorge of the Barbate river, this bright white village was first built up in Phoenician and Roman times to protect the fishing grounds below from barbarian tribes from further north. It later became an important agricultural centre under Moorish influence – the original Moorish gates are still standing. Surrounded by pastures and orange groves, Vejer has a commanding position overlooking the coast from Tarifa to Cádiz.

Vejer was largely undiscovered by the outside world until the 1980s. Interesting buildings to visit include the 14th-century **Iglesia de Divino Salvador**, built on the site of an old mosque; the **Santuario de Nuestra Senora de la Oliva**, a local chapel that houses a 16th-century sculpted image of the Virgin Mary; and the restored 16th-century Renaissance **Convento de las Monjas Concepcionistas**. The plaza on the edge of the old Moorish village offers a number of good restaurants and bars.

🚗 *Continue on the A314 to Barbate. Then take the A2231 into Zahara.*

9 Zahara de los Atunes
Cádiz; 11150

Once a thriving tuna-fishing port, Zahara de los Atunes ("of the tunas") is now a low-key resort with a magnificent, long beach, mainly used by Spaniards. It is also home to two noteworthy buildings: the spectacular 17th-century **Iglesia de Nuestra Senora Carmen**, and the ruins of 15th-century **Castillo de las Almadrabas**, which was built to protect the town from pirates and was also the residence of the Dukes of Medina-Sidonia. This town's other claim to fame is the local belief that Miguel de Cervantes (1547–1616), the Spanish author and poet, was imprisoned here for espionage. He mentions the town in *La Fregona Ilustre* (The Illustrious Mop).

🚗 *Leave Zahara de los Atunes eastwards on the A2227 passing La Zarzuela en route. After 11 km (7 miles), turn right onto the N340 to Tarifa.*

10 Tarifa
Cádiz; 11380

Windsurfing and kitesurfing capital of Europe, Tarifa is the liveliest town on the Costa de la Luz. The town was named after its Moorish conqueror, Tarif ibn Malik, who conquered the town in AD 710, making it the first Moorish possession in Spain. It is home to an assortment of brightly painted bars and sunny plazas that give it an atmosphere reminiscent of the Caribbean. The constant wind feeds the hundreds of power-generating windmills erected in the area. The smoky-blue outline of Africa's Rif mountains can be seen from the ramparts of the town's 10th-century **Castillo de Guzmán el Bueno** *(closed Mon)*. The 15th-century **Iglesia de San Mateo** houses a late Gothic interior, hidden behind its 18th-century Baroque exterior. Two-thirds of the city walls, built after the Castilians took Tarifa from the Moors in 1292, and the main gate, the **Puerta de Jerez**, are still standing.

Winds and Whales

Tarifa's strong winds are ideal for wind- and kitesurfing and the sandy beaches make the experience especially enjoyable. A multitude of other day-trip activities are also available, including scuba diving, fishing, hang-gliding and, away from the water, free climbing, trekking and horse riding. Tarifa's location is ideal for whale- and dolphin-watching and daily boat trips are available for viewing these cetaceans. Long-finned pilot whales, bottlenose dolphins, common dolphins and striped dolphins are commonly sighted in this region.

WHALE-WATCHING IN TARIFA

Foundation for Information and Research on Marine Mammals
The FIRMM conducts daily whale- and dolphin-watching boat trips.
Pedro Cortés 4, 11380; 956 627 008; www.firmm.org; open Apr–Oct, book at least two or three days in advance

EAT AND DRINK

VEJER DE LA FRONTERA
Venta Pinto *moderate*
This former staging post is now a chic but rustic restaurant serving elaborate country dishes and tapas.
La Barca de Vejer s/n, 11150; 956 450 877; www.ventapinto.com

TARIFA
La Vaca Loca *moderate*
Hugely popular – so visitors often have to wait for a table – this very Tarifa-style restaurant specializes in generous grills of excellent meats.
C/ Cervantes 6, 11380

Below Windsurfer off the beach at Tarifa

DAY TRIP OPTIONS

There are plenty of spots along the Costa de la Luz worth a day trip. This drive can be divided into two day trips with either Jerez de la Frontera (near the A4) or Vejer de la Frontera (near the A48) as base.

Sherry circuit
Start at Jerez de la Frontera ❶, famous for its sherry, and head northwest to Sanlúcar de Barrameda ❷ where all *manzanilla* sherry is made. Sanlúcar also has a great equestrian tradition. Follow the coast from here, passing the small resorts of Chipiona ❸ and Rota ❹ before reaching El Puerto de Santa María ❺, once the most important sherry-exporting port and a great spot for sampling sherries and seafood dishes.

From Jerez, take the A480 to Sanlúcar and Chipiona. Then follow the A491 and the A2075 to Rota. From Rota take the A491 and then the CA603 to El Puerto de Santa María.

Sea and sand
After spending the morning in Vejer de la Frontera ❽ and visiting its church, the Iglesia de Divino Salvador, drive down to the coast at Barbate. From here, drive to the Cabo de Trafalgar before heading down the coast to Zahara de los Atunes ❾, one of the prettiest spots on the Costa de la Luz. End the day at Tarifa ❿, which offers some excellent windsurfing and kitesurfing opportunities.

From Vejer de la Frontera, take the A314 southwards to Barbate and the Cabo de Trafalgar. Then follow the A2231 to Zahara de los Atunes. From Zahara de los Atunes, take the A2227, then the N340 to Tarifa.

The Mudéjar Route

Almuñécar to Salobreña

Highlights

- **Ancient Almuñécar**
  Wander around the ancient Phoenician port, and then relax by the beach

- **Picturesque villages**
  Follow the Mudéjar route, which winds through a string of villages in the Axarquía

- **Arab baths**
  Visit the baths hidden beneath a spa hotel in Alhama de Granada

- **Castle town**
  Walk through the picturesque streets of Salobreña to the Moorish castle

Village of Frigiliana, nestled amid rugged hills

The Mudéjar Route

The coast of the province of Granada is known as the Costa Tropical because of its microclimate, which permits the cultivation of exotic fruits. Only a short hop from the Costa del Sol, it has a rugged shoreline punctuated by often unfrequented beaches. This route follows the most scenic part of the coast and then heads inland to the picturesque villages of the Axarquía, a region said to have the best climate in Europe. After a visit to the spa of Alhama de Granada, the route returns to the coast via a dramatic mountain descent to end the journey with a walk around the old town of Salobreña.

KEY

Drive route

0 kilometres   5

0 miles   5

PLAN YOUR DRIVE

Start/finish: Almuñécar to Salobreña.

Number of days: 2.

Distance: 220 km (135 miles).

Road conditions: Generally good, although some parts of the road to Torrox are badly surfaced.

When to go: June and September are ideal. July and August are holiday months and can be crowded.

Opening hours: Most museums are open from 9:30am to 1:30pm, and from 4:30 to 6 or 8pm.

Main market days: Almuñécar: Fri; Alhama de Granada: Fri.

Major festivals: Almuñécar: Le Noche de San Juan, Jun; Frigiliana: Festival de las Tres Culturas, Aug.

Above Sandy beach surrounded by rocky cliffs in Nerja, *see p211*

① Almuñécar
Granada; 18690

A settlement was founded on the site of Almuñécar, now a cosmopolitan resort, by the Phoenicians in the 8th century BC. It was later taken over by the Romans who constructed an aqueduct and a fish-salting plant – the ruins of the latter can be seen in **Parque del Majuelo**, a pretty garden of subtropical plants. Situated above the garden is the **Castillo de San Miguel** *(closed Mon and Sun afternoon)*, built by the Romans and developed into an impressive fortress by the Moors in the Middle Ages.

🚗 *Head west along the coast and turn right towards Málaga on the Avenida del Mediterráneo. At the crossroads, turn left on the N340 for La Herradura, passing the turn-off for Marina del Este.*

② La Herradura
Granada; 18697

There are views of the beautiful bay of La Herradura as the road descends towards the sea. A detour to the left into Calle de la Carretera de la Playa, after crossing the tunnel before La Herradura, leads to the pretty yacht harbour of **Marina del Este**, a base for underwater excursions. The same road leads to a lighthouse, above the harbour, from which there are panoramic views of the countryside and the coast. La Herradura itself has a splendid beach and some restaurants that serve great seafood.

🚗 *Retrace the route to the N340 and turn left. Go straight over the roundabout, where most of the traffic leaves the N340 to join the motorway. A tunnel pierces through the headland of Cerro Gordo, marking the beginning of perhaps the most beautiful stretch of road on Spain's southern coast.*

③ Cerro Gordo
Granada, Málaga; 18697, 29787

The N340 winds along the coast offering a scenic drive crossing the magnificent headland of Cerro Gordo, which has a succession of beaches. Several 16th- and 17th-century watch-towers still stand guard along the coast. Turn right at the roundabout after Maro to visit the **Cuevas de Nerja**, a series of vast caverns discovered in 1959. Back on the N340, cross the viaduct over the Chillar river. You will see the 19th-century **Acueducto del Aguilar**, to which the viaduct runs parallel, on the right.

🚗 *Drive over a series of roundabouts, past Nerja, to turn right onto the MA5105 for Frigiliana. Go through the first, more modern part of town and descend to the parking area in Plaza de la Cañada del Ingenio. Park here to take a walk in the Old Town.*

④ Frigiliana
Málaga; 29788

Frigiliana is by far the prettiest of the many whitewashed towns in the Axarquía. The old quarter of the town is a delightful complex of small streets, alleyways, steps and tunnels, often leading nowhere, decorated with potted plants.

🚗 *Leave on the MA9012 for Torrox. Pass beneath the Caracoles hotel, descend into a valley, cross a small bridge and climb again to reach Torrox. A green metal fence on the left confirms the route. Turn right for Cómpeta on the A7207. Just before reaching Cómpeta, there is a mirador (viewpoint) over the town. At the next junction, turn right on the Avenida Sayalonga (MA112). In the town, the tourist office is on the right. Go up the slope to Plaza Axarquía and park.*

Above left Colourful doors around a courtyard, Frigiliana **Above right** Long curving beach at La Herradura

WHERE TO STAY

ALMUÑÉCAR
Los Laureles *inexpensive*
A small four-bedroom guesthouse in the back streets of the town, this place also has a swimming pool.
La Ribera Baja 14, 18690; 958 069 132; www.loslaureles.net

AROUND FRIGILIANA
Los Caracoles *expensive*
With igloo-like bungalows arranged on a hillside, Los Caracoles, 5 km (3 miles) from Frigiliana, has spectacular views.
Ctra. Frigiliana-Torrox, Km 4.5, 29788; 952 030 680; www.hotelloscaracoles.com

EAT AND DRINK

ALMUÑÉCAR
Horno de Candida *moderate*
This restaurant-school is located in the old part of the town near Plaza de las Constitución. The chefs may be trainees under supervision, but the standards are high.
C/ Orovia 3, 18690; 958 883 284

FRIGILIANA
Restaurante Al Fuente *inexpensive*
Charming little restaurant with just a few tables, serving up dishes that add North African and Dutch influences to the traditional tastes of Spain. Good gluten-free and vegetarian options.
C/ Real 32, 29788; 660 777 744; closed Wed

El Chambao de Joaquin *moderate*
Although it looks like a humble beach bar, this is a fairly sophisticated restaurant. On Saturdays and Sundays, a giant paella is cooked over a wood fire.
Paseo de Andrés Segovia 2, 18697; 958 640 044; www.elchambaodejoaquin.com

Eat and Drink: inexpensive, under €20; moderate, €20–€40; expensive, over €40

Top Typical Andalusian farm outside sleepy Cómpeta **Above** Placid waters of the spa in Alhama de Granada **Below** Andalusian spa town of Alhama de Granada

WHERE TO STAY

ALHAMA DE GRANADA

La Seguiriya *inexpensive*
A small hotel-restaurant in the Old Town, La Seguiriya is run by a flamenco singer and his family. There are six individually decorated rooms. It also has a restaurant with a terrace.
C/ Las Peñas 12, 18120; 958 360 636; www.laseguiriya.com

SALOBREÑA

Jayma *inexpensive*
This is a family-run hotel on one of the main streets of the Old Town. One room is equipped for the disabled. There are no meals served here but there are bars and restaurants nearby.
C/ Cristo 24, 18680; 958 610 231; www.hostaljayma.com

AROUND SALOBREÑA

La Casa de los Bates *moderate*
The Casa de los Bates, a 19th-century country mansion, sits on a hill overlooking the Costa Tropical, 10 km (6 miles) to the east of Salobreña. It has personalized rooms, a lovely garden and a large swimming pool.
Ctra. N340, Km 329, 5, 18600, Motril; 958 349 495; www.casadelosbates.com

⑤ Cómpeta
Málaga; 29754
The pleasant mountain of town Cómpeta acts as a service centre for the villages and houses spread across the surrounding hillsides. Its main economic activity, apart from tourism, is the production of sweet dessert wines. The sloping rectangular enclosures, used for drying the grapes, are a common feature of the homesteads of the Axarquía region.

Retrace your route back out of Cómpeta, but continue straight at the junction towards Torre del Mar and Algarrobo on the MA112 and MA111. After 5 km (3 miles), take the right turn onto the MA5104 for Archez. Continue on this road across the bridge and then on the MA4108 to Salares.

⑥ La Ruta Mudéjar
Málaga; 29753 & 29714
The Mudéjars were Muslims who stayed back in Christian territory after the *reconquista* (Reconquest of Spain), continuing to apply their artistic and architectural skills in accordance with their own traditions. Visitors can still see examples of Mudéjar craftsmanship in Archez and Salares. Stroll around these towns to see exquisite ornate brick church towers, which are minarets in all but name.

Continue on the road past Sedella and Canillas de Aceituno and follow signs for Vélez Málaga. At the bottom of the hill, turn right for Granada onto the A7205. Cross the bridge to meet the A402. Turn right and keep on the same road through Ventas de Zafarraya. In Alhama de Granada, follow signs for "Centro Urbano" to the tourist information office.

⑦ Alhama de Granada
Granada; 18120
The ancient spa town of Alhama is built on the lip of a gorge; there are great views of the canyon from behind the Iglesia del Carmen. The town is built around the main parish church, the **Iglesia de Santa María de la Encarnación** *(open for Mass daily)*. In the cellars of the the spa hotel of Balneario Alhama de Granada below the town are perfectly preserved 13th-century Arab baths *(visits 2–4pm daily, while spa patients are at lunch)*.

Retrace your route on the A402 towards Ventas. After leaving town, turn left onto the A4150 for Játar, crossing the Alhama river and passing a reservoir. Before Játar, take the badly signed left turn onto the GR3302. Skirt Arenas del Rey and continue to Fornes, taking the left turn signposted to Granada and then onto Jayena. Turn right at the next junction onto the A4050 – the Carretera de la Cabra.

⑧ Carretera de la Cabra
Granada; 18127, 18698 and 18699
The route goes through a rolling landscape high above the coast, with a sudden dramatic descent, passing under greyish-white cliffs. There are endless curves and great views all the way down the so-called "Road of the Goat", which goes through **Otívar** and **Jete** and passes a few Roman remains.

On reaching Almuñécar, do not go under the N340, but turn left and follow it parallel to a junction to pick up the N340 east towards Salobreña. Take the second marked entrance into Salobreña to reach the roundabout, next to which is the tourist information office, and park nearby.

⑨ Salobreña

Granada; 18680

The old white town of Salobreña is spread over a large rock located a little way back from the sea. This walk goes through a warren of steep, narrow streets and steps, to the Moorish castle at the top. The town is best explored in the morning and early evening to avoid the heat of an Andalusian summer's day.

A two-hour walking tour

From the car park, walk to the **Tourist Information Office** ① and follow the pavement past the roundabout, on which stands an old sugar-milling machine. Go down Avenida de Federico García Lorca. Pass by the church and market; turn right between the hardware shop and the Santander Bank, up the short Calle de los Hermanos Álvarez Quintero. Go straight on this road and up Calle Nuestra Señora del Rosario towards the fountain. Take the two flights of steps to the Plaza del Antiguo Mercado. Bear right to a hairpin bend from where a flight of steps begin. Go up the steps and into a modern arcade outside the **Museo Historico** ② (open daily, closed Mon in winter), a museum of Salobreña's history, on Plaza del Ayuntamiento.

Turn left around the square and again immediately left through Calle de la Bóveda, a 16th-century barrel-vaulted tunnel. Continue a few steps to the Pesetas restaurant for a lunch stop, which has superb views from its rooftop terrace. Otherwise, take the flight of brick steps to the right, leaving the Bóveda, and turn right at the top towards the Arab-influenced Mudéjar church, **Iglesia de Nuestra Señora del Rosario** ③. Turn left up the steps at the corner of the church. At the top of the steps, stop either at the refreshments stall located on the right, halfway up the cobbled and stepped Calle Andrés Segovia, or turn left to visit Salobreña's restored **Castillo Arabe** ④ (open daily), which has panoramic views from its magnificent ramparts.

From the castle, go down Calle Andrés Segovia and turn left at the bottom into Calle Girona, then immediately left again. This goes to the horseshoe-arched Puerta del Postigo

Colourful tile from Salobreña

gate; fork left through it for a park, the **Paseo de las Flores** ⑤.

Take the narrow steps across the street from the Puerta del Postigo, slightly to the left and downhill. There is no option but to turn left at the bottom of the first flight of steps. Take the next set of steps to the right, which leads out to a balcony. Bear right along this through a park overhung by eucalyptus trees. At the bottom of the next flight of steps, bear left down another very short zigzag flight of steps. Get on to Calle Carmen, which is just around the corner. Turn right and continue straight down Calle Bodegon to reach Calle del Cristo. At the crossroads at the bottom of this street, turn right onto Antonio Machada to reach a pedestrianized triangle on which stand the outdoor tables of the bar-restaurant Porteria. Turn left at the corner just after the bar to approach the tourist information office, where the car is parked.

Above Charming old town of Salobreña overlooking the beach

VISITING SALOBREÑA

Tourist Information
Plaza de Goya, 18680; 958 610 314; www.ayto-salobrena.es

Parking
Parking is available on the streets near the tourist information office.

EAT AND DRINK

SALOBREÑA

El Peñón *moderate*
The menu has a wide selection of seafood, some of which is barbecued over an open fire on the beach.
Playa del Peñón, 18680; 958 610 538; www.restauranteelpenon.es

Pesetas *moderate*
Good seafood dishes and tables with stunning views of the coast.
C/ Bóveda 11, 18680; 958 610 182; www.restaurante-pesetas.es; closed Mon

Historic Mountain Villages

Granada to Puente de Tablate

Highlights

- **Moorish Spain**
  Wander through the streets of the Alabaicín, the old Moorish quarter of Granada, up to the Alhambra

- **Cave houses**
  Visit the famous troglodyte quarter of Guadix

- **Renaissance fortress**
  Climb up to Castillo de La Calahorra, which stands guard over the plains

- **Villages of the Alpujarras**
  Explore the tiny villages on the slopes of the Sierra Nevada

The Alhambra and the Sierra Nevada, seen from the Mirador de San Nicolás, Granada

Historic Mountain Villages

The city of Granada, famous for the unmistakable castle-palace of the Alhambra, sits at the foot of the northern slopes of the Sierra Nevada. This route crosses the mountains at the first available pass to the east, after visiting the cave quarter of Guadix and the Renaissance castle at La Calahorra. The gentle, green southern slopes of Las Alpujarras are a rural region of beautiful walks and peaceful villages. This route makes an excellent relaxed and unhurried drive.

KEY

Drive route

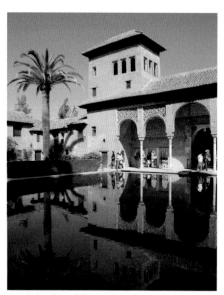

Above Intricate Portico del Partal inside the Alhambra, Granada, *see p218*

Below View over the rooftops of the old Moorish quarter, the Albaicín, in Granada, *see p218*

0 kilometres   5

0 miles   5

PLAN YOUR DRIVE

Start/finish: Granada to Puente de Tablate.

Number of days: 2, allowing a day for the walk around the Albaicín and the Alhambra.

Distance: 235 km (145 miles).

Road conditions: Some of the roads on this route are narrow and winding.

When to go: The best time to visit this region is from spring to autumn. The road over Puerto de la Ragua may be inaccessible in winter.

Opening hours: Most museums and monuments are generally open from 10am to 2pm, and from 5 to 8pm, and are closed on Mondays.

Main market days: Granada: Wed, Sat, Sun; Guadix: Sat; Lanjarón: Fri.

Shopping: The region is famous for *jarapas* (rag rugs). Look for ceramics in Purullena and cured hams in Trevélez.

Major festivals: Granada: Día de la Cruz, 3 May; Corpus Christi, May/Jun; Guadix: Feria, end Aug; Lanjarón: Fiesta de San Juan, 24 Jun.

DAY TRIP OPTIONS

The route splits into two halves: north of the Sierra Nevada and south of it. **History buffs** will enjoy a visit to the Alhambra and the cave houses in Guadix. **Mountain lovers** should head south to visit the tiny villages for a breath of fresh air. For details, *see p223*.

ACTIVITIES

Visit the Alhambra – one of the most extraordinary sights in Spain

Shop for traditional ceramic items in the roadside shops of Purullena

Taste the hams of Trevélez, dry-cured in the mountain air, and wash them down with local wine

Stroll along the dense wooded paths of the Alpujarras

Right Arid La Peza countryside en route to Purullena, *see p220*

Above Patio de los Leones inside the Alhambra

VISITING GRANADA

Parking
Parking is restricted in the centre of Granada (especially in the Albaicín) and it is best to park a little way outside the centre. There is a car park next to the ticket office of the Alhambra on the hill above Plaza Nueva. From here visitors can either walk down the hill to Plaza Nueva or take a minibus. There is a car park on Acera de Darro from which it is a 10-minute walk to Plaza Nueva.

VISITING THE ALHAMBRA

A visit to the Alhambra is best planned well ahead as visitor numbers are limited. Tickets can be bought online (www.ticketmaster.es) or booked in advance through various outlets, details of which are listed on the official website, which also has comprehensive information and a useful interactive map of the Alhambra. *www.alhambra-patronato.es; open daily 8:30am–8pm, closes 6pm in winter, night visits 10–11:30pm Tue–Sat Mar–Oct, 8–9:30pm Fri–Sat in winter*

WHERE TO STAY

GRANADA

Santa Isabel la Real *moderate*
Located in a restored 16th-century house, this hotel consists of 11 individually styled rooms around a patio. *C/ Santa Isabel la Real Nº19, 18009; 958 294 658; www. hotelsantaisabellareal.com*

Parador de Granada *expensive*
Part of the state-run Parador chain, this hotel enjoys a fabulous setting next to the gardens of the Alhambra. *Real de la Alhambra s/n, 18009; 958 221 440; www.parador.es*

ⓘ Granada
Granada; 18009

First occupied by the Moors in the 8th century, Granada's golden period came during the rule of the Nasrid dynasty from 1238 to 1492, when artisans, merchants and scholars all contributed to the city's reputation as a centre of culture. The city is overlooked by one of the most impressive sights of Spain – the fortress-palace of the Alhambra. This walk goes through the streets of Granada's Moorish quarter, the Albaicín, and then up to the Alhambra and its gardens. Avoid doing this walk in the afternoon as it can get very hot.

A two-hour walking tour

Start from the car park and walk to **Plaza Nueva ①**, below the Alhambra. Start walking down Calle de Elvira (at the end of the square, signed for Plaza de San Gil) but fork right almost immediately up Calderería Vieja. Turn right at the top to emerge onto the Plaza de San Gregorio. Keep going in the same direction, always uphill, on Calle de San Gregorio and double back at the first corner on the left. At the end of this short street, turn left again; this will lead to Placeta de San José, beneath a graceful 10th-century minaret, now a church tower of the **Iglesia de San José ②**. Continue uphill from the Placeta de San José beside the minaret on Calle San José, past the door of Carmen San Luis – *carmen* being the name of a typical well-to-do house in the Albaicín – its garden secluded behind high walls. Turn right and immediately left across

Calle de Bocanegra and straight uphill into **Placeta de San Miguel Bajo ③**. Here the route turns right on Calle de Santa Isabel la Real beside the wall of the whitewashed church. Go past the 16th–17th-century monastery of the same name. From here, the tower of Iglesia de San Nicolás on top of the hill can be seen. Turn left just before the road starts to go downhill to get to the square (up the steps) in front of the church, where there is the viewpoint, the **Mirador de San Nicolás ④**. There is a panoramic view of the Alhambra across the Darro valley from here.

Turning left at the bottom of the Mirador de San Nicolás, go past the modern mosque on the left, down the steps through Cuesta de las Tomasas and down to the **Placeta del Aljibe de Trillo ⑤**, which has a 14th-century cistern. At the bottom of the square, turn left on Azacayuela de San Pedro. Go down the steps and round the corner. Turn left on the unsigned Calle Limón to reach Plaza Escuelas, where the **Iglesia de San Juan de los Reyes** ⑥ acts as a landmark. Cross the street into Calle Zafra and go straight down it to the banks of the Darro river. At the end of the street, on the left, is the **Museo Arqueológico** ⑦ *(currently closed for renovation),* housed in the Casa de Castril, a Renaissance mansion with a lovely Plateresque portal. Turn right along the Darro and further along on the right, there is the **El Bañuelo** ⑧ *(open Tue–Sat),* 11th-century Arab baths whose vaults are lit by star-shaped holes in the roof. Continue in the same direction to return to Plaza Nueva.

From here, head towards the Alhambra. Those with the day to spare can get to the Alhambra on foot from Plaza Nueva but it is a long steep walk up the Cuesta de Gomérez and not suggested. A minibus goes up the same route here. By car, the Alhambra is approached along an access road from the southeast, which avoids the city centre. There is a car park at the entrance of the Alhambra.

Built under Ismail I, Yusuf and Muhammad V – kings of the Nasrid dynasty – the Alhambra is the most sensual piece of architecture in Spain. Although it has an austere defensive exterior when seen from the Albaicín, the Alhambra has an exquisitely decorated suite of royal chambers and courtyards at its heart. On the hillside above it is the summer palace, Generalife, which stands in water

gardens. The Generalife now provides a magical setting for some events of Granada's annual music and dance festival. After the visit, go back to Plaza Nueva and then to the car park.

🚗 *Get onto the bypass (indicated by blue signs) south towards Motril. After taking exit 132 for Sierra Nevada keep to the left and follow signs. Keep to the right lane through the tunnel and look out for a right turn for Pinos Genil and Quéntar. An access road leads to a T-junction outside Cenes de la Vega. Turn right here on the A4026. Before Pinos Genil turn left for Dudar, Quéntar and La Peza on the GR3201 for the Embalse de Quéntar. A right turn will lead to the car park, which is off a bend going left.*

② Embalse de Quéntar
Granada; 18192, 18519

This attractive turquoise-blue reservoir comes up suddenly after the town of Quéntar. From the car park, walk around and across the dam. There are some good views of the lake. The route then continues over the scenic pass of **Puerto de los Blancares** (1,300 m/4,250 ft).

🚗 *Continue on the same road (the GR3201, which is sometimes also numbered GR-SE-39) beside the lake for Purullena. Take a right turn in La Peza towards Purullena. Continue through the town to the crossroads which has a large statue of a bull. Turn left downhill on Calle Rio and continue down and then out of town on the GR4104. Keep on this road past Los Baños and Graena onto Purullena.*

Above Rugged terrain of the Sierra Nevada
Below left Belfry of the Iglesia de San José in Granada **Below right** View of the Alhambra

EAT AND DRINK

GRANADA

Mesón El Yunque *moderate*
An agreeably informal place for tapas or a meal, in a square in the Albaicín.
Plaza San Miguel Bajo 3, Albaicín, 18009; 958 800 090; www. vivagranada.com/yunque

Mirador de Morayma *moderate*
This charming patio-restaurant specializes in dishes of Granada, such as *remojón* (codfish and orange salad). *C/ Pianista Garcia Carnillo 2, 18010; 958 228 290; www.miradordemorayma. com; closed Sun eve, Sun Jul & Aug*

Eat and Drink: inexpensive, under €20; moderate, €20–€40; expensive, over €40

Above Renaissance Castillo de La Calahorra, with its domed turrets against the Sierra Nevada **Below left** Distinctive chimney of a cave house in Guadix **Below right** Streets of La Calahorra with the castle in the background

VISITING THE CAVES IN PURULLENA

Cueva Museo "La Inmaculada"
This ethnological museum, in a complex of three caves, depicts cave dwellers' lives throughout history.
Ctra. de Granada 80; 958 690 181; www. cuevainmaculada.com; open daily

ACTIVITIES IN THE SIERRA NEVADA

Hiking
Lanteira is a popular departure point for hikes. The tourist office for the area is in Guadix.
Plaza de la Constitución 15–18, 18500; 958 662 804; www.guadix.es

WHERE TO STAY

AROUND GUADIX

Cuevas La Granja *moderate*
Several caves around Guadix have been transformed into womb-like hotels. This hotel in Benalúa, 8 km (5 miles) from Guadix, has 11 self-contained cave houses, a restaurant and a pool.
Camino de la Granja, 18510, Benalúa; 958 676 000; www.cuevas.org

Casa Las Chimeneas *moderate*
The owners of this bed-and-breakfast organize walking tours, yoga and gastronomy classes. Each large bedroom has a private balcony or terrace.
C/ Amargura 6, Mairena, 18493; 958 760 352; www.alpujarra-tours.com

③ Purullena
Granada; 18519
Until the motorway arrived, Purullena was on the main road between Murcia/Almería and Granada. This explains the existence of the large open-fronted shops specializing in local ceramics on the way out of town. The brightly coloured crockery comes in all shapes and sizes. Famous for its cave houses, Purullena still has a large number of people who live in these cave homes today. The cave quarter is located above the town.

🚗 *Leave on the A4100 towards Guadix. Entering Guadix, follow the broad Avenida de Mariana Pineda into the centre. At the large roundabout, bear right for the tourist information office, which is located behind the cathedral in Plaza de la Constitución*

④ Guadix
Granada; 18500
Founded in Roman times, Guadix thrived under the Moors and after the Reconquest but declined in the 18th century. Although it has a handsome monumental town centre, most visitors make straight for the famous *barrio de cuevas*, the troglodyte quarter with 2,000 inhabited caves. These caves have been used as dwellings since prehistoric times, when people first hid in them for safety. The **Museo de Alfarería** and **Museo Etnológico** *(open Mon–Sat)*

museums show how people here live underground. For an overview, follow the "Barrio de Cuevas" signs beyond the church to the **Mirador Cerro de las Balas**. Steps from a small car park lead up to a constructed balcony overlooking the town and its mud hills pockmarked with cave dwellings. Two sights worth visiting are the 16th-century Baroque **Cathedral** and the **Iglesia de Santiago**, which has a fine coffered ceiling and a Mudéjar tower.

🚗 *From the cave quarter, return to the town centre and leave on the N324 towards Almería. Just after leaving the town, turn right onto the GR5104 (also marked GR-SE-19) for Jerez del Marquesado and Lanteira. Keep on the same road past Jerez to Lanteira.*

⑤ Lanteira
Granada; 18518
A pleasant town of winding streets lined with white houses, Lanteira serves as a departure point for hikes into the Sierra Nevada. Its name is derived from the Ibero-Roman Argentaria, City of Silver, a reminder that there was once a prosperous mining industry here, which supported two castles. Both are ruins now.

🚗 *Continue on the same road, the GR5104, into La Calahorra. Either walk from the town up to the castle or take the car further up the hill, but there are no signs on the route to help.*

⑥ Castillo de La Calahorra
Granada; 18512

Standing on the summit of an isolated hill from which to control the plains below, at the foot of the Sierra Nevada, the magnificent Castillo de La Calahorra *(open Wed only)* was the first Renaissance building in Spain. The construction of the castle was ordered by Rodrigo de Mendoza, son of Cardinal Mendoza, for his bride, and was completed between 1509 and 1512. The defiantly military exterior of La Calahorra, with its four cylindrical corner towers, is in complete contrast with the Carrara marble pillars and the palatial courtyard inside.

🚗 *Take the road towards Granada and Almeria, but at the end of the town turn off right onto the A337 for Ferreira and Puerto de la Ragua.*

⑦ Puerto de la Ragua
Granada; 18512, 18494, 18460

The ascent to the tree-shrouded 2,000-m (6,550-ft) pass across the slopes of the Sierra Nevada has some beautiful views looking back over the plains and fertile valleys. Far from the crowds of alpine ski resorts, visitors can indulge in the many sports activities such as cross-country skiing and mountain biking. In the summer, the pass is a great place to pick up the hiking trails that set off from the visitors' centre here. The pass is usually snowbound in the winter months when the slopes are used for cross-country skiing.

🚗 *Coming down from Puerto de la Ragua, turn right for Válor on the A4130, passing over the top of Laroles. Stay on this road through Válor to Yegen, Mecina Bombarón as it passes*

Bérchules and on to Juviles. After Juviles, turn right on the A4132 to the town of Trevélez.

Troglodyte Residences
In and around Guadix, a cave house is considered just as good a place to live in as a house or flat, if not better. The soft clay is easy to excavate, so an extra room can be added if needed. Underground, the temperature remains at an agreeably constant 18° C (64° F), meaning that the cave feels relatively warm in winter and cool in summer. The only drawback is the lack of natural light, but despite this, caves here are much in demand and are bought and sold (at surprisingly high prices) just like any other piece of good real estate.

Above left Flowerpots decorate the walls of a house in La Calahorra **Above right** Colourful ceramic pottery in a shop in Purullena **Below** Cave houses against a rock face, Guadix

Above Flat roofs of Pampaneira huddled together on the mountainside Below left Ruins of Lanjarón's castle on a lone hill Below right Spray of flowers adding colour to a house in Trevélez

the road enters the Poqueira Valley. Turn right by the petrol station to get onto the A4129 to visit Bubión and Capileira above. To get to Pampaneira, retrace the route on the A4132 and turn right.

⑨ Poqueira Valley

Granada; 18411, 18412, 18413

The attractive little villages tucked into the folds of the southern slopes of the Sierra Nevada are a must-visit. **Bubión**, **Capileira** and **Pampaneira** are the prettiest villages in Las Alpujarras, surrounded by dazzling views. All share similar characteristics – white houses piled on top of each other seemingly at random, all with flat gravelled roofs and sprouting eccentric chimneys. The streets are quiet and some disappear down short tunnels beneath the houses – one in Pampaneira has a stream gurgling down the middle. From Capileira, the furthest point that can be driven to independently, take a national park minibus *(bookings recommended; 671 564 406, 958 763 090)* into the heights of the Sierra Nevada.

🚗 *Leave Pampaneira on the A4132. At the bottom of the hill outside Órgiva, turn right for Lanjarón on the A348.*

⑧ Trevélez

Granada; 18417

The highest town in Spain, Trevélez stands at an altitude of 1,450 m (4,750 ft) beneath the highest mountain on the Spanish mainland, Mulhacén (3,479 m/11,414 ft). Trevélez is divided into three parts: a nondescript area of shops at the bottom selling the town's trademark cured hams, and two more *barrios* (quarters) up the hill. Calle Cuesta, starting beside the church, is the most direct way to walk up into the prettier streets.

🚗 *Continue on the A4132 to Pórtugos – where there is an unusual iron-rich spring – and Pitres. Rounding a corner,*

⑩ Lanjarón

Granada; 18420

On the threshold of Las Alpujarras, Lanjarón has a long history as a spa. It is known throughout Spain as the source of one of the country's most

WHERE TO STAY

TREVÉLEZ

Hotel La Fragua *inexpensive*
This simple whitewashed *mesón* (inn) is located in one of the highest villages in Spain, with spectacular views from the rooftop and, in winter, an open fire.
C/ San Antonio 4, 18417; 958 858 626; www.hotellafragua.com; closed 10 Jan–10 Feb

POQUEIRA VALLEY

El Cascapeñas *inexpensive*
Located in one of the prettiest villages of the Alpujarras, Capileira, this is a charmingly decorated small hotel and restaurant. It also has a well-stocked wine cellar.
C/ Carril s/n, 18413, Capileira; 958 763 011; www.elcascapenas.com

Where to Stay: inexpensive, under €70; moderate, €70–€120; expensive, over €120

popular brands of mineral water. From June to October, visitors flock to the town for various water treatments for many ailments. There are several springs and fountains where visitors can fill up a bottle – one of the most convenient is beside the road shortly after leaving town. A major festival, the Fiesta de San Juan, begins on the night of 24 June and includes a water battle. Lanjarón's only monument is a ruined castle on a bluff, south of the town. The roads to and from Lanjarón wind slowly and dizzily aound the slopes.

🚗 *Follow the A348 straight down from Lanjarón past the wind farm. Turn left at the bottom of the hill for Puente de Tablate.*

⓫ Puente de Tablate

Granada; 18660

Curiously, this name applies to three bridges of three different generations, all striding over the same gorge,

which is 45 m (150 ft) deep, at the same point. The oldest, **Puente Nazari**, was built between the 16th and 17th centuries and is used only by pedestrians. Next to it is the 19th-century bridge (with a white shrine beside it), which replaced it. Above both of these older bridges is a functional modern viaduct over which traffic passes noisily.

Above Craft shop displaying its wares in Pampaneira in the high Alpujarras **Below** View of Capileira in Las Alpujarras

EAT AND DRINK

TREVÉLEZ

La Fragua *moderate*
This restaurant concentrates on the traditional food of the Alpujarras, which includes dry-cured ham.
C/ San Antonio 4, 18417; 958 858 512; www.hotellafragua.com

POQUEIRA VALLEY

Hostal Pampaneira Casa Alfonso
inexpensive
A small *hostal* in Pampaneira which specializes in braised meats and serves local Alpujarra wines.
Avda. de la Alpujarra 1, 18411; 958 763 002; www.hostalpampaneira.com

LANJARÓN

Alcadima *moderate*
Regional favourites are given a modern twist here, and there are vegetarian and gluten-free options too.
C/ Francisco Tarrega 3, 18420; 958 770 809; www.alcadima.com

DAY TRIP OPTIONS

Using Granada as a base, the itinerary can be split into two independent day trips. A third option is to head south from Granada to the Alpujarras. The A44 and A92 motorways are easy access roads to most of the sights in this drive.

Magnificent Alhambra
The Alhambra, in Granada ❶, can take the best part of a day to see properly, with a lazy lunch in the middle. Dip into the city centre monuments and stroll around the fabulous gardens of Generalife. Then

take a walk around the atmospheric streets of the Albaicín.

With a little planning, and using a bus or two, go around the Alhambra.

Castles and cave houses
Either wander along the back road to Guadix ❹ and return along the motorway or, if time is really short, use the motorway to go straight to Guadix to see the extraordinary cave houses. The trip can be extended to see Castillo de La Calahorra ❻.

Take the motorway, A92, from Granada to Guadix and return the same way.

Mountain lovers
The best of Las Alpujarras can be seen if the last part of the route is done backwards. Take a walk around the mountain town of Lanjarón ❿ and then Pampaneira, Bubión and Capileira – picturesque villages of the Poqueira Valley ❾.

Take the A44 south from Granada towards Lanjarón. Continue towards Órgiva but before getting there, turn off left onto the A348 for Lanjarón. Continue on the A348 and, at Órgiva, get onto the A4132 to visit Pampaneira, Bubión and Capileira.

Eat and Drink: inexpensive, under €20; moderate, €20–€40; expensive, over €40

Andalusian Renaissance and Wooded Mountains

Baeza to Sabiote

Highlights

- **Colleges and palaces**
  Explore Baeza with its old university and ornate Palacio del Jabalquinto

- **Renaissance towns**
  Stroll around the superb Andalusian town of Baeza and visit the Palacio del Deán Ortega in Úbeda

- **Woods and mountains**
  Drive down the valley of the Guadalquivir river in the Parque Natural Sierras de Cazorla, Segura y Las Villas or take a hike on one of the park's many trails

Courtyard of the Palacio del Deán Ortega in Úbeda

Andalusian Renaissance and Wooded Mountains

Two preserved Renaissance towns, Baeza and Úbeda, sit on adjacent hills among the endless olive groves of Jaén province. This route crosses the plains, taking visitors up into one of Spain's best-known nature reserves, the Parque Natural Sierras de Cazorla, Segura y Las Villas. Much of the itinerary goes through dramatic landscapes and there are plenty of opportunities to stop and enjoy the views or set off on foot with a pair of binoculars in search of wildlife. Game and freshwater fish figure on menus everywhere in this region, as do some of the world's best olive oils.

Above Ornate Isabelline-style façade of the Palacio del Jabalquinto, Baeza, *see p228*

Below Panoramic view of the Collado del Almendral, *see p230*

ACTIVITIES

Take an organized nature trek or photo safari in a 4WD vehicle into restricted areas of the Parque Natural Sierras de Cazorla, Segura y Las Villas

Follow one of the many marked footpaths, which vary from easy to demanding, of the Parque Natural Sierras de Cazorla, Segura y Las Villas

Try climbing or hang-gliding in the Parque Natural Sierras de Cazorla, Segura y Las Villas

Taste the olive oils of the region, which to connoisseurs have just as much individual character as fine wines

KEY

Drive route

0 kilometres   5

0 miles   5

Cerro de Natao △
1,274 m

Fuente
Pinilla

↑ Albacete

A6202

A319

Tranco

Villanueva del
Arzobispo

A6202

A6202

N322

Casa de
Petón

Embalse
del Tranco

Bujaraiza

Isla
Cabeza
de la Viña

Alto de
Pedro Miguel
1,830 m
△

A319

Los Candelejas

**COLLADO DEL
ALMENDRAL**

Embalse de
Aguascebas

6

Coto-Rios

Parque Natural
Sierras de Cazorla,
Segura y
Las Villas

**TORRE DEL
VINAGRE** 5

A319

**PUERTO DE
LAS PALOMAS**

Embalse de
los Órganos

Burunchel

4 Arroyo Frío

La Iruela

A319

3 **CAZORLA**

Vadillo Castril

Below left Ruins of the Iglesia de Santa María in Cazorla, *see p229* **Below right** Guadalquivir river in the heart of the Parque Natural Sierras de Cazorla, Segura y Las Villas, *see p229*

PLAN YOUR DRIVE

Start/finish: Baeza to Sabiote.

Number of days: 2, allowing half a day to explore Úbeda.

Distance: 190 km (120 miles).

Road conditions: Generally good, although some roads are very windy.

When to go: June and September are ideal; the weather is warm but there are few people around. July and August are holiday months and on the weekends the roads can be busy with traffic.

Opening hours: In the winter, most museums are open from 9:30 or 10am to 6 or 8pm, though they may close on Mondays. In the tourist season, most museums remain open all day long.

Main market days: Baeza: Tue; Úbeda: Fri; Cazorla: Mon, Sat.

Shopping: Olive oil is a speciality in this region.

Major festivals: Baeza: Feria, second week Aug; Romeria de la Yedra, early Sep; Úbeda: San Miguel, 29 Sep; Sabiote: Fiesta de Virgen de la Estrella, May.

DAY TRIP OPTIONS

For those interested in **architecture** and **culture**, Baeza and Úbeda together can make up a day's sightseeing. The nature reserve in Cazorla can make a self-contained day out for **nature lovers**. For details, *see p231*.

Above Sunlight filtering into the courtyard of the Palacio del Deán Ortega in Úbeda

VISITING ÚBEDA

Tourist Information
C/ Baja del Marqués 4, 23400; 953 779 204; www.turismodeubeda.com

Parking
Parking is available in and around the Plaza de Santa Lucía.

WHERE TO STAY

BAEZA

Puerta de la Luna *expensive*
This 17th-century mansion was formerly the residence of the cathedral's canons. It has a large courtyard with a library, a swimming pool, a spa and a small gym.
C/ Canonigo Melgares Raya, 23440; 953 747 019; www. hotelpuertadelaluna.com

ÚBEDA

Parador de Úbeda *expensive*
The former residence of the Dean of Málaga, this is a comfortable place centred around an elegant patio.
Plaza de Vázquez Molina, 23400; 953 750 345; www.parador.es

AROUND CAZORLA

Parador de Cazorla *expensive*
This modern hotel, south of the village in a privileged and secluded forest setting in the heart of Cazorla's nature reserve, is a good base for walks.
23470, Sierra Cazorla, 23470; 953 727 075; www.parador.es

Where to Stay: inexpensive, under €70; moderate, €70–€120; expensive, over €120

① Baeza

Jaén; 23440
Baeza has a compact monumental centre, which makes it easy to explore on foot. Begin in the **Plaza del Pópulo** (Plaza de Los Leones), a square overlooked by two arches and two other handsome buildings, one of which is the tourist information office. From here the cathedral is uphill through the arch to the left and, opposite it, the former university with the names of students daubed on it in bull's blood. The town's most visited building, the **Palacio del Jabalquinto** *(open Mon–Fri)* is a splendid Gothic palace.

🚗 *Leave town on the J3040, then turn left onto the A316, which leads to Úbeda. Follow the purple signs for "Centro Monumental" or the yellow signs for the "tourist office". Park in or near the tiny Plaza de Santa Lucía.*

② Úbeda

Jaén; 23400
Úbeda is a remarkable assembly of Renaissance architecture with an Andalusian flavour. Much of it is due to the combination of a gifted 16th-century architect, Andrés de Vandelvira, and his two patrons – Francisco de los Cobos, secretary to Emperor Charles V, and Cobos' nephew and successor in the post, Juan Vázquez de Molina.

A one-hour walking tour

From the car park, walk up Calle Baja del Salvador to the **Plaza Vázquez de Molina** ① and take time to look at the four main buildings that delineate it. At the eastern end stands the **Sacra Capilla del Salvador** ②, a funerary chapel by Vandelvira (1509–75), with an ornate façade and interior. Framing the northern side of the square are the town hall, **Palacio del Deán Ortega** ③ *(open daily)*, former residence of the Dean of Málaga, now a parador hotel and the **Palacio de las Cadenas** ④. Across the square is the somewhat discordant church complex of **Santa Maria de los Reales Alcazares** ⑤, constructed in a mixture of styles. The doorway, for example, is Romanesque, and the cloister, Gothic.

Leave the square on Calle Juan Montilla, to the left of the town hall as you face it. Turn left at the corner of the Plaza del Ayuntamiento into Calle Corazón de Jesús. Turn right up Baja del Marqués. The tourist information office is housed in the 18th-century **Palacio de Marqués del Contadero** ⑥ on the left of this street. Turn right into the next street to return to the Plaza del Ayuntamiento beneath the **Palacio Vela de los Cobos** ⑦, a handsome urban mansion, distinguished by a gallery on the top floor and a corner balcony right below it. Turn left up Calle Juan Montilla and then left up Calle Real, the main street through the Old Town, and turn right up Calle Las Parras. At the top, turn right down Calle de las Ventanas but first take a few steps left to see **Torre Octagonal** ⑧, a remnant of Úbeda's medieval Arab wall.

Turn right off Calle de las Ventanas, through Plazuela Josefa Manuel then right into Calle de Hernán Crespo and quickly left down Calle de Cervantes. Just off this street on the right is the **Casa Mudéjar** ⑨. This rebuilt 14th-century house is entered through a porch framed by horseshoe arches. The rooms, built around the patio inside, are now occupied by the town's archaeology museum.

Continue down Calle de Cervantes past the 13th-century **Iglesia de San Pablo** ⑩. In the square beside the church (Plaza del Primero de Mayo) is a monument of the same name to **San Juan de la Cruz** ⑪, who died in Úbeda in 1591. He is best remembered for his mystical poetry.

Continue downhill past the *ayuntamiento viejo* (old town hall) back to the Plaza Vázquez de Molina. From here, retrace the route down Calle Baja del Salvador to the car park at Plaza de Santa Lucía.

🚗 *Exit Úbeda on Calle de Valencia and turn right onto the N322a. Turn right onto the N322 eastwards towards Torreperogil and Albacete. Turn right at Torreperogil onto the A315. From the roundabout before Peal de Becerro, turn left onto the A319 to Cazorla. Park in or near one of the two squares before entering the streets of the Old Town.*

❸ Cazorla
Jaén; 23470

The town clings to a steep slope beneath a rocky ridge and looks out over endless olive groves. The *casco histórico* (old town) is a warren of narrow streets leading to the **Plaza de Santa María** and the gutted but impressive ruins of the **Iglesia de Santa María**. The Moorish **Castillo de la Yedra** *(open Tue–Sun)* stands slightly out of the urban area. This mountain town serves as an access point to the nature reserve, the **Parque Natural Sierras de Cazorla, Segura y Las Villas**. On the road leading to the park are the remains of **La Iruela** castle, dramatically sited on a rock outcrop.

🚗 *Leave Cazorla on the A319, which runs beside the thin triangular park next to the tourist office, towards the nature reserve (following the brown signs). Follow the road through Burunchel to the Puerto de las Palomas.*

Above Medieval archways framing the streets of Baeza **Below left** Façade of a *posada* (inn) in Plaza de Santa María, Cazorla **Below right** Fountain in Plaza Vázquez de Molina, Úbeda

EAT AND DRINK

BAEZA

Juanito *moderate*
This renowned restaurant has served bullfighters, politicians and other VIPs.
C/ Puche Pardo 57, 23440; 953 740 040; www.juanitobaeza.com

ÚBEDA

Meson Navarro *inexpensive*
A centrally located restaurant, this place offers a well-priced *menú del día*.
Plaza del Ayuntamiento 2, 23400; 953 757 395; www.casaventura.es

CAZORLA

Las Vegas *inexpensive*
This is one of the most popular bars in town, serving tapas prepared with game, fish, mushrooms and olive oil.
Plaza de la Corredera 17, 23470; 953 720 277

Eat and Drink: inexpensive, under €20; moderate, €20–€40; expensive, over €40

Above left Botanical garden at Torre del Vinagre **Above right** Street decorated with potted plants, Iznatoraf **Below left** Nature reserve visitors' centre at Torre del Vinagre **Below right** House with a carved stone portal, Sabiote

VISITING PARQUE NATURAL SIERRAS DE CAZORLA, SEGURA Y LAS VILLAS

Safaris
C/ Martinez Falero 11, 23470, Cazorla;
686 938 375; www.turisnat.es

Hang-gliding centre
Estación de Vuelo Libre El Yelmo,
Segura de Sierra; www.fiaelyelmo.com

WHERE TO STAY

SABIOTE

Palacio las Manillas moderate
Housed in a 16th-century Renaissance
mansion, this hotel has 15 rooms.
C/ Castillo 1, 23410; 953 774 346;
www.palaciolasmanillas.com

④ Puerto de las Palomas
Jaén; 23470
There are two miradors (constructed
viewpoints) at the top of the wooded
Puerto de las Palomas (1,140 m/
3,750 ft). The first, on the right, is
the **Mirador de Paso del Aire**, with
a view northwest over olive groves
near Cazorla and La Iruela. A little
further on is the **Mirador de Puerto
de las Palomas**, which has impressive
views over the thickly wooded
Guadalquivir valley – the heart of
the nature reserve.

🚗 *The A319, still passing through the
Sierras de Cazorla park, descends to a
crossroads, the Empalme de la Valle.
Turn left here to continue on the A319,
through the Guadalquivir river valley,
towards Torre del Vinagre. After
crossing the Guadalquivir river, the
road goes through the tourist complex
of Arroyo Frío. Follow the road across
the Guadalquivir a second time to the
Torre del Vinagre.*

⑤ Torre del Vinagre
Jaén; 23470
The Torre del Vinagre is the Parque
Natural Sierras de Cazorla, Segura y
Las Villas' visitors' centre. It has exhibitions on the various ecosystems of
the surrounding mountains and
valleys. Across the road (and to the
left) is a pleasant botanical garden in
which threatened, locally endemic
species, such as the Cazorla violet,
are protected and propagated. The
garden is at its most colourful in
spring. A short road from the Torre
del Vinagre leads across the river to
another visitors' centre, next to a fish
farm, where displays deal with fish
and other aquatic life.

🚗 *Stay on the same road through the
valley but look out for the next stop at
Collado del Almendral, on the right.
A handwritten sign indicates "Parque
Cinegético" and "Kiosco". Park here
or, to skip the 800 m (875 yd) on foot,
continue on the road and park near
the gate on the right.*

⑥ Collado del Almendral
Jaén; 23470
This fenced-in area of woodland is the
closest visitors will get to Cazorla's wildlife without going on a guided
excursion. A footpath leads through
the trees, past pens in which deer are
kept. The animals will probably be
dozing in the shade but at the very
least there will be views of the
Embalse del Tranco reservoir in the
distance. The reservoir expands and
contracts depending on how wet
the year has been. Trek up to the
viewpoint at the top of the hill in the

middle of the Collado del Almendral for more spectacular views.

🚗 *After the Collado del Almendral, the A319 winds around the reservoir and crosses the Embalse del Tranco, exiting the Sierras de Cazorla park. Turn left onto the A6202 at Tranco for Villanueva del Arzobispo. Turn left onto the N322 towards Úbeda, then right onto the JA8103 for Iznatoraf.*

⑦ Iznatoraf

Jaén; 23338

There are panoramic views of the countryside from this small hilltop town – Cazorla and La Iruela are visible to the south and Sabiote to the southwest. The shady streets, decorated with potted plants, converge on the 16th-century church. Several houses have their coat of arms set into their façades. All or part of the five arched gateways, which formed part of the city's 11th-century Arab walls, still survive.

🚗 *Retrace the route to the N322 and turn right for Úbeda. After skirting around Villacarrillo, continue for another 21 km (13 miles) and then turn right onto the JV6106 to Sabiote. Park in the square beside the castle.*

Above Breathtaking view from the Mirador de Puerto de las Palomas **Below** Façade of a house in Sabiote

⑧ Sabiote

Jaén; 23410

Sabiote is a gem of an old town with beautiful streets winding uphill from its Renaissance castle and the **Iglesia de San Pedro** to the *ayuntamiento* (town hall). Many of the houses in Sabiote have ornately carved stone portals and grilled windows. Two-thirds of the town's medieval walls remain intact along with six gateways. The views from the walls and the lookouts are spectacular.

EAT AND DRINK

SABIOTE

Bar la Chispa *inexpensive*
The personal attention at this small bar makes the delicious regional dishes even more enjoyable. There are excellent desserts, too.
C/ San Gines 36, 23410; 953 773 542

DAY TRIP OPTIONS

An alternative to one long drive is to break the route into one or two separate day trips. One of these could be dedicated to the two splendid Renaissance towns with either Baeza or Úbeda (on the A316) as a base, the other to the nature reserve with Cazorla (on the A319) as the base.

Architecture and culture

The superb Renaissance towns of Baeza ❶ and Úbeda ❷ are close

enough for them to easily be visited in the same day, allowing more time for the latter. There will almost certainly be time to make the short drive to visit Sabiote ❽ as well.

Leave Baeza on the A316 straight to Úbeda. From Úbeda, follow the A6103 into Sabiote.

Nature and adventure

Visit the ruins of the church and the Moorish castle in the hillside

Renaissance town of Cazorla ❸. With Cazorla as base, visit the Parque Natural Sierras de Cazorla, Segura y Las Villas, a nature reserve, which makes a self-contained tour. Visitors can go climbing and hang-gliding or take a safari through the park to discover its flora and fauna.

Enter the Parque Natural Sierras de Cazorla, Segura y Las Villas from Cazorla and follow the A319 to Torre del Vinagre and return along the same road.

Eat and Drink: inexpensive, under €20; moderate, €20–€40; expensive, over €40

Secret Beaches

Carboneras to Vela Blanca

Highlights

- **Rocky peninsula**
  Visit the remains of Spain's last gold mines in Rodalquilar

- **Quiet beaches**
  Find a deserted beach on this fascinating coastline

- **Breathtaking views**
  Take in the beauty of the coast from one of several viewing points

- **Eighteenth-century tower**
  Explore Torre de Vela Blanca, set amid jagged cliffs

Dark volcanic rocks at Cabo de Gata, east of Almería

Secret Beaches

Spain's Mediterranean coastline still has spectacular, remote places to get away to. This route goes through the Parque Natural de Cabo de Gata in the dry southeast province of Almeria. The nature park has seen only light development, leaving many sandy beaches and secret coasts virtually untouched by tourism. The drive visits few monuments but passes through dramatic desert landscapes with breathtaking views.

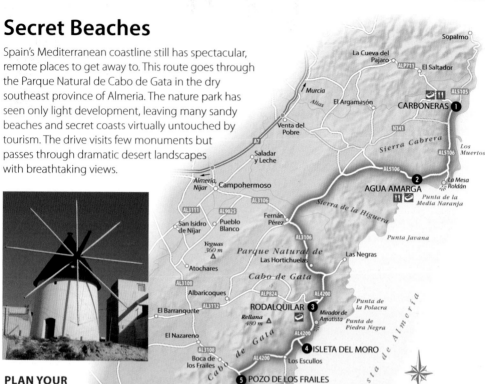

PLAN YOUR DRIVE

Start/finish: Carboneras to Vela Blanca.

Number of days: 1 day.

Distance: 60 km (40 miles).

Road conditions: All the roads in this region, except for the final stretch, are surfaced.

When to go: June and early September are ideal to visit. Ask about sea conditions at the nearest resort before swimming.

Opening hours: Museums in this region do not have fixed times, so it is best to check before visiting.

Main market days: Carboneras: Thu.

Shopping: Pick up pottery from around the region.

Major festivals: Carboneras: San Antonio, Jun; **Agua Amarga:** Santiago, Jul; **Rodalquilar:** Fiesta del Turista, Jul; **Isleta del Moro:** Virgen del Carmen, Jul.

Above Windmill at the holiday resort of Carboneras, *see p235* **Below** Whitewashed houses stretching out around the beach in Agua Amarga, *see p235*

1 Carboneras

Almeria; 04140

Named after its previous industry of charcoal-burning and towered over by a power station chimney, this former fishing village is now a booming holiday resort. It is also a point of access to the **Parque Natural de Cabo de Gata**. The Plaza de Castillo is the heart of this town. However, the main attractions of Carboneras are its several long, sandy beaches, which stretch for almost 17 km (11 miles) along its coast, and a rocky islet, the **Isla de San Andrés**.

Leave Carboneras along the seafront on the AL5106 towards Agua Amarga. Go past the Almeria turn-off and continue straight. Shortly after leaving the urban area, there is a car park for **Los Muertos** beach on the left. Next to this is a little road signposted for **La Mesa Roldán**. Turn up this road and go up to the lighthouse and watchtower for some spectacular views.

🚗 *Return to the AL5106 and resume on the road to Agua Amarga. In Agua Amarga, park on the main road.*

2 Agua Amarga

Almeria; 04149

A small resort of white houses, barely more than a hamlet on the edge of the Parque Natural de Cabo de Gata, Agua Amarga has adapted to tourism without losing its charm. It is a great place for water sports and scuba diving, and for visitors who feel like a walk, the nature reserve is a stone's throw away. Behind the beautiful sandy beach, there are streets worth exploring for their picturesque corners. The houses, both old and modern, are in the typical white-washed, cubic style of Almeria. In the hills around Agua Amarga are several old farmsteads with attractive domed wells.

🚗 *Leave Agua Amarga for Almeria, Murcia and Venta del Pobre on the AL5106. Look out for an inconspicuous turning to the left, which only has a signpost for Fernán Pérez. At the end of the road, there is a T-junction in Fernán Pérez. Turn left for San José on the AL3106 and then right on the AL4200 after Las Hortichuelas for Rodalquilar. Turn right to enter the town, fork right and head towards the church to park.*

3 Rodalquilar

Almeria; 04115

Once a run-down town, Rodalquilar is now the headquarters of the Parque Natural de Cabo de Gata. There is an information office next to the church and the **Jardín Botánico El Albardinal** nearby. Continue on the road, passing the nature reserve's buildings, to a geology museum. Beyond the museum is the site of the somewhat eerie, dilapidated remains of the peninsula's last gold mines, the **Minas de Oro de Rodalquilar**. Visitors are free to wander around the wash pans and crumbling buildings but extreme care is needed as there are no safety precautions here.

Just outside Rodalquilar, on the AL4200, is the **Mirador de Amatista**, a viewing balcony high above the sea, from which there are spectacular views of the sea.

🚗 *Leave Rodalquilar on the AL4200 and turn right for San José. Continue on this road for 4 km (2 miles) and turn left down to Isleta del Moro.*

4 Isleta del Moro

Almeria; 04118

This picturesque fishing village of low-lying white houses on an isthmus leading to an outcrop of rock and an island (the *isleta* of the name) has changed little under the impact of tourism. Most people come here to combine a day on the beach with a meal of fried or grilled fish in one of Isleta's few restaurants. Another small resort worth a stopover, just down the road, is **Los Escullos**.

🚗 *Return to the AL4200 and turn left. After Los Escullos, the road leads to a T-junction. Turn left on the AL3108 for Pozo de los Frailes.*

Above left Church in the town of Rodalquilar
Above right Turquoise blue waters seen from the Mirador de Amatista

WHERE TO STAY

CARBONERAS

Hostal San Antonio
inexpensive–moderate
Good-value small hotel conveniently located in town near the beach; ask for a room with an ocean view.
C/ Pescadores 11, 04140; 518 889 079; www.hostalsanantonio.com

AGUA AMARGA

El Tio Kiko *expensive*
All the rooms in this small Rusticae hotel have large windows and terraces with great views. There's a pool in the garden.
C/ Embarque 12, 04149; 950 138 080; www.eltiokiko.com

RODALQUILAR

Los Patios *expensive*
A minimalist hotel close to the sea, with partly glass roofs in some of the rooms so visitors can watch the stars.
Camino del Playazo, 04115; 950 525 252, www.lospatioshotel.es

EAT AND DRINK

CARBONERAS

El Dorado *moderate*
This charming restaurant and hotel is a good place for breakfast by the sea.
C/ Camino Viejo de Garrucha 24, 04140; 950 454 050; www.eldorado-carboneras.com

AGUA AMARGA

Asador La Chumbera *moderate*
A restaurant in a traditional farmhouse just outside Agua Amarga. The cuisine is Mediterranean with an Italian accent. The black *paella* is a triumph.
Paraje los Ventorrillos, 04149; 609 079 944; http://asadorlachumbera.com

Eat and Drink: inexpensive, under €20; moderate, €20–€40; expensive, over €40

Top Faro de Gata on the headland of Cabo de Gata **Above** Waterwheel in Pozo de los Frailes

VISITING VELA BLANCA

Tourist Information
There are tourist information offices en route and in San José. They provide information regarding Vela Blanca and also about visiting the Parque Natural de Cabo de Gata.
Avda. de San José 27, 04118; 950 380 299; www.cabodegata-nijar.com

WHERE TO STAY

AROUND POZO DE LOS FRAILES

Cortijo el Sotillo *moderate*
The Cortijo el Sotillo is both a hotel and restaurant built around an early 18th-century farmhouse 2 km (1 mile) from Pozo de los Frailes, when entering San José. On the menu are fresh fish, kid and lamb.
Ctra. Entrada a San José, 04118, San José; 950 611 100; www.cortijo elsotillo.com

⑤ Pozo de los Frailes
Almeria; 04117

At the centre of this tiny village is a restored waterwheel surrounded by a circular wall. Step inside to appreciate the ingenuity with which water was managed in the arid regions of Almeria. This watermill dates back to when the Moors occupied the land. There are several more watermills and windmills in this area, some of which have been restored. Continue on the AL3108 into San José. Back on the coast south of El Pozo, **San José** is the main town in this area, where all the hotels and restaurants in the southern Cabo de Gata are located.

🚗 *From San José, follow signs for Genoveses and Monsul. The road goes around the back of San José to the start of a dirt road to the beaches of Genoveses and Monsul. Take this dirt road over a saddle until the fork. Take the left turn down to the car park of the Genoveses beach.*

⑥ Genoveses
Almeria; 04118

An arc of sand between two prominent headlands, this beach is named after the Genoese fleet that took part in the Christian attack on Moorish Almeria in 1147. In common with all the beaches west of San José, no development has been permitted and there are no bars or restaurants here. Despite its lack of facilities, Genoveses is hugely popular in the summer. There are two more small beaches further down the road.

🚗 *Go back to the fork and turn left onto the upper road to Monsul, 2 km (1 mile) further on. There is a car park on the road and another one near the beach, turning left from this road.*

⑦ Monsul
Almeria; 04118

If Monsul, with its large rock placed in the middle of the sand, looks familiar, it may be because it was used as the location for a scene in *Indiana Jones and the Last Crusade* starring Harrison Ford, Sean Connery and a flock of imported pigeons. The sandy beach stretches for a long distance with calm tranquil water, perfect for diving and snorkelling. The coastline is studded with dramatic volcanic rocks.

🚗 *The track continues a little way beyond Monsul. After Monsul, the track leads to a gate. Park here to do the walk.*

⑧ Vela Blanca
Almeria; 04118

Due to the fragility of its ecosystem, the stretch of coast between Cala Carbón (near Monsul) and the headland of Vela Blanca is closed to traffic. A broad track runs along the steep slopes from one gate to another (approximately 2 km/1 mile apart), offering easy walking and spectacular views all the way. Avoid doing the walk in the hottest part of the day as there is no shade along the route. The views are different in the morning, afternoon and evening as the sun shifts round the whole day long. For views of the cape ahead, visitors need to do the walk before midday. Later in the day the sun shines on the beaches of Monsul and Genoveses.

A three-hour walking tour
From the car park go to the **eastern gateway** ① and take the broad track ahead. This track follows the contours of the coast without turning off it, so there is no possibility of getting lost.

At first glance it looks as if little life survives here, but this is a surprisingly rich habitat. The most conspicuous plant is the dwarf fan palm (*Chamaerops humilis*), Europe's only native palm tree. There is always some species or other in flower among the xerophytic flora along the side of the track and on the steep slopes. Some plants, such as the pink snapdragon (*Antirrhinum charidemi*), grow here and nowhere else in the world.

Around the first corner of the track, there is a spectacular viewpoint looking back eastwards over the beaches and headlands between here and San José. Below, the steep slopes fall into the Mediterranean as

Above left Rocky Monsul coastline in Almeria
Above right Secluded beach of Genoveses

inaccessible cliffs. Hidden beneath the waves is a marine nature reserve rich in coral reefs and beds of sea-grass in contrast to the arid and deserted hillsides around.

From here the track swings away from the sea and continues to climb leading to a ravine, the **Barranco del Negro** ②. Once across this ravine, continue to walk up to the **western gateway** ③. This is located on a saddle below the Torre de Vela Blanca, offering stunning views in both directions. Westward is the cape itself on which stands a lighthouse. Beneath it are some jagged rocks, the Arrecife de las Sirenas (Mermaids' Reef), the name referring to monk seals which used to inhabit these waters. Walk up the road to the **Torre de Vela**

Blanca ④, although it is closed to visitors there are spectacular views. The tower was built in the 18th century under Charles III as part of the coast's defences against pirate attacks. If a belligerent vessel was sighted, a fire would be lit and a smoke signal transmitted to the next towers in the chain. It is said that such a message could be sent from Málaga to Mojácar in 30 minutes.

For a longer walk (6 km/4 miles there and back), take the same road down from the saddle, descending in hairpins and passing over the top of two beaches to reach a junction near the Faro de Gata lighthouse. The only way back is by the same route; downhill from the saddle to the lower gate and to the car park.

ACTIVITIES IN CABO DE GATA

SCUBA DIVING

ISUB
Although this centre is mainly for experienced divers, there is also a beginner's "Discover Scuba Diving" course for those who want to progress. There are more than 20 diving sites along the coast of the Parque Natural de Cabo de Gata – Carboneras, Agua Amarga, Las Negras, Isleta del Moro and San José being a few of them.
C/ Babor 3, 04118, San José; 950 380 004; www.isubsanjose.com

EAT AND DRINK

AROUND POZO DE LOS FRAILES

Casa Sebastián *inexpensive*
Enjoy wonderful sea views and freshly cooked seafood straight from the grill at this local favourite by the port in San José.
C/ La Calilla 18, 04118, San José; 950 380 050

Casa Miguel *moderate*
A rice and fish restaurant on the main street at the centre of San José, 3 km (2 miles) from Pozo de los Frailes. The menu is strong on local fish and seafood. *Paella* is another good choice.
C/ Correo 43, 04118, San José; 950 380 329; www.restaurantecasamiguel.es

Taberna Kamarote *moderate*
Located by the waterside marina in San José, 3 km (2 miles) from Pozo de los Frailes, this restaurant offers a choice of sun and shade.
Puerto Deportivo de San José, 04118; 699 058 769

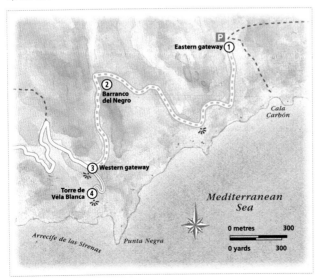

Eastern gateway ①

② Barranco del Negro

Cala Carbón

③ Western gateway

Torre de Vela Blanca ④

Arrecife de las Sirenas

Punta Negra

Mediterranean Sea

0 metres 300

0 yards 300

Eat and Drink: inexpensive, under €20; moderate, €20–€40; expensive, over €40

Mallorca's Cliffs and Coves

Palma to Alcúdia

Highlights

- **Historic city**
  Explore the capital of Mallorca, Palma, an ancient seaport with a beautiful Gothic cathedral

- **Fishing village**
  Stop by Sant Elm, a small coastal resort, by the crystal-clear waters of the Mediterranean

- **Mountain scenery**
  Take in the spectacular mountain scenery of the Serra de Tramuntana along Mallorca's northwest coast

- **Hidden beaches**
  Relax in a hidden cove by a dazzling turquoise sea

The cathedral, La Seu, overlooking the town and the harbour of Palma

Mallorca's Cliffs and Coves

The largest island of the Balearic archipelago, Mallorca offers visitors wonderful beaches, rural retreats, quiet coves and historic architecture. Beginning in the capital city of Palma, this drive weaves its way through the green foothills of the Serra de Tramuntana before emerging on the north coast. The road threads through steep valleys and past rearing peaks, where there are exquisite views out across the Mediterranean, to explore the beguiling old town of Pollença, the walled town of Alcúdia and the craggy mountains of the Península de Formentor.

Above Exterior of the Palau de l'Almudaina in Palma, see p242 **Left** Open-air market stalls in Alcúdia, see p247

ACTIVITIES

Take a walk around the historic town of Palma and visit its spectacular cathedral

Go for a swim at Sant Elm, one of the island's most charming resorts

Enjoy the spectacular views around the Gorg Blau and its reservoirs

Explore the holiest place in Mallorca, the Santuari de Monestir de Lluc

See the island's wildest scenery on the Península de Formentor

Right Looking down on the cove at Banyalbufar, see p243

Cap de Formentor

Cases Velles

Cala Castell

Cala Bòquer

Cala Sant Vicenç

Cala Solleric

14 PENÍNSULA DE FORMENTOR

MA2210

MA2200

Port de Pollença

Badia de Pollença

POLLENÇA

13 MA10

Mortitxet

Es Rafalet

Can Puig

MA2220

Port de Alcúdia

15 ALCÚDIA

Alcanada

Sa Calobra

Montaña

MA10

GORG BLAU **11**

Escorca **12** SANTUARI DE MONESTIR DE LLUC

MA10

MA2200

MA13

S. de Paries

Embalse de Gorg Blau

Embalse de Cúber

MA2130

Serra de Tramuntana

Campanet

40

37

Selva MA13

30

Lloseta

Inca

25

27

Alaró

Binissalem

Consell

17

KEY

Drive route

0 kilometres 5

0 miles 5

Below Town and monastery of Valldemossa, *see p244*

PLAN YOUR DRIVE

Start/finish: Palma to Alcúdia.

Number of days: 2, including half a day on Illa de Sa Dragonera.

Distance: 230 km (145 miles).

Road conditions: Roads and lanes are generally very narrow but are well paved and signed. There are many steep sections, especially the ascent/ descent into Sóller on the northeast and southwest side. There are a lot of hair-raising bends down to Sa Calobra, the Península de Formentor, and between Andratx and Banyalbufar.

When to go: Spring (from Apr to May) and autumn (from late Sep to Oct) are the best times to enjoy the drive. Temperatures can be too hot for comfort and the roads very crowded during summer (from Jul to Aug).

Opening hours: Museums and historic monuments are usually open from Mon to Fri, from 10am to 1pm and again from 4 to 6pm. Most churches, however, have no fixed opening hours.

Market days: Palma: daily; Valldemossa: Sun; Sóller: Sat; Pollença: Wed, Sun; Alcúdia: Tue, Sun.

Shopping: Shoppers should head to Palma which has a range of shops. Local specialities include glassware, lanterns, chandeliers, leather goods, Mallorcan textiles and ceramic tiles.

Major festivals: Palma: Sant Sebastià, mid-Jan; Carnival, Feb; **Valldemossa:** Santa Catalina Thomàs, end Jul; **Sóller:** Festes de Moros i Cristians, second Sun May; **Pollença:** Sant Antoni, mid-Jan, Corpus Christi, mid-Jun; **Alcúdia:** Romeria de la Victòria, early Jul; Sant Jaume, end Jul.

DAY TRIP OPTIONS

Visitors can explore the area covered in the drive in a series of day trips. **Wildlife enthusiasts** can head off to Sant Elm and then to the Illa de Sa Dragonera nature reserve; **architecture buffs** can enjoy the echoing cloisters of Valldemossa monastery; and **families** will delight in the safe, gently shelving beach at Port de Pollença. For details, *see p247*.

Above Rows of sunbeds lining the beach at Sant Elm **Below left** Shops along a shady street in Palma **Below right** Majestic façade of the Gothic cathedral in Palma

VISITING PALMA

Tourist Information
The main tourist office is called the Oficina d'Informació Turística. *Passeig del Born 27, 07012; 902 102 365; www.illesbalears.es*

Parking
For on-street parking, visitors have to buy a ticket from the ubiquitous ORA ticket machines. Alternatively, there are about 10 underground car parks in and around the city centre; just follow any of the signs. One of the handiest car parks is right next to the cathedral on Avenida Antoni Maura.

WHERE TO STAY

PALMA

Hotel Born *moderate*
Located in the centre of Palma, this is an appealing hotel in a lovely refurbished old mansion.
C/ Sant Jaume 3, 07012; 971 712 942; www.hotelborn.com

Brondo Architect Hotel *expensive*
Modern and elegant Bohemian chic-style hotel in the centre.
C/ Ca'n Brondo 4, 07001; 971 720 507; www.brondoarchitect.com

Palacio Ca Sa Galesa *expensive*
Set in a privileged location just a stone's throw from Mallorca's cathedral, this is a 16th-century palace.
Miramar 8, 07001; 971 715 400; www.palaciocasagalesa.com

AROUND GALILEA

El Castell Son Claret *expensive*
This 15th-century castle has been painstakingly restored into a luxurious hotel, with two restaurants, a pool, a spa and a Moorish garden.
Ctra. Es Capedellá-Galilea, Km 1.7, 07196, Es Capdellà; 971 138 620; www.castellsonclaret.com

① Palma
Mallorca; 07012
Palma's pride and joy is its cathedral, **La Seu** *(open Sun for Mass only)*, which dominates the waterfront from the crest of a hill. The interior, renovated by Antoni Gaudí (1852–1926), is the epitome of the Catalan Gothic style, its yawning nave flanked by tall and slender columns. It is one of Spain's outstanding Gothic structures. Next door is the **Palau de l'Almudaina** *(closed Sun)*, a royal residence from Moorish times. The current Gothic palace was rebuilt in the 13th century after the Moorish fortress was destroyed, and it is still sometimes used as a royal residence. Spreading northeast behind the cathedral are the narrow lanes and ageing mansions of the old town. Tucked away among the side streets are two detours – the Baroque **Basílica de Sant Francesc** *(open daily)*, notable for its exquisite Gothic cloister, and the 10th-century Moorish bathhouses, the **Banys Àrabs** *(open daily)*. About 3 km (2 miles) west of the city centre, stands the Gothic **Castell de Bellver** *(open daily)* with great views of the city and bay.

🚗 *Head west around Palma's outer ring road, the Via Cintura, and take the MA1040 north to get to Esporles.*

② Esporles
Mallorca; 07190
A world away from the teeming resorts of the coast, Esporles is a leafy little town whose elongated main street, the Passeig del Rei, follows the line of an ancient stone watercourse. This street is lined with a handful of cafés and restaurants. The town's principal sight is the 16th-century stone church.

From Esporles, drive 1 km (0.6 miles) north along the MA1100 and turn left onto the MA1101 to reach **La Granja** *(open daily)*, a handsome *finca* (country house) nestled in a tranquil wooded and terraced valley. It belonged to an order of Cistercian monks from the 13th to the 15th centuries and then to the Fortuny family. Highlights of the interior include an antique kitchen, the dining room with its paintings and the first-floor loggia. Look out also for the finely crafted, green-tinted Mallorcan chandeliers and the beautiful majolica tile-panels that embellish the walls. There are folk-dancing displays here *(Wed and Fri)* throughout the summer.

🚗 *Leave La Granja and turn south onto the MA1101, a winding country road, towards Puigpunyent. Go through Puigpunyent on the MA1032 to Galilea. Park on the street.*

③ Galilea
Mallorca; 07195
Offering a spectacular view of the southwestern Mallorcan coast, the tiny village of Galilea is a favourite haunt for artists from all over Europe. It has a few whitewashed farmsteads dotting the valley and clambering up the surrounding hills. The main sight in the village is the sturdy 19th-century church, as many of its older buildings

did not survive the attentions of marauding pirates.

🚗 *Leave Galilea on the MA1032 to Es Capdellà. At Capdellà, turn right onto the MA1031 to reach Andratx. From Andratx, take the MA1030 straight to Sant Elm. Park on the street at the entrance to the village.*

④ Sant Elm
Mallorca; 07159

Sant Elm's main street strings along the seashore with a sandy beach at one end and a tiny harbour at the other. This small resort town has a good selection of cafés and restaurants and beautiful scenery.

From the harbour, passenger boats take 15 minutes to shuttle across to the austere offshore islet of **Sa Dragonera**, a craggy hunk of rock, 4 km (2 miles) long and 700 m (765 yd) wide, that lies at an angle to the coast. A nature reserve since 1988, Sa Dragonera is home to a variety of birdlife and wild flowers. An imposing ridge of cliffs dominates its northwestern shore. Behind the ridge, a rough track travels the length of the island, linking a pair of craggy capes and their lighthouses. Boats dock at a cove-harbour halfway up the east shore, which puts both ends of the island within comfortable walking distance, though the excursion north to Cap de Tramuntana is prettier.

🚗 *From the harbour, retrace the route on the MA1030 to Andratx. At the roundabout in Andratx, take a left onto the main coastal road, the MA10. Follow this road for 18 km (11 miles) northeast to Estellencs. Park on the street in Estellencs.*

⑤ Estellencs
Mallorca; 07192

With its steep coastal cliffs and handsome terraced fields, Estellencs is the prettiest of the coastal villages. It has narrow winding alleys adorned by old stone houses and an 18th-century parish church *(no fixed opening hours)*. The church has an exquisite pinewood and candle-lit interior, where villagers gathered for hundreds of years, seeking shelter from pirates and invaders.

A steep, but driveable, 2-km (1-mile) lane leads down from the village to **Cala Estellencs**. Quiet and undeveloped, Cala Estellencs is a rocky, surf-buffeted cove that has a beach and a summertime bar.

🚗 *Return to the MA10 and continue (7 km/4 miles) to Banyalbufar.*

⑥ Banyalbufar
Mallorca; 07191

The terraced fields of Banyalbufar cling to the coastal cliffs beside the MA10. The land here has been cultivated since Moorish times, with a spring above the village providing a water supply that is still channelled down the hillside along slender watercourses into open storage cisterns. The village's main street, flanked by whitewashed houses and narrow cobbled lanes, culminates in the main square, which is overlooked by the 15th-century parish church.

🚗 *From Banyalbufar, continue on the MA10. At the junction with the MA1100, stay on the same road. At Valldemossa, park in one of the two municipality car parks. They are paid car parks, but are safe.*

Above Quiet cove of Cala Estellencs, lapped by the blue-green waters of the sea
Below Rooftop view of Galilea

VISITING SA DRAGONERA

Ferry Services
There is a passenger boat service to Sa Dragonera from Sant Elm three times a day from Feb to Apr and from Oct to Nov, as well as a more frequent service (four times a day) from May to Sep.
*Plaça de la Reina 2, 07012;
639 617 545, 627 966 264;
www.crucerosmargarita.com*

EAT AND DRINK

PALMA

Ca'n Joan de S'Aigo *inexpensive*
This long-established coffee house serves freshly baked *ensaïmadas* (pastry buns), excellent fruit-flavoured mousses and home-made ice cream.
C/ Can Sanç 10, 07001; 971 710 759

La Taberna del Caracol *inexpensive–moderate*
Housed in a charming old premises with wooden beams and ancient arches, this is an excellent tapas bar.
*C/ Sant Alonso 2, 07001; 971 714 908;
http://tabernacaracol.com; closed Sun;
reservations advised at peak times*

Sadrassana Restaurant Cocteleria *expensive*
Superb restaurant serving creative interpretations of Balearic cuisine. It's a hip spot, with an art gallery upstairs.
Plaça Drassanes 15, 07012; 971 728 515; www.sadrassana.com; closed Mon

SANT ELM

Vista Mar *moderate*
Located on the harbour, this restaurant does an excellent fish soup as well as seafood main courses.
Avda. Jaume I 46, 07159; 971 237 547

Eat and Drink: inexpensive, under €20; moderate, €20–€40; expensive, over €40

Above People relaxing on the beach at Cala Deià, Deià **Below** Monastery complex of Reial Cartoixa de Valldemossa overlooking the town

WHERE TO STAY

VALLDEMOSSA

Es Petit Hotel Valldemossa *expensive*
This restored hotel has a welcoming atmosphere and it combines old and modern decorative elements.
Uetam 1, 07170; 971 612 479;
www.espetithotel-valldemossa.com

DEIÀ

Pensión Miramar *moderate*
Perched high above and signposted from the road, this is a family-run *pensión* in a traditional stone *finca*.
C/ Ca'n Oliver s/n, 07179; 971 639 084;
http://pensionmiramardeia.com

Belmond La Residència *expensive*
Nestled in the foothills of the Tramuntana, this is a beautiful luxury hotel which has several ivy-covered stone buildings and villas.
Son Canals s/n, 07179; 971 639 011;
www.belmond.com/la-residencia-
mallorca; closed Nov–Mar

AROUND DEIÀ

Hotel Costa d'Or *expensive*
Splendid four-star hotel just east of Deià, overlooking an unspoilt coast.
Lluc-Alcari s/n, 07179; 971 639 025;
www.hoposa.es; closed Nov–Feb

SÓLLER

Hotel El Guía *moderate*
Set behind a pretty little courtyard near the train station, this is a long-established, family-run hotel.
C/ Castanyer 2, 07100; 971 630 227;
www.sollernet.com/elguia; closed
mid-Nov–mid-Mar

AROUND SÓLLER

Hotel Ca's Xorc *expensive*
Located in the hills, just off the MA10, this is an intimate boutique hotel with a beautiful swimming pool.
Ctra. Deià, Km 56.1, 07001; 971 638 280;
www.casxorc.com; closed 1 Nov–15 Apr

---

⑦ Valldemossa

Mallorca; 07170
The ancient hill-town of Valldemossa is a jumble of houses and monastic buildings. Valldemossa's status was transformed in the early 14th century, when the asthmatic King Sanç built a royal palace here in the hills where the air was easier to breathe. In 1399, the palace was gifted to Carthusian monks from Tarragona, who converted and extended the original buildings into a sprawling monastery, the **Reial Cartoixa de Valldemossa** *(open daily, except Sun in Dec & Jan)*. The monastery also houses the **Museu Municipal Art Contemporani,** which has a small collection of works by Spanish artists such as Miró, Picasso and Tàpies.

🚗 *Leave Valldemossa on the MA1130 and then take a right onto the MA10. Drive along the coast to Son Marroig, which comes up on the left of the road. Park in the car park.*

Sand and Chopin

The Reial Cartoixa de Valldemossa monastery owes its present fame almost entirely to the French writer George Sand (1804–76), who, with her companion, the composer Frédéric Chopin, lived here for four months in 1838–9. Visitors can look around Sand and Chopin's old quarters as well as the church and its echoing cloisters, where the first port of call is the antique pharmacy. There are free concerts of Chopin's piano music.

---

⑧ Son Marroig

Mallorca; 07179
An imposing L-shaped mansion perched high above the seashore, Son Marroig *(closed Sun)* was the favourite residence of the Habsburg Archduke Ludwig Salvatore (1847–1915), who lived here long enough to immerse himself in all things Mallorquín. The house is now a museum dedicated to his life and work. The Son Marroig estate comprises the house, its gardens and the wild and wonderful Sa Foradada headland, a 40-minute walk away.

🚗 *Continue on the MA10 from Son Marroig along the coast to Deià. Park on the street in Deià.*

⑨ Deià

Mallorca; 07179
Dramatically surrounded by mountains, Deià is a beautiful village located at the spot where the mighty Puig d'es Teix mountain (1,050 m/ 3,450 ft) meets the sea. Alleys of old peasant houses curl up to a country church, in the precincts of which the village's most famous resident, British poet and novelist Robert Graves (1895–1985), is buried. His old home, **Ca n'Alluny** *(closed Mon, and Sat in Dec & Jan)*, beside the main road, north-east of the village, was opened in 2006. Known also for its artistic community and upmarket cafés, Deià attracts a big international crowd.

Drive out of Deià on the MA10 and take the signed turn to reach **Cala Deià** on the left. A lovely cove flanked by jagged cliffs, Cala Deià is a great place for a swim. There is a ramshackle beach bar to keep the swimmers happy.

🚗 *Return to the MA10, which wriggles its way over the mountains before emerging at Sóller. Park on the Avinguda Gran Via while driving into town.*

Where to Stay: inexpensive, under €70; moderate, €70–€120; expensive, over €120

⑩ Sóller

Mallorca; 07100, 07101

Sóller is one of the most elegant towns on Mallorca and it is also an ideal base for exploring the surrounding mountains. The town's sloping lanes are lined with 18th- and 19th-century fruit merchants' stone houses, many of which are adorned with ornate grilles and doors – examples of Catalan Modernism. This walk starts at Sóller and steps out of town through the countryside to visit the hamlet of Biniaraix.

A two-hour walking tour

From the spot where the car was parked, head down Carrer Bauza towards **Plaça Constitució** ①, a lively square and the centre of Sóller, which is flanked by a gaggle of cafés and bisected by the tramlines that carry on down to Port de Sóller. Overlooking the square is the Gothic-Baroque **Església de Sant Bartomeu** ②, which dates back to 1236. Its most appealing features are its attractive rose window, high in the main Art Nouveau façade, and the sweeping balustrade up above. The façade was designed by the celebrated Catalan Modernist architect Joan Rubió i Bellver (1870–1952), a disciple of Antoni Gaudí. From the square, head north along Avinguda Cristòfol Colom to reach the **market** ③ with its racks of local produce and glistening fish. The market is something of a social hub for locals, who gather here to drink coffee and cognac while nibbling on the island's *ensaimadas* (pastries). Take Carrer Palou from near the market and turn right onto Carrer 11 de Maig to reach **Can Prohom** ④, one of the grandest mansions in town at Carrer de Sa Lluna. The gentry used to stay here when they came to town, donning their top hats and canes before strolling out into town. From here retrace the route to the car park.

Hop into the car and drive along Carrer Bauza and then Carrer de Sa Lluna up the valley to the tiny and extremely pretty hamlet of Biniaraix. On the way, pass orchards and farmland flanked by dry-stone walls. At Biniaraix, look out for the tiny main square, where there are lovely cafés under the shade of the palm trees. The village is popular as the starting point for long and strenuous hikes up into the surrounding mountains. After relaxing for a while, retrace the route to return to Sóller.

🚗 *Leave Sóller on the MA11. At the roundabout, turn right onto the MA10. The road climbs up into the mountains before tunnelling through to the Gorg Blau, a distance of 13 km (8 miles).*

Above Façade of the Església de Sant Bartomeu in Plaça Constitució

VISITING SÓLLER

Tourist Information
The tourist office is right in the centre of town, a few metres down from the train station in an old train carriage. *Plaça d'Espanya, 07100; 971 638 008; www.visitsoller.com*

Parking
Park on the street on Avinguda Gran Via just on entering the town.

EAT AND DRINK

VALLDEMOSSA

Restaurant Ca'n Mario *inexpensive*
Located just a few minutes from the Valldemossa monastery. Serves tasty, affordable, traditional Mallorcan food. *C/ Uetam 8, 07170; 971 612 122; http://hostalcanmario.net; closed 18 Dec–18 Jan*

DEIÀ

Restaurant Buganvilia *expensive*
The highlight of this smart hotel-restaurant is a creative menu using the very best of local ingredients, from island fish to home-grown vegetables. *Ctra. Deià-Valldemossa s/n, 07179; 971 639 000; closed 30 Oct–16 Apr*

SÓLLER

Kingfisher Restaurant *moderate*
Very accommodating place in the port area, serving seafood and meat dishes. *Calle San Ramon de Penyafort 25, 07108; 971 638 856*

Eat and Drink: inexpensive, under €20; moderate, €20–€40; expensive, over €40

WHERE TO STAY

POLLENÇA

Posada de Lluc *expensive*
This is a chic hotel in an immaculately restored old stone town house.
C/ Roser Vell 11, 07460; 971 535 220; www.posadalluc.com

Son Brull *expensive*
A very comfortable hotel that combines ancient architecture with avant-garde design.
Ctra. Palma–Pollença PM220, Km 50, 07460; 971 535 353; www.sonbrull. com; closed mid–Dec–Apr

AROUND POLLENÇA

Hotel Bahía *moderate*
Located right on the seafront, this attractive hotel occupies a 19th-century villa.
Passeig Voramar 29, 07470, Port de Pollença; 971 866 562; www. hoposa.es; closed Nov–Mar

ALCÚDIA

Ca'n Simó *moderate*
This is an appealing hotel occupying a 19th-century Mallorcan manor house.
C/ Sant Jaume 1, 07400; 971 549 260; http://cansimo.com

AROUND ALCÚDIA

Hostatgeria Ermita de la Victòria *moderate*
The old monastic quarters behind the Ermita de la Victòria, just 5 km (3 miles) from Alcúdia, have been converted into a charming *hostal*.
07400, Ermita de la Victòria; 971 549 912; www.lavictoriahotel.com

Above left Portal of the Santuari de Monestir de Lluc **Above right** Breathtaking view from the Mirador d'es Colomer **Below** Looking down the Via Calvari from the shrine at Pollença

⑪ Gorg Blau
Mallorca; 07315

A well-known beauty spot, the Gorg Blau (Blue Gorge) offers a harsh and craggy landscape in the heart of the mountains. Two reservoirs dot the bottom of the gorge. The largest reservoir is the Embalse de Cúber, which is located southwest of Gorg Blau. There is rich birdlife here and this is a good spot to see different kinds of birds of prey. To visit the gorge, visitors need to look out for the sign to Embalse de Gorg Blau.

🚗 *Continue on the MA10. After Escorca, turn left to stay on the MA10. Turn left onto the MA2140 to reach the Santuari de Monestir de Lluc.*

⑫ Santuari de Monestir de Lluc
Mallorca; 07315

Located in a valley in the middle of the mountains is the Santuari de Monestir de Lluc *(open daily)*, Mallorca's most important place of pilgrimage for over 800 years. Tourists now mingle with the pilgrims who arrive here every year to pay homage. The object of devotion, inside the basilica, is a much-revered statue of the Virgin, *La Morenta de Lluc*. The monastery's boys' choir, nicknamed *Els Blauets* (The Little Blue Boys), for the colour of their cassocks, performs in the basilica. There is a museum which houses local handicrafts and works of art.

🚗 *Leave the monastery on the MA2140 to reach the MA10. Keep on this road to arrive at Pollença. Park on the street on the south side of town.*

⑬ Pollença
Mallorca; 07460; 07470

Inordinately pretty, the narrow cobbled lanes and honey-coloured stone mansions of Pollença are a delight. Pollença has retained much of its old-world charm with narrow, twisting streets and beautiful houses. At the centre of town is the **Plaça Major**, a genial main square, which houses a cluster of laid-back cafés and is the site of a lively fruit and vegetable market on Sundays. Overlooking the square is the 13th-century **Església de Nostra Senyora dels Àngels**, with a fine rose window. Pollença's most dramatic attraction is its **Via Calvari** (Way of the Cross), a long and steep stone stairway that climbs up to a tiny hilltop shrine.

Drive out of Pollença on the MA2200 to Pollença's port 5 km (3 miles) northeast of the town. **Port de Pollença** was actually built just inland to guard against surprise attacks from pirates and this town curves through the flatlands behind its bay, the **Badia de Pollença**. The beach is the centre of attention here, a narrow sliver of sand enhanced by its sheltered waters, which are ideal for swimming. The prettiest part of the resort is to the north of the marina, where a portion of the old beachside road has been pedestrianized and planted with pine trees, known as the "Pine Walk".

🚗 *Leave Port de Pollença and drive northeast on the MA2210, Carretera de Formentor, to reach the next stop, Península de Formentor.*

⑭ Península de Formentor

Mallorca; 07470

The Carretera de Formentor goes through an extravagantly scenic route to Península de Formentor. Located at the northern end of the Serra de Tramuntana, this peninsula is a 20-km- (12-mile-) long headland of steep mountains. Three lookout points, such as the **Mirador d'es Colomer**, oversee plunging, north-facing sea cliffs. The peninsula also boasts one of the island's finest beaches, the **Platja de Formentor**. The rocky, wind-battered tip of the peninsula, the **Cap de Formentor**, is guarded by a lighthouse, rising to 260 m (850 ft), from where there are magnificent views. On a clear day visitors can see Menorca and its former capital, Ciutadella.

🚗 *Leave Cap de Formentor on the MA2210 back along the bay back to Port de Pollença. Continue on the MA2220 through Port de Pollença to Alcúdia. Park in the big car park not far from the main entrance to town.*

⑮ Alcúdia

Mallorca; 07400

The town of Alcúdia, with its old stone mansions surrounded by the sturdy remains of the old city wall, cuts a handsome profile. Situated on a neck of land separating two large and sheltered bays, Alcúdia's strategic location was first recognized by the Phoenicians and then by the Romans, who built their island capital here. The beautifully restored town is entered through the vast **Porta des Moll** gate. The town's best-looking building is the *ajuntament* (town hall), a finely proportioned 17th-century structure with an elegant stone balcony. Located on the edge of town, a 10-minute walk away, is Alcúdia's **Museu Monogràfic** *(closed Mon)*, which is packed with an assortment of archaeological bits and pieces, including Phoenician jewellery and a multitude of Roman artifacts. Right next to the museum are the Roman ruins, Alcúdia's most famous sight.

EAT AND DRINK

POLLENÇA

Restaurant Clivia *moderate*
Located in the heart of Pollença, this is a friendly restaurant offering an excellent range of Spanish dishes.
Avda. Pollentia 5, 07460; 971 533 635; closed Wed

AROUND POLLENÇA

Café La Balada del Agua del Mar *inexpensive*
This is an appealing little beachside café-restaurant, 5 km (3 miles) from Pollença, occupying an old villa. The highlights are the salads and seafood.
Passeig Voramar 5, 07470; 971 864 276; closed late Oct–Apr

Restaurant Stay *moderate*
Set beautifully on the pier, this restaurant combines contemporary design with a good international and Mallorcan menu. Lots of big salads.
Moll Nou, 07470; 971 868 020; www.stayrestaurant.com

Below left Roman ruins at Alcúdia **Below right** Nostra Senyora dels Àngels overlooking the main square, Pollença

DAY TRIP OPTIONS

Mallorca is a small island with a dense road network, so getting from one place to another rarely takes time. The MA10 accesses most of the stops in this drive. Visitors can base themselves either in Palma or Alcúdia.

Beaches and island

Spend a lazy morning on the beach in Sant Elm ❹ and then take a boat to the uninhabited nature reserve island of Sa Dragonera.

Take the MA1 from Palma, southwest towards Andratx. At Andratx, get onto the MA1031 and then the MA1030 to Sant Elm. Return to Palma the same way.

Ancient monastery and resort

Take a stroll around the Santuari de Monestir de Valldemossa ❼ and then head to Deià ❾ to spend the rest of the day in this resort town.

Leave Palma on the MA1040 towards Esporles. After Esporles, take the MA1100

left and then get onto the MA10, right, to Valldemossa. Continue on the MA10 to Deià. Return to Palma the same way.

Port town and spectacular views

Spend the day on the golden sands of Port de Pollença and then head up the Península de Formentor ⑭ for some spectacular views.

Take the MA2220 from Alcúdia to Port de Pollença and then the MA2210 to the Península de Formentor.

Eat and Drink: inexpensive, under €20; moderate, €20–€40; expensive, over €20

The White Island

Santa Eulària des Riu to Eivissa Town

Highlights

- **Charming port town**
  Explore Santa Eulària des Riu, a colourful old town in a delightful seaside setting

- **Sparkling beaches**
  Catch the sun on Cala Mastella, one of Ibiza's best beaches

- **Spectacular views**
  Take in the views at Port de Sant Miquel, a former smugglers' hideaway

- **Stunning town**
  Stroll around Dalt Vila, the exquisite heart of Eivissa Town (Ibiza)

Tourists on the beach at Port de Sant Miquel

The White Island

For many, the most beautiful of the Balearic islands, Ibiza, or Eivissa in the island's Catalan language, has a 200-km (125-mile) long coastline punctuated with small coves and pristine beaches. The island is celebrated for its nightlife, but while most tourists are bound for its bars and clubs, discerning visitors know that Ibiza has much more to offer. The island has a backbone of beautiful hills and, away from the big resorts, tiny, beguiling villages dot the landscape. This drive, which can easily be done in a day, takes in the most scenic parts of rural Eivissa.

PLAN YOUR DRIVE

Start/finish: Santa Eulària des Riu to Eivissa Town.

Number of days: 1–2, allowing for a walk around Eivissa Town.

Distance: 65 km (40 miles).

Road conditions: Generally well paved and signed, with some steep sections in the hills approaching Sant Miquel.

When to go: Spring (Apr–May) and autumn (late Sep–Oct) are the best times to enjoy the drive. Temperatures can be too hot for comfort and the roads very crowded during July and August.

Opening hours: Most monuments are generally open daily from 10am to 2pm, and from 4 to 6pm. None of the churches mentioned in the drive have set opening times. Most clubs open late at night and stay open until morning.

Market days: Santa Eulària des Riu: May–Oct: Mon, Tue & Thu–Sun.

Major festivals: Santa Eulària des Riu: Anar a Maig, first Sun May; Sant Joan de Labritja: Nit de Sant Joan, 23 Jun.

Above Old city walls of Dalt Vila in Eivissa Town, *see p253* **Right** Tourists at one of La Marina's many outdoor restaurants, Eivissa Town, *see p253*

KEY

Drive route

① Santa Eulària des Riu

Ibiza; 07840

The island's third-largest town, Santa Eulària des Riu is an attractive place, whose neat centre spreads along the seashore. Santa Eulària is crowned by the **Puig de Missa** church and cemetery. The main street, Passeig de s'Alamera, is lined with market stalls selling everything from T-shirts to jewellery. There are two town beaches, whose sands slope down into the sea, making them ideal for children. The town is at its busiest on Wednesdays as tourists make their way to the large hippy market at Punta Arabí, just 3 km (2 miles) northeast of Santa Eulària.

🚘 *From the town, take the PM810 northeast to Sant Carles de Peralta, and turn right on the country lane signed for Cala Llenya. Follow this road for some distance, and look out for signs pointing to Cala Mastella.*

② Cala Mastella

Ibiza; 07840

Located in a beautiful cove, Cala Mastella is one of northern Ibiza's prettiest beaches. Its yellow-white sands back onto a lovely terraced valley of orchards and olives. Pine trees provide shade and the waters are crystal-clear. The snorkelling is among the best in the Mediterranean. Sunbeds are available for hire and there is a beach bar selling soft drinks. Swimmers should beware of jellyfish and sea urchins.

🚘 *From Cala Mastella, head back towards Sant Carles de Peralta to rejoin the PM810. Proceed north on the PM810, which then becomes the PM811. Continue on this road until the T-junction and turn left, following the PM811 into Sant Joan de Labritja.*

③ Sant Joan de Labritja

Ibiza; 07810

Once a hippy hangout, Sant Joan de Labritja is a lovely little village of just 950 people, nestled in the foothills of northern Ibiza. The most distinctive sight of the village is its large 18th-century church, the **Església de Sant Joan**, whose thick walls dominate proceedings. The village is still a favourite haunt of expatriate writers and artists. Many of them live in tastefully modernized, bright white old peasants' cottages with nifty wrought-iron balconies and handsome wooden doors. The fertile countryside surrounding Sant Joan supports numerous farms that are proud of their organic credentials.

🚘 *From Sant Joan de Labritja, drive west on the PM811, which becomes the C733. Turn right onto a country lane signposted to Sant Miquel de Balansat, then right on the PM804 into the village centre.*

Above left Tranquil beach of Cala Mastella
Above right Whitewashed houses lining a street in Sant Joan de Labritja **Below** Colourful flea market at Punta Arabí, Santa Eulària des Riu

WHERE TO STAY

SANTA EULÀRIA DES RIU

Agroturismo Xarc *expensive*
This finely appointed country hotel, 5 km (3 miles) north of Santa Eulària, amalgamates the best of modern style with traditional features, including stone walls and wooden beams.
C'an Casmi Es Nuvells, 07840; 971 339 178; www.agroxarc.es; a minimum stay of five nights in summer; closed Nov–Feb

SANT JOAN DE LABRITJA

Can Martí *expensive*
An environmentally conscious country hotel just 2 km (1 mile) south of Sant Joan de Labritja. The four apartment-sized rooms are individually decorated and seductively charming.
Venda de Cas Ripolls 29, 07810; 971 333 500; www.canmarti.com

EAT AND DRINK

SANTA EULÀRIA DES RIU

Agroturismo Atzaró *expensive*
This luxury hotel in an old Ibizan-style house set in an orange grove serves great Mediterranean dishes with creative touches. A selection of tapas is available and they have an excellent collection of South African wines.
Ctra. Sant Joan, Km 15, 07800; 971 338 838; www.atzaro.com

SANT JOAN DE LABRITJA

La Paloma Café & Bakery
inexpensive–moderate
This relaxed, homely café serves up Mediterranean cuisine with Tuscan influences. Bread is baked fresh daily.
C/ Can Pou 4, 07812; 971 325 543; www.palomaibiza.com

Eat and Drink: inexpensive, under €20; moderate, €20–€40; expensive, over €40

Above Spectacular view over the harbour of Eivissa Town from Dalt Vila **Below left** Courtyard leading to the Església de Sant Miquel in Sant Miquel de Balansat **Below right** Way up to the 14th-century cathedral in Dalt Vila, Eivissa Town

SHOPPING IN EIVISSA TOWN

Eivissa Town has the best shopping on the island, with many boutiques and shops lining up along the main streets of the city centre. In particular, look out for the handsome ceramics of Ceramica Es Test (C/Mar 14, 07800; 971 310 321); the designer clothes of Babaz – Antik Batik (Plaça Constitució 8, 07800; 971 315 706); and the artwork and handmade items of Natura (Plaza del Parque 7, 07800; 971 394 328).

WHERE TO STAY

AROUND PORT DE SANT MIQUEL

Hacienda Na Xamena expensive
Set in the heart of a nature reserve, this is a luxury spa-hotel 3 km (2 miles) to the west of Sant Miquel. It also has a poolside gourmet restaurant.
Buzón 11, 07815, Na Xamena; 971 334 500; www.hotelhacienda-ibiza.com

EIVISSA TOWN

Ryans Marina expensive
Right on the waterfront, this boutique hotel occupies three portside buildings dating back to the 1920s.
C/ Barcelona 7, 07800; 971 310 172; www.ryans.es/hotel-ryans-marina

La Torre del Canonigo expensive
Spectacular views and a smooth ambience can be found here in this small, plush hotel, which occupies an old stone tower that was once part of the city wall.
C/ Major 8, Dalt Vila, 07800; 971 303 884; www.latorredelcanonigo.com

④ Sant Miquel de Balansat
Ibiza; 07815
Located high up in the hills, the small village of Sant Miquel de Balansat was founded in the 13th century. A must-see is the large and imposing **Església de Sant Miquel**, a 16th-century church that once provided shelter during the frequent raids by pirates. The interior of the church is unusual in that it has two chapels, one of which is adorned with bright, modern frescoes. Every Thursday at 6:15pm (May–Oct) there is a music and dance show by a local folklore group in front of the church. From the church there are lovely views of the olive groves and pine forests in the surrounding country-side and of the huddle of artisans' cottages that make up the village.
🚗 *Heading north from Sant Miquel, it is just 4 km (2 miles) along the PM804 to Port de Sant Miquel.*

⑤ Port de Sant Miquel
Ibiza; 07815
The main road from Sant Miquel to Port de Sant Miquel cuts a scenic route through a verdant valley before weaving its way down to the coast at this tiny port that was once a smugglers' hideaway. The port has a spectacular setting with jutting promontories sheltering a tiny inlet, and there is a first-class sandy beach with all the accoutrements – a beach bar, pedalos and a brace of large hotels. Nearby, on one of the hills, stands the exclusive hotel Hacienda Na Xamena hotel, which offers magnificent views.
🚗 *Doubling back from Port de Sant Miquel on the PM804, it is 12 km (7 miles) south to Santa Gertrudis.*

⑥ Santa Gertrudis de Fruitera
Ibiza; 07814
This ancient agricultural village is surrounded by apricot, peach and orange orchards, and hence its name "de Fruitera", which means "of the fruits". Now a centre of expat life, it has an excellent selection of bars and restaurants, plus the very popular Casi Todo auctioneers (www.casitodo.com), where visitors can pick up anything from clocks to paintings and doors to old cars. Visit the **Església de Santa Gertrudis**, a stern structure dating back to medieval times and long the centre of village life, though it is much less so today.
🚗 *Leave Santa Gertrudis de Fruitera going south on the PM804. After 5 km (3 miles), it joins the C733, which goes straight to Eivissa Town (Ibiza).*

❼ Eivissa Town

Ibiza; 07800

Glued to a rocky outcrop overlooking the Mediterranean, the oldest and most interesting part of Eivissa (or Ibiza) Town, Dalt Vila, dates back to the 17th century. This part of town boasts a Gothic cathedral, honey-coloured stone walls, attractive squares and chic bars and restaurants. There are fine views over the city from its walls.

Above View across the port towards the upper town of Eivissa

A two-hour walking tour

Park the car and start exploring Eivissa by the waterfront with its cafés, fishing boats, ferries and yachts. Halfway along the waterfront is a distinctive stone **obelisk** ①, which was erected in honour of those local corsairs who long protected the island from marauding pirates. Head south from near the obelisk along Carrer de Sant Elm. Turn left at the end and take the first right up Carrer de Joan Mayans to reach **Mercat Vell** ②, the Old Market.

From the Old Market, walk south up the hill to the monumental stonework of the **Portal de Ses Taules** ③, the main gateway into the old town, the Dalt Vila. Beyond the gateway, turn right for **Plaça de la Vila** ④, a broad, pedestrianized piazza, flanked by old mansions and alive with art galleries, boutiques, bars and restaurants. Down the slope from the plaza is the

A statue in the Portal de ses Taules

Baluard de Sant Joan, a stone bulwark that juts out over the town.

Go up the hill from Plaça de la Vila and take the second left along Carrer de Sant Carles, which leads into Carrer de Ignasi Riquer. This leads to the square abutting both the medieval church, the **Església Sant Pere** ⑤ (Santo Domingo), and the **ajuntament** ⑥, the town hall. A narrow walkway to the left of the town hall leads up to Carrer de Santa María. Follow it up and round to a second gateway, the **Sa Portella** ⑦. Beyond the gateway, turn left and ascend to the 14th-century **Catedral de la Verge de les Neus** ⑧, rebuilt in Baroque style in the 18th century. From here, go southwest along the ramparts to the **Baluard de Sant Bernat** ⑨, one of Dalt Vila's several surviving bastions. From here the neighbouring island of Formentera is visible in the distance. After the walk, go back to where the car is parked.

VISITING EIVISSA

Tourist Information
Passeig Vara de Rey 1, 07800; 971 301 900; www.ibiza.travel

Parking
Park on the streets close to the pier, on the area that lies between Avinguda de Bartomeu de Rosselló and Passeig de Vara de Rey.

EAT AND DRINK

EIVISSA TOWN

El Faro *moderate*
Located on the harbourfront, this is one of the best places to eat fish and take in the quayside atmosphere.
Plaça Sa Riba 1, 07800; 971 313 233; www.elfaroibiza.com

La Oliva *moderate*
A smashing Dalt Vila restaurant serving a creative menu that mixes Spanish and French cuisines. Located in the heart of the Eivissa scene, it is a very popular spot, so book ahead.
C/ Santa Creu 2, 07800; 971 305 752; www.laolivaibiza.com; closed mid-Oct–mid-Apr

La Brasa *moderate*
This first-rate restaurant, in between the port and the city walls, has a lovely garden terrace for summer dining. Meat and seafood dishes are highly recommended and the daily specials stick firmly to seasonal ingredients.
C/ Pere Sala 3, 07800; 971 301 202; www.labrasaibiza.com

Eat and Drink: inexpensive, under €20; moderate, €20–€40; expensive, over €40

General Index

Page numbers in **bold** refer to main entries.

A

Abadía Retuerta (La Milla de Oro) 149
Abies pinsapo 193
accommodation **22–3**
  booking 23
  camping 23
  casas rurales 22, 23
  facilities and prices 23
  hotels 22
  paradors 22
Acrópolis Ibérica 122, **123**
Acueducto del Aguilar (Cerro Gordo) 211
Agua Amarga 234, **235**, 237
Agüero 84, **85**
air travel **10**
ajuntament (Alcúdia) 247
ajuntament (Eivissa Town) 253
ajuntament (Girona) 102
ajuntament (Morella) 132
A Lanzada 33, **36**, 37
Albaida **141**
Albariño Wine 36
Albarracín 119, 120–21, 126, **127**
La Alberca 155, 158, **159**
Alcañiz 119, 121, **122**, 123, 127
Alcazaba de Mérida (Mérida) 176
Alcázar de Jerez (Jerez de la Frontera) 202
Alcázar de los Duques de Feria (Zafra) 177
Alcoy **142**
Alcúdia 239–241, 246, **247**
Alexander VI, Pope 140
Alfonso VII, King 168
Alhama de Granada 209–10, **212**
Alhambra 215–19, 223
Alhóndiga (Villanueva de los Infantes) 184
Almacén de los Fúcares (Almagro) 186
Almagro 181, **186**, 187
Almería
  Secret Beaches **232–7**
Almuñécar 210, **211**
Alonso VIII 167
Las Alpujarras 216, 222–23
Andalusia
  Andalusian Renaissance and Wooded
    Mountains **224–31**
  Coast of Light **198–207**
  Historic Mountain Villages **214–23**
  The Mudéjar Route **208–13**
  White Pueblos **188–97**
Anfiteatro (Mérida) 176
Anguiano 59, 65, 67
Anguiano Dancers 65
Ansó 82, 83, 86, 88, **89**
Antiga Església de Sant Francesc (Montblanc)
  113
Antigua Casa Palacio del Marqués de Torresoto
  (Arcos de la Frontera) 192
Antigua Fábrica Noguera (Beceite) 124
A Pobra de Trives 42, **43**
Aragón
  From the Mountains to the Plains **118–27**
  To the Roof of Aragón **80–9**
Aranda de Duero 147, **150**, 151
Arco de la Villa (Zahara de la Sierra) 194
Arco de Trajano (Mérida) 176
Los Arcos (Clunia) 151
Los Arcos (Teruel) 127
Arcos de la Frontera 190, 191, **192**, 193
El Arenal (Arenas de San Pedro) 157
Las Arenas de Cabrales (Desfiladero de la
  Hermida) 54
Arenas de San Pedro 155, 156, **157**, 161
Ares del Maestre 130, 131, 134, **135**
Argolibio (Desfiladero de los Beyos) 50
Asturian Cider 55

Asturias
  Ocean and Mountain **46–55**
A Teixeira (Monasterio de Santa Cristina de
  Ribas de Síl) 42
ATMs **14**
A Toxa 32, 35, **36**
Atrivm (Alcañiz) 122
Augustus, Emperor 176
Ávalos, Juan de 126
Axarquía 209, 210, 211, 212
Ayerbe **84**

B

Badia de Pollença (Pollença) 246
Baeza 225, 226, 227, **228**, 229, 231
Bajo Aragón 123
Balcón de Pirineo (Monasterio de San Juan de
  la Peña) 86
Balearic Islands
  Mallorca's Cliffs and Coves **238–47**
  The White Island **248–53**
balloon rides, hot-air 105
Baluard de Sant Bernat (Eivissa Town) 253
El Bañuelo (Granada) 219
Banyalbufar 241, **243**
Banyeres de Mariola 142, 143
Banyoles 100, 101, 102, **103**, 107
Banys Àrabs (Girona) 103
Banys Àrabs (Palma) 242
Baqueira-Beret (Val d'Aran) 96
Barajas (Valle del Tormes) 158
Baroja, Julio Caro 76
Baroja, Pío 76
Baroja, Ricardo 76
Barranc de Subenuix (Parc Nacional
  d'Aigüestortes i Estany de Sant Maurici) 95
Barranco del Negro (Vela Blanca) 237
Barrio de la Estación (Haro) 63
Barro (Llanes) 55
Barruera (Vall de Boí) 91, 96, 97
El Barco **158**
Basílica Arxiprestal de Santa María (Morella) 133
Basílica de Santa María (Castelló d'Empúries) 106
Basílica de Santa María (Vilafranca del Penedès)
  112
Basílica de Sant Francesc (Palma) 242
Basque Country 9, 11, 12, 13, 17, 26
Beatus of Liébana 53
Beceite 120, 121, **124**, 125, 127
Béjar 155, **159**
Bejes (Desfiladero de la Hermida) 49, 54, 55
Bellver, Joan Rubió i 245
Bera (Vera de Bidasoa) 71, **76**, 77
Berceo, Gonzalo de 65
Berdún 82
Bertiz estate 71, 79
Besalú 101, 104, **105**, 107
Biniés 82, **88**
Bishop of Astorga 44
Boca de Infierno (Hecho) 89
Bocairent 137, 138, 139, 140, **141**, 143
Bodegas Antonio Cañaveras **184**
Bodegas Arzuaga (La Milla de Oro) 149
Bodegas La Fabulista 61, 67
Bodegas Pago de Carraovejas (La Milla de Oro)
  149
Bodegas Ysios **61**, 67
Bodegues Torres (Vilafranca del Penedès) 112
Boí (Vall de Boí) 96
Bornos **193**
El Bosque **193**
Bosque de Irati 70, 71, **74**, 79
Briones 58, 59, **62**, 67
Bubión (Poqueira Valley) 222, 223
Bulnes 47, 48, 49, **54–5**

C

Cabo de Gata 236, 237
Cabre, Juan 123
Cáceres 164, 171, 172, 173, **174**, 175, 177
Cadafalch, Josep Puig i 112
Cadaqués 100, 101, 106, **107**
Cádiz 11, 194, 199, 200, 201, 204, **205**
Cádiz el Chico (Little Cádiz) 194
Caín de Valdeón (Posada de Valdeón) 52
Cala Deià (Deià) 244
Cala Estellencs (Estellencs) 243
Cala Mastella 250, **251**
Calatrava, Santiago 61
Calderón de la Barca, Pedro 187
Calixtus II, Pope 140
El Call 99, 102
Camacho, Valentín Rodríguez 187
Cambados 32, 33, 35, **36**, 37
El Camí de la Llibertat (Sort) 94
Camino de Santiago 34, 44, 69, 70, 72, 75, 78, 87
camping **23**
Campo de Criptana 180, 181, **182**, 183, 187
Canales de la Sierra 67
Ca n'Alluny (Deià) 244
Candelario **158–9**
Cangas de Onís 48, 49, **50**, 51, 55
Cañón del Síl 40, 41
Can Prohom (Sóller) 245
Cantavieja 132, **133**, 135
Cap de Creus 100, **107**
Cap de Formentor (Península de Formentor)
  247
Cap de Sant Antoni (Xàbia) 143
Capileira (Poqueira Valley) 222, 223
Capilla de la Virgen del Cid (Iglesuela del Cid)
  135
Capilla de la Virgen del Pilar e Iglesia de San
  Juan Bautista (Laguardia) 60
Capilla de Santa María (Xàtiva) 141
carbonera (Parque Natural de Señorío de Bertiz)
  76
Carboneras 234, **235**
car insurance 16
Carretera de la Cabra **212**
Cartoixa d'Escaladei (Escaladei) 115
Casa Bayo (Teruel) 126
Casa Consistorial (Valderrobres) 124
Casa Consistorial (Zangoza) 72
Casa de Cultura (Ciudad Rodrigo) 161
Casa de Cultura (Teruel) 127
Casa de Cultura (Villanueva de los Infantes)
  184
La Casa de las Argollas (Plasencia) 168
Casa de las Bolas (Aranda de Duero) 150
Casa de las Cadenas (Trujillo) 174
Casa del Rey Moro (Ronda) 196
Casa del Torico (Teruel) 127
Casa do Viño (Monasterio de Santa Cristina de
  Ribas de Síl) 43
Casa Maurí (La Pobla de Segur) 97
Casa Mudéjar (Úbeda) 229
Casa Museo de Pizarro (Trujillo) 175
Casa-Museo Gayarre (Roncal) 74
Casa Palacio de Cuenca (Arcos de la Frontera)
  192
Casares de las Hurdes (Las Hurdes) 169
Casa Sapera (Cretas) 123
Casas Hidalgas (Peñafiel) 148
Casa y Torre Carvajal (Cáceres) 174
Casa y Torre de las Cigüeñas (Cáceres) 174
Cascada de la Ratera (Parc Nacional
  d'Aigüestortes i Estany de Sant Maurici) 95
Castell de Bellver (Palma) 242
Castell de Guadalest (Guadalest) 142
Castell de la Zuda (Tortosa) 116, 117
Castellfollit de la Roca **105**

Castile 24, 27
Castile y Léon
  Along the Duero **144–51**
  The Spine of Castile **152–161**
Castilla La Mancha
  Don Quixote's La Mancha **178–87**
El Castillo (Alcañiz) 122
Castillo Arabe (Salobreña) 213
Castillo de Calatrava la Nueva 179, **185**, 187
Castillo de Castro Caldelas (Castro Caldelas) 43
Castillo de Don Álvaro de Luna (Arenas de San
  Pedro) 157, 161
Castillo de Enrique II (Ciudad Rodrigo) 161
Castillo de Guzmán el Bueno (Tarifa) 207
Castillo de Javier **72**
Castillo de La Calahorra **221**, 223
Castillo de la Luna (Rota) 204
Castillo de la Yedra (Cazorla) 229
Castillo de las Almadrabas (Zahara de los
  Atunes) 207
Castillo de Loarre 81, 82, 83 **84**, 85
Castillo de los Condes de Oropesa (Jarandilla
  de la Vera) 167
Castillo de los Duques de Alburquerque **157**
Castillo de Morella (Morella) 132
Castillo de Peñafiel (Peñafiel) 148
Castillo de Rochafrida (Parque Natural de las
  Lagunas de Ruidera) 180, 183
Castillo de San Marcos (El Puerto de Santa
  María) 204
Castillo de San Miguel (Almuñécar) 211
Castillo de Santiago (Sanlúcar de Barrameda)
  203
Castillo de Valdecorneja (El Barco) 158
Castillo del Águila (Gaucín) 197
Castillo (Medina-Sidonia) 206
Castillo y Murallas (Trujillo) 175
castle
  Albarracín 127
  Ponferrada 44
  Valderrobres 124
  Villafranca del Bierzo 44
Castro Caldelas 42, **43**
Catalonia
  Mountains and Valleys **90–97**
  The Catalan Heartland **98–107**
  Vineyards and Gothic Treasures **108–17**
Catedral de Girona (Girona) 102
Catedral de la Verge de les Neus (Eivissa Town)
  253
Catedral de San Martiño (Ourense) 42
Catedral de San Pedro (Jaca) 88
Catedral de San Salvador (Jerez de la Frontera)
  202
Catedral de Santa Maria (Ciudad Rodrigo) 160–61
Catedral de Santa María (Teruel) 127
Catedral de Santa María de la Asunción (Coria)
  169
Catedral de Santa Maria d'Urgell (La Seu
  d'Urgell) 94
Catedral de Santa María la Real (Iruña) 78
Catedral de Santiago de Compostela (Santiago
  de Compostela) 34
Catedral de Tortosa (Tortosa) 116
Catedral Nueva (Cádiz) 205
Catedral Nueva (Plasencia) 164, 168
Catedral Vieja (Cádiz) 205
Catedral Vieja (Plasencia) 168
cathedral
  Albarracín 127
  Guadix 220
Cava de Sant Blai (Bocairent) 141
Caves Codorniu (Sant Sadurní d'Anoia) 112
Cazorla 227, 228, **229**, 230, 231
Celorio (Llanes) 54
Ceneya (Desfiladero de los Beyos) 50
Centre d'Estudis de la Batalla de l'Ebre
  (Gandesa) 116
Centre d'Interpretació Ull de Canals (Banyeres)
  142

Centre Romànic de la Vall de Boí (Vall de Boí) 96
Centro Etnogràfico (Torre del Compte) 122
Cerro Gordo **211**
Cervantes, Miguel de 207
Chanson de Roland 75
Charles II, King 77
Charles V, Emperor 167, 186, 228
cheeses
  Picos 54
  Roncal 74
children, driving with **20**
Chipiona 201, **204**, 205, 207
Chopin, Frédéric 244
Churriguera, José Benito de 177
cider 47, 48, 49, 54, 55
Cistercian trail 117
Ciudad Rodrigo 153, 154, 155, **160–61**
Ciudadela de Jaca (Jaca) 88
Ciudadela (Roses) 106
Ciutadella (Menorca) 247
climate **9**
Clunia 145, 147, **151**
Coll de Cantó (La Seu d'Urgell) 94
Coll de la Creu de Perves (Pont de Suert) 97
Collado del Almendral **230–31**
Colegiata de Nuestra Señora de la Asunción
  (Roa) 149
Colegiata Real (Roncesvalles) 75
Commentary on the Apocalypse (Beatus of
  Liébana) 53
Communications **14**
Cómpeta **212**
Condes de Albarei 36
Congost dels Collegats (La Pobla de Segur) 97
Conjunt Megalític (Roses) 106
conquistadors 166, 171, 172, 174, 178
Consuegra 180, 181, 186, **187**
Convent de Sant Francesc (Morella) 132
Convento de las Mercedarias Descalzas (Arcos
  de la Frontera) 192
Convento de las Monjas Concepcionistas (Vejer
  de la Frontera) 206
Convento de San Nicolás el Real (Villafranca del
  Bierzo) 44
Convento de Santa Clara (Cáceres) 174
Convento de Santa Clara (Mérida) 176
Convento de Santa Clara (Peñafiel) 148
Convento de Santo Domingo (Jerez de la
  Frontera) 202
Cooperativa Agrícola (Falset) 116
Cooperativa Agrícola (Gandesa) 116
Coria 164, 165, 168, **169**
Corral de Comedias (Almagro) 180, 186, 187
Corredores (Consuegra) 187
Cosgaya (Valle de Camaleño) 53
Costa Blanca 10, 137 138, 143
Costa de la Luz 200, 201, 204, 207
Costa del Sol 197, 200, 210
Costa Tropical 210
Covadonga y los Lagos **50**, 55
Covetes dels Moros (Bocairent) 141
Cretas 121, **123**
Crist de Mijaran 96
Crist de Taüll 96
The Cubes of Memory 55
La Cubiella (Soto de Sajambre) 51
Cueva de Montesinos (Parque Natural de las
  Lagunas de Ruidera) 180, 183
Cueva de San Genadio (Valle del Silencio) 45
Cueva de Tito Bustillo (Ribadesella) 50
Cuevas del Águila **156**, 157
Cuevas de Nerja (Cerro Gordo) 211
Las Cuevas de Zugarramurdi 74, **75**
Curiel de Duero 148, **149**
currency 14

D

Daimiel 186
Dalí, Salvador 99, 100

The Dalí Triangle 107
Dalt Vila 249, 253
Danza de los Zancos 65
Deià **244**, 245, 247
Delta de l'Ebre 109, 110, 116, **117**
Deltebre (Delta de l'Ebre) 117
Denominación de Origen 54, 55, 63, 74,
  116, 184
Descenso Internacional del Sella (Ribadesella)
  50
Desfiladero de la Hermida **54**
Desfiladero de los Beyos **50**
Diada dels Raiers 97
disabled travellers **13**
Doade (Ponte do Sil) 43
driving in Spain **16–21**
  breakdown and accidents 18–19
  buying fuel 17
  caravans and motorhomes 20
  car hire 21
  cycling 20
  disabled drivers 20–21
  driving in winter 18
  driving with children 20
  insurance and breakdown cover 16
  maps 19
  motorcycles 20
  mountain roads 20
  parking 19
  paying tolls 16
  road conditions 18
  road systems 16
  rules of the road 17
  speed limits and fines 17
  taking a break 18
The Dry Marshes of Daimiel 186
dry-stone architecture 129, 130, 134
Duanes del Mar (Xàbia) 143
Durro (Vall de Boí) 91, 96, 97

E

Eivissa Town 249, 250, 252, **253**
Elcano, Juan Sebastián de **203**
Elciego 59, **62**, 63, 67
Elizondo 71, **75**, 79
Els Ports 120, 123
Embalse del Tranco (Collado del Almendral)
  230
Embalse de Mansilla **66**, 67
Embalse de Quéntar **219**
Emerita Augusta see Mérida
Erill la Vall (Vall de Boí) 91, 96, 97
Ermita de la Virgin de las Nieves (Bosque de
  Irati) 74
Ermita de Nuestra Senora de los Remedios
  (Olvera) 195
Ermita de San Antonio Abad (Acrópolis Ibérica)
  123
Ermita de San Cristóbal (Acrópolis Ibérica) 123
Ermita de San Homónimo (Monasterio de San
  Juan de la Peña) 86, 87
Ermita de San Voto (Monasterio de San Juan de
  la Peña) 87
Ermita de Santa Ana (Beceite) 124
Ermita de Santa Aúrea (Villavelayo) 67
Ermita de Santa Teresa (Monasterio de San Juan
  de la Peña) 86–7
Ermita y Castillo de Monfragüe (Parque
  Nacional de Monfragüe) 167
Escaladei 111, 114, 115, 117
Los Escullos (Isleta del Moro) 235
Església de l'Assumpció de Nostra Senyora
  (Albaida) 141
Església de Nostra Senyora dels Àngels
  (Pollença) 246
Església de San Pere de Galligants (Girona) 103
Església Sant Pere (Eivissa Town) 253
Església de Sant Bartomeu (Sóller) 245
Església de Sant Bartomeu (Xàbia) 143

Església de Sant Climent (Vall de Boí) 96
Església de Sant Feliu (Girona) 102–103
Església de Sant Francesc (Xàtiva) 140
Església de Sant Joan (Sant Joan de Labritja) 251
Església de Sant Marçal (Montblanc) 113
Església de Sant Miquel (Montblanc) 113
Església de Sant Miquel (Sant Miquel de Balansat) 252
Església de Sant Miquèu (Val d'Aran) 96
Església de Sant Pere (Xàtiva) 140
Església de Santa Gertrudis (Santa Gertrudis de Fruitera) 252
Església de Santa Maria (Alcoy) 142
Església de Santa Maria la Major (Montblanc) 113
Església de Santa Maria la Mayor (Mora de Rubielos) 133
Església de Santa Maria (Ontinyent) 141
Església de Santa Maria (Vall de Boí) 96
Espinama (Valle de Camaleño) 53
Esporles **242**
Espot **94**, 95, 97
Estany de la Ratera (Parc Nacional d'Aigüestortes i Estany de Sant Maurici) 95
Estanyola de la Ratera (Parc Nacional d'Aigüestortes i Estany de Sant Maurici) 95
Estella (Lizarra) **79**
Estellencs **243**
Ex-Colegiata de Santa Maria la Mayor (Rubielos de Mora) 134
Extremadura
  Cities of the Conquistadors **170–7**
  Roman Ruins and Unspoilt Landscapes **162–9**
Ezcaray 59, **64**, 65, 66

F

Falset 111, **116**, 117
Faro de Chipiona (Chipiona) 204
Ferrer, Eleuterio Blasco 125
ferries
  Balearic Islands **10–11**
  Illa de Ons 36
  Sa Dragonera 243
festivals **9**
Figueres 99, 100, 101, **106**, 107
Finca Villacreces 149
Font d'Almodar (Xàtiva) 140
Fonte as Burgas (Ourense) 42
food and drink **24–5**
  bars and cafés 25
  picnic shopping 25
  practical information 24
  restaurants 24
  wines 25
Foz de Arbayún **73**
Foz de Biniés (Biniés) 88
Foz de Lumbier **73**
Francisco de Orellana 174, 177
La Fregona Ilustre 207
La Fresneda 121, **122**, 127
Frigiliana 210, **211**
Fuente de Chorros 79
La Fuente de las Galeras (El Puerto de Santa María) 204
Los Fusilamiento del 3 de Mayo 142

G

Galería de Arte Arx-Arcis (Arcos de la Frontera) 192
Galicia
  Along the Sacred Shore **38–45**
  Medieval Treasures and Golden Bays **30–37**
Galilea **242–3**
Gallo Azul Café (Jerez de la Frontera) 202
Gandesa **116**
Garganta la Olla **167**
Garrotxa Volcanic Zone 107
Gata de Gorgos 138, 139, **142**

Gaucín 190, 196, **197**
Gaudí, Antoni 117, 242, 245
Gayarre, Julián 74
Gehry, Frank 62, 67
Genoveses **236**
Gerri de la Sal 97
Girona 10, 16, 99, 100, 101, **102–103**, 107
Glosas Emilianenses 64
Golden Age of Theatre 187
Gorg Blau 240, **246**
Goya (painter) 37, 142
Granada 7, 10, 210, 215, 216, 217, **218–19**, 223
La Granja (Esporles) 242
Gratallops (Vilella Baixa) 111, 115
Graves, Robert 244
Grazalema 189, 190, 191, **194**, 195, 197
Grutas de Cristal **125**
Grutas del Águila see Cuevas del Águila
Guadalest **142**, 143
Guadalupe 171, 172, 173, **175**, 177
Guadix 215, 216, 217, 219, **220**, 221, 223
Guifré el Pilós, Catalan ruler 105
Guifré el Pilós (Wilfred the Hairy) 100, 104, 105
Gumiel de Izán **150**, 151
Guzman, Santo Domingo de 150

H

hang-gliding 226, 230, 231
Haro 58, 59, 62, **63**, 67
health **12–13**
Hecho 81, 82, 83, **89**
Hemingway, Ernest 78
La Herradura **211**
hiking 107, 219
holidays, public **9**
El Hornillo (Arenas de San Pedro) 157
Hospital Real (Xàtiva) 140
Hotel Marqués de Riscal (Elciego) 62, 67
Hoyos del Espino (Valle del Tormes) 154, 158

I

Ibarrola, Agustín 55
the Iberians 123, 141, 151, 192
Ibiza see Eivissa Town
ibn Malik, Tarif 207
Iglesia-Convento de San Pablo 148
Iglesia de Divino Salvador (Vejer de la Frontera) 206
Iglesia de El Salvador (Murillo de Gállego) 85
Iglesia de la Asunción (Cretas) 123
Iglesia de la Encarnación (Olvera) 195
Iglesia de Nuestra Senora Carmen (Zahara de los Atunes) 207
Iglesia de Nuestra Señora de la Asunción (Briones) 62
Iglesia de Nuestra Señora de la Asunción (El Barco) 158
Iglesia de Nuestra Señora de la Merced (Parque Nacional de Monfragüe) 166
Iglesia de Nuestra Señora de la O (Rota) 204
Iglesia de Nuestra Señora de la O (Sanlúcar de Barrameda) 203
Iglesia de Nuestra Señora del Rosario (Salobreña) 213
Iglesia de San Andrés (Villanueva de los Infantes) 184
Iglesia de San Bartolomé (Beceite) 124
Iglesia de San Caprasio (Santa Cruz de la Serós) 87
Iglesia de San Cristóbal (Necrópolis de Cuyacabras) 67
Iglesia de San Cristóbal (Quintanar de la Sierra) 67
Iglesia de San Esteban (Castillo de Loarre) 84
Iglesia de San Francisco (Sanlúcar de Barrameda) 203
Iglesia de San José (Granada) 218
Iglesia de San Juan Bautista (Aranda de Duero) 150
Iglesia de San Juan de los Reyes (Granada) 219

Iglesia de San Martín (Hecho) 89
Iglesia de San Martín (Trujillo) 174
Iglesia de San Mateo (Tarifa) 207
Iglesia de San Miguel Arcángel (Torrejón el Rubio) 166, 169
Iglesia de San Miguel (Peñafiel) 148
Iglesia de San Pablo (Úbeda) 229
Iglesia de San Pedro (Ansó) 89
Iglesia de San Pedro (Arcos de la Frontera) 192
Iglesia de San Pedro (Ayerbe) 84
Iglesia de San Pedro (Hecho) 89
Iglesia de San Pedro (Sabiote) 231
Iglesia de San Pedro (Teruel) 126
Iglesia de San Pedro de la Rúa (Lizarra) 79
Iglesia de San Pedro y San Isidoro (Ciudad Rodrigo) 161
Iglesia de San Salvador (Biniés) 88
Iglesia de San Vicente (Potes) 53
Iglesia de San Vicente Ferrer (Plasencia) 168
Iglesia de Santa Ana (Peñaranda de Duero) 150–151
Iglesia de Santa Eulalia (Mérida) 176
Iglesia de Santa María (Aranda de Duero) 150
Iglesia de Santa María (Cáceres) 174
Iglesia de Santa María (Cazorla) 229
Iglesia de Santa María (Curiel de Duero) 149
Iglesia de Santa María (Gumiel de Izán) 150
Iglesia de Santa María de la Asunción (Arcos de la Frontera) 192
Iglesia de Santa María de la Encarnación (Alhama de Granada) 212
Iglesia de Santa María de los Reyes (Laguardia) 60
Iglesia de Santa María del Mar Mayor (Valderrobres) 124
Iglesia de Santa Maria la Coronada (Medina-Sidonia) 206
Iglesia de Santa María la Mayor (Béjar) 159
Iglesia de Santa María la Mayor (La Fresneda) 122
Iglesia de Santa María la Mayor (Ronda) 196
Iglesia de Santa María la Mayor (Trujillo) 175
Iglesia de Santa María Mayor (Alcañiz) 122
Iglesia de Santa María (Peñafiel) 148
Iglesia de Santa María (Santa Cruz de la Serós) 87
Iglesia de Santa María de la Meza (Zahara de la Sierra) 194
Iglesia de Santiago (Agüero) 85
Iglesia de Santiago (Coria) 169
Iglesia de Santiago (Elizondo) 75
Iglesia de Santiago (Guadix) 220
Iglesia de Santiago (Puente la Reina) 79
Iglesia de Santiago (Valle del Silencio) 44
Iglesia de Santiago (Villafranca del Bierzo) 44
Iglesia de Santo Domingo (Sanlúcar de Barrameda) 203
Iglesia de Santo Tomás (Haro) 63
Iglesia del Crucifijo (Puente la Reina) 79
Iglesia Santa Maria la Mayor (Ezcaray) 64
Iglesuela del Cid 130, 131, **134–5**
Illa de Ons (Praia de Paxariñas) 32, 36, 37
Illa de Sa Dragonera 241
Indiana Jones and the Last Crusade (movie) 236
La Iruela (Cazorla) 229
Iruña (Pamplona) 70, 71, **78**
Isla de San Andrés (Carboneras) 235
Isleta del Moro 234, **235**
Iznatoraf **231**

J

Jaca 82, **88**, 89
James, Apostle 34
Jarandilla de la Vera 164, 165, **167**
Jardín Botánico (Coria) 169
Jardín Botánico El Albardinal (Rodalquilar) 235
Jardín de Señorío de Bertiz (Parque Natural de Señorío de Bertiz) 71, 76, 77, 79

Jardins de la Francesa (Girona) 103
Jaume I, Violant of Hungary 114
Jerez de la Frontera 10, 195, 199, 200, 201, **202–203**, 207
Jerez de los Caballeros 171, 172, 173, **177**
Jete 212
Jimena de la Frontera 189, 190, 191, 196, **197**
Joly, Gabriel 127
Judería (Morella) 133

K
kayaking **51**, 88, 95

L
Lagos de Covadonga (Covadonga y los Lagos) 50
Laguardia (Biasteri) 57, 59, **60–61**, 67
Laguna Concejo (Parque Natural de las Lagunas de Ruidera) 180, 183
Lagunas Altas de Neila **67**
Lagunas de Ruidera 179, 181, 183
languages **12**
Lanjarón 217, **222–3**
Lanteira **220**
Las Hurdes 163, 164, 165, 168, **169**
Le Maja Desnuda 142
Los Leones (Viso del Marqués) 185
Lignum Crucis 53
Linares de Mora (Rubielos de Mora) 134, 135
Little Seville *see* Zafra
Llanes 48, 49, 54, **55**
Llavorsí (Sort) 93, 94
Llessui (Sort) 94
La Lonja (Alcañiz) 122

M
Maestrazgo 130, 132, 134
Maeztú, Gustavo de 79
Los Mallos de Riglos 81, 82, **84**
manzanilla (sherry) 203, 207
Marina del Este (La Herradura) 211
Marqués de Riscal bodega (Elciego) 62
Marquis of Santa Cruz 185
Martí I, King 114
Martinell, Cèsar 116, 117
Mas de Bunyol 119, 124
Matarraña 120, 121, 124
Matarraña river 124, 127
Mausoleo de Los Amantes (Teruel) 126
Medina-Sidonia 200, **206**
Las Médulas 39, 40, 41, **44**, 45
Mendoza, Rodrigo de 221
Mercat Vell (Eivissa Town) 253
Mérida 171, 172, 173, **176–7**
La Mesa Roldán (Carboneras) 235
La Milla de Oro 147, 148, **149**, 151
Minas de Buferrera (Covadonga y los Lagos) 50
Minas de Oro de Rodalquilar (Rodalquilar) 235
Mirador Cerro de las Balas (Guadix) 220
Mirador de Abades (Arcos de la Frontera) 192
Mirador de Amatista (Rodalquilar) 235
Mirador de Cabezoás (Monasterio de Santo Estevo de Ribas de Sil) 42
Mirador de l'Estany (Parc Nacional d'Aigüestortes i Estany de Sant Maurici) 95
Mirador de Paso del Aire (Puerto de las Palomas) 230
Mirador de Puerto de las Palomas (Puerto de las Palomas) 230
Mirador de San Nicolás (Granada) 218
Mirador del Oso (Puerto de San Glorio) 52
Mirador d'es Colomer (Península de Formentor) 247
Mirambel 129, 131, **133**, 135
Miranda del Castañar 158, **159**
Mogrovejo (Valle de Camaleño) 53
Molino Culebro (Campo de Criptana) 182
Molino El Vínculo (Zahara de la Sierra) 194
Molino Infante (Campo de Criptana) 182

Molinos 124, **125**
Mombeltrán 155, 156, 157, 161
Monasterio de Guadalupe (Guadalupe) 175, 177
Monasterio de Leyre 70, **72–3**
Monasterio de Nuestra Senora de la Regla (Chipiona) 204
Monasterio de Poio (Poio) 37
Monasterio de San Juan de la Peña 82, 85, **86–7**, 89
Monasterio de San Martiño Pinario (Santiago de Compostela) 34
Monasterio de San Millán de Suso (San Millán de la Cogolla) 65
Monasterio de San Millán de Yuso (San Millán de la Cogolla) 64–5
Monasterio de Santa Cristina de Ribas de Sil **42–3**, 45
Monasterio de Santa María de la Vid 146, 147, 150, **151**
Monasterio de Santa Maria la Real (Nájera) 64
Monasterio de Santo Estevo de Ribas de Sil 39, **42**, 45
Monasterio de Valvanera 59, **66**, 67
Monasterio de Yuste 165, **167**
Monasterio Nuevo (Monasterio de San Juan de la Peña) 86, 87, 89
Moneo, Rafael 176
Monestir de Poblet **114**
Monestir de Sant Pere de Rodes (Parc Natural del Cap de Creus) 107
Monestir de Santa Maria de Vallbona (Vallbona de les Monges) 114
Monestir de Santa Maria (Ripoll) 104, 105
Monestir de Santes Creus (Santes Creus) 112, 117
Monsul **236**
Montblanc 109, 111, 112, **113**, 117
Montsant 110
Mora de Rubielos 131, 132, **133**, 135
Morella 129, 130, 131, **132–3**, 135
La Morera de Montsant 115
Moros y Cristianos 141
Mosqueruela **134**
Mudéjar 121, 126, 174, 175, 190, 192, 203, 209, 210, 211, 213, 220, 229
Los Muertos (Carboneras) 235
Murillo de Gállego 84, **85**
Museo Arqueológico (Granada) 219
Museo Arqueólogico Municipal (El Puerto de Santa María) 204
Museo de Alfarería (Guadix) 220
Museo de Arte Sacro (Aranda de Duero) 150
Museo de Arte Visigodo (Mérida) 176
Museo de Cádiz (Cádiz) 205
Museo de la Cárcel Real (Coria) 169
Museo de la Cofía (Trujillo) 175
Museo de l'Almodí (Xàtiva) 140
Museo de la Radio (Peñafiel) 148
Museo de las Brujas (Las Cuevas de Zugarramurdi) 75
Museo de Micro-Miniaturas (Guadalest) 142
Museo de Pontevedra (Pontevedra) 37
Museo del Bierzo (Ponferrada) 44
Museo del Orinal (Ciudad Rodrigo) 161
Museo del Traje Ansotano (Ansó) 89
Museo Diocesano (Jaca) 88
Museo Etnográfico (Almagro) 186
Museo Etnográfico (Castro Caldelas) 43
Museo Etnográfico y Textil (Plasencia) 168
Museo Etnológico (Guadix) 220
Museo Histórico (Salobreña) 213
Museo Judío David Melul (Béjar) 159
Museo Nacional de Arte Romano (Mérida) 176
Museo Provincial (Cáceres) 174
Museo Provincial (Teruel) 127
Museu Soler Blasco (Xàbia) 143
Museu Comarcal (Olot) 104
Museu d'Art (Girona) 102
Museu dels Jueus (Girona) 102

Museu dels Raiers (La Pobla de Segur) 97
Museu dera Val d'Aran (Val d'Aran) 96
Museu d'Història de la Ciutat (Girona) 102
Museu Internacional de Titelles (Albaida) 141
Museu José Segrelles (Albaida) 141
Museo Vivanco de la Cultura del Vino (Briones) 58, 62
Museu Monogràfic (Alcúdia) 247
Museu Municipal Art Contemporani (Valldemossa) 244

N
Nájera 59, **64**
Napoleon 160, 193
Naranjo de Bulnes (Bulnes) 54–5
Navarra
A Circuit around Navarra **68–79**
Navarredonda de Gredos (Valle del Tormes) 158
Noguera Pallaresa valley 97
Nogueruelas (Rubielos de Mora) 134
Nogués, Xavier 116
Nuestra Señora de Muskilda (Ochagavía) 74
Nuñomoral (Las Hurdes) 169

O
Obelisk (Eivissa Town) 253
Ochagavía (Otsagabia) 71, **74**, 79
Ocuri (Ubrique) 193
Olot 100, 101, **104**, 105, 107
Olvera 194, **195**
Ontinyent 140, **141**
opening hours **15**
Oratorio de San Felipe Neri (Cádiz) 205
Order of Calatrava 122, 123
Orellana, Francisco de 174
Otívar (Carretera de la Cabra) 212
Ourense 40, 41, **42**, 43, 45

P
Padrón 33, **34**, 37
Palacio de Arizcunera (Elizondo), 75
Palacio de Bertiz (Parque Natural de Señorío de Bertiz), 77
Palacio de la Conquista (Trujillo), 174
Palacio de las Cadenas (Úbeda), 228
Palacio del Conde de Alba de Yeltes (Ciudad Rodrigo), 161
Palacio del Deán Ortega (Úbeda), 225, 228
Palacio del Gobierno de Navarra (Iruña), 78
Palacio del Jabalquinto (Baeza), 225, 228
Palacio del Marqués de Salvatierra (Ronda), 196
Palacio de los Ávila y Tiedra (Ciudad Rodrigo), 161
Palacio de los Duques de Medina-Sidonia (Sanlúcar de Barrameda), 203
Palacio de los Golfines de Abajo (Cáceres), 174
Palacio de los Marqués de San Nicolás (Briones), 62
Palacio de los Marqueses (Ayerbe), 84
Palacio de los Marqueses de Piedras Albas (Trujillo), 174
Palacio de los Reyes de Navarra (Lizarra), 79
Palacio de los Zúñiga y Avellanda (Peñaranda de Duero), 151
Palacio de Marqués del Contadero (Úbeda), 229
Palacio de Mirabel (Plasencia), 168
Palacio de Moctezuma (Ciudad Rodrigo), 161
Palacio de Mondragón (Ronda), 196
Palacio de Ongay-Vallesantoro (Zangoza), 72
Palacio de Orleans y Borbon (Sanlúcar de Barrameda), 203
Palacio de Pizarro-Hinojoso (Trujillo), 175
Palacio de San Carlos (Trujillo), 174
Palacio Domecq (Jerez de la Frontera), 202
Palacio Episcopal (Albarracín) 127
Palacio Vela de los Cobos (Úbeda) 229
Palau Alenyà (Montblanc) 113
Palau de l'Almudaina (Palma) 242

Palau del Marqués de Montortal (Xàtiva) 140
Palau-Fortalesa del Castlà (Montblanc) 113
Palma 239, 240, 241, **242**, 243, 247
Palomino (grape) 203
Pampaneira (Poqueira Valley) 222, 223
Pamplona (Iruña) see Iruña
Panes (Desfiladero de la Hermida) 54
Parada del Compte (Torre del Compte) 122
paradors **22**
Parc Nacional d'Aigüestortes i Estany de Sant
    Maurici 91, 92, 93, 94, **95**, 97
Parc Natural de El Montgó (Xàbia) 143
Parc Natural de la Serra de Mariola 138, 139,
    142, 143
Parc Natural de la Zona Volcànica de la Garrotxa
    103
Parc Natural del Cap de Creus **107**
Parc Natural del Delta L'Ebre (Delta de l'Ebre), 117
Parc Natural dels Aiguamolls de l'Emporda, 106
Parc Olímpic del Segre (La Seu d'Urgell), 94
Parque de la Isla (Plasencia), 168
Parque del Majuelo (Almuñécar), 211
Parque Escultórico de Hinojosa de Jarque **125**
Parque Nacional de Monfragüe 163, 164, 165,
    166–7, 169
Parque Natural de Cabo de Gata (Carboneras)
    234, 235
Parque Natural de Carreirón **35**, 37
Parque Natural de la Sierra de Grazalema
    (Grazalema) 189, 193, 194, 197
Parque Natural de las Lagunas de Ruidera 182,
    183
Parque Natural de Señorío de Bertiz 70, 71, **76–
    7**, 79
Parque Natural Sierras de Cazorla (Cazorla) 225,
    226, 229, 230, 231
El Parrizal (Beceite) 124, 127
Parroquia de Nuestra Senora de la O (Chipiona)
    204
Paseo de las Flores (Salobreña) 213
Passeig Joan Brudieu (La Seu d'Urgell) 94
passports **12**, 13
Pazo de Oca 31, **34**
Pazo de Xelmirez (Santiago de Compostela) 34
Pedro Ciga 76, 77
Pedro Ximénez (grape) 203
Pelayo, Don 50
Peña Alba (Valle del Silencio) 45
La Peña de Francia 154, 155, **160**, 161
Peñafiel 145, 146, 147, **148**, 149, 151
Peñaranda de Duero 147, **150–51**
Peña Sola 84, 85
Península de Formentor 240, 241, 246, **247**
Pere III, the Ceremonious, King 113
personal security **13**
Picos, cheeses of 54
Picos de Europa 48, 50, 51, 52, 55
Pilós, Guifré el 105
Pinell de Brai (Gandesa) 116
Pinofranqueado (Las Hurdes) 169
pintxos (wine) 26, 70, 79
Piscina Natural de L'Assut (Beceite) 124
Pizarro, Francisco 166, 174, 177
Pla de Santa Bàrbara (Montblanc) 113
Plaça Constitució (Sóller) 245
Plaça de Dins (Alcoy) 142
Plaça de la Llibertat (Besalú) 105
Plaça de la Trinitat (Xàtiva) 140
Plaça de la Vila (Eivissa Town) 253
Plaça del Mercat (Xàtiva) 140
Plaça dels Àngels (Montblanc) 113
Plaça Major (Albaida) 141
Plaça Major (Montblanc) 113
Plaça Major (Pollença) 246
Placeta del Aljibe de Trillo (Granada) 218
Placeta de San Miguel Bajo (Granada) 218
Plasencia 163, 164, 165, 167, **168–9**
Platja de Formentor (Península de Formentor)
    247
Platja de la Grava (Xàbia) 143

Plaza Chica (Zafra) 177
Plaza de Castillo (Carboneras) 235
Plaza de Castillo (Iruña) 78
Plaza de España (Alcañiz) 122
Plaza de España (Cretas) 123
Plaza de Santa María (Cáceres) 174
Plaza de Santa María (Cazorla) 229
Plaza de Toros (El Puerto de Santa María) 204
Plaza de Toros (Las Virtudes) 184
Plaza de Toros (Ronda) 197
Plaza de la Asunción (Jerez de la Frontera) 202
Plaza de la Duquesa de Parcent (Ronda) 196
Plaza de los Duques (Peñaranda de Duero) 150
Plaza del Arenal (Jerez de la Frontera) 202
Plaza del Cabildo (Arcos de la Frontera) 192
Plaza del Coso (Peñafiel) 148
Plaza del Pópulo (Baeza) 228
Plaza Grande (Zafra) 177
Plaza Mayor (Albarracín) 127
Plaza Mayor (Laguardia) 60
Plaza Mayor (Plasencia) 168
Plaza Mayor (Trujillo) 174
Plaza Nueva (Granada) 218, 219
Plaza Vázquez de Molina (Úbeda) 228, 229
La Pobla de Segur 91, 93, 96, **97**
Poblet 110, 111, 114, 117
Poio 31
Pollença 240, 241, **246**, 247
Ponferrada 40, 41, **44**, 45
Pont de Suert **97**
Ponte Bibei (A Pobra de Trives) 43
Ponte do Síl **43**, 45
Pontevedra 31, 32, 33, 36, **37**
Poqueira Valley **222**, 223
Port de la Bonaigua (Val d'Aran) 96
Port de Pollença (Pollença) 241, 246, 247
Port de Sant Miquel 249, **252**
Porta des Moll (Alcúdia) 247
Portal de Bové (Montblanc) 113
Portal de Sant Miquel (Morella) 132
Portal de Ses Taules (Eivissa Town) 253
Posada de Valdeón **52**, 53
Potes 48, 49, **52–3**, 55
Pozo de los Frailes **236**, 237
Prades 111, **114**, 115
Praia das Margaritas (Parque Natural de
    Carreirón) 35
Praia de Paxariñas 32, **37**
Praia de Salinas (Parque Natural de Carreirón)
    35
Praia Lontreira (Parque Natural de Carreirón) 35
Praza de Fefiñanes (Cambados) 36
Presa Romana (Consuegra) 187
Priorat (Siurana) 109, 110, 115
public holidays **9**
pueblos blancos 190, 197, 206
Puente de Tablate 215, 216, **223**
Puente del Cardenal (Parque Nacional de
    Monfragüe) 166–7
Puente la Reina 71, **78–9**
Puente Milenio (Ourense) 42
Puente Nazari (Puente de Tablate) 223
Puente Nuevo (Ronda) 196, 197
Puente Romano (Cangas de Onís) 50
Puente Romano (Ourense) 42
Puerta de Jerez (Tarifa) 207
Puerta de San Juan (Laguardia) 60
Puerta de Santiago (Trujillo) 175
Puerta del Arroyo (Jerez de la Frontera) 202
Puerta Nueva (Laguardia) 60
Puerto de la Ragua 217, **221**
Puerto de las Palomas **230**
Puerto de los Blancares (Embalse de Quéntar)
    219
Puerto de los Santos (Villarrubia de los Ojos)
    187
Puerto de San Glorio **52**
El Puerto de Santa María 201, 203, **204**, 207
Puerto del Pico 154, **157**

Puerto Lápice 179, 181, **182**, 183, 187
Puig de Missa (Santa Eulària des Riu) 251
Punta da Cruz (Parque Natural de Carreirón) 35
Purullena 217, **220**
Pyrenean valleys 94, 100

Q

Queen's Balcony (Castillo de Loarre) 84
Queso Monje Picón 54
Quijada, Don Luis de 167, 187
Quintanar de la Sierra 58, 59, 66, **67**
Quixote, Don 7, 179, 180, 181, 182, 184, 187

R

Rabita Rutta 204
Rafael Amorós (Albaida) 141
rafting 12, 82, 88, 92, 94, 95
Rafters of the Pyrenees 97
rail travel **11**
Ramón y Cajal, Santiago 84
Real Fábrica (Ezcaray) 64
Real Monasterio de San Juan de la Peña
    (Monasterio de San Juan de la Peña) 86,
    87, 89
Refugi Mallafré (Parc Nacional d'Aigüestortes i
    Estany de Sant Maurici) 95
regaderas (canals) 95
Reial Cartoixa de Valldemossa (Valldemossa)
    244
Reials Col·legis (Tortosa) 116
El Reino de los Mallos (Kingdom of Mallos)
    84, 85
Rías Baixas 32, 35, 36, 37
Ribadesella 47, 48, 49, **50**, 51, 55
Ribeira Sacra (the Sacred Shore) 40
Ribera, José de 168
La Ribera del Duero 145, 146, 148, 150, 151
Rilke, Rainer Maria 196
La Rioja
    The Land of Rioja **56–67**
La Rioja Alavesa 58, 60, 63, 67
Ripoll 99, 100, 101, **104**
Ríumar (Delta de l'Ebre) 117
Roa 147, **149**
road systems **16**
Rodalquilar 233, 234, **235**
Rodas, Gaspar de 174
Romanesque architecture 81, 85, 96, 104
Roman gold mines 45
Roncal (Erronkari) 70, 71, **74**, 79
Roncesvalles 11, 69, 71, 74, **75**
Ronda 189, 190, 191, **196–7**
Rosalía de Castro (poet) 34
Roses **106–7**
Rota 199, 201, **204**, 205, 207
Royal Chapel (Castillo de Loarre) 84
Rubielos de Mora 131, **134**, 135
Rumsey, Charles 174
Ruta de los Iberos 123
Ruta de Sant Antoni-Molins (Xàbia) 143
La Ruta Mudéjar **212**

S

Sa Dragonera (Sant Elm) 241, 243, 247
Sa Portella (Eivissa Town) 253
Sabiote 226, 227, 230, **231**
Sacra Capilla del Salvador (Úbeda) 228
safaris 230
St Eulalia 176
St Julià 133
Saint Lucas 66
Saint Xavier, Francis 72
Salardú (Val d'Aran) 96, 97
Salobreña 209, 210, 212, **213**
Salvatierra (Castillo de Calatrava la Nueva) 185
Salvatierra, Don Vasco Martín de 196
Salvatore, Habsburg Archduke Ludwig 244
Samaniego, Félix María 61
San Bartolomé (Jerez de los Caballeros) 177

Sanç, King 244
Sancho Panza 180, 184
Sancho Ramírez, King of Aragón 84
Sancho VII, King of Navarra 75
Sancho V Ramírez, King of Navarra 79
San Fermín 9, 71, 78, 79
San José (Pozo de los Frailes) 236
San Juan de la Cruz (Úbeda) 229
San Juan de la Peña 81, 83, 89
San Miguel (Gata de Gorgos) 142
San Millán de la Cogolla 59, **64–5**, 67
San Pedro de Verona (Parque Natural de las Lagunas de Ruidera) 183
Sand, George 244
Sangüesa see Zangoza
Sanlúcar de Barrameda 200, 201, 202, **203**, 207
Sant Elm 239, 240, 241, **243**, 247
Sant Joan de Labritja 250, **251**
Sant Joan de les Abadesses 99, 100, 101, 104, **105**
Sant Miquel de Balansat **252**
Sant Sadurní d'Anoia 109, 110, 111, **112**, 113, 117
Santa Cruz de la Serós 81, 86, **87**
Santa Cruz de Mudela 187
Santa Cueva (Covadonga y los Lagos) 50
Santa Eulària des Riu 249, 250, **251**
Santa Gertrudis de Fruitera **252**
Santa María de la Encarnación (Jerez de los Caballeros) 177
Santa María de Lebeña **54**, 55
Santa Maria de los Reales Alcazares (Úbeda) 228
Santa María la Real (Zangoza) 72
Santa Pau 103, **104**, 105
Santes Creus 110, 111, **112**, 113, 114, 117
Santiago de Compostela 7, 10, 31, 32, 33, **34**, 35, 37, 85
Santiago el Mayor (Zangoza) 72
Santo Domingo de la Calzada 59, **63**, 67
Santo Toribio de Liébana 49, 51, **53**, 55
Santuari de Monestir de Lluc 240, **246**
Santuari de Monestir de Valldemossa 247
Santuario de Nuestra Senora de la Oliva (Vejer de la Frontera) 206
Santuario de Nuestra Señora de las Virtudes (Las Virtudes) 184
scuba diving 207, 235, 237
Segura y Las Villas (Cazorla) 225, 226, 229, 231
Selva de Oza (Hecho) 89
Seminario Conciliar (Teruel) 127
Senda de Los Cortinales 159
Señora de la Torre (Jarandilla de la Vera) 167
Senterada (Pont de Suert) 96, 97
Serra de Montsant Nature Park 115
Serra de Tramuntana 239, 240, 247
Setenil de las Bodegas 194, **195**
La Seu d'Urgell 91, 93, **94**, 95, 97
La Seu (Palma) 242
La Seu (Xàtiva) 140
"Seven Infants of Lara" 65
sherry 25, 190, 199, 202, 203, 204, 207
Sierra de Aitana 138
Sierra de Gredos 19, 154, 156, 157, 161
Sierra de la Demanda 57, 58, 59, 64, 65, 67
Sierra de la Peña de Francia 154, 159, 164
Sierra Nevada 215, 216, 217, 220, 221, 222
Síl river 40, 41, 42, 43, 45
Siresa (Hecho) 89
Siurana 110, 114, **115**, 117
Sóller 241, **245**
Son Marroig **244**
Sort 93, **94**, 97
Soto de Sajambre 49, **51**
Sotres (Bulnes) 55
Subenuix (Parc Nacional d'Aigüestortes i Estany de Sant Maurici) 95
The Sun Also Rises (Hemingway) 78
Suspiro waterfall (Parque Natural de Señorío de Bertiz) 77

T

tapas 24, **25**, 26, 27, 34, 48, 78, **79**, 190, 203, 204
Tarifa 10, 199, 200, 201, 206, **207**
Taüll (Vall de Boí) 96
Teatre Municipal (Girona) 102
Teatre-Museu Dalí (Figueres) 106, 107
Teatro Romano (Mérida) 176
Templo de Diana (Mérida) 176
Teruel 119, 120, 121, **126–7**
Theatre, Golden Age of 187
tipping **15**
Toros de Guisando 153, 155, **156**, 161
Torre Abacial (Laguardia) 60
Torre de Reloj (Ayerbe) 84
Torre de San Martín (Teruel) 127
Torre de Telefonica (Cádiz) 205
Torre de Vela Blanca (Vela Blanca) 234, 237
Torre del Alfiler (Trujillo) 175
Torre del Bujaco (Cáceres) 174
Torre del Compte **122**, 123
Torre del Vinagre **230**
Torre dels Cinc Cantons (Montblanc) 113
Torre Exenta (Santo Domingo de la Calzada) 63
Torre Octagonal (Úbeda) 229
Torre San Roque (Valderrobres) 124
Torre Tavira (Cádiz) 205
Torrejón el Rubio **166**, 169
Torreón de San Esteban (Teruel) 126
Tortosa 110, 111, **116**, 117
Tourist Information **15**
Trajan, Emperor 43
Tramullas, Pedro 89
Travel Insurance **12**
Tresviso (Bulnes) 54, 55
Trevélez 217, **222**, 223
Troglodyte Residences 221
Trujillo 163, 164, 165, **166**, 167, 169, 172, 173, **174–5**, 177

U

Úbeda 225, 226, 227, **228–9**, 231
Ubrique 191, **193**, 197
Uztárroz 74

V

Val d'Aran 11, 92, 93, **96**, 97
Valderrobres 119, **124**
Valdezcaray (Ezcaray) 64
Valencia
    Behind the Costa Blanca **136–43**
    The Land of the Templars **128–35**
Vallbona de les Monges 111, **114**, 117
Vall de Boí 93, **96**, 97
Vall Fosca (Pont de Suert) 97
Valldemossa 241, **244**, 245
Vallderrobres 121, **124**, 127
Valle de Camaleño **53**, 55
Valle del Alberche 153, **156**, 161
Valle de Baztán 71, 79

Valle del Cuco 146, 149
Valle del Silencio 39, 40, 41, **44–5**
Valle del Tormes **158**
Vandelvira, Andrés de 228
Vega, Félix Lope de 187
Vega de Liébana (Puerto de San Glorio) 52
Vega Sicilia (La Milla de Oro) 149
Vegabaño (Soto de Sajambre) 51
Vejer de la Frontera 200, **206**, 207
Vela Blanca 233, 234, **236–7**
Venta del Quijote (Puerto Lápice) 182
Vera de Bidasoa see Bera
Via Calvari (Pollença) 246
Via Nova (A Pobra de Trives) 43
Viajeros (Laguardia) 61
Vielha (Val d'Aran) 11, 93, 94, 96
Vilafranca del Cid (Iglesuela del Cid) 134, 135
Vilafranca del Penedès 111, **112**, 117
Vila Vermella 114
Vilella Baixa 114, **115**, 117
Villafranca del Bierzo **44**, 45
Villanueva de los Infantes 181, **184**
Villarrubia de los Ojos **187**
Vinseum (Vilafranca del Penedès) 112
Las Virtudes 181, **184**, 187
Visas **12**
Viso del Marqués 181, 184, **185**, 187
Viu de Llevata and Sarroca de Bellera (Pont de Suert) 97
Vultures, feeding 124, 127

W

Western Andalusia 27, 194
whale-watching 207
The White Towns 194
windsurfing 199, 200, 207
wines **25**
    Albariño 36
    cathedrals 117
    La Fabulista 61
    Priorat 115
    La Rioja 63
    tasting 7, 146, 151

X

Xàbia 137, 138, 139, 142, **143**
Xàtiva 137, 138, 139, **140–41**, 143

Z

Zafra 171, 172, 173, 176, **177**
Zahara de la Sierra 191, **194**, 197
Zahara de los Atunes 199, 201, 206, **207**
Zurbarán, Francisco 37, 177

Acknowledgments

Dorling Kindersley would like to thank the many people whose help and assistance contributed to the preparation of this book.

Contributors
Mary-Ann Gallagher has written more than 20 travel guides. She has written for and edited numerous guidebooks for DK, *National Geographic* and *Footprint Handbooks*, among others.
Nick Inman is a full-time author, editor and photographer. He has written for or contributed to over 50 travel guides, mainly on Spain and France.
Phil Lee has been a travel writer for over 20 years and his work has been published in many magazines and newspapers. He also writes regularly for *Rough Guides*.
Chris Moss is the travel editor at *Time Out* magazine, London. He contributed to DK *Eyewitness Travel Guide to Argentina* and is the author of *Patagonia: A Cultural History*.
Nick Rider has a PhD in history and has written books on France, Spain and Mexico. He has also contributed to DK *Eyewitness Travel Guides to France, Spain, Mexico, Great Britain and Poland*.
Richard Trillo is a travel writer and editor. He is the author of *Rough Guides to Kenya, West Africa, The Gambia* and *World Music* and was formerly Rough Guides' Director of Communications.
Suzanne Wales is a freelance writer who writes for publications such as *Wallpaper**, *Vogue* and *The Australian Newspaper*, and contributes to documentaries and television reports on various Spanish issues.
Greg Ward has written several different guides to Hawaii, as well as books on the USA, the Southwest USA, the Grand Canyon, the Blues, American History and many other topics.

Fact Checkers
Cristinà Barrallo Calonge, Fran Bastida, Paula Canal
Proofreader
Devabrata Kar
Indexer
Cyber Media Services Ltd.

Design and Editorial
Publisher Douglas Amrine
List Manager Vivien Antwi
Managing Art Editor Jane Ewart
Project Editor Michelle Crane, Georgina Palffy
Project Designers Shahid Mahmood, Kate Leonard
Senior Cartographic Editor Casper Morris
Cartographer Stuart James
Managing Art Editor (Jackets) Karen Constanti
Senior Jacket Designer Tessa Bindloss
Jacket Designer Meredith Smith
Senior DTP Designer Jason Little
DTP Designers Jamie McNeill, Natasha Lu
Picture Research Ellen Root
Production Controller Linda Dare

Revisions Design and Editorial
Louise Abbott, Lynette McCurdy Bastida, Maria Victoria Cano, Emer FitzGerald, Mohammad Hassan, Priyanka Kumar, Sonal Modha, Rada Radojicic, Susana Smith, Nikky Twyman, Vinita Venugopal, Ajay Verma

Special Assistance
Bernard Byrne, Paula Canal, Juan Marcos Carillo, Serge Defaix, Lara Dunston, Elizabeth Furbear, Cristina Garcia, Maribel Izcue, Arma Kleinepier, Cécile Landau, Kate Leonard, Xavier Ribas, Marie Aude Serra, Matt Wright

Photography
Alex Havret, Nick Inman, Chris Moss, Alex Robinson, Tara Stevens.

Additional Photography
Max Alexander, Stephen Bere, Joe Cornish, Lydia Evans, Joan Farre, Emma Firth, Heidi Grassley, Neil Lukas, Malcolm McGregor, John Miller, Kim Sayer, Colin Sinclair, Tony Souter, Linda Whitwam, Peter Wilson, Bartlomies Zaranek Rough Guides: Ian Aitken, Demetrio Carrasco, Neville Walker.

Photography Permissions
Dorling Kindersley would like to thank the following for their assistance and kind permission to photograph at their establishments:
Casa Leonardo, Casa-Museo Rosalía de Castro, Caudalíe Vinothérapie Spa at Hotel Marqués de Riscal, Elciego, Hotel el Convento Parador de Cambados, Parador de Sto. Estevo, Posada el Bosque.

Picture Credits
Placement Key- t=top; tc=top centre; tr=top right; cla=centre left above; ca=centre above; cra=centre right above; cl=centre left; c=centre; cr=centre right; clb=centre left below; cb=centre below; crb=centre right below; bl=bottom left; bc=bottom centre; br=bottom right; ftl=far top left; ftr=far top right; fcla=far centre left above; fcra=far centre right above; fcl=far centre left; fcr=far centre right; fclb=far centre left below; fcrb=far centre right below; fbl=far bottom left; fbr=far bottom right.
Every effort has been made to trace the copyright holders, and we apologize in advance for any unintentional omissions. We would be pleased to insert the appropriate acknowledgments in any subsequent edition of this publication.
The publisher would like to thank the following individuals, companies and picture libraries for their kind permission to reproduce their photographs:
4Corners Images: SIME/Schmid Reinhard 9br; **Alamy Images:** Graham Lawrence 79tl; [Holandaluz] Vincent de Vries 20tr; **The Bridgeman Art Library:** Map of Spain, from 'Blaeus Grooten Atlas, Oft Werelt-Beschryving...' by Joan Blaeu (1596–1673) 1648–65 (coloured engraving), Spanish School, (17th century) / © Royal Geographical Society, London, UK 28–29; **Photolibrary:** Jeronimo Alba 224–225; Paco Ayala 17tr; Alan Copson 2–3; Kevin George 162–163; Jose Antonio Jimenez 6cl; Sabine Lubenow 248–249; Juan Carlos Munoz 38–39; Fabian von Poser 1c; Jose Fuste Raga 8; Antonio Real 30–31

Sheet Map Picture Credits
Front: SuperStock: age fotostock/Jordi Sans..

Cover Picture Credits
Front: SuperStock: age fotostock/Jordi Sans.
Back: Dorling Kindersley: Nick Inman c; Chris Moss l; Tara Stevens r. Spine: SuperStock: age fotostock/Jordi Sans t.
All other images © Dorling Kindersley
For further information see: www.dkimages.com

Phrase Book

IN AN EMERGENCY

Help!	¡Socorro¡	soh-koh-roh
Stop!	¡Pare!	pah-reh
Call a doctor!	¡Llame a un médico!	yah-meh ah oon meh-dee-koh
Call an ambulance!	¡Llame a una ambulancia!	yah-meh ah oo-nah ahm-boo-lahn-thee-ah
Call the police!	¡Llame a la policía!	yah-meh ah lah poh-lee-thee-ah
Call the fire brigade!	¡Llame a los bomberos!	yah-meh ah lohs bohm-beh-rohs
Where is the nearest telephone?	¿Dónde está el teléfono más próximo?	dohn-deh ehs-tah ehl teh-leh-foh-noh mahs prohx-ee-moh
Where is the nearest hospital?	¿Dónde está el hospital más próximo?	dohn-deh ehs-tah ehl ohs-pee-tahl mahs prohx-ee-moh

COMMUNICATION ESSENTIALS

Yes	Sí	see
No	No	noh
Please	Por favor	pohr fah-vohr
Thank you	Gracias	grah-thee-ahs
Excuse me	Perdone	pehr-doh-neh
Hello	Hola	oh-lah
Goodbye	Adiós	ah-dee-ohs
Goodnight	Buenas noches	bweh-nahs noh-chehs
Morning	La mañana	lah mah-nyah-nah
Afternoon	La tarde	lah tahr-deh
Evening	La tarde	lah tahr-deh
Yesterday	Ayer	ah-yehr
Today	Hoy	oy
Tomorrow	Mañana	mah-nya-nah
Here	Aquí	ah-kee
There	Allí	ah-yee
What?	¿Qué?	keh
When?	¿Cuándo?	kwahn-doh
Why?	¿Por qué?	pohr-keh
Where?	¿Dónde?	dohn-deh

USEFUL PHRASES

How are you?	¿Cómo está usted?	koh-moh ehs-tah oos-tehd
Very well, thank you.	Muy bien, gracias.	mwee bee-ehn grah-thee-ahs
Pleased to meet you.	Encantado de conocerle.	ehn-kahn-tah-doh de koh-noh-thehr-leh
See you soon.	Hasta pronto.	ahs-tah prohn-toh
That's fine.	Está bien.	ehs-tah bee-ehn
Where is/are …?	¿Dónde está/están …?	dohn-deh ehs-tah/ehs-tahn
How far is it to …?	¿Cuántos metros/ kilómetros hay de aquí a …?	kwahn-tohs meh-trohs/ kee-loh-meh-trohs eye deh ah-kee ah
Which way to …?	¿Por dónde se va a …?	pohr dohn-deh seh bah ah
Do you speak English?	¿Habla inglés?	ah-blah een-glehs
I don't understand.	No comprendo.	noh kohm-prehn-doh
Could you speak more slowly, please?	¿Puede hablar más despacio, por favor?	pweh-deh ah-blahr mahs dehs-pah-thee-oh pohr fah-vohr
I'm sorry.	Lo siento.	loh see-ehn-toh

USEFUL WORDS

big	grande	grahn-deh
small	pequeño	peh-keh-nyoh
hot	caliente	kah-lee-ehn-the
cold	frío	free-oh
good	bueno	bweh-noh
bad	malo	mah-loh
enough	bastante	bahs-tahn-the
well	bien	bee-ehn
open	abierto	ah-bee-ehr-toh
closed	cerrado	thehr-rah-doh
left	izquierda	eeth-key-ehr-dah
right	derecha	deh-reh-chah
straight on	todo recto	toh-doh rehk-toh
near	cerca	thehr-kah
far	lejos	leh-hohs
up	arriba	ah-ree-bah
down	abajo	ah-bah-hoh
early	temprano	tehm-prah-noh
late	tarde	tahr-deh

entrance	entrada	ehn-trah-dah
exit	salida	sah-lee-dah
toilet	lavabos, servicios	lah-vah-bohs, sehr-bee-thee-ohs
more	más	mahs
less	menos	meh-nohs

SHOPPING

How much does this cost?	¿Cuánto cuesta esto?	kwahn-toh kwehs-tah ehs-toh
I would like …	Me gustaría …	meh goos-ta-ree-ah
Do you have …?	¿Tienen …?	tee-yeh-nehn
I'm just looking, thank you.	Sólo estoy mirando, gracias.	soh-loh ehs-toy mee-rahn-doh grah-thee-ahs
Do you take credit cards?	¿Aceptan tarjetas de crédito?	ah-thehp-tahn tahr-heh-tahs deh kreh-dee-toh
What time do you open?	¿A qué hora abren?	ah keh oh-rah ah-brehn
What time do you close?	¿A qué hora cierran?	ah keh oh-rah thee-ehr-rahn
This one	Éste	ehs-the
That one	Ése	eh-she
expensive	caro	kahr-oh
cheap	barato	bah-rah-toh
size (clothes)	talla	tah-yah
size (shoes)	número	no-mehr-oh
white	blanco	blahn-koh
black	negro	neh-groh
red	rojo	roh-hoh
yellow	amarillo	ah-mah-ree-yoh
green	verde	behr-deh
blue	azul	ah-thool
antiques shop	la tienda de antigüedades	lah tee-ehn-dah deh ahn-tee-gweh-dah-dehs
bakery	la panadería	lah pah-nah-deh ree-ah
bank	el banco	ehl bahn-koh
bookshop	la librería	lah lee-breh-ree-ah
butcher's	la carnicería	lah kahr-nee-theh-ree-ah
cake shop	la pastelería	lah pahs-teh-leh-ree-ah
chemist's	la farmacia	lah fahr-mah-thee-ah
fishmonger's	la pescadería	lah pehs-kah-deh-ree-ah
greengrocer's	la frutería	lah froo-teh-ree-ah
grocer's	la tienda de comestibles	lah tee-yehn-dah deh koh-mehs-tee-blehs
hairdresser's	la peluquería	lah peh-loo-keh-ree-ah
market	el mercado	ehl mehr-kah-doh
newsagent's	el kiosko de prensa	ehl kee-ohs-koh deh prehn-sah
post office	la oficina de correos	lah oh-fee-thee-nah deh kohr-reh-ohs
shoe shop	la zapatería	lah thah-pah-teh-ree-ah
supermarket	el supermercado	ehl soo-pehr-mehr-kah-do
tobacconist	el estanco	ehl ehs-tahn-koh
travel agency	la agencia de viajes	lah ah-hehn-thee-ah deh bee-ah-hehs

SIGHTSEEING

art gallery	el museo de arte	ehl moo-seh-oh deh ahr-the
cathedral	la catedral	lah kah-teh-drahl
church	la iglesia, la basílica	lah ee-gleh-see-ah, lah bah-see-lee-kah
garden	el jardín	ehl hahr-deen
library	la biblioteca	lah bee-blee-oh-teh-kah
museum	el museo	ehl moo-seh-oh
tourist information office	la oficina de turismo	lah oh-fee-thee-nah deh too-rees-moh
town hall	el ayuntamiento	ehl ah-yoon-tah-mee-ehn-toh
closed for holiday	cerrado por vacaciones	thehr-rah-doh pohr bah-kah-cee-oh-nehs
bus station	la estación de autobuses	lah ehs-tah-ee-ohn deh owtoh-boo-sehs
railway station	la estación de trenes	lah ehs-tah-thee-ohn deh treh-nehs

STAYING IN A HOTEL

Do you have a vacant room?	¿Tienen una habitación libre?	tee-eh-nehn oo-nah ah-bee-tah-thee-ohn lee-breh

double room	**habitación doble**	ah-bee-tah-thee-ohn doh-bleh
with double bed	**con cama de matrimonio**	kohn kah-mah deh mah-tree-moh-nee-oh
twin room	**habitación con dos camas**	ah-bee-tah-thee-ohn kohn dohs kah-mahs
single room	**habitación individual**	ah-bee-tah-thee-ohn een-dee-vee-doo-ahl
room with a bath	**habitación con baño**	ah-bee-tah-thee-ohn kohn bah-nyoh
shower	**ducha**	doo-chah
porter	**el botones**	ehl boh-toh-nehs
key	**la llave**	lah yah-veh
I have a reservation.	**Tengo una habitación reservada.**	tehn-goh oo-na ah-bee-tah-thee-ohn reh-sehr-bah-dah

EATING OUT

Have you got a table for …?	**¿Tienen mesa para …?**	tee-eh-nehn meh-sah pah-rah
I want to reserve a table.	**Quiero reservar una mesa.**	kee-eh-roh reh-sehr-bahr oo-nah meh-sah
The bill, please.	**La cuenta, por favor.**	lah kwehn-tah pohr fah-vohr
I am a vegetarian.	**Soy vegetariano/a.**	soy beh-heh-tah-ree-ah-no/na
waitress	**la camarera**	lah kah-mah-reh-rah
waiter	**el camarero**	ehl kah-mah-reh-roh
menu	**la carta**	lah kahr-tah
fixed-price menu	**el menú del día**	ehl meh-noo dehl dee-ah
wine list	**la carta de vinos**	lah kahr-tah deh bee-nohs
glass	**un vaso**	oon bah-soh
bottle	**una botella**	oo-nah boh-teh-yah
knife	**un cuchillo**	oon koo-chee-yoh
fork	**un tenedor**	oon teh-neh-dohr
spoon	**una cuchara**	oo-nah koo-chah-rah
breakfast	**el desayuno**	ehl deh-sah-yoo-noh
lunch	**la comida/ el almuerzo**	lah koh-mee-dah/ ehl ahl-mwehr-thoh
dinner	**la cena**	lah theh-nah
main course	**el primer plato**	ehl pree-mehr plah-toh
starters	**los entremeses**	lohs ehn-treh meh-sehs
dish of the day	**el plato del día**	ehl plah-toh dehl dee-ah
coffee	**el café**	ehl kah-feh
rare	**poco hecho**	poh-koh eh-choh
medium	**medio hecho**	meh-dee-oh eh-choh
well done	**muy hecho**	mwee eh-choh

MENU DECODER

al horno	ahl ohr-noh	baked
asado	ah-sah-doh	roast
el aceite	ehl ah-thee-eh-teh	oil
las aceitunas	lahs ah-theh-toon-ahs	olives
el agua mineral	ehl ah-gwa mee-neh-rahl	mineral water
sin gas/con gas	seen gas/kohn gas	still/sparkling
el ajo	ehl ah-hoh	garlic
el arroz	ehl ahr-rohth	rice
el azúcar	ehl ah-thoo-kahr	sugar
la carne	lah kahr-neh	meat
la cebolla	lah theh-boh-yah	onion
la cerveza	lah thehr-beh-thah	beer
el cerdo	ehl therh-doh	pork
el chocolate	ehl choh-koh-lah-teh	chocolate
el chorizo	ehl choh-ree-thoh	red sausage
el cordero	ehl kohr-deh-roh	lamb
el fiambre	ehl fee-ahm-breh	cold meat
frito	free-toh	fried
la fruta	lah froo-tah	fruit
los frutos secos	lohs froo-tohs seh-kohs	nuts
las gambas	lahs gahm-bahs	prawns
el helado	ehl eh-lah-doh	ice cream
el huevo	ehl oo-eh-voh	egg
el jamón serrano	ehl hah-mohn sehr-rah-noh	cured ham
el jerez	ehl heh-rehz	sherry
la langosta	lah lahn-gohs-tah	lobster
la leche	lah leh-cheh	milk
el limón	ehl lee-mohn	lemon

la limonada	lah lee-moh-nah-dah	lemonade
la mantequilla	lah mahn-teh-kee-yah	butter
la manzana	lah mahn-thah-nah	apple
los mariscos	lohs mah-rees-kohs	seafood
la menestra	lah meh-nehs-trah	vegetable stew
la naranja	lah nah-rahn-hah	orange
el pan	ehl pahn	bread
el pastel	ehl pahs-tehl	cake
las patatas	lahs pah-tah-tahs	potatoes
el pescado	ehl pehs-kah-doh	fish
la pimienta	lah pee-mee-yehn-tah	pepper
el plátano	ehl plah-tah-noh	banana
el pollo	ehl poh-yoh	chicken
el postre	ehl pohs-treh	dessert
el queso	ehl keh-soh	cheese
la sal	lah sahl	salt
las salchichas	lahs sahl-chee-chahs	sausages
la salsa	lah sahl-sah	sauce
seco	seh-koh	dry
el solomillo	ehl soh-loh-mee-yoh	sirloin
la sopa	lah soh-pah	soup
la tarta	lah tahr-tah	pie/cake
el té	ehl teh	tea
la ternera	lah tehr-neh-rah	beef
las tostadas	lahs tohs-tah-dahs	toast
el vinagre	ehl bee-nah-greh	vinegar
el vino blanco	ehl bee-noh blahn-koh	white wine
el vino rosado	ehl bee-noh roh-sah-doh	rosé wine
el vino tinto	ehl bee-noh teen-toh	red wine

NUMBERS

0	**cero**	theh-roh
1	**uno**	oo-noh
2	**dos**	dohs
3	**tres**	trehs
4	**cuatro**	kwa-troh
5	**cinco**	theen-koh
6	**seis**	says
7	**siete**	see-eh-the
8	**ocho**	oh-choh
9	**nueve**	nweh-veh
10	**diez**	dee-ehth
11	**once**	ohn-theh
12	**doce**	doh-theh
13	**trece**	treh-theh
14	**catorce**	kah-tohr-theh
15	**quince**	keen-theh
16	**dieciséis**	dee-eh-thee-seh-ees
17	**diecisiete**	dee-eh-thee-see eh-the
18	**dieciocho**	dee-eh-thee-oh-choh
19	**diecinueve**	dee-eh-thee-nweh-veh
20	**veinte**	beh-een-the
21	**veintiuno**	beh-een-tee-oo-noh
22	**veintidós**	beh-een-tee-dohs
30	**treinta**	treh-een-tah
31	**treinta y uno**	treh-een-tah ee oo-noh
40	**cuarenta**	kwah-rehn-tah
50	**cincuenta**	theen-kwehn-tah
60	**sesenta**	seh-sehn-tah
70	**setenta**	seh-tehn-tah
80	**ochenta**	oh-chehn-tah
90	**noventa**	noh-vehn-tah
100	**cien**	thee-ehn
101	**ciento uno**	thee-ehn-toh oo-noh
102	**ciento dos**	thee-ehn-toh dohs
200	**doscientos**	dohs-thee-ehn-tohs
500	**quinientos**	khee-nee-ehn-tohs
700	**setecientos**	seh-teh-thee-ehn-tohs
900	**novecientos**	noh-veh-thee-ehn-tohs
1,000	**mil**	meel
1,001	**mil uno**	meel oo-noh

TIME

one minute	**un minuto**	oon mee-noo-toh
one hour	**una hora**	oo-na oh-rah
half an hour	**media hora**	meh-dee-a oh-rah
Monday	**lunes**	loo-nehs
Tuesday	**martes**	mahr-tehs
Wednesday	**miércoles**	mee-ehr-koh-lehs
Thursday	**jueves**	hoo-weh-vehs
Friday	**viernes**	bee-ehr-nehs
Saturday	**sábado**	sah-bah-doh
Sunday	**domingo**	doh-meen-goh

Driver's Phrase Book

SOME COMMON ROAD SIGNS

aduana	customs
apagar luces de cruce	headlights off
aparcamiento	car park
atención al tren	beware of trains
autopista	toll motorway
autovía	toll-free motorway
callejón sin salida	no thoroughfare
calle peatonal	pedestrians only
calzada deteriorada	bad surface
calzada irregular	uneven surface
cambio de sentido	crossroads
carretera cortada	road closed
ceda el paso	give way
centro ciudad	city centre
centro urbano	town centre
circule despacio	slow
circunvalación	circular road
cruce	crossroads
desvío	diversion
desvío provisional	temporary diversion
encender luces de cruce	headlights on
escalón lateral	no hard shoulder
escuela	school
final de autopista	end of motorway
firme en mal estado	bad surface
hielo	black ice
información turística	tourist information
obras	road construction
ojo al tren	beware of trains
paso a nivel	level crossing
paso subterráneo	subway
peaje	toll
peatón, circule a la izquierda	pedestrians, keep to the left
peatones	pedestrians
peligro	danger
peligro deslizamientos	slippery road surface
precaución	caution
prohibido aparcar	no parking
prohibido el paso	no trespassing
puesto de socorro	first-aid post
salida de camiones	construction exit
vado permanente	in constant use (no parking)
vehículos pesados	heavy vehicles
velocidad controlada por radar	automatic speed monitor
zona azul	restricted parking zone
zona de estacionamento limitado	restricted parking area

DIRECTIONS YOU MAY BE GIVEN

a la derecha/izquierda	on the right/left
después de pasar el/la ...	go past the ...
la primera a la derecha	first on the right
la segunda a la izquierda	second on the left
todo recto	straight on
gira a la derecha	turn right
gira a la izquierda	turn left

THINGS YOU'LL SEE

aceite	oil
agua	water
aire	air
apague el motor	turn off engine
aparcamiento subterráneo	underground car park
área de servicios	service area, motorway services
cola	queue
completo	full
entrada	way in
estación de servicio	service station
garaje	garage
gas-oil	diesel
gasolina	fuel
gasolinera	petrol station
introduzca el dinero exacto	exact change
nivel del aceite	oil level
presión	air pressure
presión de los neumáticos	tyre pressure
prohibido fumar	no smoking
recoja su ticket	take a ticket
reparación	repairs
salida	exit
sin plomo	unleaded
solo para residentes del hotel	hotel guests only
taller (de reparaciones)	garage (for repairs)

THINGS YOU'LL HEAR

¿Lo quiere automático o manual?
Would you like an automatic or a manual?

¿Su permiso/carnet de conducir, por favor?
May I see your driving licence?

Su pasaporte, por favor.
Your passport, please.

USEFUL PHRASES

I would like some petrol/oil/water.
Quería gasolina/aceite/agua.
keh-ree-a gassoh-leena/athay-teh/ahg-wa

Fill it up, please!
¡Lleno, por favor!
yeh-noh por fa-vor

35 litres of unleaded petrol, please
Póngame treinta y cinco litros de sin plomo, por favor
ponga-meh traynti theenkoh leetross deh sin plohmoh, por fa-vor

Would you check the tyres for me, please?
¿Podría revisarme los neumáticos, por favor?
podree-a revee-sarmeh loss neh-oo-mateekoss por fa-vor

Do you do repairs?
¿Hacen reparaciones?
ah-then reparrath-yoh-ness

Can you repair the clutch?
¿Pueden arreglarme el embrague?
pweh-den arreh-glarmeh el embrah-geh

There is something wrong with the engine.
Hay algo que no va bien en el motor.
i algoh keh noh va byen en el moh-tor

The engine is overheating.
El motor se calienta demasiado.
el moh-tor seh kal-yenta deh-massyah-doh

I need a new tyre.
Necesito un neumático nuevo.
neh-thessee-toh oon neh-oo-matikoh nweh-voh

Can you replace this?
¿Pueden cambiarme esto?
pweh-den kam-byar-meh es-toh

The indicator is not working.
El intermitente no funciona.
el een-tair-mee-ten-teh noh foon-thyoh-na

How long will it take?
¿Cuánto tiempo tardarán?
kwan-toh tyem-poh tar-da-ran

I'd like to hire a car.
Quería alquilar un coche.
keh-ree-a alkee-lar oon kot-cheh

How much is it for one day?
¿Cuánto cuesta para un día?
kwan-toh kwesta parra oon dee-a

Is there a mileage charge?
¿Tiene suplemento por kilómetro?
tyeh-neh soo-ple-men-toh por kee-lo-met-roh

When do I have to return it?
¿Cuándo tengo que devolverlo?
kwan-doh teng-goh keh devo-lvair-loh

Where is the nearest garage?
¿Dónde está el taller más cercano?
don-deh esta el tayair mass thair-kah-noh

Where is the nearest petrol station?
¿Dónde está la gasolinera más cercana?
don-deh esta la gas-soh-lee-neh-ra mass thair-kah-na

Where can I park?
¿Dónde puedo aparcar?
don-deh pweh-doh appar-kar

How do I get to Seville?
¿Cómo se va a Sevilla?
koh-moh seh va a sevee-ya

Is this the road to Malaga?
¿Es ésta la carretera de Málaga?
ess esta la karreh-teh-ra deh malaga

Which is the quickest way to Madrid?
¿Cuál es el camino más rápido para Madrid?
kwal ess el kam-ee-noh mass rapee-doh parra madreed

USEFUL WORDS

automatic	**automático**	*owtoh-mateekoh*
bonnet	**el capó**	*ehl kapo*
boot	**el maletero**	*ehl malleh-teh-roh*
brake	**el freno**	*ehl freh-noh*
breakdown	**una avería**	*oo-nah avveh-ree-a*
car	**el coche**	*ehl kotcheh*
car park	**el aparcamiento**	*ehl apar-ka-myen-toh*
caravan	**la caravana**	*lah karra-vah-na*
clutch	**el embrague**	*ehl embrah-geh*
crossroads	**el cruce**	*ehl kroo-theh*
driving licence	**el permiso/**	*ehl pair-meesso/*
	el carnet	*ehl kar-neh*
dual carriageway	**la autovía**	*lah owtoh-vee-a*
engine	**el motor**	*ehl moh-tor*
exhaust	**el tubo**	*ehl too-boh*
fanbelt	**la correa del**	*lah korreh-a del*
	ventilador	*ven-teela-dor*
garage (for repairs)	**un taller**	*oon tay-air*
gear	**la marcha**	*lah mar-tcha*
gears	**las marchas**	*lahs mar-tchass*
headlights	**las luces**	*lahs loo-thess*
	de cruce	*deh kroo-theh*
indicator	**intermitente**	*een-tair-mee-ten-teh*
junction	**el cruce**	*ehl kroo-theh*
mirror	**el (espejo)**	*ehl esspeh-hoh*
	retrovisor	*retroh-vessor*
motorway	**la autopista**	*lah owtoh-peesta*
number plate	**la matrícula**	*lah matree-koola*
petrol	**la gasolina**	*lah gassoh-leena*
petrol station	**una gasolinera**	*oo-nah gassoh*
		-leeneh-ra
rear lights	**las luces traseras**	*lahs loothess-*
		trasseh-rass
road	**la carretera**	*lah karreh-teh-ra*
spare parts	**los repuestos**	*lohs reh-pwestoss*
spark plug	**la bujía**	*lah boo-hee-a*
speed	**la velocidad**	*lah velothee-da*
speedometer	**el cuenta-**	*ehl kwenta-*
	kilómetros	*keelomeh-tross*
steering wheel	**el volante**	*ehl voh-lanteh*
tow	**remolcar**	*reh-molkar*
traffic lights	**el semáforo**	*ehl seh-mafforoh*
tyre	**el neumático**	*ehl neh-oo-matee-*
		koh
van	**la furgoneta**	*lah foorgoneh-ta*
wheel	**la rueda**	*lah rweh-da*
windscreen	**el parabrisas**	*ehl para-bree-sass*
windscreen	**el limpia-**	*ehl leempya-*
wiper	**el parabrisas**	*ehl parabreessass*

SPECIAL EDITIONS OF DK TRAVEL GUIDES

Road Signs

SPEED LIMITS AND GENERAL DRIVING INDICATIONS

Give way

Compulsory stop

Your route has priority

Your route no longer has priority

Give way to oncoming traffic

Your lane has priority over oncoming traffic

Speed limit

No overtaking

No stopping

Crossroads ahead

Roundabout

Minimum distance separation required

No entry

Traffic light

60 km/h maximum speed

WARNING SIGNS

Caution, left-hand bends

Slippery road surface

Risk of snow and ice or slippery road

Road works

Risk of rockfalls

Wild animals

Children crossing

Pedestrian crossing

Speed bumps

Unspecified danger

Level crossing without barriers

High winds

Steep downhill decline

Road narrows

Road narrows on right